BRITISH SOCIALIST FICTION, 1884–1914

CONTENTS OF THE EDITION

VOLUME 1
General Introduction
1884–1891

VOLUME 2
1892–1900

VOLUME 3
1901–1906

VOLUME 4
1907–1910

VOLUME 5
1911–1914

BRITISH SOCIALIST FICTION, 1884–1914

Volume 4
1907–1910

Edited by
Deborah Mutch

PICKERING & CHATTO
2013

Published by Pickering & Chatto (Publishers) Limited
21 Bloomsbury Way, London WC1A 2TH

2252 Ridge Road, Brookfield, Vermont 05036-9704, USA

www.pickeringchatto.com

All rights reserved.
No part of this publication may be reproduced,
stored in a retrieval system, or transmitted in any form or by any means,
electronic, mechanical, photocopying, recording, or otherwise
without prior permission of the publisher.

Copyright © Pickering & Chatto (Publishers) Limited 2013
Copyright © Editorial material Deborah Mutch 2013

To the best of the Publisher's knowledge every effort has been made to contact
relevant copyright holders and to clear any relevant copyright issues.
Any omissions that come to their attention will be remedied in future editions.

BRITISH LIBRARY CATALOGUING IN PUBLICATION DATA

British socialist fiction, 1884–1914.
1. Political fiction, English – 19th century. 2. Political fiction, English – 20th
century. 3. Socialism – Fiction.
I. Mutch, Deborah, 1965– editor of compilation.
823.8'0803581-dc23

ISBN-13: 9781848933576

This publication is printed on acid-free paper that conforms to the American
National Standard for the Permanence of Paper for Printed Library Materials.

Typeset by Pickering & Chatto (Publishers) Limited
Printed and bound in the United Kingdom by Berforts Information Press

CONTENTS

Introduction	vii
Clarion	1
Robert Blatchford, 'The Sorcery Shop. An Impossible Romance' (1906–7)	3
McGinnis, 'An Idyll of the Dover Road. A True Story' (1907)	105
Glanville Maidstone, 'His Sister. A Little Spangle of Real Life' (1907)	107
Grace Potter, 'He Was a Valuable Dog' (1907)	109
R. B. Suthers, 'The Peasants and the Parasites. A Fable' (1908)	111
A. Neil Lyons, 'Little Reggie Writes Home. A Childish Document, Edited' (1908)	115
Victor Grayson, 'The Myopian's Muddle' (1909)	119
Victor Grayson, 'A Dead Man's Story' (1909)	123
A. Neil Lyons, 'My Lady's Chariot' (1910)	127
Glanville Maidstone, 'Nightmare Bridge' (1910)	131
Justice	135
Anon., '"Happy Valley." A Fairy Tale' (1907)	139
C. L. Everard, 'The Eternal Feminine' (1908)	143
Charles Allen Clarke, 'The Red Flag' (1908)	147
Edward Hartley, 'The Man in the Street. High Rates, Officialism and Socialism' (1909)	255
W. Anderson, 'The Fool and the Wise Man' (1910)	261
Labour Leader	263
Margaret Holden, 'A Scene in Eden Street' (1907)	265
Ernest Smith, 'Socialist Red' (1908)	269
Arthur Laycock, 'The "Retired" Street Sweeper' (1909)	271
Nellie Best, 'At a Servant's Registry' (1910)	275
Social Democrat	279
Frank Rosamund, 'For the Syndicate' (1907)	281
Prosper Mérimée, 'The Capture of the Redoubt', trans. Jacques Bonhomme (1908)	285
M. L. Pitcairn, 'Because They Understood Not' (1909)	289
F. J. Maynard, 'Unemployment: A Tragedy in Little' (1910)	297

Socialist Review	301
A. L. Grey, 'A Martian's Visit to Earth. Being a Literal Translation into English of the Preface to an Account by a Martian of his Visit to England' (1909)	303
Eric Dexter, 'Faith the Healer' (1910)	311
Teddy Ashton's Weekly Fellowship/Teddy Ashton's Weekly	319
William Siddle, 'A Stormy Wooing. The Smart Young Man and the Smarter Woman' (1907)	321
Teddy Ashton, 'Bill Spriggs in the Pantomime' (1908)	325
Editorial Notes	331
Silent Corrections	359

INTRODUCTION

In terms of political advancement, the period covered by this volume was one of both success – as the number of members of the Labour Representation Committee (LRC; the Labour Party after 1906) in the House of Commons rose from two to twenty-nine after the 1906 election – and division – as the Labour Party executive board moved closer to the Liberal Party in a bid to ensure electoral success, to the consternation of many outside of Parliament. Socialists who were sceptical about the usefulness of parliamentary socialism, such as Robert Blatchford (1851–1943) and Henry Mayers Hyndman (1842–1921), began a call for unity between socialist groups in order to ensure a strong and independent socialism. Even within the Labour Party there were concerns about the drift towards Liberal politics, and there was a call for Independent Labour Party (ILP) branches to be allowed to run their own candidates in elections without restrictions by national party policy. This dissatisfaction rumbled on until the 1909 Labour Party conference, when the executive board – the 'Big Four' of James Keir Hardie (1856–1915), James Ramsay MacDonald (1866–1937), John Bruce Glasier (1859–1920) and Philip Snowden (1864–1937) – threatened to resign if the motion was passed. The threat forced a retreat, but the motion only failed by 244 votes to 146.[1]

That fiction was still central to the socialist argument is evident in the attitudes to its inclusion in the periodicals during this time of division. Hardie had sold the *Labour Leader* to the ILP in 1905, and it was now edited by Glasier. Parliamentary success in the 1906 election was perceived by the executive board as a move in the right direction. As a consequence of either Glasier's different editorial style or the sense that on the strength of polling figures there was less need for multiple genres of persuasion in the *Labour Leader*, the volume of fiction was significantly reduced. The *Labour Leader* had not been the most prolific publisher of fiction, but the reduction was evident: while the period 1900 to 1904 saw long serializations by Margaret McMillan (1860–1931), Farquhar Auchenvole (n.d.), 'K. O'B.' (n.d.) and George Eliot (1819–80) in synopsis, in the period between 1905 and 1908 it published only two short serials by Katherine Bruce Glasier, one being extracts from an earlier work, and no serial at all in 1905. On the other hand, both the Social Democratic Federation (SDF; the Social-Democratic Party by late 1907) and Blatchford turned to fiction to further their arguments. *Justice* serialized Charles Allen Clarke's (1863–1935) 'The Red Flag', the third of only four serialized fictions in the period covered by this collection (Henry Baxter's (n.d.) 'David Dexter, Socialist' would follow in 1909–10), while Blatchford turned to utopian fiction in the *Clarion*. Although there were a number of areas where the socialism of Hyndman, the SDP, Blatchford and the *Clarion* overlapped, there was a marked difference between the serial literatures.

The *Clarion* continued to publish a great deal of humorous fiction by A. Neil Lyons (1880–1940), including 'Sixpenny Pieces' (1907–8); didactic short fiction in the form of fable and parable, represented here by R. B. Suthers's (1870–1950) 'The Peasant and the Parasites' (1908), Victor Grayson's (b. 1881) 'The Myopian's Muddle' (1909) and Glanville Maidstone's 'Nightmare Bridge' (1910); and realism in McGinnis's 'His Sister: A Little Spangle of Real Life' (1907) and Grace Potter's (n.d.) 'He Was a Valuable Dog' (1907). (McGinnis was a pseudonym used by Robert Blatchford, and Glanville Maidstone is also assumed to be Blatchford; see the *Clarion* headnote on p. 2 for further details.) But the most important piece of fiction published in the *Clarion* during the years covered by this volume is Robert Blatchford's 'The Sorcery Shop', serialized between 9 November 1906 and 22 March 1907. Blatchford's serial is important for two reasons: it is his final piece of lengthy fiction before he embarked on his crusade to warn Britain of the growing German threat,[2] and it is a version of *Merrie England* written as utopian fiction. Furthermore, the serial is the only one included in this collection to carry an explanation of the author's reasons for writing the piece – an interesting but rare addition to any of the socialist fictions published in the periodicals. 'A Few Explanatory Remarks by the Author' followed the conclusion of the *Clarion* serial but opened the story in the bound version, giving the reader a different experience and possibly a different approach to reading the story. Authorial intent is clearly explained as Blatchford claims, 'I have written this story for propagandist purposes, and because I thought it might be easier to write and to read than a revised edition of "Merrie England"' (p. 103).

Open propaganda in socialist periodical fiction is not unusual; in addition to the clearly propagandist fables, there are long discursive passages in H. J. Bramsbury's 'A Working Class Tragedy' (*Justice*, Volume 1) and Lillian Claxton's 'Nigel Grey' (*Labour Leader*, Volume 2). What is different is that these stories are allowed to present their politics as an integrated part of a whole fiction, whereas Blatchford describes 'The Sorcery Shop' as 'more of a Socialist tract than a story' (p. 103). This is not how subsequent critics refer to 'The Sorcery Shop' – most describe it as a 'novel' – but the position of the explanatory remarks at the beginning of the bound publication and Blatchford's denial of the work as fiction must have been intended to raise different expectations to those of the serial reader.

Blatchford described his story as 'utopian romance' and explained that the work was intended 'To indicate the possibilities of communal efforts, to show what might be done with England by a united and cultured English people, and to meet the common arguments brought against Socialism' (pp. 103–4). The intended impact of the utopian genre on the material world was similarly recognized by one of the *Clarion*'s reviewers of the fiction, who wished for 'a few million copies' to be distributed so that 'a new light would dawn' and 'nobler natures would be aroused'.[3] As argued in the General Introduction, the socialist movement in both Britain and the USA had grasped the use of utopian fiction as a spur and motivation for political and social change. What had changed between *Merrie England* and 'The Sorcery Shop' was Blatchford's idea of who would lead the way to utopia.

In *Merrie England*, Blatchford, writing under his pseudonym 'Nunquam', addressed his criticism of society to 'John Smith, of Oldham a hard-headed workman, fond of facts',[4] and that is what *Merrie England* gave the reader: facts about working-class living conditions, British agricultural production, sources of wealth and much more, with many chapters giving suggestions for further reading. Yet between the publication of *Merrie England* in 1893 and 'The Sorcery Shop' in 1906–7, the ILP had grown, the LRC had been formed and there was a clear movement towards a working relationship with the Liberal Party, even if the Gladstone–MacDonald pact was generally unknown. All of this took parliamentary socialism further and further away from Blatchford's ideas of socialist independence; the working-class voter had not moved far from his previous political position. As Anna Vaninskaya has argued of Blatchford's utopias, '[a]fter the clearest possible case had been presented, Mr Smith could still choose to vote for Tories or Liberals'.[5] Nevertheless, Blatchford's exasperation with the Liberal leanings of 'Mr Smith' and the Labour Party shifts his target for propaganda, as 'The Sorcery Shop' presents the socialist utopia to the upper- and middle-class Members of Parliament. Thus utopia is revealed to General Storm, the Tory landowner, and Mr Jorkle, the Liberal capitalist businessman, both of whom are Members of Parliament and are therefore positioned as potential engines for change.

The story concludes back in old England, as General Storm considers the visions of New Manchester in New England. Their guide, Mr Fry the wizard, by Chapter III 'had already given up [on Jorkle] as hopeless in his philistinism' (p. 16), but the experience affects the General. Jorkle and Storm return to their gentlemen's club as a parade of the unemployed pass the building; Jorkle dismisses the marchers and returns to his privileged lifestyle, ordering champagne, oysters and his motor car, but the General is less indifferent. Nevertheless, there is uncertainty about the effect of utopia on him as the fiction ends with his contemplation: '"Hah! Dammit! Hah! What a devilish odd dream. Hah! by Jove! The – the unemployed. Hah! the unemployed! Hah! Damn!"' (p. 103). There is no indication as to the General's attitude to past and present events; the 'Damn' may be a suggestion of dismissal or irritation with the public spectacle, or an exclamation of impatience with his renewed sense of responsibility. Or it may be that the realization of hardship and the possibility of change have now become apparent. What is clear is that the Tory General is unable to dismiss the experience, as the Liberal Jorkle does. The bound version reproduced the *Clarion* text but changed the General's final words: rather than the ambiguous 'Damn!', the bound text ends with 'God! God!'[6] The appeal to a higher power changes the tone, and the General's invocation to a deity could also be read in a number of ways. In light of Blatchford's dismissal of religion in the *Clarion* series of articles published as *God and my Neighbour* in 1903, it may suggest the General's approach to be useless and impractical. Alternatively, Blatchford did not discuss established religion in 'The Sorcery Shop', so the reference might suggest a re-awakening of the General's Christian values.

Charles Allen Clarke's 'The Red Flag' occupies a completely different literary position to Blatchford's fantasy: where Fry shows Storm and Jorkle the results of socialism, Clarke describes the necessity of socialism. The first twelve instalments present detailed descriptions of Mrs Wilkinson, her companion, May, and their experiences of being 'on tramp'. The reader is presented with the filthy conditions deemed acceptable for the homeless, the undignified treatment of the homeless by workhouse staff, the constant threat of physical or sexual abuse suffered by female tramps, and the hunger, isolation, death and suicides caused by such conditions. It is not until Chapter IX that there is any respite from the misery of homelessness, and even then that misery is only relieved by a presentation of one of the causes: the wealthy, lascivious capitalist whose bequest of almshouses places moral restrictions on the inhabitants not practised by himself. 'The Red Flag' was written by Clarke during what his biographer calls 'his most left-wing phase',[7] and it is the most overtly political of all his fiction.

Where Blatchford's 'Sorcery Shop' connected to reality through its inverse representation of social wrongs by showing them as social 'rights', Clarke's fiction connected with reality by drawing social investigation into the fiction. The serial begins with a reference to the borrowed material, as Clarke acknowledges his debt to 'Mrs Higgs' and her book *Glimpses into the Abyss*. This study of tramp life, published in 1906, was an anthology of Mary Higgs's (1854–1937) previous journalistic investigations, including 'Five Days and Five Nights as a Tramp among Tramps, which was originally published in 1904 and anonymously attributed to 'A Lady'. It is this account that Clarke uses as the template for his fictional portrayal of Mrs Wilkinson and May. By using a non-literary account of homeless life, Clarke sets out his selection of the aspects of reality used to make his political point. The separation between 'realism' and 'truth', as addressed in the

General Introduction, lies in the choice of what will be used to give the impression of 'reality' in fiction, and as Clarke directs the reader to the work of Higgs, he sets out his vision of the hardships of unemployment.

Clarke's fictionalized version of Higgs's account begins with her second chapter, 'A Night in a Common Lodging-House', rather than with the first chapter, 'A Night in a Municipal Lodging-House', presumably because the experience depicted in the first chapter is not as harrowing. Clarke repeats Higgs's description of the communal room in the common lodging house, the filth of the house and the verminous bedding presenting to the reader a picture of dirt and degradation very close to that of Higgs. Where Clarke differs from Higgs is in the description of the human inhabitants. While Higgs presents the inhabitants of the lodging house in a tone of barely suppressed horror, Clarke presents a more positive image without entirely sanitizing the scene. The main focus of Higgs's account is 'a huge negro with a *wicked* face';[8] Clarke instead presents the reader with a well-read cobbler who quotes Shelley. Higgs questions the veracity of the wedding ring worn by two women in the room, including the woman she assumes is with the 'negro', while Clarke makes no such suggestion of the cobbler's wife or the mothers in the room. Higgs separates herself from the inhabitants by giving only a visual description of the people, whereas Clarke's Mrs Wilkinson and May speak with some of the other lodgers, learning the cause of homelessness through Jim Campbell's story and the experiences of life on tramp from others. Both acknowledge that there is bad language, loose morals and alcohol swirling around the homeless, but Clarke nevertheless depicts a choice available to them, allowing some to behave with decorum and decency, and separating these from the less decorous but without imposing a moral judgment on those who behave differently.

Rather than projecting forward to an idealized socialist future, Clarke stretches the boundaries of his fiction to include fact in the same manner that Benjamin Disraeli (1804–81) had used the parliamentary blue books as the basis for *Sybil* (1845). But rather than relying on the investigation to describe a social class with which he had no involvement (as Disraeli did), Clarke combines journalism and social investigation to create a fiction that embedded comfortably within a periodical arguing for socialist change. There has never been a clear separation between the journalism and the fiction carried by a periodical, and critics have recognized the important influences of each on the other; for instance, Matthew Rubery's *The Novelty of Newspapers* 'challenged the assumed divide between the period's literature and journalism ... by demonstrating how the newspaper was integral to the Victorian novel's development'.[9] The porousness of the periodical and newspaper page, discussed in the General Introduction, is evident here as the boundaries of Clarke's fiction open and draw in Higgs's investigative work.

During this period, the *Clarion* carried two short fictions by Victor Grayson, the new and independent socialist MP for Colne Valley in West Yorkshire. Grayson was flamboyant, unpredictable and critical of the parliamentary Labour Party for what he – and his local group, the Colne Valley Labour League – saw as its abandonment of the working classes and the unemployed: 'The CVLL wanted a non-trade unionist to stir up the Labour Party in parliament and question its sheep-like support of the Liberal line'.[10] His separation from the Labour Party, his association with the Marxist SDF (the SDP from October 1907) and the generally anti-party-political *Clarion*, and his involvement in the attempt to develop a unified British Socialist Party did not endear him to prominent Labour members like MacDonald and Glasier, who worked to distance the Labour Party from the socialists. Grayson's short stories 'The Myopian's Muddle' and 'A Dead Man's Story', although not in any sense different from the socialist use of the short story, do suggest his critical attitude to the Labour Party's dilution of socialism.

'A Dead Man's Story' is a fairly standard use of the short story form. The narrator recounts a dream and so separates the fiction-within-fiction; the story is distanced from the narrator's 'reality' in the same manner as Blatchford's 'The Sorcery Shop' and other utopian or dystopian fictions. The dream, consisting of the narrator's conversation with a ghost, is a similar form to that of Glasier's 'Andrew Carnegie's Ghost: A Red Letter Night at Skibo Castle. A Christmas Story' (*Labour Leader*, Volume 3). But where Glasier's ghostly conversation was held between living millionaire Andrew Carnegie and his grasping inner consciousness, Grayson presents the reader with a conversation between the narrator and a suicide. The latter gives all the reasons for choosing death over life: unemployment, starvation, economic entrapment and imprisonment on the assumption by the legal system that the unemployed must all be potential thieves. The story ends with a direct statement on the necessity of social, political and economic change: 'Life must be made worth keeping. It must be as free as the sun and as dignified as the stars' (p. 125).

'A Myopian's Muddle', on the other hand, is a direct and scathing attack on both the Labour Party and their supporters. Grayson takes the original form of the fable, with its origins with Aesop the slave and the necessity of encoding social criticism, and applies it to socialist and labour politics. The naming of the groups within the story – the Myopians and the Panopians – separates the short-sighted workers/voters with the all-seeing employers/politicians whose clarity of vision is used to benefit themselves and enslave the workers. The metaphor is extended to include a criticism of religion, as the Fakir soothes Myopian discontent with stories of happiness in a faraway land. But the most scathing criticism is reserved for party politics. The building of a circular railway to convince the Myopians that progress to Utopia was being made while no change in circumstance was being implemented is a direct critique of the British parliamentary system as it stood. Grayson's story destroys the illusion – propounded by the employers and politicians who benefit from it – that voters have any effect on the running of the country or on the decisions made by others that affect their lives.

Up to this point, Grayson's criticism of parliamentary politics is the same as the arguments raised throughout the socialist movement. But his story's departure from others lies in his criticism of the Labour Party as indistinguishable from other political parties. The circular parliamentary journey to nowhere is steered by a driver in a blue uniform, which clearly signifies the Conservative Party through its party colour. Meanwhile the conductor is dressed in a red uniform, the colour of socialism; but instead of offering a real political alternative, his shout of 'All change here!' (p. 120) signals the start of a journey back to the beginning. The interchange of 'red' and 'blue' omits the Liberal 'yellow'. This might be read as the absorption of 'red' or socialist ideas by the Liberal Party, as the 'People's Budget' of 1909 benefited the workers to a certain level without making any changes to the structure of political power; or it might be read as an accusation of the collusion of the Labour Party with the established political parties – an accusation made particularly barbed by the association with Conservatism and not the Liberalism that MacDonald was drawing the party towards. The 'young man' who tries to open the eyes of the Myopians is clearly both Grayson himself and the socialism he and others are trying to elevate above party politics. But the young man is thrown off the train, which carries on turning in party-political circles – a prophetic conclusion, as Grayson would lose his seat in the 1910 election and the socialists outside of the Labour Party would lose the contest for control of the party.

This was a crisis point for the socialist movement, and authors such as Blatchford, Clarke and Grayson drew the fight for socialism and the arguments for the necessity of socialist political independence into their very different genres. But despite the differences between genres, the message is clear, and there is a harmony in the clarion calls through the fiction that desires to be echoed in reality through British socialist politics.

Notes
1. M. Pugh, *Speak for Britain! A New History of the Labour Party* (London: Vintage, 2011), p. 71. The 'Labour Party' was an umbrella title for the separate socialist groups and trade unions that constituted the party. A member at this time could not be a directly affiliated member of the Labour Party but would become a member by joining one of the affiliated socialist groups (the ILP and the Fabians being the largest) or one of the affiliated trade unions.
2. L. Thompson, *Robert Blatchford: Portrait of an Englishman* (London: Victor Gollancz, 1951), p. 127.
3. A. E. Fletcher, 'A New Utopia', *Clarion*, 2 August 1907, p. 2, quoted in C. Waters, *British Socialists and the Politics of Popular Culture, 1884–1914* (Manchester: Manchester University Press, 1990), p. 51.

4. 'Nunquam' [Robert Blatchford], 'Merrie England', *Clarion*, 4 March 1893, p. 8.
5. A. Vaninskaya, *William Morris and the Idea of Community: Romance, History and Propaganda* (Edinburgh: Edinburgh University Press, 2010), p. 187.
6. R. Blatchford, *The Sorcery Shop* (London: Clarion Press, 1907), p. 199.
7. P. Salveson, *Lancashire's Romantic Radical: The Life and Writings of Allen Clarke/Teddy Ashton* (Huddersfield: Little Northern Books, 2009), p. 68.
8. 'A Lady' [M. Higgs], 'Five Days and Five Nights as a Tramp among Tramps' (1904), *The Workhouse, The Story of an Institution*, at http://www.workhouses.org.uk/Higgs/TrampAmongTramps.shtml [accessed 7 February 2013].
9. M. Rubery, *The Novelty of Newspapers: Victorian Fiction after the Invention of the News* (Oxford: Oxford University Press, 2009), p. 4.
10. J. Dickenson, *Renegades and Rats: Betrayal and the Remaking of Radical Organisations in Britain and Australia* (Melbourne: Melbourne University Press, 2006), p. 128.

CLARION

Robert Blatchford, 'The Sorcery Shop. An Impossible Romance', *Clarion*, Chapter I, 9 November 1906, p. 1; Chapter II, 16 November 1906, p. 7; Chapter III, 23 November 1906, p. 9; Chapter IV, 30 November 1906, p. 7; Chapter V, 7 December 1906, p. 7; Chapter VI, 14 December 1906, p. 1; Chapter VII, 21 December 1906, p. 1; Chapter VIII, 28 December 1906, p. 1; Chapter IX, 4 January 1907, p. 1; Chapter X, 11 January 1907, p. 1; Chapter XI, 18 January 1907, p. 7; Chapter XII, 1 February 1907, p. 7; Chapter XIV, 8 February 1907, p. 7; Chapter XV, 15 February 1907, p. 1; Chapter XVI, 22 February 1907, p. 7; Chapter XVI [continued], 1 March 1907, p. 1; Chapter XVII, 8 March 1907, p. 1; Chapter XVIII, 15 March 1907, p. 5; Chapter XIX, 22 March 1907, p. 1.[1]

McGinnis, 'An Idyll of the Dover Road. A True Story', *Clarion*, 5 April 1907, p. 1.

Glanville Maidstone, 'His Sister. A Little Spangle of Real Life', *Clarion*, 19 April 1907, p. 7.

Grace Potter, 'He Was a Valuable Dog', *Clarion*, 4 October 1907, p. 12.

R. B. Suthers, 'The Peasants and the Parasites. A Fable', *Clarion*, 24 January 1908, p. 3.

A. Neil Lyons, 'Little Reggie Writes Home. A Childish Document, Edited', *Clarion*, 22 May 1908, p. 1.

Victor Grayson, 'The Myopian's Muddle', *Clarion*, 12 March 1909, p. 8.

Victor Grayson, 'A Dead Man's Story', *Clarion*, 26 March 1909, p. 3.

A. Neil Lyons, 'My Lady's Chariot', *Clarion*, 8 July 1910, p. 1.

Glanville Maidstone, 'Nightmare Bridge', *Clarion*, 15 July 1910, p. 1.

Robert Blatchford continued his warnings, begun in 1904, of the dangers of German naval expansion, and his articles in the *Clarion* (1891–1935) were joined and supported by similar articles by Fred Jowett (1864–1944) and Henry Mayers Hyndman. Although these warnings were greeted with a cry of 'jingo' from all sides of British socialism, Blatchford maintained his concern about potential German invasion and control of the seas and continued to explain the German necessity of looking outside its own borders because of its inability to be self-sufficient in providing food for its expanding population.[2] In 1909, at the invitation of foreign editor Fenton Macpherson, a former ILP member and contributor to the *Labour Leader*, Blatchford continued his campaign in the pages of the imperialist *Daily Mail*. For a short period between 1906 and 1907, Victor Grayson (b. 1881) was the *Clarion*'s political editor before his election as socialist MP for Colne Valley in West Yorkshire in 1907. Sales of the *Clarion* reached a peak of 83,000 in 1910 shortly before Blatchford resigned the editorship and passed the control of the paper to his daughter, Winifred.

Many of the authors included in this selection had previously published in the *Clarion*. Blatchford regularly published under the pseudonym McGinnis (sometimes spelled M'Ginnis). He might have also used the pseudonym Glanville Maidstone; there is no record of an author of this name, but Robert Peel Glanville Blatchford (Glanville being a family name) was born in Maidstone, Kent. Blatchford's full biography can found in the headnote for the *Clarion* in Volume 2, p. 3, while biographical details for R. B. Suthers and A. Neil Lyons are presented in the headnote for the *Clarion* in Volume 3, pp. 2–3. However, Grace Potter has not been identified.

Only Albert Victor Grayson had not previously published in the *Clarion*. Grayson's birth was registered in Liverpool, but there were rumours that his parents were not his birth parents. Grayson joined the ILP in 1905 and was renowned as an orator. He was elected as an independent socialist MP for Colne Valley in 1907 and proved combative, pushing the socialist cause in the House of Commons, but he lost his seat in the first 1910 general election. He stood for Kennington, south London, in the second election of 1910 but failed to secure the seat. He published his ideas on socialism in A. P. Orage's *New Age* and Blatchford's *Clarion* and was on the committee of British Socialist Party until he, the ILP and the *Clarion* group were marginalized by Hyndman and the SDP. He retired from the Party in 1912. Marriage and a brief spell in Australia followed until his wife's death and his return to Britain. Grayson disappeared in September 1920 and was neither seen nor heard of again.

Notes
1. In the serialization of 'The Sorcery Shop', Chapter XII, titled 'A Question of Finance' and published in the issue for 1 February 1907, was followed in the issue for 8 February 1907 by Chapter XIV, 'The Navvies'. This printing error was corrected in the bound text, published later in 1907, when 'The Navvies' was amended as 'Chapter Thirteen'.
2. P. Ward, *Red Flag and Union Jack: Englishness, Patriotism, and the British Left, 1881–1924* (Woodbridge: Boydell Press, 1998), p. 111.

Robert Blatchford, 'The Sorcery Shop. An Impossible Romance' (1906–7)

[9 November 1906]

Chapter I. The Ink Well.

The smoke-room of the Directorate Club – sometimes playfully called the "Guinea Pigs," because the membership was confined to directors of public companies – was rich and solid, like its illustrious owners; but it was not homely. It smelt of stale tobacco; it had a northern aspect; its chairs and sofas bore themselves unpropitiously; its colours were harsh and sombre. Indeed, a casual visitor with no intimate comprehension of the financial soul to guide him, must have thought it marvellous that such an extravagance of carved mahogany, and stamped leather, and gilt moulding, and tapestry curtain, and pile carpet had resulted in a effect so mean and comfortless.

On one particular morning, a raw, bleak morning, in early May, the home of the Guinea Pigs looked its unfriendliest and hardest.

On this occasion there were only three members present. Two of them, seated at a table on which stood a tray of biscuits and two glasses of sherry and bitters, were talking. The other sat bolt upright in a huge armchair, reading a copy of the "Times."

The gentlemen at the table were very important personages indeed; for one of them was Major-General Sir Frederick Manningtree Storm, Conservative M.P. for South Loomshire, and the other was Mr. Samuel Jorkle, Liberal M.P. for Shantytown East.

The Honourable Member for Shantytown East was a highly respectable and influential professional patriot and financier; one of those great captains of industry who have made England what she is, and are somewhat extravagantly proud of the achievement. The dream of his life was to form a combine of all the big noses in Ivory and Old Bones, and to perpetrate a corner in false teeth.

Mr. Jorkle was, for so eminent and successful a financial magnate, somewhat undistinguished in appearance. He was, to be candid, a bald, pompous, corpulent man of sixty, with watery eyes, thin lips, a bulbous nose, a gold cable watchchain, a diamond ring, gold-rimmed pebbles,[1] and flat feet.

Major-General Sir Frederick Storm was a distinguished and richly decorated professional homicide; a vicious, choleric, brave, arrogant, gouty, liverish, obtuse old Tory of the bluest blue, who had defended his country upon a hundred fields, where the inscrutable degrees of Providence had destined her to exploit recalcitrant natives. He believed himself, with a strange sincerity, to be an honourable and exemplary member of the better classes.

In appearance he was the typical aristocrat, retired from the army, well-dressed well-groomed, tall, and lean; his sharp face, dyed purple with Southern wine and Eastern suns. He wore the grizzled, fierce moustaches of the old *sabreur*,[2] and his hard grey eyes stared insolently at the world from under their heavy white brows.

"The worst of it is," said Mr. Jorkle – they were talking about the Socialists – "that all the preposterous advertisement they are getting just now in the Press may have the effect of making capital shy."

"It will have the effect of making capital *bolt*, sir," answered the Major-General, emphasising the pun.

"Of course," said Mr. Jorkle, pursing up his thin lips, "I don't believe that any sensible person will take their hysterical nonsense seriously, but – the boom should be stopped."

"Take them seriously?" said the General; "*I'd* take them seriously in a way they would like precious little. A parcel of illiterate, lazy tub-thumping levellers. I'd level 'em, by George!"

"Ah," sighed Mr. Jorkle, "the idea of the fools imagining they could carry on the country without capital! Capital, sir, is wings and feet and heart and lungs. Abolish capital, and the cock won't fight, sir."

"Abolish capital?" cried the honourable and gallant member for South Loomshire, "*I'd* abolish 'em, dammit!"

These were the very words of that remarkable man.

"If they ever did get a Socialist State," continued Mr. Jorkle, "which God forbid, they would very soon have enough of it. Nice place it would be, with all the incentives to enterprise destroyed; individuality crushed out; intellect subordinated to the petty tyranny of illiterate and unintelligent demagogues; all the life and spirit of the nation paralysed by a machine-like system of espionage and interference; the nation stagnant at a dead level of mediocrity, and life reduced to a horrible penal round of dull and colourless monotony." The Honourable member for East Shantytown paused, with one hand a little raised; his earnestness had betrayed him into something very like a speech.

"Pooh, pooh, sir!" cried General Storm, hotly, "I say pooh, pooh! Who is going to trust those unwashed ragamuffins with the helm of Government? One might as well select a Cabinet from the prisons and idiot asylums. A Socialist State, begad! – Pretty kettle of fish! Dustmen paid as well as a field-marshal, Jack as good as his master. Prime Minister, in a flannel shirt, dropping aitches all over the House,[3] by George! And a Chancellor of the Exchequer trying to squeeze estimates out of nowhere, after he has killed the goose that laid the golden eggs! If I'd my way with the fools, dammit –"

Here the honourable and gallant gentleman was interrupted by a question from the little man behind the "Times."

"You have, I presume, studied Socialism on its practical side, General Storm?" said the little old gentleman.

The two great men stared at the questioner in silence, for a few moments. The gold spectacles seemed to say, "What are you, sir?" The monocle seemed to ask, "Who the devil are *you*, and how dare you speak to me without an introduction?"

The stranger smiled, and took a pinch of snuff.

He was small and thin, with a hairless, wrinkled face, and bushy grey hair. He might have been any age between sixty and ninety. He was dressed in old-fashioned black garments, with a black satin stock and Gladstonian collar.[4] His lips flickered with dry, satirical smiles, and his eyes twinkled and gleamed out of the deep, pent-house shadows of his brows, like sparks of green and blue fire.

After an interval of frosty silence the General spoke. "I did not know, sir," he said coldly, "that Socialism *had* a practical side. You – er – you have the advantage of me, sir."

"I beg your pardon, General," said the old gentleman, with a bow, "my name is Fry; Nathaniel Fry, of Wells and Wells, in Simmery Axe."[5]

"Wells and Wells," said Mr. Jorkle, doubtfully; "may I ask what they are in?"

"Art," said Mr. Fry.

"Art!" The gold rims looked surprise; the monocle contempt.

"Yes, sir; black and white."

"You don't mean newspaper work!" exclaimed Mr. Jorkle.

Mr. Fry laughed softly and tapped his gold snuff box. "No," he said, in a slow distinct way; "no, sir. I mean art. Black art, and white art; or, as I should prefer to call it, black magic, and white magic. I am a wizard, a magician."

Having made this amazing statement, as calmly as if he had been declaring himself a dealer in jute, the queer little man took a pinch of snuff, and offered the box to each of the two great men in turn.

Then, the offer being politely declined, he closed the box with a snap, and, as he did that, a flash of blue fire burst from under the lid.

Mr. Jorkle laughed. The General looked on in contemptuous silence.

"Hullo!" said Mr. Jorkle, "magic?"

"H'm! The fact is," said Mr. Fry, "this is a curious box." With that he took another pinch of snuff, and, after I having it, blew from his nostrils a long, thin, spiral of bright green smoke. It was no ordinary smoke either, for it floated across the room in writhing rings until it swirled and twisted itself into the letters "N. Fry." "My signature, gentlemen," said the little man with an odd laugh.

"Gad!" exclaimed the General, thawing somewhat, "that's a deuced clever trick, by George! Beats Maskelyne and Cooke![6] Hey?"

"You flatter me," said Mr. Fry. He placed the snuff-box on the table. "Will you oblige me by opening it?" he asked.

Mr. Jorkle raised the lid, and started as a white mouse leaped out, and, tumbling off the table, banished in a puff of smoke on the carpet.

The magnets laughed. And the General declared that 'pon his word Mr. Fry "ought to be on the halls."[7]

The old gentleman shrugged his shoulders deprecatingly. "Toys," he said, "toys to amuse the young."

"Toys!" exclaimed Mr. Jorkle, in his bland patronising manner. "I call it exceedingly clever conjuring."

"Pardon me," said Mr. Fry, "I should not call it conjuring. I should call it magic." Then, as the magnates smiled, he added, "You do not believe in magic?"

"Haw!" said the General, "hardly, at this time of day."

"Perhaps," said Mr. Fry, "you will allow me to show you something less elementary."

"With pleasure," said Mr. Jorkle, "but don't be too magical, Mr. Fry. Don't turn us into dumb waiters, or umbrella stands." And Mr. Jorkle laughed ponderously over his own wit.

"My dear sir," said Mr. Fry, gravely, "I assure you that our firm would never presume to take such a liberty. But will you kindly step with me into the lift for a moment?"

The magnates seemed to think this was taking a good deal of trouble for the sake of a mere joke, but after a brief hesitation assented, and the three gentlemen stepped out upon the landing. "Rabbit," said Mr. Fry, to the attendant, "kindly allow us to go down in your lift. We shall return shortly."

To Mr. Jorkle's surprise, the commissionaire made no objection. The three gentlemen entered the lift, Rabbit closed the door, Mr. Fry touched the button and they descended.

"Gentlemen, allow me," said Mr. Fry, as the lift came to a stop, and he opened the door and bowed his guests into an apartment upon which neither of them had ever before set eyes.

It was a circular room, the walls panelled in brown oak, the ceiling panelled in brown oak, the floor of brown oak parqueterie.[8] There was no furniture of any kind: there were no pictures nor decorations, no windows, nor firegrates, nor doors; but from the centre of the ceiling a large opalescent globe lamp was suspended, giving a soft bright light.

The magnates looked at their strange host and at each other in mute surprise. The lift rose slowly through the ceiling; the panels closing after it. Then Mr. Fry spoke.

"Gentlemen," he said, "this is my private office, at No. 70, Simmery Axe."[9]

"Simmery Axe!" said Mr. Jorkle, "oh, come!"

"If you will be kind enough to glance out of the window, Mr. Jorkle," said the host. "Ah, I forgot." As he spoke he clapped his hands and a circular window opened in the oaken wall, as the rose aperture opens in a camera. "Now, sir," said Mr. Fry.

Mr. Jorkle stepped to the window and looked out. "Yes," he said doubtfully, "yes, yes, that is Simmery Axe, or seems to be. But how we have got from the West End to the City[10] in a few seconds and by way of the club lift, I don't pretend to understand."

"Magic," remarked the General, dryly.

"Thank you, sir," said Mr. Fry, "allow me to offer you a glass of the best wine in the world. Light!"

As he uttered the word "Light" in a sharp tone a handsome youth in evening dress appeared. He did not come in, nor up, nor down; he appeared.

"Yes, sir," said Light.

"Refreshments, Light," said Mr. Fry, "and a nice, clean goblin."

"Yes, sir."

Light touched his nose, and an electric bell rang. Immediately there rose through the floor a handsome old oak table and three of the most luxurious armchairs that ever lured a human being to slumber.

"Be seated, gentlemen, please," said Mr. Fry quietly. "Light, the wine."

Light smiled, produced a large decanter of wine from the tail pocket of his dress coat; drew three ancient cut-glass beakers from his sleeves, and vanished.

"Well, upon my word, Mr. Fry," said Mr. Jorkle, "you beat all the magicians I've ever seen. Good God! what's that?"

The General looked round sharply, and beheld, standing at his elbow, a fearsome creature, like a frog, in a page boy's livery.

"That," explained Mr. Fry, placidly, "is one of our goblins. He is spotty, but innocuous. Spots, get the ink-well ready for use." Spots saluted and vanished.

"Now, gentlemen," said Mr. Fry, as he filled the glasses, "the club wine is good, as I need not tell you. But I think – I hope – this is better. Gentlemen, my respects."

The host and his guests gook their wine simultaneously. As they replaced the empty glasses upon the board, Mr. Jorkle sighed and the General said emphatically, "By George! By George, sir, that is a devilish good wine. If magic can make a wine like that –" Here the General stopped speaking and stared at the picture in the panel opposite to his chair. "Hallo!" he said, after a pause, "that's a deuced pretty girl. Hah! Reminds me of a girl I met – hah – at Penally[11] – hah – let me see – it must have been in the sixties – hah – devilish sweet sort of a girl – hah – hum."

The General hahed and hummed himself into a silent reverie. Somewhere a thrush began to sing. As Mr. Fry refilled the glasses the glug glug of the bottle reminded Mr. Jorkle of a brook – a brook in a green, green wood. And that was strange, for Mr. Jorkle had not heard a brook prattle for more than thirty years.

"If you gentlemen believed in magic," said Mr. Fry, with a curious smile, "I should say that this is magic wine."

"Magic or not," said the General, "we'll finish it, by George."

They sat and finished the wine in silence. And the thrush went on singing, and the pretty girl in the picture seemed to look on smilingly, and the General curled his moustaches and gazed sternly at the toe of his patent leather boots.

At length Mr. Fry rose and clapped his hands, whereupon a panel in the wall slid silently back, and saying, "This way, gentlemen, if you please," the host led the way into another room.

This was a domed room, the roof cunningly contrived to represent the night sky in which the stars sparkled like gems. In the centre of the marble floor was a circular black pool, some seven or eight feet in diameter, and surrounded by a flat pewter edge.

"That," said Mr. Fry, pointing to the black pool, "is the Ink Well. You have doubtless heard of the magic properties of ink."

"Ha, yes," said the General, "Indian devilry. Look into blot of ink in the hand, and see wonders, don't you know, and that sort of thing."

"Precisely. Many marvels have been seen in ink. With your permission, I will show you some."

Again the wizard clapped his hands, and a pear-shaped car or cabinet came down through the roof and settled upon the black pool, like a balloon floating in water.

"Our Crystal Car, gentlemen," said the wizard. He whistled and a door opened in the car, and, saying, "Kindly follow me," he stepped in and sat down. The others followed; the door was shut, and the car sank swiftly into the darkness.

"How do you get your light?" asked Mr. Jorkle; "there are no lamps, and the walls seem to be opaque."

"Certainly," replied the wizard. "They are solid crystal, and are immersed in black ink; but the car is lined with moonbeams."

The General coughed, and, to change the subject, remarked; "Talking of light, that's a smart young fellow, that Light of yours."

"Yes," said Mr. Fry, mildly, "an excellent fellow. Quite a superior fellow. He is a thief."

"A thief!"

"Well, he was a thief. He tried to steal my watch. That is how I first came to know him. And I brought him over to Simmery Axe on a broomstick, and taught him the business. He is very clever in the lighter branches."

"Not the light-fingered branches?"

"Eh! Oh no. He is very good at dreams. His nightmares are really works of art. I hope to make him head of the haunting department soon. He is so clever with the ghosts. There is not a ghost in England who wouldn't do anything to oblige Light."

"Indeed," said the General, "oh, I will not trouble you with idle questions. I don't mind where we may be going, so long as we are not bored when we get there, don't you know; but – hah – I hope we shall be back I time for lunch."

"Oh," said Mr. Fry, "but I hope you will lunch with me there."

"With pleasure," said Mr. Jorkle, "for I am hungry; but I don't know where 'there' may be."

"There is here," answered the wizard, as the car came to rest. "And now gentlemen, we are in an impossible country, inhabited by impossible people, who do impossible things, and are impossibly happy. I hope you will be amused. Allow me to open the door."

[16 November 1906]

Chapter II. Paradise Regained.

The three stepped out into a great green wood. Around them the tall, proud beeches lifted their long, sinuous boughs, like arms held up in gladness to the spring. The young green foliage was more luminous than gems; the glints of blue sky 'twixt silver branch and emerald plume glowed like old stained glass in a cathedral window; the mossy path was dappled with fluttering, soft lights and tender shadows; and in the balmy sea-green twilight overhead a blackcap sang passionately with the exceeding joy that almost makes chords with pain.

The wizard's guests looked round them curiously. "Fine timber," said Mr. Jorkle.

"Lots of game about here, eh?" remarked the General.

"To be sure, to be sure," answered the little man, with his dry smile; "timber to sell, and game to kill. Why not?"

He remained silent for a moment, standing in a pool of quivering golden sunlight, and looked at the two Philistines[12] with a puckering of his face, and a queer gleam in his eyes. Then, as he drew forth the magic snuff box, and tapped the lid, he said, in clear-cut and deliberate words: "In this strange country, gentlemen, there is no selling and no killing: none."

"What!" cried his guests, staring at him blankly.

"In this country," the little man went on, "they have neither money nor guns; not a weapon, not a cartridge; not a banknote, bill, nor coin. I told you it was an impossible place." He took a pinch of snuff, and the three walked on in silence.

In a little while they reached the fringe of the wood; and came out upon a broad plateau, the grass of which was cut short, like a lawn. From this the land fell away in a gentle slope, now all ablaze with the brilliant yellow flowers of the gorse. Round the foot of the slope wound a broad, shallow stream, so clear that the pebbles on its speckled bed were quite plain to the eye. The stream was crossed at interval by light wooden bridges, simple but elegant in design; and hard by one of these a great blue heron stood amongst the flowering rushes, complacently preening his feathers.

Mr. Fry halted on the crown of the slope and waved his hand. "I think, gentlemen," he said, "you will like this view."

Beyond the green lawn, and the golden gorse, and the silver stream, spread out a gracious plain. It was such a plain as the philistines had never dreamed of; but they were not good at dreams.

It was an orchard plain, a plain of flowering trees, in the midst of which was built a city. The roofs and towers and gables of the town stood up like red and white islands out of a vast sea of blossom.

"A fair sight, a fair sight on a fine May morning," said Mr. Fry.

For a while the Philistines gazed silently at the marvellous dream city and its sea of flowers. They saw the red roofs glowing amid the billows of delicate pink and white. They saw the domes and towers of marble palaces, and the graceful shaft of a tall campanile with a gleaming golden crown.[13] They heard the rhythmic hurry of a carillon, sounding wonderfully from some distant belfry and the throbbing and champing music of a marching band, afar off in the hidden streets. Below them ran the chuckling river; above them spread the glistening azure sky; behind them the thrush sang rapturously in the leafy wood. The dew-washed air was swept with the perfume of blossom and flower, and suffused by the sun with a rosy glow.

The old wizard, in his rusty black, stood looking at his companions with his sparky eyes to mark the effects of the vision.

"Hah!" came at last from the General. "Hah! Where the devil *are* we, Mr. Fry?"

Mr. Fry, his hands under his coat tails, his legs apart, and his head inclined to one side, stood like some crafty and satirical old crow watching a Cockney with a gun.

"What town is this, sir?" asked Mr. Jorkle.

"Gentlemen," said the wizard, smiling slily, "have you ever heard of Manchester?"

His guests laughed.

"Manchester," Mr. Fry continued, "is a dirty, unhandsome, smoky city. Rich, but mean. Eh?"

"Beastly hole!" said the General.

"Well, gentlemen," said the wizard, spreading his legs wider, and looking more like a crow than ever, "*this* is Manchester." He waved his hand towards the flowery plain. "This city of health and beauty, of happy homes, and noble palaces, of trees and flowers, this Paradise regained,[14] is Manchester – Manchester under impossible conditions."

The Honourable Member for Shantytown East adjusted his spectacles, Major-General Sir Frederick Mannintgree Storm put up his monocle. Both regarded the wizard sternly for some moments. Then Mr. Jorkle asked curtly, "What building is that – the big marble place, with high towers?"

Mr. Fry laughed silently before he answered. Then he said, "That, sir, is the Hulme Town Hall."[15]

"Town Hall!" exclaimed the General. "It looks like a royal palace, by George! I began to think the King had come to live here, by Jove!"

"There is no king," quoth Mr. Fry.

"No king!" The two guests started. Then the General said tartly: "No king! You don't mean to say there's a beastly president, dammit."

"There is no president," quoth Mr. Fry.

"But, but," cried Mr. Jorkle, swelling with consequence, "there must be – er – somebody. What kind of government have they here?"

The wizard, in his driest tones, replied: "Sir, this healthy, wealthy, and happy people, this great people, have no government at all: none of any kind, sir."

"Must be a devilish queer place to live in," said the General.

"It is," replied the wizard, with a kind of tender gravity, "the happiest nation the world has ever known."

"I'm glad I don't live here, at any rate," said Mr. Jorkle.

"I too," said the General.

"Well, gentlemen, we shall see, we shall see," said the wizard, smiling; "but, now, suppose we walk into the town and get some lunch."

"Haw," said the General, "they do eat and drink, then? That's better. I began to think the natives were a lot of beastly angels."

"The Manchester people used not to be angels," remarked Mr. Jorkle.

"Hah! Didn't look it certainly," assented the General; "used to be an undersized, smoke-dried lot of little beggars, by Jove, with bandy legs, hah, and that sort of thing."

"Let us walk on," said Mr. Fry; "we shall meet some of the people by the way."

On this the three followed the winding path through the scented gorse, and crossed the bridge where the heron stood.

"Cool customer, that bird," said the General, surprised that the heron showed no fear.

"Yes," said the wizard, "all the wild things hereabouts are very bold," and he added quietly, "the people love them so."

Crossing a strip of meadow, where the primroses and violets were so thickly intermixed that the sward suggested some wonderful Oriental carpet, the three came into the highway.

"This," said the Wizard, "is the Chester Road."

It was a wide road, so wide that after the first glance Mr. Jorkle remarked, with characteristic astuteness, "land must be cheap about here."

But the wizard shook his head. "Land," he said, "is very dear. It is so dear that the most popular hero, the greatest benefactor of the people, could not beg, nor buy, a single square foot to all his own. The land here, like the air and the sea, is *pro bono publico*."[16]

Mr. Jorkle looked at the General. They both looked at the Chester Road.

"You will notice certain peculiarities about this road," said Mr. Fry. "You will observe that it is a wide road, with a broad band of well-kept grass along each side, nearest the gardens. You will observe that the houses are very handsome and homely, and are all detached, each standing in its own garden. There are no walls nor hedges between these gardens and the road. As a matter of fact, there is not a lock nor a fastening in all Manchester."

"Good God!" said the General.

"You will notice, further," Mr. Fry went on, "that the avenue which runs the whole length of this long road is composed wholly of fruit trees."

"And do you mean to tell me, sir," Mr. Jorkle asked warmly, "that people here are so honest that they will not steal the fruit from these trees, and that no thief will ever enter these houses?"

"'Honest' is not the right word," answered the wizard; "the people here would no more think of robbing each other's houses than you and Sir Frederick Storm would think of stealing each other's spoons."

"But, hah, dash it all, Mr. Fry," said the General, "don't they steal the fruit? Don't the boys, begad, hook the apples?"

"They take the apples, no doubt, if they want them," said Mr. Fry; "but they don't *steal* them. The apples are grown by the people, for the people to use. Moreover – ha, here are some of the natives."

As he spoke two young men, dressed in cricketing flannels, came out of an adjacent garden and walked toward the three. They were tall men, with bronzed complexions, dark hair, and grey eyes.

"Come," said the wizard, "these Manchester men are not stunted and crooked, General. They are handsome, alert, well-set-up fellows, and more than common tall. You might find a couple of finer men in the Life Guards,[17] and – you might not. Eh?"

"Hah!" said the General, "they are smart, upstandin' chaps, certainly. Yes, begad, and they carry themselves like men. But these are gentlemen, of course."

The wizard shook his head. "There are no gentlemen here," he said, "and no ladies."

"Hah," said the General, "that reminds me, what are the women like?"

"The women?" Mr. Fry wrinkled up his eyes and laughed. "Oh, the women. I'm afraid I'm not magician enough to describe them. They worship their women here; consequently, my dear General, the women are – like that." He turned his eyes towards a lawn on his right.

There was a woman standing in the pathway, trimming the flowers. She met their look with a bright, friendly smile, and "a good morning, friends," that sounded as fresh and merry as he laughter of a child.

The three raised their hats and returned the greeting as they passed. And there was silence for a little while. Then Mr. Fry said, "*that* is a woman." And the General, curling his moustache, replied, "Yes, by George, that *is* a woman."

"But," Mr. Jorkle said, in a puzzled, half querulous tone, "she must be a lady. She has the bearing of a lady. She is dressed as a lady. Besides, only well-to-do people could live in a road like this."

"My friend," said the wizard, in his dry way, "*all* the people of this country are well-to-do people. They are the wealthiest and happiest people the world has ever known."

"They are," said the General emphatically, "a devilish handsome people, if they are at all like those we have seen."

"Those houses," Mr. Jorkle said, "would let for a hundred a year in England."

"Black hair," mused the General, "dusky and fine; a figure like a goddess, a smile like a baby, and purple eyes. Hah! Hang it, Fry, couldn't you conjure one or two into Simmery Axe?"

"H'm! Do you think," said Mr. Jorkle, "that you could conjure some lunch?"

"Why, of course," answered the wizard, "we will go and lunch with the goddess."

"Do you know her?" asked the General rather eagerly.

"I know the country; that is enough, said Mr. Fry, and he at once set off, and the others, somewhat doubtfully, followed him.

The goddess saw them turn, and actually walked out into the road to meet them.

"Madam," said the wizard, "we are three strangers, and –"

"You would like some lunch," struck in the goddess, with a beautiful smile. "Please come in. I will ask my daughter to get something. You would like it in the garden, I suppose, so that you can sit and look at the cherry trees, and the white lilac?" With another of her wonderful smiles, she added: "I am Mrs. Arthur Lascelles.[18] My husband is at the Town Hall; he is putting up a new lightning rod on the tower."

"Madam," said the wizard, "I thank you. My name is Fry. Allow me to introduce my friends, General Storm, and Mr. Jorkle."

The introductions were made, the gentlemen bowing, and Mrs. Lascelles performing an elegant curtsey, and the party walked into a beautiful garden, where the guests sat down at a table under a great lilac tree, while the lady withdrew to arrange about the lunch.

"Well, this is a most extraordinary place," said the General. "Do you mean to say you never met this lady before?"

"Never," answered the wizard, "but I know the customs of the country. She would see that we were strangers by our dress. Pleasant smile, hasn't she?"

"It is the most deadly smile I've ever seen," said the General. "A smile like that would play the devil with a whole station.[19] *What* did she say her husband was up to?"

"Painting rods on a roof," said Mr. Jorkle, with a sardonic chuckle.

"It is," said the General, "the damdest, most extraordinary thing I've ever heard or seen in four continents. I suppose her man's a hod-man,[20] or a blacksmith, or something impossible, and he lives in a villa, and his wife's a wood nymph, or a siren, and has purple eyes and stands free lunches to tramps."

"Here comes her daughter," said the wizard, as a tall and exceedingly pretty girl emerged from the French window and walked across the lawn, carrying a tray with some goblets and dishes on it.

The three arose and went to her assistance. Introductions followed, the table was set, and the lunch began. It was excellent of its kind, and consisted of soup, a curry with rice, a pumpkin pie, potato straws, stuffed olives, some first-rate bread and – iced water in an Arabian carafe.

"The people here," Mr. Fry explained, "do not drink any kind of alcoholic liquors. There is not a drop of wine, spirits, or beer in the country."[21]

"Ha!" said the General, "precious good job, too, by George! But I should like a whiskey and soda."[22]

"Very good," said the wizard. "Light!"

"God bless my soul!" exclaimed the General, "you don't mean to say –"

"Sir," said Light, quietly. He had "appeared."

"Whiskey and soda, please," said Mr. Fry.

Light produced a decanter of old Irish whiskey from his left ear and a syphon of soda water from his waistcoat pocket, and vanished.

The General, who was getting beyond the reach of surprise, said "thanks awfully," and helped himself. The other gentlemen drank water.

A few minutes later Mrs. Lascelles and her daughter came out and asked their guests if the lunch had been to their liking.

"It was magnificent, thank you, madam," said Mrs. Jorkle.

"Especially the curry," the General remarked, and added that he supposed it was a vegetable curry.

"Naturally," replied the hostess.

"Hah, to be sure," said the General. "I mean that you had put no meat into it."

"Meat?" said Mrs. Lascelles with a look of surprise. "What is meat?"[23]

The General looked at Mr. Fry, who said, "The General has been much abroad, and is learned in Eastern spices." Then, with a meaning glance at Sir Frederick, he said, "Meat is unknown here."

Here Charlotte Maud – so Miss Lascelles was named – created a diversion by asking the guests if they were going to the choral festival?

"Ah, and where is the festival?" inquired Mr. Fry.

"It is at the Town Hall at two o'clock. Mother is singing, and I shall be playing the violin. We have a band of a hundred and fifty, and a chorus of three hundred. There will be a great many people there: quite ten thousand. I do hope you will come."

"Certainly," said Mr. Fry. "It will please us greatly."

"I'm sure it will, sir," said Charlotte Maud, " the music is very good indeed, and we have a new soloist, a soprano, with a marvellous voice. Her name is Dorothy Suthers.[24] She is a weaver. She made the rugs for the Mother's Parlour in the City Hall. They say she is to sing at the opera in London next season."

"We shall take care to be in time," said the wizard, and, having once more thanked their hostess in suitable terms, the three travellers set out for the Town Hall.

When they had gone a little way, the General, taking out his cigar case, said "I say, Mr. Fry, do these peculiar people smoke?"

The wizard shook his head.

"What nonsense!" exclaimed Mr. Jorkle.

"You will admit, I think," said the wizard, "when you have seen something of them, that these people appear to be very healthy and happy: and, after all, smoking, drinking, and meat eating are only habits, and bad habits at that."

"Quite so, quite so," the General remarked; "most drinks and all meats are gouty, I know: but I like a bottle of wine, or a whiskey peg,[25] and I must have my cigar. Yes, hang it all, I must have my cigar."

"But," protested Mr. Jorkle, "will these impossible persons try to force their fads upon us?"

"Oh, no," answered the wizard; "but in Rome – it is as well to humour the Romans. I mean to say, these people would be as much shocked to hear you speak of eating roast beef as you would be to hear a Chinaman lamenting the absence of roast dog. Drinking whiskey or wine they would regard much in the way we regard the taking of opium. As for tobacco smoking, it would appear to them to be a foolish and unclean habit. As it *is*." And Mr Fry produced his snuff box and took a pinch.

"Hah! I say, dash it all, look here," said the General, stopping abruptly and turning to his companions, "this is becoming noxious. I'm not asleep, am I? Jorkle, I'm not asleep."

"I shouldn't like to risk an opinion," said Mr. Jorkle. "What do you think about *me*?"

"I've always found you particularly wide awake," answered the General. "What I want to know is am I awake myself? I don't think I could dream such an excellent vegetable curry, and I couldn't dream you, Jorkle. Look here, what are the odds against Blow-the-Man-Down for the Derby?"

"Six to four," said Mr. Jorkle, briskly, "how did Spanish pig iron close last night?"

"Three-sixteenths down, and still sluggish," said the General, without hesitation. "What about Liver Pill Consolidated?"

"Fitful with a tendency upwards," said Mr. Jorkle.

"We are *not* asleep," cried the General, "and the prima donna at Covent Garden *does* make hearth-rugs, and the man who mends lightning rods is married to a purple-eyed Venus; and the population of Manchester are all vegetarians and non-smokers, and teetotallers, who don't know the meaning of the word 'damn.' I begin to think Mr. Fry's right: this is not conjuring, it's magic!"

"Perhaps," said Mr. Jorkle, grumpily, "but all the same I should like to ask Mr. Fry some questions."

"I shall be delighted to answer them, sir," said the wizard, "but, as it is now a quarter to two, I should suggest that we wait until after the concert. That avenue of red and white thorn trees, on the left, leads to the great square, called Fountain Square. Let us make haste."

As the three turned into the lane of scented hawthorns some distant bell broke out into a joyous, silvery peal.

[23 November 1906]

Chapter III. The Festival.

"Have you ever seen anything like this? If you have it must have been in your dreams." The wizard addressed himself to the General; he had already given up the other man as hopeless in his philistinism.[26]

The three stood at the entrance to Fountain Square, observing the scene each through the lens of his own personality.

"No," said the General, "I have never seen anything like this, even in a dream. Paris – no! Vienna – no! It's not quite English, and it's not quite foreign: it's neither ancient nor modern. Hah! It's a most surprising place, begad! Hah! hum! hah!"

"There's no traffic," said Mr Jorkle, sulkily; "it's like a playground."

The three stood looking on. The great square presented an animated picture of rich colour, and noble form, and eager, happy human life. The place was a garden; a garden of green lawns, and bright spring flowers, and sparkling fountains, and stately trees – a garden surrounded by marble palaces, and canopied by a blue and smokeless sky. Here the people – the beautiful, brave, impossible people – gathered in their thousands, walking, lounging, laughing, talking as though the square were occupied solely by troops of friends.

It was at the people the General looked with the keenest interest; and as he looked he frowned. The wizard noticed it directly.

"Yes," he said, answering the half-formed, unspoken thought, "yes, General, you are right; we are out-classed. Our racial pride may resent the fact, but it is there. We have never seen a people so physically handsome, so vigorous. We have never seen such manly men, such womanly women. We have never seen a people so intelligent, so fearless, so free. You are a judge of such things. How say you?"

"Hah!" replied the General. "They do look beastly fit and jolly."

"Gentlemen," said the wizard, "the point I wish to press home to your minds is the fact that these people are *happy*. They are happy, happy, happy."

"They are fine animals, I admit," said Mr. Jorkle, "but they seem to me to be dressed too gaudily."

"Gaudily," cried the wizard.

"Gaudy? No," said the General. "They are dressed perfectly, by George! Hah. I've never seen people dressed so well, nor so well groomed and set up, not a crowd, don't you know. The clothes are awfully jolly, begad; and, hah, there's men and women inside the clothes, sir. Look at those fellows; what Grenadiers they'd make! Look at the women, Jorkle. Gad, sir, the women are a – er – a revelation! They are the kind of women we've been looking for all our lives, sir. Hah! Hang it all! Yes." The General frowned and twisted his moustache.

"General," said the wizard, "you have hit the bull's-eye. These are the most womanly women our earth has yet borne. They are better than beautiful. Look at their faces. They have clear skins; clean, firm, and gentle mouths; eyes full of courage and loving kindness; hair like the glory of night and day. You might truly say of any one of these, 'her face is like the Milky Way in the sky, a meeting of gentle lights without a name.'[27] What is your opinion, Mr. Jorkle?"

"My dear sir," answered the great financier, coldly, "I have not studied the subject. I have had something more important to do. And at *our* time of life, Mr. Fry, feminine beauty is a closed book."

"I'm damned if it is," quoth the General.

The wizard took a pinch of snuff. "Let us go to the concert," he said.

The concert hall was circular in form. The seats, placed in concentric crescents, from the bow of the orchestra and stage, rose in a gradual and unbroken slope from the level of the floor to the great window which ran like a broad jewelled belt of light completely round the walls. The hall contained ten thousand chairs, and every seat was occupied.

The wizard led the way down the wide central aisle, almost to the stage, where he turned, so as to face the audience. "Gentlemen," he said, smiling. "I have ventured to take a slight liberty, which I hope you will condone. In order that we may be able to observe freely, and to converse freely upon all we see and hear, I have – ah – presumed so far as to disembody myself and you. We are, therefore, for the present, invisible, inaudible, and intangible. The advantages of this arrangement are obvious."

The wizard produced his snuff box, and looked inquiringly at his companions.

Mr. Jorkle swelled, frowned and glowered through his gold-rimmed glasses. The General drew himself up very straight, stared very hard, coughed, and said: "Hah! Confound it, sir, you don't stick at trifles."

"It is nothing," said the wizard; "a wave of the hand will put it right, and it enables us to look at the people and to talk about them without being rude. I hope you do not object."

"I – er – I don't know that I wish to stare at people," said Mr. Jorkle, "and – er – had my consent been asked I should decidedly have declined to be – er – disembodied. Of course, the – er – the arrangement is quite temporary."

"Look here, dash it all," said the General, "are we to understand that we are a couple of demnition ghosts?"

"That is the idea," answered the wizard, calmly.

"Then – hah – it seems to me," said the General, his eyes hardening and his figure stiffening, "that – hah –" But he here became conscious that he was standing close to one of the most superlatively beautiful women he had ever seen, and after a few more hahs and hums, the cold light faded out of his eyes, and he concluded, rather lamely: "Hah, it seems to me, Jorkle, that the – hah – situation has something to – hah – recommend it."

Mr. Jorkle shrugged his shoulders, and the wizard bowed. "For instance," said the latter, "I being invisible and inaudible to these people, can ask you to observe their faces, and especially the faces of the women –"

"You seem to be vastly interested in the women," remarked Mr. Jorkle.

"Ha! ha! ha!" laughed the General. "I've noticed that, Jorkle. Ha, ha! Our friend the magician is quite a dog, begad! Hah! By Jove!"

The wizard tapped his snuff box, and smiled inscrutably. "I'm afraid," he said, "that you have not quite caught the idea, gentleman. I wish you to observe the women with especial care because in attempting to understand these impossible people we shall find the women of the utmost importance. You smile, General; but my purpose is deeply serious, I assure you."

"Ha! Of course, of course," said the General, smiling more than ever. "Hah, an old Colonel of mine, when I was a subaltern, once pointed out a sentry to some of us youngsters. Hah! He said: 'There's a real soldier, gentleman, there's a clean, smart soldier, properly drilled and properly dressed. Hah! That man's a picture. If I had a cup of coffee and a biscuit I could sit and look at that man all day.' Ha! Dash it all, Fry, I feel exactly like old Square-toes. I could stand and look at these ladies all night, dammit, and never ask for a coffee or biscuit at all. Hah! by George, sir, they are worth it! Ha, ha, ha! sly dog, sly dog!"

The wizard contracted his eyes until they were mere specks of fire. "Very good," he said, "that is what I ask; but there is no need to make a night of it." Then, turning to Mr. Jorkle, he said: "You will notice, sir, I think, that the faces of these ladies are, as it were illuminated by intelligence and kindness. They remind me of the 'Shining Ones' in Bunyan's dream.[28] High intelligence, sweet goodwill, look frankly from their wonderful eyes. The lady just before us, whose charms caused the General to change front just now," – the wizard's eyes twinkled – "may be taken as a type. Her beauty is suffused with a kind of tender graciousness. Like all the women in this impossible country, she is enfolded in love, – and crowned with honour. *That* is what I want you to observe, sir. The women here have a new atmosphere, an atmosphere of sweetness and *light*."[29]

"Yes, sir," cried a brisk voice, and Light appeared.

"My good lad, I'm sorry," said Mr. Fry, "I did not call you. I mentioned your name by chance."

"Very good, sir," said Light, and vanished.

"Hah! that chap Light of yours," said the General, "is rather – hah! sudden, Hah! almost jumpy, begad."

"You will soon get used to him, General," said the wizard. "Ah, here is the conductor. Tut! *Light*."

"Sir."

"A programme. Thank you. The concert, gentlemen," said the wizard, coolly, as he unfolded the programme, "is in honour of the spring. It opens with a Spring Song, for band and chorus, and I see there is a solo by Miss Dorothy Suthers, the lady who makes the hearthrugs. And – here she comes."

The soloist came forward and made a profound curtsey, smiling upon the vast audience with the bright, pleased look of a child amongst very dear and familiar friends. In response to their obeisance all the men in the hall rose and bowed, while the women touched their lips with their right hands and then lightly extended their right arms. This was the regular form of welcome when a lady was the performer. There was no applause.

Turning, after a look of surprise at the strange formality, the General regarded the young singer with keen interest. Miss Dorothy Suthers was a young and beautiful brunette, rosy and dimpled, with hair like black floss silk, pouting lips as red as haws, and the soft eloquent brown eyes of a gazelle. She wore a dress of amber silk with crimson bows and a handsome belt of silver, cunningly engraved.

"Phew!" said the General, "what a little gem, she is!"

"She is," said the wizard, "a sweet bouquet of all the pretty loves and delicate graces. I could find in my heart to steal her."

"She has an eye that would charm a duck off the water, by George!" said the General.

"I begin to think –" Mr. Jorkle began; but the General said: "Don't; don't begin it at your time of life, Jorkle," and then the conductor lifted his long white hand, and the music commenced.

"Do you like music, General?" the wizard asked.

"Hah! oh, yes," said the General. "Hah! it's all right, don't you know."

"Oh," said the wizard. "It is all right? I see. And you, Mr. Jorkle?"

"I don't object to it, in moderation," replied that great man, "but I am not exactly musical."

"Not exactly! H'm!" said the wizard. "Then we need not stay, but I should like to hear the opening of the Spring Song, and that lovely child's solo."

"Why," Mr. Jorkle exclaimed, "nearly half the orchestra are women!"

"Why not?" said the wizard. "You will remember that Miss Lascelles told us she played in the band. Ah! There she is flushed with music, and wreathed in smiles."

While Mr. Fry was speaking the solo began. Out of the soft pleading of the string and cooing of the reeds welled up a sudden, passionate, delicious gush of song:

> Under the greenwood tree
> Who loves to lie with me,
> And turn his merry note
> Up to the sweet bird's throat.[30]

Then, as the violins worked themselves up into an eager hurry, and the reeds gurgled and warbled the voice increased in volume, filling the great hall with its joyous challenge.

> Come hither, come hither, come hither!

And as the basses boomed and the horns awoke, the chorus of three hundred lusty and fresh voices took up the refrain:

> Here shall he see
> No enemy
> But winter and rough weather.

The three were now well up the aisle, almost at the door. They paused to hear that storm of joyous song, and to wonder at the voice of the mat-maker ringing through it all like the sound of a silver trumpet.

"By – *Jove*!" cried the General, "what a *ripping* voice."

"And do you mean to tell me, Mr Fry," said Mr. Jorkle, "that this young person does not get paid for singing?"

"Certainly, sir," answered the wizard, "she is not paid."

Mr. Jorkle shrugged his shoulders disgustedly. "Then," said he, "what does she do it for?"

The wizard laughed. "Upon my word, Mr. Jorkle," said he, "that is a quite surprising and unforeseen question. What does the skylark sing for?"

"Hah!" said the General, "the little beggar sings because he's glad, I suppose. I sing in my bath, for some such reason. Hah! but nobody would think of paying me. Jorkle, do you sing when you have made a particularly wicked and successful deal?"

"Well," said the wizard, "shall we go? There is a choral symphony called 'Evolution,' which is very fine, I hear. The first part is called 'The Realms of Chaos and Old Night,' and was composed by the great Russian, Vronsky; the second part, called 'War,' is by the French composer, Metin; the third part is by an Englishwoman, Miss Mildred Thompson.[31] But, perhaps, Mr. Jorkle is anxious to get to the heckling."

"I'm not in a hurry," said Mr. Jorkle, "but I have an important appointment in town to-night, and must not be late."

"Have no fear, sir; have no fear," said the wizard. "We are working by one of our best chronometer repeater Dream Watches. This watch" – he took from his pocket as he spoke a large white-faced, antique gold watch – "is one of our best lines. It keeps dream time, enables one to serve seven years penal servitude between two snores, or ride five hundred miles in a runaway railway engine and fall over a bottomless precipice while a fly is walking across one's nose. A most useful instrument. We sell a great many of them for presents. Hah! Excuse me. I will just embody myself for a moment."

They had come out into a corridor, and a tall, fair lady was walking slowly towards them. She was dressed in black: dressed as ladies were dressed in London – their London. She was beautiful, and possessed of great charm; but her gait was languid, and her air listless, or bored.

Mr. Fry walked straight up to her, raising his hat and holding out his hand, and said: "You here, Adelaide! What can have brought you?"

"I wanted to see you," said the lady; "are you sorry I have come? Are you tired of me?"

"Nonsense," answered the wizard. "You know I was always pleased with you. I like you better than any of the others."

The lady smiled, rather sadly, perhaps, and said: "How sweet of you. You spoiled me. You know you did. You always spoil your girls. But I am *very* fond of you for all that." She laid her daintily gloved hand upon the old man's arm, and looked at him affectionately.

"I'll tell you what," said the General to Mr. Jorkle, "we seem to be devilishly out of it. Hah! You'll notice that old Simmery Axe hasn't – hah – embodied *us*. It's not – hah – quite playing the game. Hah! At the same time – hah – as we can see and hear, we had better walk on. Hey?"

"Certainly," said Mr. Jorkle; "but, for a man of his years, I must say –"

"Hah! no," said the General, "I think you're off the wicket, Jorkle. The old witch doctor is not *that* sort. But I don't relish being left with the reserves when there's fun going on at the front, and – hah – by George, I won't stand any more of this disembodiment. Hah! confound his impudence!"

The two walked to the end of the corridor, where in a few minutes, the wizard joined them.

"I beg ten thousand pardons," he said, as he came up. "Allow me." He made a couple of peculiar passes with his hands. "We are now re-embodied. I hope I have not kept you waiting long. It was rather – rather an unexpected meeting. The lady you saw me speak to is one of my heroines. Er – a while ago I used to write novels. That lady – Miss Adelaide Langdale – was in one of them, and it seems I have – I have, quite inadvertently, done her an injustice."

"In what way?" asked the General. "Well," said Mr. Fry, "I left off the story in such a way as to suggest that Adelaide would probably marry a Mr. Tennant. I did not exactly say so; but left the matter open. You follow?"

The General nodded, and said, "Hah! yes."

"Well," the wizard went on, "it seems she did not want to marry at all, and that she regarded Tennant as a good deal of a bore. Consequently the poor child had no future. Absolutely none."

"But there are plenty of men in the world; hang it!" said the General.

Mr. Fry rubbed his nose in a perplexed way. "No," he said, " not in her world. But I'll write another book, and let her reappear. That's only right. The worst of it is she wants me to alter her; and I hate altering my people. She says I made her too sweet. She says I idealise too much, and that her own sweetness is positively cloying to her. She is really a charming girl. I suppose you saw that?"

"Hah! Dash it all! That was our share of it," said the General.

"My dear sir," exclaimed the wizard, "I'm sorry. I was rather thrown out and forgot my manners. I'm very sorry – really."

"Sorry be hanged!" said the General, testily. "It isn't cricket."

The wizard laughed. "Well," he said, "we must try to do better next time. And now I must attend to Mr. Jorkle's questions. Light!"

"Sir!"

"Throw up a small pavilion of some kind in the beech wood. One of our magic card houses will do; and put decanters, cigars and pipes; we may have a long sitting."

"Yes, sir."

"Gentlemen," said the wizard, "will you oblige me by turning round three times: like this. Thank you. There is our pavilion in the green glade; you can just see it through the beeches. This is the wood we walked through before we entered Manchester."

[30 November 1906]

Chapter IV. The Pavilion.

"Our little card pavilion, gentlemen," said the wizard, with one of his gracious gestures of the hand, "built with a pack of our magic playing cards. The exterior, walls, and roof, are made by the backs of the cards. How does the design appeal to you? It is quaint and pleasing I think. I like the way the maroon and purple are woven together, and the dim thread of gold, playing at hide-and-seek in the pattern, like a merry thought in a grave discourse. I had the design from an old Florentine who was burnt for heresy. He is a very courteous and tasteful spectre, who haunts the palaces, suggesting to his patients nothing more unpleasant than a kind of warm and mellow melancholy, such as belong to the frail perfume of *pot-pourri*, or the rustle of autumn leaves. Hem! The faces of the cards, as you see, make the inner walls and ceiling. I like the idea of centreing the court cards at intervals. They suggest the panelled portraits of old queens and kings. The ceiling is set diagonally, you will notice. The floor is of knaves and fives, and we use the ace of spades for a table. Please sit down. These card chairs are strong and resilient. Ah I see Light has forgotten to place me a churchwarden,[32] he has been called away. He has, in fact, gone on a business trip into the seventeenth century to clear up the origin of the haunting of Fitshaubock Castle. It seems there is a little dispute between two highly reputable and gifted phantoms upon a matter of succession."

The wizard coolly drew a long clay pipe down his sleeve. "Now, gentlemen," he said, "there is tobacco in the inexhaustible jar on the table; there are cigars in the arms of the brown clay god; and the fat black flagon will yield you any kind of liquor you wish to pour out. If you will excuse me, I will take tea, since I am to be heckled."

The three sat down; Mr. Fry and Mr. Jorkle facing each other; the General, seated at the table, making the third point of a triangle, as it might have been, and, indeed, was, planned for a triangular duel.

Mr. Jorkle pursed up his lips and pondered heavily. Mr. Fry leaned back in his chair, crossed his legs and puffed slowly at his pipe.

Now, the General was not an imaginative man, or, perhaps, his imagination was somewhat atrophied from lack of exercise, but as he sat looking from the wizard to Mr. Jorkle, and from Mr. Jorkle to the wizard, he experienced a slight thrill, not unlike the thrill of expectation before a battle.

Having in his time enjoyed a considerable variety of bloodshed, and confronted antagonists of many creeds and colours, he was a keen judge of fighting men and their qualities. And as he compared the pompous, lumbering guinea pig with the lean, keen, alert little wizard, he curled his long moustaches, and slightly raised his heavy white eye-brows.

The wizard's figure was relaxed and still, his hand lay loosely and lazily over the arm of the chair, his face was wrinkled in a smile of satirical good humour; but his half-closed eyes gleamed with a strange fierceness, as they watched intently the man before him.

The General thought first of the eyes of an owl he had once seen in the act of killing a mouse. Then he remembered a certain puissant master-at-arms from Seville, whose ferocity and power were wrapped softly and elegantly in folds of grace and stripes of humour, as the soul and sinews of a panther in its satin skin.

"Looks just like that devil Trefada," was the General's mental comment, "and, gad, if Jorkle isn't spry he'll be through him before he can say damn."

"I suppose we are to assume, sir," said Mr. Jorkle, in his most ponderously important board-room manner, "that this place we are in, or seem to be in, is a Socialist state, or city?"

"It is a kind of commune," said the wizard.

"Ah! Then the first questions I shall ask will concern the relations of the sexes; the marriage laws, the laws of divorce, and the control and education of children." Mr. Jorkle put up his glasses and looked severely at Mr. Fry.

The wizard sat motionless and silent for a few seconds. Then he said; "Certainly, Mr. Jorkle. General, may I borrow your hat? Thank you." He placed the General's silk hat upon the table, waved his pipe over it, and lifting it up, disclosed a sculptured group of three figures in marble.

"Gentlemen," said Mr. Fry, "I am glad Mr. Jorkle has begun with the position of woman, because that is the beginning of the whole matter, and almost the end. If you will look at this small statuary group you will see that it represents a mother and her son and daughter. The son is a boy of, say, fifteen; the daughter perhaps two years younger. It is a great conception, greatly carried out; the figures are noble types. That, however, is by the way. This is a model of the colossal work which stand in the great Rose Garden at Hoxton – not our Hoxton.[33] This group, which was executed by the famous sculptor, Denis Maxted, has a deep and sacred significance for the English people – the impossible people of whom we are now to talk. Well, gentlemen, can you guess the name of the woman – the mother in that composition?"

"You say there is no queen," said the General. "Hah! it isn't Charity. No – I – hah! give it up."

"And I also," said Mr. Jorkle.

"That figure," said Mr. Fry, "is Britannia!"

"Britannia!"

"She has, you see, no helmet, no trident, no lion. Britannia does not rule, nor menace, now; she protects, she cherishes. She is the emblem of England, and you see she is a woman, and a mother. She protects and cherishes – the children."

"Ha! very charming, and poetical, and – er – all that," said Mr. Jorkle, "but not explicit."

The wizard resumed his seat and his pipe. "I venture to infer," he said, mildly, "that you speak in the interests of morality."

"You are quite right, sir," said Mr. Jorkle, with an ominous little nod, "quite right."

The wizard took a few puffs at his pipe, then went on in a very soft and quiet voice: "It does you great credit Mr. Jorkle, that you retain so pure and unselfish an interest in morality" – (puff, puff) – "coming, as you do, from such a barbarous – and basely immoral country – as the England we know."

"I hope, sir," said Mr. Jorkle, "that in this Utopia they have not improved upon our moral rags and tatters by – er –simply going naked – and unashamed."

The wizard smiled, then said, slowly: "The foundation and pattern of this State, sir, is the family."

Mr. Jorkle started and frowned. "Go on, sir, go on," he said, "and be explicit, pray."

"The heart of this civilisation," Mr. Fry continued, "is the family; the heart of the family is the woman – the mother. When *these* English speak of England as the motherland they use a true figure of speech. When the Englishman of our England speaks of the motherland he lies."

"Hum! And about those marriage laws?" said Mr. Jorkle.

"As I said before," the wizard answered, "there are no laws here. But there are customs. One of those customs is the custom of marriage – the custom of strict monogamy."

"And – er – suppose a man gets sick of his wife," said Mr. Jorkle, "does he leave her?"

"Ah! You are thinking of our England," said Mr. Fry, "and the system of marital slave-owning. Here if a husband showed his wife that he had ceased to love her she would be likely to leave him."

"And what becomes of the children?" cried Mr. Jorkle, triumphantly.

"The children," said Mr. Fry, "until they are of age to act for themselves, belong to the mother."

"The devil they do," said the General; "hah! What do the men say to that?"[34]

"The men say that it is quite just and expedient," said the wizard, "this may seem strange to you, because in our England we do not reverence nor honour women."

"Oh, come, dash it all, that's going too far," the General protested.

"Excuse me," Mr. Jorkle struck in, "suppose a man leaves his wife, or that she leaves him, is he at liberty to take another wife?"

"Do you mean may he marry again?" said the wizard.

"Yes. Or – yes, of course," Mr. Jorkle answered.

The wizard smiled. "It was," said he, "a woman, the excellent Mrs. Glasse who said, 'first catch your hare.'[35] You must not forget that the position of woman here in no way resembles her position with us. Here if a husband leaves his wife he finds it very difficult to find another. The women here are very proud, their ideal of purity is very high, and they are completely independent. No woman here marries for bread. No woman dreads a future of solitary indigence. There is no poverty in this country. Every wife is economically independent of her husband. Imagine then a divorced husband going out tainted and a failure to pay court to one of these free women. The maidens here set their entreatments at a higher rate than a demand to parley. They are free. They are men's equals. They are honoured, and it is a case of *noblesse oblige*.[36] But, indeed, it is not often that marriage is a failure amongst these people. When a couple do discover that they are ill-sorted they may part; but generally they make the best of it, for the children's sake. But woman or man divorced has but a poor chance of a second marriage."

"But such marriages *do* occur?" said Mr. Jorkle.

Mr. Fry nodded. "Sometimes," he said.

"And what then, sir, is the fate of the children?"

"I will ask you, because it is very necessary to ask you," said Mr. Fry, "to remember what in our country would be the fate of the children in similar circumstances. And I will remind you that here no sordid, miserable money troubles exist. The children can find homes in a hundred households. They can take food anywhere. Every house is open, every table free to them, and, still more happily, every heart is open to them also. No child here is denied food, no child is denied instruction, no child is denied love. Children here are not regarded as a burden, but as a blessing. There is scarcely a parent in this beautiful, impossible land who would not rush open-armed to succour any child who needed a mother and a home. Picture to yourself this state of things, and then" – the wizard paused, and with a glance like the thrust of a rapier, concluded "and then, in the interest of morality, Mr. Jorkle, remember London – our London: the moral London for the preservation of whose purity you are so concerned."

"Yes, yes," said the financier, "but I am not yet satisfied as to the perfection of this place."

"Perfection!" said the wizard. "Is there any question of perfection? Your idea, I take it, was to show that this place was morally worse than our England. If I show it to be morally very much better, I submit that you are answered."

"Come," said Mr. Jorkle, with a forensic air, "what about free love in this moral state?"

"All love here is free; that is why the relations of the sexes are so happy and so pure."

"But I always understood," the magnate persisted, "that under Socialism free love would ride rough-shod over every moral restraint, and that the family ideal would be destroyed. Do you mean to say it is not so here?"

"Some Socialists may have given cause for such a fear,"[37] said the wizard, "but there are few English Socialists who would endorse such extravagant ideas. And I have shown you, not only that no such state of things exists here, but also why it does not exist."

"I'm afraid," said Mr. Jorkle, "that I do not quite follow."

"But," said the wizard, "you understand my repeated assertions that the women here are entirely free, and are held in honour and in reverence. How then could a state of immorality be possible?"

"Hah! I must say the men here seem to be devilishly gallant," remarked the General.

The wizard looked at him in a peculiar way. He seemed amused but not pleased. "My dear sir," he said, "in using the word gallant you seem to indicate that you have not fully understood the situation of affairs in this country."

"Well," said the General, "I am – hah – anxious to learn, don't you know."

"It always seems to me a very odd thing," said the wizard, "that in our highly moral and cultured society if a man speaks reverently or affectionately of women his meaning is monstrously misconstrued. I believe that the woman who stands nearest to the general masculine imagination is Aspasia.[38] I remember once remarking that sex was the greatest fact in human life, and being told by the educated yahoo to whom I was speaking that it was not so important as hunger. 'For,' said that extraordinary person, 'in a hungry man the naked Venus herself might appeal in vain.' Are *you* thinking of Venus, General?"

"Hah! Confound it all, no," said the General, "but of what the dickens are you speaking?"

The wizard laughed. "Upon my word, it *is* Venus who is standing in your light, and in Mr. Jorkle's light also. Why, gentlemen, our barbarous society has so confused you that it is necessary to explain to you the meaning of some of the commonest words in our tongue."

"We await instruction, sir," said Mr. Jorkle.

"Good," said the wizard, "when we speak of woman we mean woman, and not *a* woman; of the least admiral type. For sex includes motherhood, sisterhood, maidenhood. It includes the holy relationships of sister and brother, of father and son, of children and mother, of husband and wife. Don't forget, mother, gentlemen; don't forget mother. These people have remembered mother, and have seated her upon the throne."

"You don't mean to say that woman wears the breeches, dammit?" exclaimed the General.

"My dear General," laughed the wizard, "you really are magnificent."

"Then we are to understand that no such thing as immorality exists in this wonderful paradise?" said Mr. Jorkle.

"You are to understand, gentlemen," said the wizard, "that this is the most moral people the world has ever known, and you are to understand that this is so because woman here is wholly free, and truly honoured."

"Hah! Honour bright?"[39] asked the General.

"It is the simple truth," replied the wizard, "and now, allow me to make a few comments upon the moral state of *our* England."

"Oh, well," said the General, with an eloquent shrug.

"In our highly moral and civilised country, as we know it, to sin and shame," said the wizard, "woman is generally regarded, and treated, as an inferior. Amid our mockery of bows and compliments, we tell her to her face that she cannot reason, that she has a weak sense of honour, that she is frivolous, inconstant, vain, and incapable of self-government. In our highly moral England, for whose purity Mr. Jorkle is so jealous, we hang women, we imprison them, we dress them as felons, and treat them as brutes. In our moral empire you may see women, old and young, working like beasts of burden. In many of our shops, and factories, and theatres, the women must sacrifice their honour and life. I need not remind you of the condition of the London streets at night. You have eyes and you have seen. But have you seen women and girls working in gangs in the fields like slaves? Have you seen a grey-haired matron carrying sixty pounds of chain on her shoulders? Have you seen pregnant women at the anvil making nails? Have you seen women carrying heavy loads of clay upon their backs? Have you seen the condition of women tramping the roads, rotting as paupers in our accursed workhouses, begging in the streets? Do you know the endless drudgery and abasement of the many thousands of overworked and underpaid general servants in our happy England? Do you know the rascally rates of wage allowed to women and girls in the majority of our industries? Are you conscious, in your moral zeal for the status of women under Socialism, that there are millions of English women existing in ignorance, in degradation, in semi-starvation? Have you ever studied the highly moral statistics of drunkenness, illiteracy, disease, over-crowding, crime, and prostitution in our glorious and highly moral Empire? You know of course, a good deal about these things. You know more than you dare to confess. And you come here" – the little man suddenly turned a blazing look upon Mr. Jorkle – "and have the effrontery to catechise me upon the moral condition of the Socialist State."[40]

The wizard relighted his pipe, and said: "You ask me about the status of women here. I tell you. I tell you; and mark it well, that in this country there is no such thing as an untaught, poor, or degraded woman; there is no such thing as a courtesan; there is no such thing as the sale and barter of women's flesh and women's honour; there is not a woman tramp, beggar, or slave; there is not woman destitute of home, of hope, of love. Ah! and I will add, gentlemen, that there is not a man who, could he hear of the dastardly, brutal, and immoral state of our England, would not loathe us as a nation of unclean and blackguardly savages. I hope, gentlemen, that I make my meaning plain."

"Hah! you certainly do," said the General, laughing, "and – hah – now I am wondering, don't you know, how you have rid these people of all their – hah – natural coarseness."

"They have simply rid themselves of the unnatural cussedness which has made, and still keeps *our* England what she is," said the wizard; "and now, gentlemen, let us go and visit some of these people in their homes."

"Hah!" said the General, "with pleasure. Hah! This *must* be a deminition dream. Hah! Jorkle, if you had not such clumping feet I would ask you to tread lightly on my gouty toe. Hah! Dash it all! It's – hah – it's marvellous, don't you know, and – hah – that sort of thing."

"Seems to me," said Mr. Jorkle, with surly rudeness, "that it's a question of facts."[41]

"My good sir," said the wizard, with a kind of smiling sternness, "if it is unwise to be rude to the equator,[42] it is sheer folly to beard a sorcerer in his den. But you shall test the facts, and I will restrain my professional longing to transform you into an earwig. Puff!"

The wizard gave a sudden whiff of his breath, and the card house fell with a clatter about their ears.

[7 December 1906]

Chapter V. Mother.

The three left the wood by the path they had taken in the morning; but after crossing the bridge where they had seen the blue heron Mr. Fry turned from the high road and led the way through the unfenced orchards. Here, as they walked over the plushy moss, on which the fluctuating lights and shadows wrought living patterns in green and blue and russet and gold, the proud piping of the blackbird from the crown of a tall poplar was checked by a sudden peal, like the clashing ripple of sweet shrill bells, of children's laughter.

"Look!" said the wizard.

"Listen!" said the General.

In the branchy primrose-spangled orchard, where the gnarled trunks gleamed like oxidised silver, and the massed blossoms were defined in delicate pink loveliness against the glistening purple sky, a troop of little children were at play.

In front strutted a sturdy black-eyed urchin, bearing a flowered spray of thorn, and after him marched, two-and-two, some three score boys and girls. They were bareheaded and bare-legged, were dressed in gaily-coloured spring clothing, and bore themselves with a mock solemnity and parody of pomp, of which their elastic step and laughing eyes made the drollest paradox. As they marched they sang, to an air that had pleased twenty generations of little people:

> Who shall walk in sunny ways,
>   Gay with love and roses;
> She whose mirth makes winter days,
>   Bright as summer posies.
>
> Gird her waist and crown her hair,
>   With proud silver lilies,
> Throne her in a lordly chair
>   Of golden daffodillies.
>
> Little men and little maids,
>   Take your merry play-time;
> Merry are the orchard glades
>   In this merry May-time.
>
> Sing the song the throstle sings
>   When the dew is falling,
> Dance like elves in fairy rings
>   When the Spring is calling.[43]

"Hah! Reminds me of the time when I got my jacket dusted for playing with the shepherd's children on Bideford Green," remarked the General.[44]

"And does it remind you of the slum children in the stifled warrens of Shantytown East, Mr. Jorkle?" asked the wizard.

"No," replied that gentleman; "what it does remind me of is my intention to ask about the education of children in this – er – State."

"Ask, then," said the wizard.

"Well, to begin at the beginning," said Mr. Jorkle, "what kind of elementary schools have they here?"

The wizard smiled. "They have none at all," said he.

Mr. Jorkle fairly gasped. "Do you mean that the children are not educated?" he exclaimed.

"On the contrary, they are beautifully educated."

"Although there are no schools!"

"Because there are no schools."

"How, then, are they educated?"

"My dear sir, before I tell you how they are, I must tell you how they are not educated."

"You have my best attention, sir."

"Well, they are not educated as children in our England are educated, because in the two Englands the ideals of life are very different, and the end in view not being the same, the means are not the same, naturally."

"And pray in what does this great difference consist?"

"People in our England are split up into classes, into religious sects, into political parties, and then our England is devoted to empire and to trade. But here they have no classes, no religious sects, no political parties, no empire, and no trade."

"And what is the positive to which all these negatives point?"

"Well, and in our England we want the children loaded with the special party bias; and each one of the two-and-seventy jarring sects hankers for the power to give a particular religious squint to their poor little souls, and then, for the sake of trade and the empire, their poor little minds have to be drugged and shackled, so that they shall be diligent and submissive workers, or masterful and ambitious rulers, according to the station of life into which it has pleased our peculiar British Providence to drop them."

"Well, well, well! But what about these children here?"

"And in our England we have the children regimented in educational barracks, and taught the educational goose-step, according to code. By machine-made scholastic drill-sergeants, in order that the dears may be as much alike as possible, and shall obey orders with mechanical docility and precision in the great national campaigns for trade and empire."

"Yes, yes! And here?"

"Here they want the children to be happy and healthy, and to grow up into good and capable women and men."

"Therefore?"

"Therefore they have burnt the code, dismantled the barracks, discharged the drill sergeants, and – gone back to *mother*."

"To mother?"

"Yes. Mother is politics, religion, drill sergeant, elementary school, and many much better things, all rolled into one."

"Do you mean to say these children are left to the teaching of a parcel of women?"

"Happily, yes. What are all elementary schools but substitutes, and bad substitutes, for mother? It is only in societies where the vanities of cast, the bitterness of sects, and the greed of trade have made drudges or toys of the women that educational barracks and scholastic drill sergeants are tolerated."

"But I thought the Socialist idea –"

"Ah, you have been importing Socialist ideas from Germany. There are, I believe, some doctrinaire German Socialists who would take the children from their mothers and regiment and goose-step them into battalions and divisions of uniform citizens;[45] but in this county they prefer to put their trust in mother."

"Mother must be devilishly well-informed and clever," said the General.

"Sir," the wizard answered, "there is no wisdom so deep as love."

"Oh!" said Mr. Jorkle, "and what do these wonderful mothers teach their children?"

"A very great deal that the wisest minister of education ever got into a code. For one cannot catch sunbeams in traps."

"I'm afraid – you – are – er – too romantic. Do you suggest – er – to *me*, that a comprehensive and systematic elementary education can be replaced by the smatterings and petting of a woman?" Mr. Jorkle grew quite hot and red with scornful indignation. But the wizard answered in his usual dry and imperturbable manner:

"Indeed, that is the idea. But what is it, my dear sir, that *you* suggest to *me*? You have been officially concerned with education, I believe?"

"I have that honour."

"You have that honour. And do you suggest to me that the flower-sweet and heavenly-wise mother, whose breast is the cradle of all womanhood and manhood, whose immeasurable love and matchless intuition win the reverence of the wise, shall be driven out, with all her healing tenderness and purifying graces. That her children may be delivered up to *you*?"

"I suggest – er – that the proper educational authorities, the – er – trained capacity of – er – the specialist must excel the – ah – irregular sentimentality – of – in short, my experience of mothers is that they are quite unqualified to teach."

"*Your* experience of mothers. In *our* England. Yes."

"Upper-class women are too frivolous and idle; lower-class women are too ignorant. I know nothing of the Utopian women here; but ours are hopeless. Er, I cannot endorse your opinion of the sex. What do *you* say General Storm?"

"Hah! My mother was a good woman," said the General.

"I give thanks," said the wizard, "that we have many such, even in our England."

"Well" – Mr. Jorkle shrugged his shoulders – "let us descend to vulgar detail. What do these wonderful mothers teach their wonderful children?"

"Primarily the mother teaches her children to be truthful, and clean, and kind. With kisses, and songs, and stories, with silver precepts and a golden example, with gentleness, sagacity, and affection, she makes them happy and good, so that in their merry voices and shining faces one discerns the sparkling signs that they are well-mothered bairns."[46]

"Yes, but –"

"What of book learning? Mother teaches the rudiments. First of all the three R's.[47] All these children read and write beautifully. How many of our children can? As for mere arithmetic, it has been much simplified by the disuse of money. There are no money sums now to worry little heads. The children learn a few simple rules."

"And is that all?"

"Oh, no. Nearly every child is taught to draw, to model, or to carve, or to do all those things; and every child is taught to sing, and to dance, and to play some instrument. This applies to the young children. Most of them can sing and play, and dance and draw and carve, and can read and write the universal language,[48] as well as English, before they are in their teens. They pick up other things as well; botany, astronomy, geography, gardening – many things. And, of course, their physical training is attended to. There father helps. The children, boys and girls, all swim, and row, and play at cricket and many other games."

"And when do they begin to work?"

"Oh, at different ages. Naturally they are eager to work before they are old enough to be indulged. But some are allowed to do a little work when they are thirteen; others a year of two later."[49]

"Then they have actually no schooling?"

"Work, as, of course, you know, is educational. But there are some kinds of work that demand special knowledge. For instance, a boy who wishes to go in for architecture, or navigation, or engineering, needs to be more than a skilled mechanic, or mason, or what not. And to supply the necessary training there are schools and classes. They are all voluntary. For a boy who is learning to be a mason may not wish to be an architect. He may prefer to develop a taste for music, or painting, or mathematics. Well, he goes to the schools and studies these things. That is what I mean by saying that boys may begin work at thirteen. They really begin to learn to work. For no boy is allowed to do the work of a man. And you will find that work here is very light and pleasant. Nobody need work more than three or four hours a day, unless he wishes to."

"Do you mean some of the men work longer than they are compelled to work?"

"Why not? Do not thousands of men in our England work longer than they need to work? Do not you, for instance? Most men here work nearly twice the regulation time. But they often put in the extra hours at a different sort of work. You must understand that with these people work is a pleasure, not a task. And in all the higher arts and crafts the men get so interested in the work, and so enamoured of it, that it is not easy to drive them away from it. But this is a digression. We were speaking of education. The idea with these people is not to waste the time and powers of a girl or boy over the acquirement of useless knowledge. It would be folly to worry our pretty mat-maker with chemistry or vulgar fractions. She makes mats; and excellent good mats, I'll dare warrant; but her soul is in her song."

"All very fine. But who discovers the bent of each child?"

"Why – mother. Who should be so competent?"

"But you say all the children learn to draw and to sing."

"I spoke generally. Of course where a child shows no aptitude for one study another is substituted."

"But can all the mothers draw?"

"Oh, most of them. But, of course, where teachers are needed they can be had from the schools. Often enough the neighbouring families will club together for lessons. Then one of the parents or older children will direct the musical and art studies. Remember this is a nation of craftsmen, and artists, and musicians."

"And you mean to say that this loose system, or no system, works out satisfactorily?"

"It is not a loose system; it is a sound one. You will find, moreover, that although the children here are not perverted and worried, and crammed, as they are with us, yet the men and women are infinitely better educated than ours. In our England they begin to forget just at the age when in this new England they begin to learn."

"Hah! how do you account for that?" asked the General.

"Why," said the wizard, "it's our ridiculous system. We stuff a boy with scraps of mathematics, and history, and Latin, and Greek; and then send him into the vulgar scramble to scratch for a living on the commercial rubbish heap. The young man is so busy and so anxious over his business, and his future, that in a few years his expensive "education" has leaked away. But here a boy chooses his work and his studies. Perhaps he will be a ship-wright. Well, he goes to his work without a scrap of anxiety as to his wages, or his situation, or his future, and he begins, outside his limited working hours, to learn to know or to learn to do the things which interest him."

For instance, there is Miss Hilda Parker, a very sweet girl friend of mine. She is a librarian, and for four hours a day she is in attendance at the library; but she is far better known as a painter of English landscape. She is a splendid artist;

and in her spare time makes musical instruments and studies natural history. Her knowledge of moths and butterflies is wonderful; she is quite an authority. Yet she is only a girl. Or, take the case of Lascelles, who mends lightning rods. Now he is the brilliant Arthur Ballantyne Lascelles, about the finest novelist in this country. In the same way the Astronomer-General is a master of rose culture, and designer of tapestries and mosaic. T. Groom, the leading authority on languages, didn't know a word except of English and Esperanto when he was nineteen. He has learnt it all since then, in the spare time when he was not doing repousse work in copper."[50]

"And does he still punch copper?" asked the General.

"No," said the wizard; "his time is mostly occupied in consultations. He is in great demand on the Continent; but he does a little pottery work when he can, and it's certainly hard on him that he can get so little time for real happy work."

"And the lightning rod man," said the General, "is a literary man? Hah! That may somewhat account for the Venus. Hah! What sort of a fellow is he?"

"I don't know him," the wizard answered, "I've seen him on the cricket field. He goes in first for England."

"Hah! Good bat, hey?"

"Very fine. A good-looking man, too; tall and well-built. He has a big thing in off-drives, and cuts like William Gunn."[51]

The General curled his moustaches. "Heh!" he said, "I should awfully like to see some cricket – *here*, don't you know."

"That isn't difficult to manage," answered the wizard; "they take their cricket very seriously," he added.

"So I should imagine, sir," Mr. Jorkle said, "so I should imagine."

"But they don't play bridge, nor gamble on the racecourse – *nor* the Stock Exchange," the wizard said, drily.

"Hum! I should like to talk to some of these angelic paragons," Mr. Jorkle observed.

"And so you shall," cried the wizard. "Look, there is a young man mowing a lawn; let us go and speak to him."

[14 December 1906]

Chapter VI. The Dunce.

The wizard stepped out between two scented cherries, and spoke to the brown-skinned mower: "Good day, friend; you have a pleasant task this pleasant day."

The young man stayed the scythe and stood up. He was lithe and well-looking, with merry blue eyes and crisp-curling brown hair.

"Yes, sir," he said, "mowing is happy work, and, as you say, it is a handsome, genial afternoon."

"And who," asked the wizard, "lives in that pretty, vine-covered house beyond the bee-hives?"

"A very dear friend of mine," the youth answered, "my sister Kate."

"And do you live with her?"

"No, sir. She is married. She is Mrs. Norris. Her husband is Mr. Joseph Norris, the tile painter. You may have heard of him; he is Assistant Astronomer General."

"I have heard of him. He explained the nature of spiral nebulæ."[52]

"Yes. Would you like to meet my sister, sir?"

"Very much, I thank you. But you have not introduced yourself."

"Oh, I'm Tom Thewlis, and nobody. I mean I'm only Kate's brother. But come this way, friends, my sister will be glad of a gossip."

The tall youth stalked across the lawn and through a quiet rose garden, followed by the three. When close to the house he shouted, "Kate!" and Kate appeared in the green twilight of the trellised porch; a living picture of happy womanhood, in a living frame of flowers. The General involuntarily exclaimed "Hah! Oh!" and turned it into a cough; and even Mr. Jorkle almost smiled. For Mrs. Norris was irresistible. It was not only her superlative prettiness that told; it was her charm; her radiant good humour, her glowing kindness, her transparent candour. Joy seemed to sparkle all about her, like spangles of sunlight on a lake. As for her beauty, its secret was one of light and colour. She was a symphony in red and brown. She had thick-clustered chestnut hair, laughing hazel eyes, arched brown eyebrows, a clear brown skin, ripe full lips and a dimple in each rosy cheek. She was of medium height, wide shouldered, deep-chested, with a full round throat; and her figure, for all its soft curves, suggested power; a happy, beneficent, tender strength.

Young Thewlis, who had anticipated the effect she would produce upon the visitors, smiled his satisfaction. "Kate," he said, "here are three strangers, who would like to rest and chat a while."

"Madam," said the wizard, "if we do not intrude, I should like my friends to see your house, and to have the pleasure of some little conversation with you and your family." He then made the necessary introductions, and the hostess courteously ushered them into her home.

"You see, gentlemen," said the wizard, as they entered the sitting-room, "it is a good deal in the old English style; but with a difference. Open beams in the ceiling panelled walls, polished oak floor. The window takes the whole south side, and is a deeply curved bay, with a seat built in. Except the piano, the harp, and the chairs there is no furniture. Only one picture, but a fine one. Ah! the corn lands at harvest time; all blue, and gold, and sunshine. Your paining, Mrs. Norris? No? The panels are decorated with paintings mostly seas and clouds. Perhaps these are your work, madam?"

The hostess shook her curly head. "No, sir," she said, smiling, "I'm not clever at all. My husband painted two of the panels; the others were done by friends. The harvest picture was painted by Miss Marion Walker, and was given to me as a wedding present."

"Thank you," said the wizard; "I must tell you, gentlemen, that one cannot buy pictures here. One paints one's own, or gets them as presents. And, talking of presents, the most prized are those which are the handiwork of the donor. For instance, if a young man gives his sweetheart a bracelet or a belt, it is always one of his own make. Or he will give a book of his own binding, or a picture of his own painting, or what not. But the girl expects a present to mean some thought and labour expended for her sake. That is so, madam?"

"Of course," said Mrs. Norris.

"And, again," said the wizard, "these people like to do a great deal for themselves. All these chairs, I suppose, would be made by the family or friends. Look at the carving."

"It must be very expensive furniture," remarked Mr. Jorkle.

"Ah! In a sense," said the wizard. "But here things are made lovingly, and lastingly. These chairs will be sound and good two centuries hence. All work here is done well, and so is 'cheap' in the end. With us, as I need not remind you, it is otherwise."

"I understand, madam," said Mr. Jorkle, "that you educate your own children."

"I – oh, no," replied Mrs Norris. "Of course, I teach them the simple things children should know. But one does not educate children. One nurses them, and spoils them."

"I'm – ha – afraid I don't understand," said the financier.

Mrs. Norris laughed. "I mean that one mothers them," she said, "that's all."

"Ha! But what, for instance, do you teach your own children?"

"Only what other mothers teach theirs. I should rather say they learn than that I teach."

"But what do you teach or they learn?"

"They learn to read and write, and to sing and play. And we tell them about the world, and the stars, so that they will know where they live. There is a great mechanical model of the solar system at the Town Hall. There they see the planets and the earth, and the sun, and the moon. So they understand about the seasons and the tides, and all that. And we teach them to make a map of the house and garden, and then show them where London is, and where France and America are. And – well, we sing to them, and talk to them, and tell them stories. Some mothers teach their children to draw, but mine go to my sister's for that. I'm not clever at all."

"Don't believe her, sir," said the brother; "she is as clever as a squirrel. There isn't a cleverer woman in Manchester."

"Why, what can I do, you silly child?" said the hostess, with one of her happy dimpled smiles.

"Do!" said the boy. "You can make other people do things. Anything you like."

"Nonsense, Tom!"

"You can; because you can make anybody love you. Isn't that clever? Look at her guilty blush; she knows."

"I know you are a goose," said his sister; "but if it comes to making people love me, what about Laura?"

"Oh, Laura! That's different," said the youth.

"Yes, it's genius." Mrs. Norris turned to Mr. Fry. "My sister Laura," she said, "is so beautiful – is really so *beautiful*, that even the women cannot be stern with her."

"She is too bad, Laura," said the boy; "she *likes* people to make fools of themselves over her."

"My dear," said his sister, "how can you wonder. Besides –"

"Besides," said Tom, "she has never done anything useful in her life."

"Oh, Tom!" Mrs. Norris looked quite hurt. "Never done anything useful? But is not genius useful? The poet, the painter, the singer; what is their genius for? It is to make joy, my dear. And who can look at Laura and not be glad? Her beauty, that is her genius; her gift to us, that is how she sings her song."

"She gives pain," said Tom, sturdily; "You give happiness, more than anyone, Katie; but she gives pain."

"Well, then," said Mrs. Norris, with another of her wonderful smiles, "if you and I, Tom, try to do good, let some of it count for Laura. Besides, it does a man no harm to be hurt as she hurts. It does him good very often."

"Would *you* do what she does, Kate?" asked the boy.

"I couldn't, dear, I couldn't, or perhaps I might. You are too serious, Tom, for a boy. And Laura is not so very bad. And she is so very, very lovely." Mrs. Norris sighed, smiled, and, turning to the wizard, said: "Our children are in the orchard playing, all except Bernard, and Bernard is a dunce."

"How do you mean, a dunce?" asked Mr. Jorkle.

"He's lazy, that's all," said Tom. "I was when I was his age."

"He *isn't* lazy, Tom; and he isn't stupid," said the mother; "if you loved him as I do you'd understand. You see, sir," she continued, addressing Mr. Jorkle, "Bernard is rather a peculiar boy. I think the lessons don't interest him. He is inattentive and forgets."

"But," said Mr. Jorkle, "don't you try means to make him learn?"

Mrs. Norris raised her dark eyebrows and pouted prettily. "Make him learn – *make* him?" she said; "why, he doesn't *like* it."

"He likes to sit in the woods, and moon,"[53] said Tom; "he does a lot of that. He's doing it now."

"But – ha – what are you going to make of him madam, at that rate?"

"Why, now, sir, I cannot even guess," said the mother; "but my father was just such a boy, and yet – you have heard of Dr. Thewlis."

"Certainly, certainly," said Mr. Fry, "and was he your father?"

"Yes. And he destroyed consumption. He abolished consumption entirely." She turned to Mr. Jorkle, smiling. "So you see, sir, how hard it is to judge. The slow boy often makes the great man. My dear father did one grand thing. Think how much we all owe him. And some day Bernard may wake up and make us all ashamed that we ever thought him stupid. No, sir, with a boy like that one can do nothing but wait; only love him and hold him closer."

Mr. Fry looked from her soft, kindling face to his companions, and said, as he tapped his snuff box, "Well, gentlemen, you hear. Do you think still it would be wise to take children from such a mother, and hand them over to be ground up in your damned scholastic machinery?"

"I don't agree with you at all, sir," cried Mr. Jorkle.

"Ah," said the wizard, "but if you were in Bernard's shoes?"

"Here is Bernard," said Mrs. Norris, and as she spoke a boy of about nine vaulted over the sill of the open window and ran into her arms. The mother stooped, gave him an affectionate and lusty hug, and kissed his short black hair. "Where have you been to, Bernard dear?" she asked.

The boy looked up at her. He was not yet aware of the strangers. "I've been in the Long Wood, mummy," he said.

"And what were you doing, dear?"

"Nothing, mummy."

"Nothing? Your uncle Tom says you are a dunce."

The boy turned a pair of serious dark eyes upon his uncle, then upon his mother. "I'm all right, mummy," he said. He snatched her hand, kissed it, and ran out of the room, laughing. A few moments later he appeared in the orchard, running in a business-like way, with steady swiftness.

"That boy's all right," said the General; "he's got a good eye in his head. Hah! He'll go far and do much. And – hah – the lady is quite right. I tell you she *is*, Jorkle."

"Pooh!" said Mr. Jorkle, "Mr. Fry has bewitched you. It's downright madness."

"It's clean old English sense," cried the General. "Hah! it is, Jorkle. All your schoolmasters are a parcel of old women, begad. I always thought you were, and now I – hah – I see it, don't you know. Hah! They trampled all over us with their damned clump-soled intellects. Dash it all they assaulted and battered us, by George! Hah! we were governed a devilish deal too much, and – hah – that sort of thing."

"As a soldier," said Mr. Jorkle, "I should expect that you would believe in discipline."

"So I do," the General answered, "so I do, by George – for soldiers. Hah! but I'm talking about cram. You cane a boy, begad, because he doesn't remember how many penny farthing candles you can sell a fool for one and ninepence. Hah! dash it all, we don't want a nation of demnition tallow chandlers. That boy's one of the Drake and Dampier breed.[54] He doesn't learn lessons; he teaches 'em. He doesn't – hah – build jerry cottages; be builds nations. You can get the other sort for a pound a week to sell candles in five languages. Hah! dash it all, Jorkle, you are in the trade yourself. But if you met that boy in a cavalry charge when he is ten years older he'd have your whiskers off before you could say Jack Robinson.[55] Hah! Hang it all, some fellows are all words and figures don't you know? But you can tell a doer, and a goer, and a stayer, by the turn of his eye. Hah! Hum! And there you are, dammit."

"Very good, very good, General," said Mr. Jorkle, sourly, "and when are you going to turn Socialist?"

"Socialist be hanged!" exclaimed the old soldier, "I'm none of your Socialists. But – hah – I know facts when I see 'em. Hah! I know a man from a mermaid."

"I daresay, but what has that to do with the question?" Mr. Jorkle asked.

"Hah! Everything," said the General, "every big and little thing in the world. You fellows think a man is filled with cram, as a demnition doll is filled with sawdust. I've been in the swim, and I know better. It isn't a question of – hah – cram; it's a question of guts. Hah! Don't tell me. You have clerks in your office who could cipher your head off. There's a thumping difference between turning a Latin verse and turning an Afghan flank."[56]

"The education is useless, General," said Mr. Jorkle.

"Not at all. Hah! But men may fight with axes, or with rifles. It's the stomach that wins."

The General turned to Mrs. Norris, "Madam," he said, "I'm – hah – delighted to have met you. Hah! You have talked jolly good sense, and – hah – that sort of thing. Hah! and have done it so prettily that my – hah – my poor friend here doesn't understand that he's beaten."

"I don't think I understand a great deal of what you say, sir," said the lady, laughing, "but I know you have spoken very kindly of my boy and I feel that you are right, as well as kind. And I thank you very much. Is there anything I can do for you?"

"Hah! Well," said the General, "what do you fellows say? I don't want to hear any more about children's lessons, myself, don't you know. I want to have a look at the men. Hah! Besides, we have already trespassed too long upon this lady's kindness. What do you say, Jorkle?"

Mr. Jorkle shrugged his shoulders, but said nothing.

"Well, sir," said Mrs. Norris to the General, "if you mean that you would like to see some of our men at work, I am sure my brother will act as a guide. But to-day it is too late. Though, of course, you would find many of them working at home. Mr. Norris is up at the observatory, taking out some calculations."

"What I should like to see," said the General, "is some – hah – good big beefy navvies shifting dirt, or some fellows throwing a bridge across a valley, don't you know, and that sort of thing. Hah! These are the fellows that count. Music and stars are all vey fine; but – hah – it's the bullocky beggars with shovels and picks that make civilisation possible. Hah! You know what I mean, madam."

"*I* know what you mean," said the wizard, "better than you know yourself, General, for you are talking rank Socialism. But I don't think this lady understands what 'beefy navvies' and 'bullocky beggars' are, and the laughter which she is so heroically subduing probably arises from the fact that she regards us as odd-looking, badly dressed, old fossils, who converse in the unknown tongue."

"Oh, it isn't that," cried Mrs. Norris; "but I feel so ignorant when I listen to your talk, for though it is English I cannot understand half of it; and then your friends look so serious, and seem angry without being so, and – and" – (here the laughter shook in her kind voice) – "your friend Mr. Jorkle seems to have such contempt for our poor lessons, and is so serious about it, that – that – oh! please let me show you the garden. Perhaps you will like our rose trees; some of them are already in bloom."

"Hah! With pleasure, madam," said the General, "and – hah – if you don't mind laughing at us we should regard it as – hah – friendly, and that sort of thing. Hah! If you can get any fun out of us we shall be awfully glad, don't you know. Hah! I shall be glad to think that such a weary old fogey as myself can be – hah! a source of innocent merriment, don't you know, and – hah – that sort of thing."

"I'm sure you are very unkind to yourself, and very kind to other people," said Mrs. Norris, "and you are not at all like what you say, though you do look rather troubled and sad. I fear you are tired, and have come far. So you must sit amongst the rose trees and I will get you some refreshment. Then Tom will fetch my husband, and we will dine together, if you can afford us so much time."

"We are most grateful, madam," said the General; "hah! our time is all our own."

"Oh, how jolly!" said the hostess; "then you can come with us to the ball?"

"The ball?"

"Yes. There is a ball, a festival ball, in honour of the May. And Laura will be there. Oh, here comes Mr. Norris."

[21 December 1906]
Chapter VII. Tomtit Lemon.

The entrance of Mr. Norris, the Assistant Astronomer-General, and expositor of spiral nebulæ, was somewhat informal, considering the eminence and gravity of that gentleman's position. Heralded by a chorus of shrill screams and boisterous laughter, the great man bundled suddenly into view amongst the apple trees, a score of long-legged boys and girls at his heels, and bore down full tilt upon his homestead, kicking before him a football, improvised from a twisted hay-band. Panting and flushed, the astronomer dribbled the ball through the orchard, and was in the act to score a goal through the garden gate, when the ball was cleverly whisked away from him by a wild-eyed maiden with poppy-red cheeks and streaming hair, who sent it flying back into the ruck, and then sat down vigorously amongst the primroses.

"There you go, Tomtit Lemon," said the eminent scientist, panting and leaning against the gate, "just when I was going to kick a goal. How would *you* like it?"

The girl, breathless and laughing could only gasp, "Oh, Mr. Norris! Oh, oh!"

"Oh, Mr. Norris!" repeated the astronomer as he helped her to rise; "a nice trick to play an astrologer. I shall consult the stars about this. I shouldn't wonder if Saturn made himself exceedingly unpleasant about it."

"Oh, Mr. Norris," panted the girl as she pushed her hair out of her eyes, "oh, how you *did* run."

"No flattery, miss," said the philosopher; "*that* won't save you. And now, my dear, come along and have some lemonade and toffee. Hallo! Here's company."

The Assistant Astronomer-General, holding the girl by the wrist, came forward. He was a stout, strongly-built man, with close-cropped black hair, keen dark eyes, and a smile that displayed the perfection of his white teeth. "Gentlemen," he said, "I hope I have not kept you waiting. If it is celestial business, we will begin by comforting ourselves with apples and staying ourselves with flagons. Kate, the times are sadly out of joint when a solid and responsible citizen cannot dribble a hay-band home from the observatory without being set upon by a mob of rudesbys. Take the prisoner, prithee and kindly introduce me to the ambassadors from Norway."[57]

"My dear," said his wife, gently drawing the girl to her side, "these three guests are strangers, and are interested in our ways of work and the training of children. Perhaps, if you can be serious, you may give them some information."

The astronomer listened with a smile, and the introductions having been made, sat down under the mulberry tree and looked at his guests inquiringly.

"My friend, Mr. Jorkle," said the wizard, "is somewhat concerned about your methods of education. He fears that they are inadequate."

"Indeed?" said the astronomer. "Well, perhaps he is right. But our system is the same as the system in vogue in other countries. From Japan to Canada and from St. Petersburg to Gibraltar the system varies very slightly."

"And – er – what is the system?" asked Mr. Jorkle.

"Well," said the astronomer, with his cheerful smile, "I hardly know how to explain. We teach the children to read and write, and give them a few elementary ideas about Nature; and then, as they grow up, each youth follows his own bent. If a boy or girl takes to art or science, the way is made smooth."

"You teach science, then?" said Mr. Jorkle.

"Yes; to those who are interested. I think most of our women and men know something of science. You see, it is of such very great importance."

"But you do not compel them to learn?"

"Compel them! No. If it comes to that we do not compel them to eat their food, or play at cricket, or fall in love."

"You find the young people apt to learn?"

"Naturally. Now, there's Tomtit Lemon. She's only fourteen, and she's a tomboy, and a ringleader in all kinds of mischief; but if you ask her you'll find she has plenty of sense. She can swim, and run, and bat and bowl like a boy, she has a wicked eye and a witty tongue; but she knows that wisdom is better than rubies."[58]

Mr Jorkle glanced dubiously at the pretty child, and said, "You are sure of that?"

"Oh," said the astronomer, "ask her. Here, Tomtit, when are you going to the classes?"

The girl looked up shyly, and removed a rosy apple from her rosy lips. "I think in about a year, Mr. Norris," she said.

"And what do you want to learn, my dear?" asked the astronomer.

"Oh, I want to learn *everything*," the child answered eagerly.

"Don't be greedy, Tommy; don't be greedy, darling."

The girl laughed. "Oh, I am a greedy pig," she said, "but I want to know such a lot. Daisy Sergeant is only sixteen, and she is learning chemistry, and geology, and wood-carving, and the theory of music, and mathematics, and languages. And I want to learn them all. And astronomy, too. I *love* astronomy."

"Do you learn astronomy?" asked Mr. Jorkle.

"Oh, only a very little yet, sir," said the child.

"Hum! And do you know any of the constellations?"

"Oh, yes, sir, all of them. But I like the star clusters, and the nebulæ, I often look at he lovely cluster in Cancer through the big town hall telescope, and the nebulous suns in the Pleiades.[59] I *love* the Pleiades."

"Ha! What do you mean by nebulous suns?"

"New suns, sir. Suns that are forming out of star dust."

"Who – er – told you that?"

"Mother told me, sir. But I read about it in the books. And we have photographs of the nebulæ. The Pleiades are lovely."

"Hum! And do you learn history?"

The child shook her head. "Not much, sir," she said. "We don't like history. It is so horrible. We don't like to read about battles, and murders, and executions. Mother says it is the nightmare period. It is all over now, mother says, and it is better to forget bad dreams."

"You don't read about Julius Caesar and the Kings of England?"

"No sir."

"Then do you know nothing about the past?"

"The past, sir? I know about evolution, a little. About the beginning of life, and the descent of man, sir; and about the geologic periods, millions of years ago. We see all those things in the Town Hall, sir, and mother tells us stories about them, Jim and I often go out finding fossils."

"Ha! And what will you be when you are a woman?"

"He means what will you work at," said Mr. Norris.

"Oh," cried the girl, her eyes sparkling with pleasure, "I shall help Jim to make microscopes."

"That will do, Tomtit, thank you," said the astronomer. Then, turning to Mr. Jorkle, he said, "You see, sir, it is as I told you. The child has plenty of sense. But why should you think she would not wish to learn?"

"Hum! But – well," said Mr. Jorkle, "I understand, Mr. Norris, that your own son is not a very keen learner."

"Oh!" The astronomer smiled. "You mean Bernard. Bernard's a bit of a pickle. But he's very young. He has a mind though. And in such cases it is wise to be very cautious. There is always danger in tampering with a young brain. It is so easy to destroy the originality of a child's mind; as easy as rubbing the bloom off a peach. And what a tragedy it would be to maim a new soul before it got its strength."

At this moment Master Bernard appeared at the house door and hailed Miss Lemon. "Hya, Tomtit! Come and bowl for me and Dicky Brewster."

The girl ran off at once, and Mr. Norris called out, "She'll bowl you out, Bernard."

"Hah! By Jove, Jorkle," said the General, "she'd have bowled *you* out precious soon if you hadn't played for safety."[60]

"What do you mean?" asked Mr. Jorkle.

"Oh – hah – what a humbug you are, Jorkle," said the General. "You know as much about astronomy as most of us do. You know the names of the planets and a few of the constellations, and that sort of thing."

"Speak for yourself, General."

"So I do. Hah! That's just it, don't you know. I'd no idea there were nebulæ in the Pleiades. And neither had you. Hah! A jolly lot you know about evolution. Hey!"

"Science with us," said Mr. Fry, "is caviare to the general. It is not too much to say that we have not yet got over the superstitious dread and dislike of science which the church originated, and still nurses. But here science is on quite a different footing. The best scientific knowledge and the best scientific brains are held by right for the service of the nation. These people are as generous in the scientific expenditure as ours are in their expenditure upon law courts, battleships, and prisons. The result of this wise liberality will be apparent to you when you get amongst the people. For the present I need only remark that the general death rate for England and Wales – *here* – is less than five in the thousand."

"Oh," said Mr. Jorkle, "that reminds me. Even assuming that the average health is abnormally good here, there must the cases of disease."

"Certainly," said the wizard.

"Well – er – in a country where everybody has to work what becomes of a weakling or a cripple?" he asked.

The wizard looked to Mr. Norris for a reply. Mr. Norris showed signs of surprise. "What becomes of a weakling or a cripple?" he asked. "Why, what should become of him? He is taken care of?"

"By the State?" asked Mr. Jorkle.

"By the State? I don't know what you mean by 'the State.' There is young Bailey, son of a friend of mine. He has an incurable spinal trouble. Well, so you ask what we did with him?"

"Certainly."

"How curious! Bailey had the best medical advice, and acted upon it. So they took a house near Heacham, on the Norfolk coast, and went to live there. The young man has the best attention. His sister looks after him. A nurse is engaged to nurse him. A doctor visits him. He has every comfort. Of course. What else can be done?"

"And – er – who pays – I mean?" said Mr. Jorkle. "Is all this at the expense of the community?"

The astronomer rubbed his chin thoughtfully, and looked puzzled. "I'm afraid," he said, "that I don't understand. Of course, if a man is sick his people nurse him and tend him. And if they cannot manage it themselves they have help. Naturally."

"But – the burden falls upon somebody," protested the financier.

"My dear sir," said Mr. Norris, "you puzzle me. If a member of your own family were sick, or disabled, would you not do all you could for him?"

"Certainly."

"Certainly. Obviously. Well, the nation is a large family. When a member of the family is ill or helpless, the family go to his assistance. What do you mean by the burden? There is plenty for all – more than we want. We have lots of food, and medicine and houses. We have many doctors. What are doctors and nurses for? You must be joking."

Mr. Jorkle coughed. "And suppose," said he, "that a man is lazy, and pretends to be sick."

"Pretends!" said the astronomer. "Pretends to be sick! Why in the name of reason should a man be such a fool?"

"Well, to avoid working."

"Upon my word," exclaimed the astronomer, "you *are* joking! Of course, if a man did not want to work – which seems absurd – he would not want to rust and moulder away in a sick room. Unless he were *mad*, and then, of course, he would be sick in reality."

"Then, do you mean to say you have no loafers?"

"Loafers? What are loafers?"

"Men who are too lazy to work."

"Well" – Mr. Norris looked very much astonished – "perhaps there may be men who would rather go to sleep in the sun, like pigs, than do healthy and interesting work. But if there are such men they have sense enough not to own their folly. Why, they wouldn't be *respected*."

"The fact is, Mr. Jorkle," said the wizard, "you cannot see things from the standpoint of these people. Here a man who shirked his work would be regarded much as we regard a gentleman who cheats at cards."

"Good God!" exclaimed the General.

"Yes," said the wizard, "it is so. With us work is regarded as degrading. Work is a task – a task imposed by poverty, or by incapacity to live by the work of others. Here work is regarded as honourable. Not only that; it is regarded as pleasant."

"Well. It *is* pleasant," said Mr. Norris. "It is pleasant, just as cricket or dancing is pleasant. It is not only pleasant to do work, but here is the added pleasure of seeing that it is good when it is done. I paint tiles. But I tell you I envy the men who have more active work to do. I never see the Channel Tunnel without wishing I had had a hand in that glazed brickwork. It is beautiful. Twenty miles of brick tunnel, as smooth and bright as the inside of a telescope. And there's the great observatory on Goathland Moor.[31] Fancy the joy of making the six-foot lens and mounting the machinery, and building the tower. Why, I know two brothers who didn't speak for months because one of them got a job as a mason there and the other was too late. I can tell you such work as that is sought after, and no wonder."

"There is no mistake about it, Jorkle," said the General, producing his cigar case, "this is a wild and dizzy dream."

"And where," asked Mr. Jorkle, who looked worried and pale, "where in the case of a great work like the Channel Tunnel do you get the capital?"

The astronomer shook his head. "Capital?" said he; "what's that?"

"Well," Mr. Jorkle explained, "who provides the bricks, and feeds and lodges the workmen?"

Mr. Norris leaned back in his chair and smiled. "Why," he said, "what a funny question. All those things were sent down to Dover from the farms and stores, of course. Brick-setters have to be fed while they build a tunnel just as they have to be fed while they build our houses. But, of course, when the local stores cannot supply all that is wanted other stores have to be drawn upon. But, tell me, what do you mean by capital?"

The wizard laughed. "Not now, Mr. Norris, if you don't mind," he said, "for here comes your wife, and I believe she is calling us to dinner."

"Hah!" said the General, "by George, that is capital!"

[28 December 1906]

Chapter VIII. The Ball Rooms.

Lascelles, the lighting-rod man, was as handsome as his wife. He stood up to the General's shrewd gaze in complete justification of the lady's choice; a tall, straight, active man, with blue eyes and golden hair, perfectly dressed, perfectly groomed, perfectly bred, serene, intellectual, strong.

"Ha! It's a fine room!" said the General, "and a ripping band, by Jove."

"I suppose you've been a dancer, General, in your day," said Mr. Jorkle; "for my part, I never *can* imagine what people see in it."

Mr. Lascelles turned his blue eyes upon the corpulent financier with a look of astonishment, in which there glimmered a light of amusement.

"Do you mean, Mr. Jorkle," he asked, "that you can find nothing in a ball-room to appeal to you?"

"That, sir," Mr. Jorkle answered, "is accurately what I do mean."

"Hah! Jorkle," said the General, "never was young, nor hah! – human."[62]

"And what, Mr. Lascelles," asked the financier, "what, may I inquire, can you see to interest a man of – er – sense?"

"Sense!" Mr. Lascelles repeated. "If you use the word as implying a sense of beauty, I can see a very great deal here to appeal to such a sense."

"Hah – beauty," said the General, "I've heard of little but beauty all day. I'm not a feminist myself."[63]

"But it seems to me," said Mr. Lascelles, that it is not a mere question of femininity. There are many beautiful women here, certainly. But the men are worthy of them. And this is a beautiful hall, is it not? And you get beautiful colour, and fine perfume, great banks of newly-cut violets. And the music is sublime. Listen to that waltz. Then look at the dresses. So you have youth, and strength, lovely women, handsome men, noble architecture, light, colour, joy, life, the scent of spring meadows, and the magic of passionate music, all blent together as subtly as the odours of many sweet flower in a garden. What more can you ask, sir?"

Mr. Jorkle began to frown and to swell with the answer to this challenge; but before he could get a word out, Mr. Lascelles was called away. Directly he was gone, with the promise of an early return, Mr. Fry took his place, and repeated the question. "What more could you ask, Mr. Jorkle?"

"More! More!" exclaimed that gentleman. "It's all stupid rubbish. Childish triviality. What is the use of it? All this noise and scramble? A parcel of men and women spinning round and round in each other's arms, like dancing Dervishes.[64] It isn't sensible. Hah! It isn't modest. And I notice, too, Mr. Fry, that these perfect people are just as absurdly dressed or undressed as the dancers in our own ridiculous society functions. It's – er – it's intolerable, sir. Quite!"

The General shrugged his shoulders, laughed, and curled his moustaches. "Hah! Jorkle," he said, "you are a confounded old Turk. You don't know it, but you are. You want a pretty woman rolled up in a bale of flannel and muzzled – hah – like a bad dog. Hah! You're not flesh and blood; you're a waxwork, dammit!"

"You have the morals of a soldier," said Mr. Jorkle, "I hope *you*, Mr. Fry, do not approve of this immodesty of exposure."

"Immodesty?" said the wizard. "I am not conscious of any immodesty in this room."

"Well, I *am*, sir; I *am*," cried Mr. Jorkle.

"But," protested Mr. Fry, "as the ladies are not –?"

"You mean if they are ignorant they are not immodest," Mr. Jorkle frowned, "do you think, then, that the effect of such an exhibition is good?"

"The effect upon whom?" the wizard asked.

"Upon the men."

"Ah!" said the wizard, "now you are coming to the point. The effect upon you is bad. Upon the General and me it is not bad; it is good. So that all the immodesty exists in your own imagination."

"You say the effect upon you is good?"

"Certainly. The effect of beauty is good. Beautiful painting and sculpture appeal to the better nature of a man. And there is no picture, no sculpture as beautiful as a beautiful woman. How beautiful these women are judge for yourself."

"He must," said Mr. Lascelles, who had just joined them, "for no one can tell him. It is very humiliating to an author to acknowledge it, but no man, not the greatest poet, has ever been able to give in words a definite pictures of a woman's beauty."

"Hah! By Jove!" said the General; "how do you account for that?"

"Easily enough, to my sorrow," Mr. Lascelles answered. "There are no comparisons."

"Hah! Um! I should have thought there were heaps," said the General.

"Try, then. There is a young girl right opposite to us, smiling at her partner while she fastens her glove. What is her smile like? What in the wide theatre of lovely nature resembles it? Look at her soft grey eyes. You cannot name the colour of them. Can you compare them to at star? There is no humour, no love, no kindness in a star. There is no change of expression in a star. There is nothing in the whole range of Nature so beautiful as a woman's eyes: not even the eyes of a child. So there is nothing to which you can compare them."

"Hah! That's true enough," said the General.

"Well, again," said Lascelles, "who can describe the beauty of a woman's throat? You can see the beauty, you can feel it. But there is nothing to compare with it. Her neck is like the swan's! What a clumsy simile! A woman's neck is no more like the neck of a swan than a woman's hand is like a lily. There is no flower petal to compare with a woman's skin. All the beauties of all the flowers, and birds, and springs, and dawns cannot match the loveliness of a woman. She is the glory of glories, the wonder of wonders." Mr. Lascelles turned to Mr. Jorkle. "You will agree with me in this," he said.

"I – er – never trouble my head about such things, sir," Mr. Jorkle answered, gruffly, "and as I am quite out of my element here, I shall go into the garden and smoke a cigar."

"Our friend," said the wizard, as the great financier ambled way, "is of a temperament difficult to describe."

"Jorkle," said the General, "is – hah – the kind of man who marries his cook."

"You have, General," the wizard exclaimed, "the happy directness of speech which I have often admired in military men."

"Hah!" said the General, laughing. "I *was* on the wicket that time. Hah! And I'm only just beginning to understand – hah – in my old age, don't you know, how devilish immoral and debasing the Jorkle person is. I have always – hah – loved women, and been – hah – ashamed to say so, and that sort of thing. And – hah – hang it – it was hogs of the Jorkle breed who made me ashamed. Hah! I ought to be kicked, don't you know? I had a mother, and a wife, and – hah – ought to have known better. Hah! Why, it makes me sick to own, but I've been afraid, dammit! I've been afraid of the Jorkles. Hah! Fry, we are *all* afraid of the Jorkles. It's as you said, sir, we have forgotten mother. By God, we have as a nation, dishonoured our good old mothers! Hah! Dammit all! Yes. Hah! – I suppose one couldn't get a whiskey-and-soda?"

"I'm sure you deserve one," said the wizard, smiling. "Let us walk round the room first, and have a look at the dancers; then we will see if we can call up Light."

Leaving Mr. Lascelles, the two walked down the side of the great hall, listening to the music and observing the dancers. In the swimming rhythm of the wonderful waltz the couples glided past them, and they confessed to each other in their looks, with all the frankness of their years, the strength of the appeal which all this youth and joy and beauty made to them. There was no need of words between them. The old soldier, in all his long and wide experience, had never been present at a scene so happily brilliant, so humanly perfect. The wizard knew this; the General made no effort to conceal it. So they roved on in silent communion until they reached the end of the room farthest from the orchestra. There they stood for some minutes without a word. When at last the wizard spoke, he might have been reading his companion's thought, or feeling. "All the grace and beauty of life: the glamour of romance," he said, "softly touch one here. We see what we have never before seen; feel what we have never before felt. But it is a dream – a vision of happiness in another planet. Not for us the Promised Land. We have missed it. We are too late."

The General nodded gravely, his eyes still fixed upon the dancers. Then, with a hoarse, rumbling sound that was partly a sigh and partly a cough, he said, "Hah! Hum! And all these are working people?"

"The people of this nation," answered Mr. Fry, "are all working people."

"They – hah! – look so refined and intelligent, and that sort of thing," said the General; "they have such style; they are so well dressed. Hah! They are perfect, don't you know?"

"They *are* perfect," the wizard sighed. "They are graceful, cultured, beautiful, and happy."

The General curled his moustache and frowned.

"Come," said the wizard, sharply, "come this way."

He turned towards a door. The General followed him. The next moment they were in a dark passage. The wizard led the way in silence. It was a long passage and there were several turnings. As they went, a sound of music came to them from the direction toward which they were moving.

"Another dance room?" asked the General.

"Yes," replied the wizard, "here." He snatched back a curtain, and, taking the General's arm, led him into a great hall.

"Good God!" exclaimed the General, and stopped dead, gazing round him in astonishment.

It was a ballroom, one of great size, but dingy, unclean, tawdry, and it was occupied by a dense crowd of dancers suited to the environment. The crowd consisted for the most part of young men and young women, differing sadly in dress, in manner, and in appearance from the dancers in the hall the two had just left. Most of the faces were anæmic, few were pretty. The girls generally were lean of figure, with stooping shoulders. The men were generally coarse, gawky, undersized. The dress was crude in cut and colour, as badly made as it was badly worn. There was plenty of noise, but no sign of real happiness; instead a boisterous hilarity, or dreamy lassitude. Many of the girls were laughing stridently; many of the men were smoking; not all of them were sober. One loutish youth, with a dirty collar and dirty hands, who was waltzing with a rather pretty and very young girl, had a clay pipe in his mouth, and was smoking over his partner's shoulder. A girl of twenty, with beautiful, but untidy auburn hair, and a faded peony drooping at the breast of her crumpled muslin frock, was walking unsteadily amongst the dancers, with a glass of muddy beer in her hand, and was calling out in a hoarse screech for "Bill 'Arry."

The wizard looked at the General, and took a pinch of snuff.

"Hah! What the devil's *this*?" demanded the Honourable and Gallant member.

"This," the wizard answered, "is Manchester – the *other* Manchester, *our* Manchester. These are working people. *Our* working people. This is the happy and admirable state of things which the opponents of socialism are so afraid that any change must spoil. Here you have the popular type and popular pleasure, as they *are*. Here you have the fruits of liberty, of education, of morality, of religion – as understood by Jorkle. This is real. This is practical! Well, are you proud of it?"

The General looked blankly at the crowd and grimly at the wizard; then he said, "Oh, damn!"

"Exactly," said the wizard; then turning suddenly away he clapped this hands and shouted, "Light!"

[4 January 1907]

Chapter IX.

The three lay in their cobweb hammocks, in the cobweb tent spun in the woods by Light's magic spiders, and smoked their cigars before sleeping.

"Hum! hah! As far as we've got," said the General, "these people seem to be jolly and healthy, and that sort of thing. But it seems to be me that – hah – life in such a country must be beastly mild, don't you know."

"You mean dull?" asked the wizard.

"Deadly dull," said Mr. Jorkle.

"Why?" asked the wizard.

"Well – hah – no sport, don't you know," said the General.

"Shooting, for instance?" Mr. Fry suggested.

"Yes; well, shootin', certainly," said the General.

"I never could understand, General," said the wizard, "what pleasure there can be in shooting birds?"

"Hah! Hang it," said the General, "it's the – hah – sport."

"But why," asked the wizard "do you like it?"

"Well – don't you know? – hah – of course," the General answered, " the bird flies up, and you let go, and you – hah! Hit it. Hah! The sport is in hitting it. Hitting the mark."

"But, it seems to me," said the wizard, "that would be an equally good excuse for shooting babies."

The General was puzzled. The idea was too abstract for him. He stared blankly across the tent at Mr. Fry; then looked earnestly at the glowing tip of his cigar. Then he said, "But – hah – we *don't* shoot babies, dammit."

The wizard laughed. "My dear General," he said, "you are most delightfully English, and one must deal with you in the hardest of hard facts. Now, it is a fact that since the birds cannot defend themselves to shoot them is cowardly, and, since they suffer pain, to shoot them is cruel. These people would regard such 'sport' with horror; therefore, they do not feel the loss of it, any more than *you* feel the loss of the more ancient sports of throwing Christians to the lions, or baiting Jews, or roasting heretics. But to come back to your feeling that life here must be dull. It seems to me that you are really raising the question of how these people amuse themselves."

"Well," said the General, "that's about what I – hah – want to get at. How *do* they amuse themselves?"

"Good," said the wizard. "I think that both you gentlemen will admit that the first essential to amusement of any kind is health. A really healthy man can find amusement in felling trees, or running in a paper chase, or climbing rocks, or throwing stones at a post. But a man in bad health cannot, as the Irish say, 'take any delight out of himself,' under the most auspicious circumstances, simply because there is no delight in him. Well, these people are wonderfully and unprecedentedly healthy. And then, another deadly foe to amusement is care: what we call worry. A worried man is like a sick man – very, very hard to amuse. Well, these people have fewer cares than any people our earth has ever bred. What we call business worries, or money troubles, have no existence here. So these men and women come to the feast of pleasure with keen and healthy appetites, and hunger is the best sauce."

"But the question is," said Mr. Jorkle, "what do their wonderful appetites find to feed on?"

"Hah! Just so," said the General, "what do the beggars play at?"

"They play at many things," answered the wizard, "and you will perhaps be surprised when I tell you that one of their chief amusements is work."

"Work!"

"Yes. For work is a pleasure when it is not imposed as a toil. Even in our England many find recreation in work. You must have met with the amateur gardener, the amateur cabinet-maker, the amateur sailor, the amateur builder. Well, in this country almost every man or woman works at several trades. The tailor, the potter, the weaver, will go haymaking, or will take a barge on the canals, or will work on a ship to America or India. The sailor or the navvy[65] will settle down for a year in one of the cities and cultivate tomatoes, or help to build houses, or will lay pavements, or carve hand-railing. When a new road is to be made, or an old one mended, all the men will pour out of their workshops and houses and set about the job as if they were preparing a lawn for a garden party. They can all work, and they all like to work. To them work is sport."

"The deuce it is," said the General.

"I don't," said Mr. Jorkle, "find my workmen very eager to do anything."

"No," the wizard answered, "because they *are* your workmen, and they would think themselves fools, and would be thought fools, to do more for you than they are paid for. But these people are their own workmen. They do not work for *your* profit, nor for the profit of any one person. They work for the general good, and for their own pleasure. There are no masters and no servants here. But you have seen the same kind of thing in summer camps. The men pitch the tents, and dig the trenches, and carry water, and chop wood, and build fires, and peel potatoes. The ladies make the tea, and lay the table, and wash the cups. Nobody wishes to shirk the work. It is for the general comfort; it is part of the fun. Well, that is how it is here, but on a larger scale and a more permanent basis."

"I think I see the idea," said the General. "Hah! There may be something in it."

"There is everything in it," the wizard answered; "or what is possible to a small party of friends is possible to a large nation of friends."

"Granted a complete change of human nature," said Mr. Jorkle.

"No," said the wizard; "granted a complete change of circumstances. The chief difference in this case is the difference between class servitude and equality."

"Well," said Mr. Jorkle, "but, besides mending roads and digging drains, what have these people to amuse them?"

"Well, as you have seen," said Mr. Fry, "they have music and dancing."

"And, besides?"

"Well, there is art."

"But all men are not artist, nor are all men fond of music."

"True. Then we have literature and science."

"You call those amusements?"

"I do. But I will pass them by, and come to sports and pastimes. And, to begin with, there are cricket and football. These games are played all over the world.

Last week England beat France, in Paris, by one wicket. This week England plays Russia in London, and Germany at Manchester. The Russians are very strong; they beat the Indians last week at Moscow, and the Indians are a very fine team."

"Good," said the General; "go on."

"Well. Besides cricket and football, there are rowing, sailing, skating, swimming, cycling, and all kinds of indoor and outdoor athletics. Most of which have county championships, and international championships, attached to them. And there are baseball, lacrosse, and tennis, and golf clubs. And there are the theatres."

"All jolly good things," said the General.

"Surely," said the wizard, "and then there are all the social pleasures. Here they have pic-nics and festivals, for instance with music and games, and dancing in the open air. This week is the May Festival, and everybody goes out to enjoy the beauties and joys of the Spring."

"H'm! Sounds rather rustic; but I daresay it's all right," said the General.

"Yes," said the wizard, "these people can dance, and sing, and play, and have been taught to use their eyes. They find great delight in the skies, and fields, and flowers, and birds; and I might say they find even more delight in each other. You can understand, I am sure, General, that a young man need not feel bored by a ramble in the woods with one of the beautiful girls we saw to-night at the ball."

"Hah! By Jove!" said the General.

"Well," said the wizard, "with good health, beautiful towns and country, pleasant work, pleasant games, music, theatres, dancing, cricket, rowing, sailing, cycling, art, science, literature, and the liveliest and sweetest women ever seen, surely these people need not be sad nor dull for lack of sport and occupation."

"It sounds all right," said the General.

"Oh, it *sounds* fair enough," said Mr. Jorkle.

"Thank you," said the wizard, "and now, gentlemen, let us turn our attention to *our* England, and ask ourselves questions about the amusements of the people there."

"Hah! That's fair, certainly," said the General, "but what an artful customer you are, Fry. Well, you have no shooting here, anyhow."

"And," said the wizard, "supposing that shooting and fishing are sports, how much of such sports do the people get in England now? I think you'll find that fox-hunting and pheasant shooting, and salmon and trout fishing are sports for the well-to-do. The people never have the chance to try them."

"Hah! That's true, certainly," said the General, "but the working classes have their fun too, I suppose."

"Well, let us see what fun they have, and how much of it," said the wizard. "First of all, you will admit – Mr. Jorkle has already admitted – that they don't get much fun out of their work. Their work is largely mechanical, a monotonous uninteresting task, done for others, and under the orders of others, and for the advantage of others. For what art of invention is there in the work of the farm labourer, the stoker, the tailor, the seamstress, the charwoman or the domestic servant? The great mass of the workers are merely wheels in a great machine; they are turned round and round by other wheels. Then they live in ugly and gloomy streets and work in unhealthy and unpleasant shops or factories. And they work long hours; from eight to twelve a day. Their towns and cities are not beautiful, and they see very little of the country. Ask the men and women in our own big towns a few simple questions about trees, or birds, or flowers. There are millions of people in our England who have never seen the sea, who have hardly ever seen a wood, or a field, who have never played cricket, nor rowed a boat, nor swam fifty yards in clean water. The average British citizen does not know a titmouse from a yellowhammer, a grayling from a chub, a bee from an elm. The average British citizen never looks at the sky, nor at the birds nor flowers. He does not know good literature or art, or drama, or music, from bad. He could not make a picture frame, a copper tray, a silver bracelet, a kitchen poker, nor a three-legged stool. He could not cook a dinner, nor graft a slip on a tree, nor dig a straight trench, nor steer a boat, nor splice a rope, nor mend a kettle, nor break a ball from the off.[66] What do the masses in our towns ever see of Nature? What do the labourers in our villages ever see of art or hear of music? In our England the great bulk of the people have no artistic nor intellectual pleasures. Have you ever been to the average village concert? Have you ever been to the cheap popular music-halls and theatres? Have you ever studied the cheap popular fiction?

"With these people, in this new England, life itself is beautiful. With us life is sordid, ugly and monotonous. For our people there are the vilest music-halls, the most fatuous plays, the most egregious novels, the most banal music, but there is betting and the public-house. But the whole of this new English nation has the best literature, art, music, sport, and athletics; better than the rich with us, and besides that, these people have more culture, finer health, and a greater capacity for enjoyment. Go into the crowded quarters of London, Glasgow, Manchester, and the Black Country, and see what the homes and the lives of the workers are like and how much and what manner of amusements fall to their lot; and then ask yourselves whether here in this fair and happy England, life is dull and slow? Why, the majority of our people do not know *how* to enjoy themselves. They have only learnt to worry and to work."

"Oh, you exaggerate," said Mr. Jorkle.

"No," said the wizard, "I am speaking of things I know and have seen. Go into the towns and see the children in the block buildings playing behind iron bars, like animals in cages. Go and watch the youth and maidens of the East End on a Bank Holiday. Go to Southend or to Blackpool, and observe a holiday crowd."

"Well, after all," said Mr. Jorkle, "life should be something more serious than a pic-nic. Work is more important than play."

The wizard laughed. "You are changing front," he said, "we were speaking about play. You had both suggested that these people here had not enough of play. But when we come to speak of work I shall try to convince you that the new England beats the old in both play and work."

"I shall be hard to convince," said Mr. Jorkle. "So far, I have seen only indications of trifling and pleasure-seeking. Music and dancing are poor equipments for the stern work of the world. I'm afraid these Utopians would fare badly in the rush and hurry of modern life."

"Ah!" said the wizard, "now you are thinking of the ruthless scuffle and fevered rush of *our* England. There is no such madness here. And, indeed, I must confess I have no patience with those stupid phrases of the hurry of modern life. The hurry! Look at the hurry of London life. What is it all about? To what end? What do the people hurry for? What comes of it?

"While five millions of frantic superficial Cockneys were hurrying and scrambling and hustling and bragging in the welter of their unlovely Babylon, desperately, jauntily, and noisily producing an infinite deal of nothing, Charles Darwin, in his quiet Kentish homestead, was silently at work – making a new religion and a new thought."[67]

"Hah! Well played, Fry, well played, magician!" cried the General. "Hah! We *do* make a deuce of a row, don't you know, about nothing. Hah! Do you think one might have a – hah – whisky and soda?"

"Light!"

"Sir?"

"Whisky and soda and cigars."

"Now, Mr. Jorkle," said the wizard, "you want to talk about work."

But the only response from the Honourable Member for Shantytown East was a loud snore.

[11 January 1907]

Chapter X. Men or Misers?

"What I don't understand, Mr. Fry," said the Honourable Member for Shantytown East, as he put down his coffee cup and took out his cigar-case, "is how you expect to get the business of the world done when you have removed the only powerful incentive to human effort."

"You mean money?" asked the wizard.

"Surely. What else?" Mr. Jorkle lit his cigar, and leaned back in his chair with his thumbs in the armholes of his waistcoat.

"You think," the wizard asked, in his soft voice, "that the one powerful incentive to human effort is money hunger?"

Mr. Jorkle coughed. "Is there any doubt about it?" he demanded.

The General curled his moustaches and looked sharply at Mr. Fry through his monocle.

"You agree with Mr. Jorkle, General?" the wizard inquired.

"Hah! Yes. Hang it, of course," said the General.

Mr. Fry nodded. "Then," said he, "you think that Nelson, Wellington, Gordon, and Clive[68] fought for money?"

"Oh! Hah! Well, don't you know? There are exceptions to every rule."

"I see. Then, the patriot, the lover, the philanthropist, the poet, the artist, and the prophet are exceptions, and the miser is the rule?"

"We are not talking about misers," said Mr. Jorkle.

"No. But we shall have to talk about them." Mr. Fry took a pinch of snuff. "I see, gentlemen," he said, that you have not outgrown the dismal axiom of the dismal science.[69] I will repeat it for you so that we may see what it is made of. I think it goes thus: The social affections are accidental and disturbing elements in human nature; but *avarice* is a constant element. Do you endorse that statement?"

"Certainly," said Mr. Jorkle.

"And you believe," said the wizard, "that avarice is the strongest incentive to human action."

"Certainly."

"Then, men will do more for money than they will do for love or honour?"

"Hah! *most* men," said the General.

"But you will admit that an average man, not very good nor very bad, but just a normal, natural man, if he could save life or avert a public disaster, would do it, even if he knew he would not be paid?"

"Yes. I suppose so."

"But a normal, natural man, would not take life nor bring disaster upon his fellows out of sheer wantonness, and with no hope of personal benefit from the crime."

"Of course not."

"Well, I think that proves that men will do good for its own sake; but that they will not do evil for its own sake."

"I, hah! don't quite see what you are driving at."

"I am suggesting that men will do good for the sake of the good; but that they will not do evil except for gain."

"What of it?"

"Why, I submit that such being the case the love of good is a constant element in human nature, and that avarice is only an accidental and disturbing element."

"Oh! now you are up in the clouds."

"Let us, then, descend to mother earth. Suppose a man were offered a million pounds to invent a machine. Would he be able to invent it if he did not possess the necessary brains?"

"Of course not."

"But, given the necessary brains, he could invent the machine, if he wished, although no prize were offered?"

"Naturally."

"It seems then that it is genius that invents machines and not greed."

"Nobody denies that."

"But you really believe that a man possessed of the genius to invent a much-needed machine, or to do a much-needed work, can only be induced to act by the hope of pecuniary reward."

"I believe," said Mr. Jorkle, "that a man will try harder for money than for anything else."

"But do you admit that genius can and does work without hope of gain."

"Oh – sometimes."

"Sometimes. And you admit that greed can accomplish nothing without genius."

"That is not the argument."

"It is part of the argument. For it seems to show that genius is stronger than greed, and that genius is not dependent upon greed for its impulse to action."

"Hah! I said before, there are exceptions," remarked the General.

"Well," said the wizard, "you are a soldier. Do you think the millions of soldiers who have entered the army, fought, suffered, died, have been actuated by the fierce desire to grasp the opulent reward of fourpence or a shilling a day?"

"Hah. Soldiers are different! Hang it."

"Soldiers are exceptions. And the volunteers and yeomen who went out to South Africa,[70] did they all go for the munificent pay?"

"Hum! An exceptional case."

"Another exception? You gentlemen have read history. Do you think that Socrates, Aristotle, St. Paul, Copernicus, Caxton, Newton, Herschell, Darwin, Shakespeare, Cromwell, Rembrandt, Dante, Nelson,[71] and the rest of the world's benefactors and heroes worked and died for money?"

"Again – exceptions."

"I hope the exceptions will not overwhelm the rule. But does not history prove that for the sake of love, for the sake of duty, for the sake of truth, for the sake of pity, for the sake of faith, men and women have chosen poverty, obloquy, torture, and death; have laid their heads upon the block, have resigned their bodies to the flames, have suffered imprisonment, execration, murder?"

"No one can. Men and women have done these things, and will again. But when did man or woman do as much for money?"

"Men will do anything for money."

"I beg your pardon. Men will not *die* for money. Money has had myraids of slaves, but money never had a martyr. In the temple of Mammon the Christian adage reads: 'What shall it profit a man if he gain the whole world and lose his own life?'[72] Men will lie for money, steal for it, kill for it, fight for it; but they will not die for it. Now, millions have died for honour, for love, for religion, for freedom, for patriotism. How, then, can it be true that the lust for money is the strongest passion of the human heart."

"Then, what, according to you, *is* the strongest human incentive?" asked Mr. Jorkle.

"Not greed. I should like to say that love is the strongest human passion. But let us say that the love of approbation is stronger than greed for money, and let that serve."

"But I do not admit it."

"Very well. Let us try it. And first of all let me ask you why men are so greedy for money."

"You admit, then that they are greedy?"

"I admit that, under existing conditions, most men wish to have money. But I have first of all to point out to you that only a very few love money, or desire money, for its own sake. The man who loves money for its own sake is a miser. The normal man desires money for the sake of what it will buy. Therefore it is not the money he covets, but those things which money will bring."

"Of course."

"Of course. And now, let us see what money does bring, or is expected to bring, and then we shall begin to get nearer to the real motives of human nature."

"Proceed."

"Well, not to go too wide, I may claim that money is expected to bring ease, and pleasure, and power, and admiration. Is that so?"

"Agreed."

"Then we find that men do not strive for money, but for ease and pleasure, and power, and admiration. So that when we speak of avarice we really mean the love of ease, and pleasure, and power, and applause."

"It amounts to the same thing."

"I beg your pardon. It does nothing of the kind. Since money is only a means to an end, and not the end itself, it follows that were other and better means to the same end attainable the greed for money would cease to move men at all."

"You are arguing in a circle."

"I hope not. Men wish for power, and luxury, and ease, and admiration. They believe that money will bring these things. They believe, many of them, that these things are the most desirable prizes of life, and that without money they cannot be obtained. But if you could convince them that there are better things than luxury, and power, and applause, and ease, and that these more desirable ends could be attained without money, they would cease to care for money. Do you agree?"

"If you could convince them; but you cannot convince them."

"Well, let us leave that point, and see where we have arrived. You began by accepting the axiom that avarice is the strongest motive power of human nature. I have shown you that only misers love money. I have shown you that what the bulk of mankind desire is ease, and pleasure, and power, and applause.

"Now, power is like money; it is only valuable for what it will bring, and it is expected to bring pleasure and admiration. So with ease, it is another form of pleasure. Therefore, we may reduce our terms to two – pleasure and admiration; and we may say that the most active motive power in human nature, under present conditions, is the love of pleasure and admiration. I say under present conditions. I will tell you why I make that stipulation.

"As society is at present constituted nearly every man gets as much money as he can. What are the ordinary motives for this conduct? Plutocrat says, 'I can make a fortune out of the cotton trade, and why should I not? If I don't make it some other man will; and perhaps the other man will be a rogue.' You see, men cannot trust each other. Under the operation of unfettered individual enterprise, life is a scramble. A man knows he could live on less than ten thousand a year, and he knows that multitudes are hungry. But if he foregoes the making of a fortune it will not benefit the poor. Some other man will seize on what he relinquishes, and the scramble will go on. So men amass wealth because they think they might as well do it as let another do it in their stead.

There is another thing. Plutocrat will tell you he has a wife and family to provide for. He knows the world too well to leave a widow and children to the tender mercies of his brother graspers. It is every man for himself and the weakest to the wall. So he will grind other people to make money to prevent other people from grinding his children. He is right in a great measure. It is his duty to provide for his wife and children. And under our present system of robbery and murder by individual enterprise the widow and the orphan will find none to pity and defend them – unless they can pay for value received.

"Again, in a commercial era and in a commercial nation wealth is the reward of merit, the crown of honour, and the sign of virtue. Every Englishman dreads failure. Wealth stamps him with the hall-mark of success, and truly that hall-mark is borne by some very spurious metals; some most evident Brummagem jewels.[73]

"But this assumption is based upon an error. Wealth is not the hall-mark of merit. The most gifted and virtuous are not the most wealthy. Many of the wealthy have neither gifts nor virtue. Amongst the world's best and greatest women and men it would be hard to find one who ever possessed the wealth of a Chicago packer of diseased meat.[74] Probably the king of a Yankee iron or meat or railway trust has more wealth than ever fell to the lot of a hundred of the worthiest and noblest of the human race from Jesus Christ to Darwin."[75]

"Well, you cannot alter human nature."

"I do not propose to try. It is only necessary to make the best of human nature as it stands. And to do that it is only necessary to alter the conditions."

"And you think people can be persuaded to agree with these new and untried theories?"

"They are *not* new, and they are *not* untried. And in the first place I want to show you that you do not believe your own axiom."

"What do you mean?"

"You say that unless men are bribed with wealth they will not do their best; that only for payment can we get the best services of the best men."

"Certainly."

"And then you oppose the payment of members of Parliament, because to pay members would be to lower the tone and impair the *personnel* of the House. Payment of members would open the way to a hoard of mercenary, self-seeking adventurers. You hold that men of the highest character and the greatest talent have always served the state for the sake of duty and of honour; and that such men work better for honour than for money."

"Again: they are exceptional men."

"Still more exceptions. Tell me: do you find the amateur cricketer or football player less keen or faithful then the paid player? Do you believe that the crews in the University boat race do not row their best and try their hardest? Do you trust the skill and devotion of the lifeboat men? And how do you explain the existence of the yeomanry and the volunteers?"

"But you propose that all men should be on a level. You would pay the doctor no more than the docker. Do you expect that to result in anything but deterioration?"

"I expect it to work, as it does work now, the whole world over, successfully. But now let us go and see the building of a new bridge over the Irwell,[76] and we will discuss that question by the way."

[18 January 1907]

Chapter XI. A Talk on the Bridge.

The three followed the line of the stream for half a mile, than paused a while on the centre of an old stone bridge, its grey front starred with golden lichen, and watched the evolutions of a shoal of roach in the clear water. The fish, a full fathom below the surface, moved "in wavering morrice"[77] amongst the slim reeds and delicate water grasses. Every scale on their silver sides, every quiver of their coral gills, every ripple of their pearly fins, could be distinctly seen as they curved and glided in and out amongst the tall green stalks, their mouths opening and closing stupidly, and their great flat, dim eyes staring; and below them could be seen the dappled bed of the brook, with here a gleam of sunlight from a polished pebble, and there a bubble sparking like a gem. Suddenly a water vole dropped into the stream with a plop, and the shoal sprang outwards in a star-like radiation of sparks of silvery light, and were gone.

"By George!" said the General, "that was sharp. Looked like the bursting of a shell, by Jove!"

"It was a pretty sight," said the wizard, "and this must be very pure and sweet water."

"Hah!" The General took out is cigar case. "Jorkle said just now that you proposed to pay the doctor no more than the docker. Is this so?"

The wizard, smiling, asked, "Why not?"

"Why not?" Hah! What kind of doctors would you get? Hah! It's absurd."

"Well," said the wizard, "put it the other way about, and say that the docker is paid as much as the doctor."

"But – but it's the same thing, by Jove!"

"No, General. For when you say it is absurd that a doctor should be paid no more than a docker you are presuming that a docker is not well paid. That is to say, you are confusing the idea of our present England with the idea of this England. With us a labourer is badly paid, badly fed, badly clothed, badly housed, and badly educated; and you are supposing that in this ideal country a doctor will fare as badly as a docker fares with us.

"But here the labourer is well fed, well housed, well clothed, well educated, and well respected. The labourer in this England has, in fact, everything that is necessary to a happy, healthy, and honourable human life. And if the labourer has everything that is good for him, what can the doctor want more?"

"But – hah! hang it all, what encouragement is there for a man to become a doctor, don't you know?"

"Let me ask you a question. Suppose a collier were paid as well as a major-general, would you be willing to give up your profession and go to work in a coal pit?"

"Hah, no! No, of course not!"

"Exactly. So that you feel that there is some other attraction besides the mere rate of wages."

"But," said Mr. Jorkle, "that is a superficial argument. A doctor needs an expensive education. A docker does not."

"To be sure," said the wizard, "and the community pays for the doctor's education, and keeps him while he acquires it. Therefore, the community is not in his debt on that score."

"Yes, yes," said the General, "but, my good man, to be a doctor, or an editor, or a statesman, or an artist, a man has to work harder than he has, don't you know, to be a labourer. Isn't it right that he should be paid for his extra labour, and – hah! – that sort of thing?"

The wizard nodded. "Good, General, very good," said he, "and I will not pretend that a man who works for ten hours a day does not confer on the community more than one who works for five hours a day, nor will I pretend that a man of genius is of no more value to the community than a man of normal intelligence."

"Very well, then. Hah! That seems to settle it. Hah! you admit that it is just that a man who is worth more should be paid more, and that sort of thing?"

"You suggest that we should pay the superior person superior wages because he confers extra benefits upon us."

"Exactly."

"But suppose we feel that by paying a lot of money to one who is a benefactor we convert him into a menace or an injury to the community. Suppose we feel that to give a benefactor riches is to make the boon into a bane."

"But – er – justice," said Mr. Jorkle; " a man must be paid the value of his labour."

"Well," the wizard answered, "you do not propose that we should pay for anything we do not get; but only for what we do get."

"Of course,"

"And you do not pretend that we are to accept a man's services if we would rather decline them?"

"No."

"Well. Suppose we say to the doctor, 'we would rather not employ you than make you a rich man. Go, then, and doctor yourself!' Or, suppose we say to the poet, 'We would rather not give you riches for your songs; go, then, and sing them to yourself.' How would the doctor and the poet fare then?"

"But that would be foolishness."

"Not at all. We have to consider the good of the community. If a rich man is a danger to the community we are within our right in refusing riches to any member of the community."

"Then you would have no doctors?"

"It does not follow. There would be men able and willing to do that or any other kind of work, on the terms we offer."

"Then you would be exploiting those men?"

"Well, yes. You must remember that we do not compel a man to confer upon us the benefit of his genius. But what he has to give must be given: we do not buy."

"Hah! That seems beastly unfair, don't you know?"

"Unfair! It's – er – it's robbery."

"Pardon me. The community says to the genius: 'We have decided to conduct this commonwealth upon certain lines. If you like to conform to the rules made for the general good and the general safety, you are welcomed to abide with us. If not, you are at liberty to go elsewhere. If you care to give we shall be glad to accept. If you do not care to give we shall not take.' What right has the genius to complain of such terms? Where is the robbery?"

Mr. Jorkle swelled with indignation. "Then," said he, "you Socialists are prepared to accept services without paying for them?"

The wizard laughed. "The folly of all theories of value," he said, "lies in the attempt to reduce all human relations to terms of money. You cannot pay for all services in money, because there are some services that cannot be counted in money."

"Hah! What services?" asked the General.

"Suppose, General," said the wizard, "that you were young and single, with an income of five thousand a year. And suppose you loved a very beautiful and sweet woman. And suppose she was willing to marry you, although a man with five hundred thousand a year had proposed to her."

"Well?"

"Would you marry her?"

"Of course, I should."

"Would you think you had done wrong to marry her, when she could have married a richer man?"

"Hah! Assuming that she – hah! – cared for me," said the General, "I should think I did quite right to marry her – by George!"

"Very well. You would exploit her. But suppose she said to you: 'I love you better than any other man, but Mr. Blank will pay me more to marry him than you can pay me.' Would you honour and admire her as much as if she gave herself for love?"

"Of course not."

"Would you think it quite right, and proper, and pleasant for your mother, your friend, or your wife to ask you to pay for every kiss or kindness – in money?"

"Hah! hang it, no."

"Could you reckon up in money how much a mother, a sister, a comrade, or a child is worth to you?"

"Hah! What beastly rot."

"If you brought in a wounded comrade off the field of battle, under fire, would you expect to be paid – in money?"

"Hah! The idea!"

"Could you reckon up the value of William Shakespeare or Horatio Nelson in L.S.D.?"[78]

"Pooh!"

"Do you believe that James Watt, Christopher Columbus, Sir Francis Drake, George Stephenson, Lord Clive, Caxton, Rembrandt, and Beethoven[79] received the full value of their services – in money?"

"Of course not."

"Suppose the value could have been estimated in millions, and paid to them, do you suppose they would have been better off with a thousand millions than with one million?"

"Perhaps not. Hah! Enough is as good as a feast."

"Enough is better than a feast. And now I will give you a line of poetry from Swinburne's 'Child's Song,' which throws a flood of light upon all theories of value. It is this:

> Gold is worth but gold,
> Love's worth love.[80]

And now let us get back to the subject of our treatment of the superior persons. In a community like this every man – *every* man – has all that a man needs. Would it be reasonable for the superior person to sulk and refuse to benefit his fellows because he was refused more than he needed? If we give him all the essentials to a healthy and happy human life. If we give him esteem and love to boot, what can he ask for more? There is nothing he can take or we can give. He has all life can yield.

"And, again, it is a mistake to suppose that a man of genius works for money. His incentive is not gain – it is genius. The reward of the giver is in the giving. The reward of the artist is his art. The singer, the painter, the healer, the discoverer, must sing, or paint, or heal, or discover. In no other way can he be happy. You don't need telling that such men as Bruno, Galileo, Copernicus, Luther, St. Paul, Cromwell and Darwin[81] did their work not only without encouragement and without pay, but in despite of opposition, of vilification, of persecution, of torture even, and peril of death.

"The genius is the spoilt child of Nature. He has joy in his work, in his gifts, in his power. You might pay a Shelley to sing, or a Nelson to fight, or a Rubens to paint, or a Spencer to think, but no wealth you could heap upon such men would suffice to bribe them to cease to work, or to study, or to sing. It *is* more blessed to give than to receive, and why should a man be paid by men because he has been more blessed by Nature?"

"Hah! there's something in what you say. But – hah! it seems to me to apply only to exceptional men."

"And it is of exceptional men we are speaking. But I think you are wrong, and that it is true of all women and men under natural conditions."

"Nonsense!" cried Mr. Jorkle.

"Well," said the wizard, "let us see. I will cite a quite common and familiar instance. Both you gentlemen have been present at many parties in your own homes or in the homes of friends. You will notice at these parties that the clever guests entertain the less gifted. That is to say, one guest sings, another plays accompaniments, another performs juggling or conjuring, or other parlour tricks, and so on. But did you ever find at any party that the amateur tenor, or baritone, or pianist, or reciter, or violinist asked to have two dinners and a double or treble allowance of wine and cigars because two-thirds of the guests merely acted as audience or spectators?"

"Hah! But, hang it, that is amongst friends."

"Just so. And what is possible in a small gathering of friends is possible in a large community of friends – as a Socialist commonwealth must be."

"And, pray," asked Mr. Jorkle, "how, in such a perfect brotherhood, are you going to allot the work? How do you persuade a man that he is to be a road-mender, and not a civil engineer; a mason, and not an architect; a printer, and not an author?"

"Why," asked Mr. Fry, "how do you persuade a member of a college eleven that he is to field at long on and not at point, that he is to go in ninth and not first, that he is to keep wicket and not bowl? In an amateur choral society, how do you convince a tenor that he is to sing in the chorus and not to take the solos? But come, let us go on the new bridge which is building, and put some of your questions to the workmen. Light!"

"Sir?"

"The flying machine."

"Yes, sir."

[1 February 1907]

Chapter XII. A Question of Finance.

The bridge, a noble stone structure, was nearly finished. As the Three approached they came upon a mason engaged in facing a large block of marble. Close to him, upon a scaffold overhanging the river, a younger man was chiselling the face of a water nymph.

The wizard stepped up to the mason and came to the point at once. "My friend," he said, "I should be greatly obliged if you would answer me a question.

I ask, not out of curiosity, but because these friends, who are travellers from over sea, have some difficulty in understanding English methods."

The mason stopped working and looked at the strangers with some wonder, and perhaps a little amusement. "Ask what you please, friend," he said, smiling.

"Well," said Mr. Fry, "my friends see you doing this plain mason's work, and a younger man doing sculptor's work and they do not quite understand that. They ask why you are content to work as a mason while another man works as a sculptor."

The mason looked from one of the visitors to the other with a puzzled and doubtful smile. "I don't," said he, "quite understand, I'm afraid. I am a mason. George, there is a sculptor. Each does his own work, of course."

"But," said Mr. Jorkle, "*why* are *you* a mason, and why is *he* a sculptor?"

The person rubbed his chin, and glanced at the sculptor. "Well," he said, "we cannot all be sculptors, or the bridge would never be built."

"Yes, yes," said Mr. Jorkle; "but why do you consent to do the rougher work and leave another man the art work?"

"Why?" The mason laughed, and the sculptor smiled, and looked over the parapet to listen. "Why?" asked the mason. "I should think that needs no telling. George does the art work because he is an artist. I do the plainer work because I am not an artist."

"But," said Mr. Jorkle, "do you think that is fair?"

"Well, friend," the mason answered, "your questions astonish me, I must say. Do you ask me if it is fair for a man to do the work he is best fitted for?"

"But," Mr. Jorkle persisted, "don't *you* want to be a sculptor?"

The mason and sculptor looked at each other and laughed. Then the former said, "No; I don't want to be a sculptor; and I could not be one if I did want."

Mr. Jorkle considered for a moment. Then he said, "But why do you consent to be a mason?"

"Well," answered the mason, with the same look of amused surprise on his bronzed face, "I'm doing this work because it wants doing, and because I like to work in the open air."

"Do you mean to say you *like* the work?" asked Mr. Jorkle.

"Well enough," said the mason. "The bridge was wanted and, of course, we like to see it done and done well."

"And you don't ask for better work?"

"Better work? I think I can guess what you mean. Did you ever see a band were all the violinists played first fiddle?"

"Of course not."

"Well? The second fiddles and the second trombones play their parts, and the conductor does his business; and the whole band are satisfied if they play the piece well. You don't expect the hundred and fifty men and women to refuse to play because they cannot all be conductors, do you. Are you making fun of us?"

"No, no," said Mr. Fry. "We are not making fun of you. Our friend thinks every man will naturally want to lead."

"Well," said the sculptor, "that is the queerest idea I have come across for a long time. Jack here bowls for Lancashire. I am only a change bowler. Do you think I shall want to go on first when he is a far better bowler? We want to win the match."

"And build our bridge," said the mason.

"And are you contented," asked Mr. Jorkle, "to go on all your life chipping stone blocks."

"Oh, I did not say that," said the mason. "I've been on two voyages to India and one to New Zealand; and sometimes I go and work on the corn lands, or do a little roofing."

"But don't you wish for more intellectual work?"

The mason shook his head. "Why should I?" he asked. "I have no leaning that way. I like to do plain work, and when I've finished I like a game of cricket or football, or a ramble in the country. George is fond of art and books, and we both grow roses. But, of course, George spends a lot of time over his sculpture. He will work here for hours after I've gone home to the garden." The mason smiled and resumed his work as though there were no more to be said. Mr. Fry thanked him, and the Three walked on.

"And what," asked the wizard, "did you think of our friend the mason, Mr. Jorkle?"

"He was a very unambitious man," said Mr. Jorkle.

"And I think," answered the wizard, "that he emphasised a common error of the political economist."

"In what way?"

"Why, the average man is *not* ambitious; is not rapacious. The average man likes an easy and pleasant life, and does not want to be bothered."

"Hah! Do you think so," asked the General.

"Certainly," said the wizard; "and that is why it is so easy for a few greedy or ambitious men to get the money, or the lead, and keep it."

"And does not that show," said Mr. Jorkle, "that equality is impossible?"

"Well," said the wizard, smiling, "it may show that. But it certainly does not prove what you were trying to prove, that without the whip of poverty or the spur of greed all men would want to be kings."

"Hm!" Mr. Jorkle puffed out his cheeks and stopped half-way across the bridge. "Perhaps you will now answer me a question as to ways and means. If all the people in the Utopia have abundance, it follows that they must consume more than is consumed in – say, England. Therefore more must be produced.

Increased production means increased labour. Yet you say these people only work a few hours a day. How do you account for that?"

"Hear, hear! Well put, Jorkle," cried the General.

The wizard took out his snuff-box and looked slily at his two friends. "So," he said, "I have been expecting that question. Let us sit here on this seat in the sunshine while I answer it."

"Hah! It seems to me you have got a tough task, don't you know," said the General.

The wizard took a pinch of snuff. "It is not a hard question at all," he said, "but my answer will take some time." He looked thoughtfully at the river for a few moments, and the General lit a cigar.

"Now," said the wizard, "you are tacitly admitting that in our England the majority of the people have not enough of the necessaries of life. And you suggest that if they are to have enough they must produce more. Eh?"

"Certainly."

"It is not certain, however. For if we assume that a great deal of the wealth produced in our England is wasted, it may be possible, by stopping the waste, to supply all the wants without extra labour.

"And, again. If in our England it is true that millions of men and women produce nothing at all, it may be possible, by setting all to work, to produce enough for all without increasing the labour of the present workers.

"And, again, by a more general and judicious use of labour-saving machinery it may be possible to produce more wealth with less labour."

"Well?"

"Very good. Let us first look into the question of waste. In our England we pay 275 millions in rent. Here there is no rent. In our England we pay 340 millions in interest. Here there is no interest. In our England we pay some 200 millions in profits. Here there are no profits.

"Now, add those sums together and we get a total of 815 millions. Reckon the average workman's wage, at thirty shillings a week, or £75 a year, and we find that in our country we pay, under these three heads alone, the earnings of nearly eleven millions of men. All that is wasted.

"But that does not exhaust the tale of our waste. We waste also 196 millions in drink. We waste many millions in tobacco and cigars. We waste something like 70 millions on soldiers, sailors, ships, guns, and ammunition. All that is saved here. Then in our England we waste more millions upon judges, lawyers, prisons, and police. Here they save all that.

"In our England, again, we spend a vast amount of money on banks, coinage, bank notes, cheques, book-keepers, cashiers, commercial travellers, overseers, commission agents, time-keepers, and other middle men. Here all that is saved.

"And in our England we spend more millions upon insurance; and we spend a lot upon pensions, and the Royal Family. Here all that is saved.

"And in our England there is an immense expenditure of money on churches, and ministers, and missionaries. Here no man takes his religion from paid preachers.

"And in our England the competitive system exposes us to much waste of labour and money: as, to mention a common example, there will be six milkmen delivering milk in one street, while only one postman delivers all the letters.[82]

"And, again, there is the enormous waste of money in advertisements.

"Then in this country the people do not eat flesh meat of any kind; and it is very much cheaper and healthier, to live on a vegetable diet.

"And in our England there are millions of idle persons, all of whom have to be clothed and lodged and fed at the expense of the industrious producer.

"For instance, in London alone there are nearly one hundred thousand persons in workhouses, prisons, hospitals, or lunatic asylums. All these persons, and those who govern or guard, or attend upon them have to be maintained.

"In London alone there are eighty thousand unemployed, thirty thousand vagrants, and as many abandoned women. These people produce nothing; but they are all consumers.

"Now, in this country there are no paupers, no beggars, no tramps, no thieves, no drunkards, no abandoned women, and no unemployed.

"There are in this country fewer sick, fewer infirm, fewer insane, therefore there are fewer nurses and doctors.

"You can see for yourself how enormous the saving must be here.

"But consider. We have one million adults who have not even a pretence of any employment. We have nearly two millions of domestic servants. We have nearly half a million of soldiers, sailors, and pensioners. We have still larger armies of tramps, thieves, beggars, paupers, prisoners, policemen, jailors, lawyers, parsons, lunatics, sick, deformed, and unemployed. We have the legion butchers, graziers, poulterers, the fishermen, book-keepers, publicans, barmaids, pot men, brewers, advertisement canvassers, and all the rest.

"Then we have all the jockeys, flunkeys, tailors, milliners, jewellers, perfumers, upholsterers, artists, gardeners, florists, ladies' maids, coachmen, huntsmen, and countless others who wait upon and work for the idle rich.

"Here all these crowds of men and women are usefully employed. Need I point out the great increase in the producers, which these facts imply?

"But there is yet another point to be made. In our country the improvement and use of machinery is left to chance and private enterprise. Here the whole nation is concerned in the matters of producing and distributing necessary things. You can easily imagine that under such circumstances this people must have made immense advances in all matters of labour-saving and wealth-producing machinery.

"We find, then, that certainly not half of our population is engaged in the production of the necessaries. We find that of their gross production more than two-thirds are wasted. We find that here all that waste is saved, and that the whole population is regularly and wisely employed; and we find that the labour-saving appliances here are infinitely better than our own.

"Well, estimating from the capacity of the best machinery in use in our countries, Mr. Atkinson, an American statistician,[83] declares that one man can produce bread for one thousand; that one man can produce cotton cloth for 250 persons; and that one man can make boots and shoes for 1,000 persons.

"Why, then, should it be necessary for the people in this country to work hard or long hours?

"To give you an example of the amounts wasted by the idle rich in our England, let me take the case of a millionaire's yacht, built at a cost of £150,000. Such a yacht uses up the year's labour of 2,000 men for one year. Reckoning the average wage of 30s. weekly.

"Now, supposing one man capable of producing bread for one thousand persons, it follows that the two thousand men employed on that yacht would produce bread for two millions of persons.

"This will give you an idea of the saving effected in this country, where everybody works, where nobody wastes, and where the machinery is of the very best.

"Consider these facts, and tell me why these people should not be able to provide themselves with abundance at the cost of four hours' work a day for each man."

The wizard paused, and took another pinch of snuff.

The General knocked the ashes off his cigar, and looked inquiringly at Mr. Jorkle.

Mr. Jorkle coughed. "It wants thinking about," said he. "It is a question of figures."

"It is, I think," said Mr. Fry, "a question of common sense."

[8 February 1907]

Chapter XIV. The Navvies.

"Well, General," said the wizard, tapping his snuff box, "here are your men of might, broad-built, brawny, and big; knights of the pick and spade. How do they like you?"

The General put up his monocle, and glared critically at the men: a party of navvies at work in a cutting. "Hah!" said he, "this is something like it. These are the fellows that make a country into a nation, begad!"

There were some two hundred men at work. They ran tall, and broad, and were muscular and brown. Around their wrists they wore the professional strap; around their legs, below the knees, the proper things.[84] They were dressed in the good old fashion: in moleskin trousers and blue or woollen grey shirts; were mostly bareheaded, and wore their collars open at the throat.

They worked, as is the manner of the craft, steadily and deftly, with out haste and without pauses, planting their heavily-shod feet solidly, and putting the weight and power of their ponderous shoulders into the push and heave of the spades.

"They are very like our own men," said the General, "except, by George, their faces. Hah! Yes, their faces are finer, don't you know."

"Of course," said the wizard; "they are educated men; cultured, many of them."

"Cultured!" exclaimed Mr. Jorkle. "But, of course, I forgot, even the dustmen in this place are perfect gentlemen."

The wizard consulted his watch. "It is close upon lunch time," he said; "I should suggest that we disembody ourselves. Then we can listen to their talk. Do you object?"

"Oh, not at all," said the General, "this isn't a ballroom, dash it all."

As he spoke a youth rose up from behind a heap of earth and began to ring a hand-bell, mellow and full-toned, and not unlike a sheep-bell, but louder.

At this sound the men stopped working and drew off to the opposite side of the cutting, where they began to wash their hands at troughs, laid, apparently, for that purpose.

These ablutions completed, the navvies formed into groups, and began their lunch, and the three drew near to one party and stood to listen to their talk.

The talk was begun by a red-haired giant, who was seated on a heap of stones. This man said to another, almost as big as himself, but black-haired and sallow, "I see you are home again, Ullathorne. Where have you been wandering this time, and how has the world used you?"

The dark man looked at the speaker and said, "I've been in Germany. Didn't you know? I went to sing at a festival in Stuttgart, and I took it into my head to walk through the Black Forest country, and sing for my supper."

"There are bonny wenches in that country, Frank," remarked a burly, bearded man, who sat near.

"There are in all countries, I give thanks," said Ullathorne, smiling; "and I daresay that is what Arthur Shirley wants to hear about."

"Rubbish!" said the giant; "tell me about the Guest Houses. Have they anything out of the common in that line?"

"Very good, very good indeed," said Ullathorne; "quaint, high-gabled houses, with plenty of clever carving. The best of them is at a little town near Stuttgart

– I forget the name. There were some Japanese travellers put up there a couple of years ago, and they decorated the principal sitting-room in their own fashion. You can almost hear the birds sing, and see the flowers nod in the wind."

"Ah," said Shirley, "There's a new guest house at Oldham since you went away, Frank. It stands right amongst the tulip beds, and looks like a crystal beehive. The dining room is circular, and the panels are painted with children and women alternately. Some of the children were painted by Dora Sutcliffe: she was half a year at the work. And you know what *they* will be like."

"If they are like Dora they will be worth seeing," said Ullathorne.

"They are wonderful," said Shirley. "*I* think they are great. What do *you* say, Jack Fergusson, you have seen them?"

The man addressed, a fine, jolly fellow of thirty-five, who was peeling apples as though he loved them, glanced at Ullathorne and laughed. "Oh," he said, "Dora Sutcliffe paints bairns well, none better, and Frank will be the last man in the world to deny it. But the finest guest house I've ever stayed at is at Nice."

"Yes, yes," said Shirley, "the one with the Odyssey pictured in the hall. I've heard of it."

"Oh, I say, Arthur," said the bearded man, "have you seen the new translation of the Odyssey?"

"You mean the one by Miss Pearce, I suppose?" said Shirley. "No, I'm not much of a bookworm. It's good, isn't it?"

"Wonderful," said the bearded one. "It's the real thing. The real, impossible, miraculous thing. It gives the literal story, and it gives the spirit and the movement, and the music of the Greek. And done by a girl!"[85]

"Which Miss Pearce is it?" asked Ullathorne.

"Oh, *the* Miss Pearce," Fergusson answered, "Stella Mary Pearce; no other."

"What!" exclaimed Ullathorn, "the gargoyle girl?"

"Yes," said the man of the beard, "the same. She must be a reincarnated Greek. Those gargoyles are unique."

"True," remarked Shirley. "I saw some on a hall at York. Never saw such funny faces in my life."

"Oh, by the by, what is this about Frank Donne and Marie Summerscale?" asked Ullathorne.

"Haven't you heard?" asked Fergusson.

"No."

Fergusson shrugged his shoulders and frowned. "Tell him, Arthur," he said. But Shirley said, "No. You tell him, Philip."

"How much do you know?" the bearded man inquired of Ullathorne.

"Nothing definite," was the answer; "a tragedy, I heard. What is it?"

"H'm! It's a sad affair," said Philip. "You knew Donne, didn't you?"

"Yes. Well. He was a splendid chap."

Philip nodded gravely. "He was," he said. "Well, you know that he was married to Miss Summerscale?"

"Of course. That's two years ago."

"Yes. Well, they were very happy. And when they had been married about a year they went to live in Kent, at Ashford."

"Yes."

"One day Mrs. Donne was walking through the woods and she met Percy Langdale. Did you know him?"

"No."

"Well. He was a Manchester man, and had known Marie Summerscale when they were both children. He had gone to manage a farm in the weald of Kent some years before. And they met in the wood that day by accident, if there is such a thing as accident."

"There's such a thing as Fate," said a serious, quiet man, who sat close by.

"Fate? Call it that if you like, Will. Anyhow, Donne's wife and Percy met in a green glade, and their souls ran together like quicksilver."

"Oh, oh, oh," Ullathorne sighed softly.

"That's how it was," said Philip; "they wandered along together in a dream. They parted, and went their ways. What they felt, or said, or did, what sort of a fight they fought with Fate, no man knoweth. But the trial was too hard for them, and they went away in a month."

"She left poor Donne? *She* did, little Marie?" said Ullathorne.

Philip nodded. "So it was," said he, "and that isn't the worst, as you will have heard."

"They were lost at sea!" said Ullathorne.

"Yes. In the Channel. All three. Marie and Percy had left for America from Dover. Somehow in the Channel, off Beachy Head,[86] in a rough sea, Marie fell overboard. Langdale jumped in after her. Just then poor Donne, who had come out on the same boat to try to part them, came on deck. He shouted to the officer on the bridge and then he jumped over also. And that was the end. The ship was going full speed. There was a heavy sea, and it was dark. Nothing was ever heard of seen of them again."

"Terrible, terrible!" said Ullathorne.

"Yes. You may say so, Frank," said Shirley. "Donne was a splendid fellow, and Marie was as pretty as a bunch of roses in a silver vase. And to think of their being whiffled out like that before they had learnt the taste of life. It was hard fortune."

"Ah," said Philip; "yes, if that was the end. But, you know, I cannot believe it is the end. And I feel sure that those two poor young things will be happy yet."

"Perhaps," said Ullathorne; "but if not, poor Donne met a hard fate."

"And so did Marie," said Philip.

"Well" – Ullathorne spoke doubtfully – "it's not a new story; it has happened before and will again; but I must own that I don't understand it."

"What don't you understand?" asked Philip.

Ullathorn frowned thoughtfully. "I don't understand those sudden and violent passions," he said. "Why didn't Langdale go away?"

"He did go away," said Philip; "but he came back."

"He must have been very weak," said Ullathorne.

"Weak?" Philip paused and looked thoughtful, then he turned to the quiet man. "Come, William the Silent," he said, "what is your opinion?"

The whole company looked hard at William. From a man habitually silent wisdom is expected.

William shook his head. "Philip," said he, in a quite voice, "*you* know, without asking me. Shirley here does not care for books; you do."

"What of it?" Shirley asked.

"Men differ," said William, laconically.

"Explain, silent one, explain," demanded Shirley.

William fixed his soft, kind gaze upon the giant. "Frank Ullathorne," he said, "would have gone away, and wouldn't have come back."

"Of course," said Ullathorne; "then, why did Langdale go back?"

"Ah, my lad, my lad," said William, "Langdale was in love."

"And suppose I had been I love?" asked Ullathorne.

"You," – William shook his head – "you would never be in love as Landgale was. And, besides, *she* was in love with *him*."

"But," cried Ullathorne, "do you mean that a man and a woman are helpless slaves – to love."

"*Some* men, and some women," said William, "and some love."

"Well," said Ullathorne, "it seems impossible to me. I cannot realise it."

William stroked his strong chin and looked serious. "It is a hard puzzle, men," said he; "it's a puzzle as old and inscrutable as death and eternity. You are very sure of yourself, Frank. And I know you are a calm, strong man, and not passionate and emotional as some men are. But, forgive me if I express a doubt."

"Oh, be candid," said Frank. "What is your doubt?"

"I doubt *you*," said William, "I mean that, cool and firm as you are, you could not, in my opinion have kept away, under certain circumstances."

'You mean if I had loved the woman as much as Langdale loved her?"

William shook his head. "No," he said, "I mean if *she* had loved you as she loved him."

Ullathorne stood up, brushing away the crumbs from his clothes. "I don't think I'm as weak as you think," said he.

"Ah!" – William smiled – "but are you sure that in such cases it is the weak who fall?"

"What do you mean?"

"I think the weak often stand, just because their passions are not strong enough to overthrow them."

"Then you think Marie – poor child – was stronger than a woman who remains a loyal wife?"

"I don't know. These things, as the old Greeks used to say, are on the knees of the gods. It must have been a great love that carried those two off their feet, and great loves don't live in little hearts."

At this moment the youth struck again upon the bell, and the men rose and moved away to their work. As they went, Philip said to Shirley: "If we get along as well as we have got along so far, we shall have this job finished a week sooner than we hoped."

"I think we shall," the big man answered; "but I'm sad when I think of Percy Langdale. He was a good friend, and a good man."

"There is another life," said Philip.

"I think not," said Shirley; and the shovels began to move again, and Ullathorne, as he strode to his place, sang in a rich, sonorous baritone voice an old song of the sea.

"Well," said the General, "hah! I keep getting surprises. Who the dickens would expect navvies to talk like that?"

"I should judge from the conversation," said Mr. Jorkle, "that this highly moral people are very little better than their neighbours."

"Oh, hang it, Jorkle," cried the General, "what a Puritan you are! I think the men talked men's talk, don't you know. Hah! What do you expect of flesh and blood, begad?"

"I expect," said Mr. Jorkle, "some decent feeling and proper conception of morality. Have these people any kind of religion?"

"Oh, come," said the General, "don't try to sell us a lame horse! I've seen a good many religions in my time, but I never saw one that – hah! – didn't leave room for a sprinkling of sinners. And – hah! – I have found the society of the saints rather a demnition bore at times."

"You are a heathen, General," said Mr. Jorkle. "But you, Mr. Fry, what have you to say for your paragons? Did you notice that during the whole course of that – er – edifying discussion nobody said a single word of condemnation of the crime?"

"I did sir," said the wizard, "but I also noticed that there was a great deal of pity and sympathy which, I submit, are much better things."

"I don't agree with you," said the financier.

"I am sorry," said the wizard.

The General laughed.

"And I think," said Mr. Jorkle, warmly, "if that is the kind of thing your Socialism leads to I should like to ask you to remember –"

"The – hah! – name of Sir Gorell Barnes,[87] dammit," said the General.

"I think," said Mr. Fry, "we might do worse than lunch. Light!"

[15 February 1907]

Chapter XV. In The Guest House.

The dining hall of the Guest House[88] stood in the middle of a cherry orchard, and through its open casements there flowed the delicate but searching perfume of the enchanted blossoms.

It was a large room, of oblong shape, with windows running in a band the whole length of the walls on both sides. Above the windows was a frieze of dim cobalt blue, with here and there a painted swallow flying. Below the windows the walls were grounded in dappled green of many tints, from apple to ivy, and against this dense retiring background were painted growing tulips of all the varied hues of that gracious flower: pearly and silver whites, shell pinks, rose reds, ruby, amber, citron, amethyst, buttercup yellow, frail violet, regal purple, glowing orange; the sunshine lighted them up like jewels. From the panelled-oak ceiling swung graceful copper lamps. The floor was of polished yew. There were many round tables placed about the room. These had tops of hammered copper, and across each one was thrown a narrow cloth of stainless white.

At one of these tables sat the Three. And when the lunch had been laid by two bright young boys, and when the invaluable Light had conjured long slim bottles from nowhere and had vanished like the flame of a blown-out candle, the General held up a tall and taper glass, and looked affectionately through his monocle at the shining golden wine.

"Hah! There are times, don't you know," said the General, "when wine is as indispensable to a dinner as drums are to a march. I – hah! – drink is a devilish bad thing, don't you know, and – hah – no good to King or country. But, dash it all, life is so often a beastly bore, and one meets so many – hah – impossible persons, and what with blunt razors and damned Radicals, and the – hah vagaries of the climate, one gets so hipped and raw, don't you know, and so disgusted, that – Hah! dammit! A bottle of wine is a beneficent creation, and one of the kindest works of God, and – that sort of thing. Hah! Hum!"

The General beamed at the golden nectar, in which a point of light sparkled like a gem, spread his fingers benevolently over this waistcoat, drained the beaker of hermitage[89] with respectful deliberation, smacked his lips, smiled, and said: "Hah! This is one of those auspicious occasions."

"Sir," said the wizard, smiling, "you have my most cordial sympathy. But still, as you say, drink is evil, and men are better without it."

The General nodded, and refilled his glass. "Men are," he said, "better, on the whole, without it. But – hah – it is a thousand million pities, don't you know, that such divine elixirs as dry champagne and ripened port and chastened hermitage should serve one jade's tricks after all, like a lovely fickle woman. Hang it!"

"There are," said Mr. Fry, "certain mellow joys, and rosy dreams, and glowing inspirations, which Dionysus[90] alone of all the gods seems able or willing to bestow. And, as you say, General, there are ragged and peevish moments when one is grateful for the power to cast that dreamy veil of rose colour betwixt one's weary soul and the ugly meanness of the workaday world. And – when it comes to a cigar!"

The General sighed.

"Pooh! Rubbish!" exclaimed Mr. Jorkle. "I see no such wonders in this stuff. Drink is well enough, and does no great harm if people are moderate. But you are a pagan epicure, General, and I'm afraid Mr. Fry is as bad."

"Hah!" cried the General, "listen to Mr. Faith-and-works[91] Jorkle! Listen to the Smite-the-Amalakites[92]-Financier! Hang it, Jorkle, you never give thanks. You are one of those fellows who wouldn't raise his hat to 'Rule Britannia.' You'd pass the saluting point with a pipe in your mouth. You despise a girl's liking for chocolate, and expect a handsome woman to be happy in a frock of last year's cut. If it comes to that, a goat doesn't care for strawberries. Our friend the sorcerer and I have palates, by Jove! You're a – hah – blessed calculating machine, by George! – Stick to your last, my dear man; heckle the wizard. Hah! *We* will drink the wine."

"Upon my word, General," said the financier, "you seem to have the gift of tongues; but, if I understand your sentiments, it appears to me they are not respectable."

"It is an old discord," said the wizard, "the old antagonism between the feudal spirit of chivalry and the commercial spirit of Mammonism. The General resents your utilitarian intolerance of human pleasure, your Puritanical intolerance of human weakness. There are some lines of Swinburne's that seem to express the feeling behind our revolt:

> Wilt thou yet take all, Mr. Jorkle? But these thou shalt not take,
> The laurel, the palms, and the pæan, the breast of the nymphs in the brake;
> Breasts more soft than a dove's, that tremble with tenderer breath,
> And all the wings of the loves, and all the joys before death.[93]

"And I hold that the General is right, and that if you take 'all the joys before death,' and offer us nothing but the reek of chimneys and a heap of money with which we may buy nothing but safes, and bonds, and coffins, you are tendering a very sorry bargain, and I, for one, will not deal with you."

"Hear! Hear!" cried the General; "that's the idea. What's the good of money, don't you know, if nothing's worth buying?"

"Very well," answered Mr. Jorkle, "you have my permission to wallow in the epicurean style, and to write odes to the public-house. And, now, Mr. Fry, to turn from your magic-lantern show of a Utopia, I should like to ask you whether you believe it possible to make England into a country like this?"

"Why not?" asked the wizard.

"Because," said Mr. Jorkle, "there are only two ways in which you could establish Socialism in England. One way is by means of a revolution; the other is by a gradual change in the laws. In the case of a revolution you would suddenly take the affairs of the nation out of the hands of experienced and capable masters, and hand them over to ignorant and incompetent men; the result of which would be failure. In the case of ultra-Socialist legislation, you would alarm the capitalists and they would take their capital out of the country."

"Good," said the General, "what do you say to that, Mr. Fry?"

"Well," said the wizard, "let us deal first with the results of a revolution. I don't believe there will ever be a revolution, and I don't consider such violent measures necessary. But suppose it came to that. You assume that the present rulers and wealth-holders have a monopoly of all executive knowledge and ability. I think you are mistaken."

"Tell us, then," said Mr. Jorkle, "who is to manage the business of the State after a sudden expulsion or displacement of the present managers?"

"We are to consider," said the wizard, "two chief problems. First, who is to conduct the Government? You will remember that after the revolt of the American colonies against British rule the Americans formed a Government, and constructed a constitution. They managed very well without the heaven-sent legislators of King George's Parliament. And the French, after de-throning Napoleon the III, seemed to have no difficulty in replacing his Government.[94]

"And you will know, as well as I, that the new men who enter a Cabinet or department generally work as well as those they replace. Mr. Birrell, Mr. Lloyd George, and Mr. John Burns[95] seem to be as capable as their confrères, or their predecessors."

"Yes. But that is gradual replacement," said Mr. Jorkle.

"Very good. And you want some score of men to make up a government. Do you suppose the country could not find them? Or do you suppose that all the capable men would be against the revolution, and only the incapables for the revolution? If that were the case how could the revolution be successful?"

"It never would, begad!" said the General.

The wizard laughed. "But," said he, "we are supposing it has been successful, and that implies that in the ranks of the revolutionary party there must be many able men."

"Not necessarily able administrators," said Mr. Jorkle.

"Come, come," said the wizard, "you know very well, Mr. Jorkle, that the standard is not a very high one. You know that outside Parliament there are thousands of men as able as any M.P., and you know that brains are not confined to any particular class. On the local governing bodies, in Parliament itself, in the Trade Union, and in the co-operative movement there are men of the working classes who have proved themselves the equals of the titled and the wealthy in matters of administration and management.

"And you know very well that in the commercial world there is hardly a single business to which one individual head is indispensable. The manager of a great railway, or shipping firm, or factory, or trust, may be a very able man. But he has to depend in a great measure upon his lieutenants, and in the event of his death or retirement the business would go on. But all this seems to me rather profitless discussion. Let us leave the case of revolution and consider the other and quieter means of establishing Socialism in this country.[96] Your argument, I understand, is that the first steps towards establishing a Socialist State in England would so alarm the rich that they would take their capital out of the country."

"That is so," said Mr. Jorkle.

"And you really believe that, Mr. Jorkle?"

"Well," said the General, "I'm jolly well sure Jorkle would take his capital, and I'm quite as sure of myself, by George!"

"I am surprised," said the wizard, "to find two such men labouring under the delusion that it would be possible for them to take their capital out of the country. Do you really believe, gentlemen, that you, or the other capitalists could do what you suggest?"

"Certainly," said Mr. Jorkle

"Hah! Confound it, *yes*!" said the General.

The wizard took a pinch of snuff. Then he said, "Mr. Jorkle, would you mind telling how your capital is made up – of what it consists?"

"Well, various investments," said Mr. Jorkle; "railways, cotton mills, house property, and shares in the South African mines. Chiefly those four things."

"And yours, General?"

"Mostly land. I've something in coal mines, and something in jute."

"Very good," said the wizard; "now, suppose you and all the other capitalists in England decide to take your capital out of the county. Mr. Jorkle has to carry away part of the permanent way and rolling stock of the railway, he has to carry away several cotton mills and their machinery, and some streets of houses. You, General, have to remove your landed estates, part of a coal mine, and a jute factory."

"Confounded nonsense!" cried the General.

"We should simply withdraw our capital," said Mr. Jorkle.

"What you are thinking of," said the wizard, "is the idea of selling your shares, and with the money setting up new businesses in some foreign country.

"But you would be anxious to sell because you believed that the businesses would be no longer profitable, or no longer safe. That being the case, who would be willing to buy?

"And supposing you could and did sell these concerns. Then the men who bought them would replace your capital with their own, and so the capital would still be in the country, after all. *You* would have gone out of the country, but the capital would remain.

"But allow me to suggest a case. Suppose the nation decided to take over your house property, land, railways, and mines, by means of some system of compulsory purchase. What could you do? Foreigners would not buy your property at a higher price than the people offered you. You could not take the land and mines and mills and houses away. You could not take away nor sell the rents and profits to come.

"Many municipalities now make their own gas. Suppose *all* the municipalities began to make their own cotton goods, jute goods, boots, clothing, soap, and ironmongery. How could you prevent them making those things and selling and buying those things? What need they care if you shut down your mills and went to America or China?"

"But – hah! that would be robbery, by George! I would be unjust, by Jove!" exclaimed the General.

"It would be immoral," cried Mr. Jorkle.

"But," said the wizard, calmly, "we are not now discussing the morality of the transactions. That by and by. We are discussing the possibility of doing these things.

"Now, suppose you shut down your mills. The municipal mills will be rid of your competition. Your work people will be working for the municipality and your profits will have disappeared. What, then can you take out of the country? All your wealth is created by the workers. *They* will remain in the country and work to create wealth for themselves."

"But – but it is organised plunder!" said Mr. Jorkle.

"Never mind that. Suppose it to be organised, can you prevent it? Can you show me any reason why it should not succeed?"

"There would – hah – be bloodshed first," exclaimed the General, hotly.

"I don't see why," said the wizard, coolly. "You have seen the gas, tram, and waterworks pass from private hands into the control of the municipalities. Why should there be bloodshed over the cotton mills and soap factories?"

"It isn't honest, dammit!" cried the General.

"Wait a little. Suppose the people offered to buy your jute mills. You would want a fancy price."

"Not at all. I should want a fair price – an honest price."

"Well, that would be the price of the second-hand buildings and machinery, no more. To ask for twenty years' purchase of the profits of the concern would be absurd. That would be asking the people to pay twenty years' value of their own work. They are not going to buy their own skill, and their own bodies. Those are already their own property. So they can say: 'We will give you a second-hand price for the mills and machines. If that does not suit you we will build municipal mills and leave you.'"

"Yes, yes," said Mr. Jorkle, "but the workers do not create *all* the value. Our administration counts for a great deal."

"You mean your management?"

"Yes."

"Very good. Then we propose to discharge you, and engage other managers, at lower salaries. What right have you to complain? You act in the same way towards those in your employ."

"I never heard such bosh in my life," said Mr. Jorkle, rudely.

"My dear sir," answered the wizard, taking another pinch of snuff, "you have all of you been all your lives labouring under a false idea. You think your capital employs the workers; it is the workers who employ your capital."

"Hah! Do you mean to say, sir," said the General, very red in the gills, "that you would defend the confiscation of my land?"

"There," said the wizard, "we come to the question of morality. I will discuss that with you presently; but now let us go out and smoke a cigar in the orchard."

[22 February 1907]

Chapter XVI. The Earth For All.[97]

"You – hah – mean to say," said the General, angrily, "that it would be right to rob me of my land?"

The wizard blew a smoke ring and smiled. "I do not defend robbery," he said; "I defend the recovery of stolen property. Socialism is not a thief, it is a policeman."

"But, dammit, I have as much right to my land as you have to your hat," cried the General, hotly.

"I beg your pardon, and I beseech your indulgence, General," said the wizard, "for I am obliged to say that you have no right to your land, no right, legal nor moral."

"No legal right! No moral right! Hang it!" the General said, glaring. "What do you mean, sir?"

"Let us begin with the law," said the wizard, quietly. "The law of England does not recognise private ownership of land. According to the law all land is held in trust of the King."

"On what authority – hah – do you make that statement, sir?" demanded the General.

The wizard blew another ring. "I will give you," said he, "three good authorities: Sir William Blackstone, Sir Edward Coke, and Sir Frederick Pollock.[98] Those are eminent lawyers you must admit."

"Well, and what do they say?"

"Sir William Blackstone says:

> "Accurately and strictly speaking, there is no foundation in nature or in natural law why a set of words on parchment should convey the dominion of land. Alloidal (absolute) property not subject in England now has, it being a received and now undeniable principle in law that all lands in England are holden mediately or immediately of the King.[99]

"I think that is quite explicit. But I will quote the other authorities. Sir Edward Coke says:

> "All lands or tenements in England in the hands of the subjects, are holden mediately or immediately of the King. For, in the law of England, we have not any subject's land that is not holden.[100]

"Could anything be more clearly and confidently expressed? Sir Frederick Pollock says:

> "No absolute ownership of land is recognised by our law books, except in the Crown. All lands are supposed to be held immediately or mediately of the Crown, though no rent or service may be payable, and no grant from the Crown on record.[101]

"Legally, therefore, my dear General, the so-called owner of an estate in England only holds that estate as on a kind of lease from the Crown. The Crown giveth and the Crown can take away."

"But – hah – that," said the General, "is merely a legal theory."

"Well," answered the wizard, "it is the law; and it proves what I said, that you have no legal right to the land."

"And what about moral right?" said Mr. Jorkle.

"Well," the wizard answered, "there is no moral right. Private ownership of land rests upon one of three excuses. First of all, there is the right of conquest. But that is not a moral right; it is only robber's law: the law of might.

"Land won by the sword must be held by the sword. Do you stand to the law of conquest, General?"

"Why not?" the General asked.

"Because," said the wizard, "you would fall by it. For if you claim that land belongs of right to those who are strong enough to take it, you admit that you have neither legal nor moral cause of complaint against those who are strong enough to take it from you.

"Say you hold the land justly yours because William of Normandy won it from the English people, and gave it to your ancestor, and you must admit the right of the English people to win it back from you, if they can, and hold it for themselves."

"But what nonsense," said Mr. Jorkle; "nearly all land, I should say all, privately held in England has been bought and paid for."

"If you say that you show a very small knowledge of the facts," said the wizard; "much land now held has been actually stolen, or has been held by right of gift from those who originally stole it. But that by the by. Let us now look at the moral right of the purchaser of land."

"Just so," said the General.

"No man," said the wizard, "can have a moral right to own land given to him or sold to him, unless it can be proved that the giver or seller of the land had a moral right to the land he gave or sold.

"If I stole the General's watch and gave or sold it to you, you would have no moral right to keep it. Your moral right would be the right to demand from me your money back. You cannot justly, nor legally, hold stolen property upon the plea that you bought it of the thief.

"Now, here can be no original private right to land. The original right to land is the right of the whole people: the right of the inhabitants of the earth to all the land thereon."

"And on the strength of this sophistry you propose to rob us of our property!" exclaimed Mr. Jorkle.

"I beg your pardon," said the wizard. "I do not propose to do anything of the kind, and I don't think the Socialists propose to do anything of the kind. We deny that any man has a moral or legal right to own our country, or any part of it; but we do not propose to take all he possesses without any payment, and leave him to starve."

"And, pray," asked the General, "what do you propose?"

"Well," said the wizard, "my idea is that the land should become the property of the nation, and that those who now claim the right to the land should be paid a reasonable sum."

"And I call that tyranny and robbery," said the General, "and – hah – lawless and immoral."

The wizard smiled. "The present laws," he said, "have been mostly made by the rich; very largely by the rich holders of land. Do you expect us to obey them?"

"Certainly; dammit!" said the General.

"Why?" asked the wizard.

"Because – hah – the laws are the laws of the land," the General answered.

"And are you, General, prepared to obey the laws of the land?" the wizard inquired.

"Hah! of course," said the General.

"Very good," said the wizard, "then if the Legislature makes new laws, a law for the compulsory purchase of land, for instance, you will obey it? For Parliament is Parliament, is it not, whether it be a Parliament of landlords or of the people?"

"But such a law – hah – is a piece of unprecedented injustice!" said the General.

"Why, no," said the wizard; "I will show you precedents. It has always been held that private rights must yield to public necessity. If a Bill be got to construct a railway, or a reservoir, or other public convenience, the land needed can be, and has been, bought by compulsory purchase, and not at the owner's price. But now I will give you two precedents of a very striking kind. I will ask you to compare your claim to the ownership of land with the claim of an author to his book, and of an inventor to his invention.

"A landlord does not make the land; he holds it.

"But if a man invent a new machine or a new process or if he write a poem or a book, he may claim to have made the invention or the book, and may justly claim payment for the use of them by other men.

"An inventor or an author has, therefore, a better claim to payment for his work than a landlord has to payment for the use of the land he calls his. Now, how does the law act towards these men?

"The landlord may call the land his all the days of his life, and at his death may bequeath it to his heirs. For a thousand years the owners of an estate may charge rent for it, and at the end of the thousand years the estate will still be theirs, and the rent will still be running on and growing ever larger and larger. And at any suggestion that the estate should lapse from the possession of the owners and become the property of the people, the said owners will lustily raise the cry of 'Confiscation.'

"The patentee of an invention may call the invention his own, and may charge royalties upon its use for a *space of fourteen years*.[102] At the end of that time his patent lapses and becomes public property without any talk of compensation or any cry of confiscation. Thus the law holds that an inventor is well paid by fourteen years' rent for a thing he made himself, while the landlord is *never* paid for the land he did not make.

"The author of a book holds the copyright of the book for a period of forty-four years or for his own life and seven years after, whichever period be the longer.[103] At the expiration of that time the book becomes public property. Thus the law holds that an author is well paid by forty-four years' rent for a book which he has made, but the landlord is *never* paid for the land which he did not make.

"If the same law that applies to the land applied to books, and to inventions, the inheritors of the rights of Caxton and Shakespeare would still be able to charge, the one a royalty on every printing press in use, and the other a royalty on every copy of Shakespeare's poems sold. Then there would be royalties on all the looms, engines, and other machines, and upon all the books, music, engravings and what not; so that the cost of education, recreation, travel, clothing, and nearly everything else we use would be enhanced enormously. But, thanks to a very wise and fair arrangement, an author or an inventor has a good chance to be well paid, and after that the people have a chance to enjoy the benefits of his genius.

"Now, if it is right and expedient thus to deprive the inventor or the author of his own production after a time, and to give the use thereof to the public what sense or justice is there in allowing a landowner to hold land and to draw an ever-swelling rent to the exclusion, inconvenience, and expense of the people for ever? And by what process of reasoning can a landlord charge an author with immorality or confiscation for suggesting that the same law should apply to the land he did not make that the author cheerfully allows to be applied to the books he does make?

"For the landlord to speak of confiscation in the face of the laws of patent and of copyright seems to me the coolest impudence.

"And you will notice that when the patent of fourteen years, or the copyright of forty-four years has expired, the inventor or author gets *nothing*.

"But you object that it would be robbery to take your land from you after you have drawn the rent for centuries.

"And when we propose to treat you much better than law and custom treat the *creators* of books and machines, and to pay you a reasonable price for the land you never made, you call out that you are being robbed. And what do you think of yourselves?" The wizard puffed at his cigar and smiled.

"Hah! Hang it all!" said the General, "two blacks don't make a white, don't you know? The patent and copyright law may be rot, and that sort of thing, but that's no reason why you should steal my land, by George!"

"There are no blacks," said the wizard; "we don't complain of the patent and copyright law. They are founded upon the just and sensible principle that the good of the nation must over-rule the profit of the individual.

"Land is necessary to the nation. Without land the people cannot produce, nor enjoy the necessaries of life. Without land they cannot have food, clothing, houses, nor fuel; they cannot have woods, fields, gardens, nor streams; they cannot have air, nor exercise, nor health.

"And the landlord would have us believe that it is immoral and dishonest of the people to refuse to pay him an enormous and ruinous tax upon their industry, and pleasure, and health. I never did believe that, and some day the masses of the people will cease to believe it. Then you will be lucky if you get anything for your land at all."

"Hah! And suppose the people – as you call them, begad – robbed us of our land and shared it out amongst them – hah – how much better off would they be?" the General demanded.

"You think, then," said Mr. Fry, "that Socialists propose to divide the land? But there you are quite wrong.

"Socialists have no more idea of taking the land from its present holders and 'sharing it out' amongst the poor than they have to taking the railways from the railway companies and sharing the carriages and engines amongst the passengers.

"When the London County Council municipalised the tram service they did not rob the companies, nor did they share out the cars amongst the people.

"*Socialism* does not mean the 'sharing out' of property; on the contrary, it means the collective ownership of property.

"Socialism does not mean one acre and half a cow[104] for each subject; it means that Britain shall be owned intact by the whole people, and shall be governed and worked by the whole people, for the benefit of the whole people.

"Just as the Glasgow tram service, the Manchester gas service, and the general postal service are *owned*, managed, and used by the citizens of Manchester and Glasgow, or by the people of Britain, for the general advantage.

"Under Socialism no citizen would be allowed to call a single inch of land his own. All the land would belong to the people, and would be used by the people, for the best advantage of the people."

"And do you suppose," said Mr. Jorkle, "that the people would be content with such an arrangement, and would not quarrel as to who should have the best land?"

"My dear sir" said the wizard, "do the guests at a *table d'hôte* quarrel over the best cuts, and the best sauces? There is enough for all. Some like to live in the hills, and some in the valleys; some like the breezy East Coast, and some the milder South. All parts of our islands are habitable and pleasant, and the people would be free to move about. There would be room for all, and air and sun, and water and land for all."

"Ah!" said Mr. Jorkle, "and how do you propose to evade the natural law that at the means of subsistence increase the population increases?"

"You mean," said the wizard, "that if people were more prosperous they would have more children, and so there would again be poverty."

"Just so," said Mr. Jorkle, "and I have never met anyone who could answer the argument. But what do you say, sir?"

"I say it isn't true, that's all," answered the wizard; "the fact is, that the wealthier, better fed, better educated classes have fewer children than the indigent and ignorant."

"I deny it," said Mr. Jorkle; "it is a natural law."

"A natural fiddlestick," said the wizard, snapping his fingers. "Suppose that it is a natural law – which it isn't – do you suppose a community of educated and intelligent men and women are going to submit to it? It is a law easy to control and is controlled in most of the more highly civilised States at present. An ignorant people might breed beyond subsistence point, and enlightened people would not."

"And who is going to teach the people this wisdom?" asked Mr. Jorkle.

"Ah!" repeated the wizard, "who, indeed? *You* don't seem to have taught them much."

"Well," said the General, emphatically, "all I've got to say is that – hah – I will not give up my land without a fight. Hah! that's flat!"

The wizard and the General looked each other steadily in the face. Then Mr. Fry said, gravely, "General, you are a fighting man. It is your trade. I do not deal in blows and bullets, only in reasons. I hope it will never come to fighting. I feel sure it never will. If it does I hope you will be beaten." The wizard threw away his cigar, and the three walked slowly and thoughtfully towards the Guest House.

[1 March 1907]

Chapter XVI. Under The Cherry Tree.

"Apart from the dishonesty of Socialism," said Mr. Jorkle, pausing under a cherry tree, "I object to the idea because of its absurdity. It would result in stagnation, in retrogression. Abolish competition, and the world would drop back into ignorance and savagery. Struggle is the order of Nature; or, as a great thinker has expressed it: 'Society flourishes by the antagonism of its atoms.'[105] The truth of that axiom is obvious." Mr. Jorkle looked at the General, and swelled with satisfaction.

"Good," said the wizard. "'Society flourishes by the antagonism of its atoms.' And you, like your great thinker, regard Society as a welter of blind forces: like a heap of maggots in a grease pot. You don't seem to be aware that the atoms of which Society is composed are thinking and feeling men and women. And you mistake aphorism for argument. It is quite easy to make such aphorisms. Allow me to offer you a few. War is better than peace. How do you like that? A house divided against itself shall stand. What say you? Union is weakness. These axioms are quite as terse, and no more absurd, than that of your great thinker."

"Mere theory," said Mr. Jorkle.

"Well," answered the wizard, "let us be practical. If a hundred men had a hundred loaves of bread, and if they piled them in a heap and fought for them, so that some got none, and some got more than they could eat, and some were trampled upon in the scuffle, that would be competition. But it seems to me a wiser and better way would be to share the bread out equally, so that each man got enough."

"Bah! I am talking about competition in trade," said Mr. Jorkle.

"Ah! And you think competition in trade is good because you always compare it with monopoly, and never with co-operation," said the wizard.

"What's that?" said the General, "I don't quite follow."

"I say," replied the wizard, "that seeing competition seems better, from your point of view, than monopoly, you rest content, and do not compare it with co-operation. For instance, we know that if a railway company has a monopoly of the traffic in a certain district the public is not so well served as where there are two competing lines. It is so in most cases. A firm which has a monopoly of trade can raise the prices and lower the quality of its goods. But let another firm enter into competition, and the public will get better goods at lower prices."

"That – hah – is just what we say," said the General.

"And it is true enough," said the wizard, "but though to the consumer of milk it may be better that there should be competition amongst milk dealers, we are not to conclude that competition is the *best* system; but only that it is better than monopoly.

"But there is another plan: that of co-operation. The private monopolist raises the price, and puts the profits in his pocket. But a municipal department for the supply of milk would always be better for the consumer than a private monopoly, because it could and would sell the milk at cost price."

"Yes, yes," said Mr. Jorkle, "but it would increase the cost by inferior management."

"I think not," said the wizard. "I claim that it would decrease the cost. Of course, a milk trust, or private monopoly, would reduce the cost, because it would avoid the heavy charges for competition. And I am told that the New York Milk Trust began by dispensing with the services of fifteen thousand men. And where municipal departments have taken over the trams of the gas or water supply, it has been found possible to run the trams at reduced fares, to pay the employees better wages for shorter hours, and to hand over substantial balances in relief of rates. And it is evident that such competition must always beat private competition, for two reasons: the first reason is that the municipality can produce more cheaply; the second reason is that no private firm can afford to trade without making some profit, where the municipality can do without any profit at all."

"And do you think it fair," exclaimed Mr. Jorkle, "for a corporation to enter trade with the citizens' capital, against private dealers?"

"Why not?" said the wizard. "Is it fair for two men to trade as partners?"

"Of course it is."

"And is it fair for half-a-dozen companies, or private firms, to form a trust?"

"Why not?"

"But it is not fair for two hundred thousand citizens to form themselves into a municipal co-operative society and supply their own wants?"

"No. It is not fair to the private trader."

"The trust is fair to the private trader; but the municipal supply is not fair?"

"Certainly not."

"It is fair for the citizens to buy their milk of Smith and Company, or of Jones and Company, or of the Northern Milk Trust, or of the Amalgamated Dairy Company; or even to import tinned milk from abroad; and it is fair for the citizens to form new dairy companies, or new milk trusts; but it is *not* fair for them to call their milk trust a municipal milk supply."

"It is using public money to crush private enterprise."

"Then may I keep a cow and provide myself with milk?"

"That is another thing."

"Or may a whole street, or a whole district, club up to run a dairy and find their own milk?"

"That is different also."

"I see. It becomes unfair when *all* the streets and districts join, and organise the mild supply on the best lines. The citizens are not to combine, because the Trans-Atlantic Tinned Milk Trust want to sell their condensed milk, or because the Bucolic Dairy Company want to make dividends."

"Well: it is an interference with the liberty of the individual."

"I really fail to see that. The individual has a perfect right to offer milk for sale; but he has no right to compel me to buy it. On the contrary, I have a perfect right to combine with others to provide milk, and a perfect right to decline to buy it from any particular dealer. You do not think, do you, that the individual has an abstract right to make profits out of his fellow citizens against their will?"

"Hah! Look here," said the General, "that reminds me, don't you know. You seem to think that private profit is public loss. Hah! If a man gets wealth he has to spend it, and he finds useful employment, and – hah – increases trade, and that sort of thing."

The wizard laughed. "What! isn't that old error dead yet?" he asked. "Do you really believe that the expenditure of the rich is good for the poor?"

"Hah! Of course it is, hang it. If I buy a saddle it's good for the saddler," exclaimed the General.

"Excellent, excellent, General," said the wizard, "but you have omitted something."

"Hah! What have I omitted?"

"You have omitted the debit side of the account. Where does the money come from?"

"Come from? Out of my pocket, dammit."

"Yes. But how does it get into your pocket?"

"Why – hah –"

"Wait a moment, General. A landlord has a rent roll of £100,000 a year. Where does he get it? He gets it in rent from the farmers. They get the money by the sale of their produce. It is as much as they can do to make both ends meet. And the farm labourers, who raise all the produce are very poor.

"Now, the landlord is rich. He is rich because the farmer and his men are poor; they are poor because he is rich.

"But the landlord buys a pair of boots from the village shoemaker. He finds him employment.

"And the labourer goes with out boots.

"Well. The labourer earns the money, the shoemaker makes the boots, and the landlord wears them.

"Does that prove the landlord is a useful member of Society? If the landlord did not take the labourer's earnings the labourer could buy boots, and so the shoemaker would have work, and the labourer would be well shod.

"Suppose I said to a farmer, 'You give me five shilling a week out of your earnings, and I will find employment for a man to make cigars. *I* will smoke the cigars.'

"What would the farmer say? Would he not say, 'Why should I employ you to smoke cigars which I pay for? If the cigar maker needs work, why should I not employ him myself, and smoke the cigars myself, since I am to pay for them?

"To say that the extravagance of the rich finds useful employment for the poor, is more foolish than to say that the drunkard finds useful employment for the brewers.

"The drunkard may have a better defence than the duke, because he may perhaps have produced, or earned the money he spends in beer, whereas the duke's rents are not produced by the duke nor earned by him.

"That is clear, is it not? And yet a few weeks since I saw an article in a London weekly paper in which we were told that the thief was an indispensable member of Society, because he found employment for policemen, gaolers, builders of gaols, and other persons.

"The excuse for the thief is as valid as the excuse for the duke. The thief finds plenty of employment for the people. But who *pays* the persons employed?

"The police, the gaolers, and all the other persons employed in catching, holding, and feeding the thief, are paid out of the rates and taxes. Who pays the taxes? The British public. Then the British public have to support not only the police and the rest, but the thief as well.

"What do the police, the thief, and the gaoler produce? Do they produce any wealth? No. They consume wealth, and the thief is so useful that if he died out for ever, it would pay us better to feed the gaolers and police for doing nothing than to fetch the thief back again to feed him as well.

"Work is useless unless it be productive work. It would be work for a man to dig a hole and then fill it up again; but the work would be of no benefit to the nation.

"Do not imagine, as some do, that increased consumption is a blessing. It is the amount of wealth you produce that makes a nation prosperous; and the idle rich man, who produces nothing, only makes his crime worse by spending a great deal."

"But," said the General, "I was talking about trade, not land."

"Well," said the wizard, "we were speaking of profits; and the same reasoning applies. For before a man can return money to the community he must take it from them, in profits. If you make a profit out of us by selling us milk, and then buy a saddle, you buy the saddle at our expense, and use it yourself."

"But you have not yet answered my argument," said Mr. Jorkle. "I said that to abolish competition would be to throw the country back into a state of stagnation, and barbarism, and dull monotony, and I defy you to contradict me."

The wizard bowed, and looked serious. "Gentlemen," he said, "You are still under the impression that Socialism would be unjust, and impractical; and that it would be in its effects disastrous!"

"That is our belief," answered Mr. Jorkle.

"Let us sit down here, for a little while," said the wizard, pointing to a seat in the warm sunshine. "I want to tell you some facts."

[8 March 1907]

Chapter XVII. Mote and Beam.

"Gentlemen," said the wizard, smiling and tapping his snuff-box, "When I hear your expressions of virtuous indignation against Socialism I am tempted to conclude that you have come direct from heaven. Instead of which I understand you are modern Englishmen, and live in London. Surely it was from London I brought you, was it not?"

"Where else?" asked Mr. Jorkle.

"But," said the wizard, "If you come from England, and from London, it seems to me that you are exceedingly fastidious. Is it possible that you do not know London, or have your forgotten it?"

"There are worse places than London, by George!" said the General. "Hah! you may take that from me."

"Socialist places?" the wizard asked.

"No! Hang it, of course not," said the General.

"Well," said the wizard, "but I understand that when you condemn Socialism you speak as Englishmen and not as angels. Or what am I to understand?"

"As Englishmen. What else?" asked Mr. Jorkle.

The wizard put on his gold-rimmed spectacles and looked mildly at his companions.

"It is astonishing," he said, "it is incredible. You actually compare the Socialist ideal unfavourably with the modern British fact."

"There are worse places than England," the General repeated.

"Yes, granted," said the wizard, "but you seem to believe that there can never be any better. And I say you must have forgotten England if you ever really knew it.

"Listen! England is full of poverty, of ignorance, of crime, vice, drunkenness, and disease. Do you deny this?"

"Tut, tut. You exaggerate," said Mr. Jorkle; "you have been misled by Socialists and demagogues."

The wizard smiled. "You are mistaken," he said. "I will show you the facts without quoting a single word from any Socialist. Let us deal first with the poverty."

"The Right Honourable H. Campbell-Bannerman, our present Prime Minister,[106] is not a Socialist. He said a few years ago that there were in our country over ten millions of persons always on the verge of destitution."

"Oh! Bannerman!" said the General.

"You do not consider him a good authority?" said the wizard. "I will quote from a speech made by the late Marquis of Salisbury, then the Tory Prime Minister."[107] The wizard took out a pocket-book, turned over the leaves, and read:

> They looked around them and saw a *growing* mass of *poverty* and *want of employment*, and of course the one object which every statesman who loved his country should desire to attain was that there might be the largest amount of profitable employment for the mass of the people.
>
> He did not say that he had any patent or certain remedy for *the terrible evils which beset us on all sides*, but he did say that it was time they left off mending the constitution of Parliament, and that they turned all the wisdom and energy Parliament could combine together in order to remedy the *sufferings* under which *so many* of their countrymen laboured.

"You will notice, General, that his lordship speaks of the terrible evils which beset us on all sides, and that he expresses the opinion that the poverty is increasing, and he confesses that he has no remedy to suggest."

"He might have begun with the drink traffic," growled Mr. Jorkle.

"Oh," said the wizard, quietly, "you admit drunkenness, then?"

"Of course," said Mr. Jorkle.

"And you admit, I suppose, the vice and the crime, and the ignorance, and the disease?" said the wizard.

"There is a great deal of crime," said Mr. Jorkle; "nobody denies it."

"Nobody can deny it," said the wizard; "but do you deny the poverty?"

"I think it is exaggerated," said the financier, sulkily.

"So? Then our two Prime Ministers were mistaken? Possibly they were mislead by Socialist demagogues." The wizard opened the pocket-book again. "I will give you," said he, "an opinion expressed by the Right Honourable Joseph Chamberlain." He read:

> For my part neither sneers, nor abuse, nor opposition shall induce me to accept as the will of the Almighty, and the unalterable dispensation of His providence, a state of things under which *millions lead sordid, hopeless, and monotonous lives, without pleasure in the present, and without prospect for the future.*

"I hope," he said, "you do not call Mr. Chamberlain a Socialist. At any rate, the opinions I have quoted are not challenged. They are supported by overwhelming testimony. Allow me to read you a few words of General Booth's." Again the wizard turned to the pocket-book and read:

> 444 persons are reported by the police to have attempted to commit suicide in London last year, and probably as many more succeeded in doing so. 200 persons died from starvation in the same period. We have in this one city about 100,000 paupers, 30,000 prostitutes, 33,000 homeless adults, and 35,000 wandering children of the slums. There is a standing army of out-of-works numbering 80,000, which is often increased in special periods of commercial depression or trade disputes to 100,000. 12,000 criminals are always inside Her Majesty's prisons, and about 15,000 are outside. 70,000 charges for petty offences are dealt with by the London magistrates every year. The best authorities estimate that 10,000 new criminals are manufactured per annum. We have tens of thousands of dwellings known to be over-crowded, unsanitary, or dangerous.[108]

"From that statement it appears," said the wizard, "that I do not at all exaggerate when I say that this country is full of vice and crime, of poverty and disease. And General Booth is no Socialist.

"Now, gentlemen, you have there a picture of London. But it is not by any means a complete picture. It does not give the background of ugly streets, and mean buildings, and blatant advertisements. It says nothing about ignorance, nor drink. It does not mention the idle rich, nor their senseless luxury. It ignores a venal Press, and a cynical Parliament, and an effete religion.

"Allow me to add a few touches to the picture. In London one and a quarter millions of persons get less than a guinea a week per family. During every year more than two and a quarter millions of persons receive poor-law relief in the British Islands. In England and Wales 72,000 persons in workhouses, hospitals, infirmaries, or asylums. In London alone there are 100,000 persons in workhouses, hospitals, prisons, or industrial schools. In London one person out of every four will die in a workhouse, a hospital, or a lunatic asylum. Throughout the British Islands about 55 per cent. of the working-class children die before they reach five years of age. Of those deaths about four-fifths are preventable.

"Now, in a Socialist State there would not be, there *could* not be, a thief, a loafer, or a beggar; there would be no ignorance, no poverty, no preventable disease; therefore, there would be no drunkenness, and little vice. And you are afraid that socialism would spoil our beautiful civilisation."

"Yes, but – hah – look here," said the General, "liberty's a jewel, don't you know. We don't want a crowd of officials poking their noses into our private lives – hah – and making slave of us. Dammit!"

"Slaves! Overseers!" said the wizard. "Do you know anything of the lives of the workers? Here is a cutting from a daily paper. It is part of a letter sent by a shop girl of Brixton:

> For many hours a day we are little better than slaves, at the beck and call of employer and customer. We have not a minute to ourselves, and are surrounded by a network of rule and regulations.

"Mr. Jorkle must know how severe is the discipline in offices, and how strict is the labour in factories. There is no whip, but there is a more terrible instrument – the sack!

"You gentlemen talk about the danger of slavery under Socialism as though Englishmen and women were at present free. You draw horrible pictures of a monotonous and cheerless life under Socialism as though England to-day were merrie and fair. But our England is sordid and ugly. Think of the houses, the costumes, the amusements of the people.

"Have you ever seen the regiment of city clerks in uniform marching out from the railway stations to business? Have you seen the streets they live in, the schools they are crammed in, the offices where each man is a cog in a machine?

"Have you ever seen the vast districts of houses which Ruskin called 'brick boxes with slate roofs,' the houses all ugly, and all inconvenient and all alike; street after street of them, one street so like another that a man would go wrong if he did not see the name on the corner? Have you ever considered the working lives of the millions of spinners, weavers, colliers, shopmen, tailors, chair-makers – what not? Do you not know that these people perform the same tasks, at the same hours, for years – for a lifetime? Do you find that painters, and poets, and playwriters, and musicians are free to give their genius its bent? Or do you know that most of these men must work to the market: 'must please to live'?

"You are afraid for the morals of the people under Socialism. Listen to Mr. Joseph Chamberlain." The wizard opened his pocket-book once more and read:

> The ordinary conditions of life among a large proportion of the population are such that common decency is absolutely impossible; and all this goes on in sight of the mansions of the rich, where undoubtedly there are people who would gladly remedy it if they could. It goes on in presence of wasteful extravagance and luxury, which bring but little pleasure to those who indulge in them; and private charity is powerless, religious organisations can do nothing to remedy the evils which are so deep-seated in our social system.[109]

"That seems to me a calm and moderate statement of a very painful and disgraceful fact. Let me add to it an official statement of the conditions of life in Scotland:

> Much has been done in the way of improvement in various parts of Scotland, but 22 per cent. of Scottish families still dwell in a single room each, and the proportion in the case of Glasgow rises to 33 per cent. The little town of Kilmarnock, with only 28,447 inhabitants, huddles even a slightly larger proportion of its families into single-room tenements. Altogether, there are in Glasgow over 120,000, and in all Scotland 560,000 persons (more than one-eighth of the whole population), who do not know the decency of even a two-roomed house.

"Do not think this state of things is confined to Scotland, or to a few towns. It is estimated that three and a quarter millions of persons in these islands live in overcrowded dwellings, the average being three persons to one room.

"You denounce Socialism as though the present condition of England were perfection. But here are the facts, and no man can deny them:

"Large numbers of honest and industrious people are badly fed, badly clothed, and badly housed.

"Hundreds of thousands of people die every year from preventable diseases.

"The average duration of life amongst the population is unnaturally short.

"Very many people, after lives of toil, are obliged to seek refuge in the workhouse, where they die despised and neglected, branded with the shameful brand of pauperism.

"It is an almost invariable rule that those who work hardest and longest in this country are the worst paid and the least respected.

"The wealthiest men in our nation are men who never did a useful day's work.

"Wealth and power are more prized and more honoured than wisdom, or industry, or virtue.

"Hundreds of thousands of men and women, willing to work, are unable to find employment.

"Through competition millions of men are employed in useless and undignified work, and all the industrial machinery of the nation is thrown out of gear, so that one greedy scramble may overreach another.

"It is not only the wrong of this that I resent, it is the *waste*. Look through the slums and see what childhood, girlhood, womanhood and manhood have there become. Think what a waste of beauty, of virtue, of strength, and of all the power and goodness that go to make a nation great is being consummated there by ignorance and by injustice.

"For, depend upon it, every one of our brothers or sisters ruined or slain by poverty or vice, is a loss to the nation of so much bone and sinew, of so much courage and skill, of so much glory and delight.

"In spite of their manifold disadvantages, some few of the workers have displayed fine qualities of mind and body.

"There was William Smith, the greatest English geologist, he was a poor farmer's son, and chiefly self-taught; there was Sir William Herschel, the great astronomer, he played the oboe in a watering-place band; there were Faraday, the book-binder, and Sir Humphry Davy, the apothecary's apprentice, both great scientists; there were James Watt, the mathematical instrument maker, and George Stephenson, the collier, and Arkwright, the barber, and Jacquard, the weaver, and John Hunter, the great anatomist, who was a poor Scotch carpenter.[110]

"Cast your eyes, then, my critical friends, over the Registrar-General's returns, and imagine if you can how many gentle nurses, good mothers, sweet singers, brave soldiers, and clever artists, inventors, and thinkers are swallowed up every year in that ocean of crime and sorrow which is known to the official mind as 'The high death rate of the wage-earning classes.'"

The wizard shrugged his shoulders and rose. "Enough of your grand modern England," he said; "I will take you now across this Socialist England, and you shall make your own comparisons."

The General and Mr. Jorkle rose.

"Hah! you know the old wheeze about a – hah – fellow convinced against his will,"[111] said he.

"Yes," the wizard answered, "I can only show you the country; you must see it with your own eyes. Light!"

"Sir."

"The flying machine."

[15 March 1907]

Chapter XVIII. The Magic Balloon.

The flying machine rose like a huge iridescent bubble, changing its brilliant hues in the May sunshine, and passed swiftly over the fertile lands and spacious towns of the new England. The three looked down from the small silver car at the noble panorama of blossoming woods, clean rivers, picturesque villages, and well-kept, winding roads. The wizard quoted from Milton:

> Straight mine eye hath caught new pleasures,
> Whilst the landskip round its measures;
> Russet lawns and fallows grey,
> Where the nibbling flocks do stray:
> Mountains on whose barren breast
> The labouring clouds do often rest;
> Shallow brooks and rivers wide.[112]

"It certainly is a very bright, rich country," said the General, "and all the houses trim and healthy. Hah! No smoke nuisance, by George! And that sort of thing."

"You never saw Lancashire look like this, General," answered the wizard, "and you must remember that there is not a thief, a beggar, nor a destitute human being in the country. That there are no ignorant, unloved children, no workhouses, no prisons, no slums."

"Hah!" said the General; "How is it done, by Jove?"

"Hypnotism," suggested Mr. Jorkle.

The wizard laughed. "The change," said he, "is due to the changed ideal of the people: to a rearrangement of society upon more practical and more human lines."

"I should like that explained," said the General.

"Well," said the wizard, "this is a planned and ordered society. *Our* English society is a barbarous anarchy. We believe in an open scramble for money, and tell ourselves it is all for the best because a few succeed in winning luxury, superfluous wealth, and honour. The misery, the vice, the awful waste and suffering and ignorance we regard as inevitable."

"So they are," said Mr. Jorkle, with a grunt.

"These people do not think so," said the wizard. "They have faced the problem in a reasonable and humane spirit, and have solved it."

"Hah! What problem?" asked the General.

"The problem," said the wizard, "may be expressed in various ways. I should express it thus: Given a country and a people, find how the people may make the best of the country and themselves."

"And how do they answer it?" Mr. Jorkle asked.

"Not in our way," said the wizard; "they begin by deciding as to the essentials to a happy and useful human life, and they then arrange that those essentials shall be brought within the reach of all."

"Hah! very good," said the General; "but what *are* the essentials, hang it?"

"I think you will agree with me," said the wizard, "that the essentials to a proper human life may be divided into two kinds: bodily essentials and mental essentials."

"Well?" said the General.

"The bodily essentials," said the wizard, "are food, clothing, shelter, and fuel, chiefly."

"Hah! Yes."

"These should be found for all. For no man can be healthy nor happy unless he has enough food, proper clothing, and a pleasant home.

"On the other hand, an excess of these things is not good, but bad. No man needs two houses to live in, two beds to sleep in; no man is the better for over-eating or over-drinking.

"These people would despise a glutton or an idler, and would regard it as insanity to allow one citizen to be hungry or houseless while another wasted food and wealth which he could not use."

"Hah! Well, I must say," remarked the General, "that sounds sensible. Hah! I've always thought, don't you know, that it was devilish hard lines that any fellow should – hah! – be destitute, and that sort of thing, if it could be prevented. But how *can* it be prevented?"

"These people," said the wizard, "make the country and all its resources the property of the whole people. And besides that they make the welfare of every citizen the care of the whole people."

The General shook his head. "No, no," said he, "that will not work. Hah! there must be private property, dammit."

"Very well," said the wizard, "I will give you an illustration form the Army." The General laughed.

"In an infantry regiment," said the wizard, "does not each soldier have a rifle an accoutrements served out to him?"

"Certainly."

"Does any other soldier ever try to take them away from him?"

"Of course not."

"Are not all the arms and accoutrements the property of the King?"

"Quite so."

"In the field does not each company have cooking kettles?"

"Yes."

"Are not those kettles the property of the King?"

"Yes."

"Are they not used for the good of the whole company?"

"Yes."

"Does A Company ever take away the kettle of B or C Company?"

"No."

"But if A Company's kettles were lost on the march would not the other companies supply them, giving, say one kettle each to A Company?"

"Of course."

The wizard took out his snuff-box. "Well, General, " he said, "what can be done in the army with cots and beds, and barracks, and utensils, and arms and ammunition, can be done in a nation with houses and food and clothing. And I will point out to you that where there is food, or other necessaries for all, no person need begrudge another person his share."

"But is there enough for all?" exclaimed Mr. Jorkle.

"I have already told you so, and why," said the wizard. "But now I want to give the General another example from his own profession."

"Go ahead," said the General.

"Well," said the wizard, "in the army, I believe, the rations are served out to the men every morning, and each company gets a fixed allowance of bread and meat, per head."

"Just so."

"Would you think it a better plan to pile all the day's rations up on the barrack square, and let the men fight for them?"

"Of course not."

"No; for then some men would starve, and some would be hurt, and some would have more than they could eat. That would be bad for the regiment, would it not?"

"Rather."

"Yes. And it is bad for the nation. You want your whole regiment to be well fed and well drilled, and well armed, because then they are healthier and more efficient. But you do not want all the people well fed, and well taught, and well cared for. You prefer a scramble, with the result of much misery, ignorance, poverty, and death for the many, and useless luxury and baneful idleness for the few, to an efficient and prosperous and happy *nation*."

The wizard took a pinch of snuff and looked at the General keenly.

"Hah! Go on, dammit," said the General. "What next?"

"We have been speaking only of the physical essentials to a proper human life," said the wizard, "but there are the higher essentials. These are love, parentage, fellowship, knowledge, morality, culture, and amusement. I need not again remind you that a very poor share of these essentials falls to the lot of the bulk of the people in *our* England. You know that. But have you ever asked yourselves why it is so?"

"Hah! Give me your opinion, if you don't mind," said the General.

"With pleasure," said the wizard; "the masses are ignorant and poor, I believe, because the successful classes and the privileged classes have a base and erroneous ideal of life. What do you think, Mr. Jorkle?"

"I will hear you out first," answered the financier.

"Good," said the wizard. "The privileged classes prize material wealth. Their ideal of life is riches and power. They fear that if the masses get knowledge and equal opportunities their own luxury and ease and authority will be taken from them. Therefore, they oppose real education, and real reform. They would rather allow the masses to be ignorant, inefficient, and unhappy; they would rather allow the children to peak and pine and die, than so long as their own flesh pots, and trinkets and fopperies and pride."

"All men are selfish. It is every man for himself," said Mr. Jorkle.

"Yes," said the wizard, "in *our* England, it is; because our people know no better. But when one has physical health and comfort one can be happy without luxury and waste. And these people recognise that fact. Real happiness comes by higher paths. Real happiness comes by service, by achievement, by purity of morals, and loftiness of mind. Give a man health, respect, food, a home, a wife and children, congenial recreation and congenial work, and he is happier than a millionaire or an emperor.

"There is not a rich man in this new England, and I might almost venture to say that there is not an unhappy man. My dear General, what do you say?"

The General coughed, frowned, stared hard through his monocle, and replied in the following eloquent speech: "Hah! look here, Mr. Fry – hah! Hang it all! You speak devilish well, don't you know, and – hah! you mean well, and that sort of thing. But – hah – I know my world, dammit, and it won't *do* sir. No by George, it will *not* do!

"Hah! If men were angels – well, if men were honest, and brainy, and good, and – hah – that sort of thing, it might work. But they are mean, and greedy and devilish stupid, don't you know; and they have always been the same dash it, as history proves right slip bang up to the hilt. Hah! Yes.

"Hah! Look at London. What can you make of such a mob of bounders? Talk about silk purses and sow's ears![113] Hah! It is always six to four[114] if you meet a stranger that he's an ass, or a cad, or man on the make. Ours is a jerry-made society of – hah – jerrymanders.[115] We have jerry builders, and jerry dealers, hang it! We have jerry peers, and jerry baronets, and a jerry-built Parliament. Look at the army! Hah! Look at the Press! How many men could you trust with your bank book, or your daughter, or the secrets of your business? Hah! I'm an old man, by George! I've seen the world and mixed with men and women, by Jove! And I don't believe that our jerry-built society can be reformed, don't you know, by a jerry-made Democracy. Men are mixed, hah! Men are bad. You can't raise them, nor mend them, nor save them. They don't know how to be good. Hah! They don't want to be good! Hah! They never will be good, dammit! And as for Socialism – Hallo! What place is that?"

The balloon was floating slowly over a noble city. The three looked down upon the silvery river, spanned by graceful bridges; they saw the wide avenues, the spacious squares, the gardens, fountains, towers, and spires, and the red roofs of innumerable houses. As far as the eye could reach the city spread, rosy, glittering, and beautiful; and below them, over the domes and chimneys sang the sky-larks.

"You don't know this place, General?" said the wizard.

"I certainly don't," said the General.

"Well," said the wizard, "this is London."

"London! Hah! London!" the General looked eagerly over the side of the car.

"London," said the wizard, gravely. Then he opened the snuff-box, took a pinch of snuff, and sneezed. And at that sneeze the bubble balloon burst, and with a short, harsh cry in their ears, the General and his companions began to fall through the air.

[22 March 1907]
Chapter XIX. Happy England.

Major-General Sir Frederick Manningtree Storm M.P., stared in a bewildered way at his friend Jorkle. The Honourable Member for Shantytown East returned the gaze. "God bless my soul!" exclaimed the General, "I – hah – I must have been dreaming!"

"Hum! I've been asleep myself," said Mr. Jorkle. "What's that row?"

"It's a band," replied the General. "Hallo! What's going on there? Hey?"

Several Guinea Pigs were standing up at the windows of the smoke-room and looking into the street. A strident brass band was approaching from the East.

The General approached one of the windows, followed by Mr. Jorkle. "What's the fun, doctor?" the General asked.

"Oh, only the hungry army," said the doctor, with a yawn; "One more procession of Tired Tims and Weary Willies. Look at them. A cake of soap would last the whole demonstration a week."

"Unemployed?" asked Mr. Jorkle.

"Yes, they are unemployed," said a tall young man in riding costume; "haven't been employed for yeahs and yeahs."

Mr. Jorkle shrugged his shoulders and left the window. "Bickers," he said to the waiter, "put me up a dozen natives[116] and a bottle of champagne in the luncheon-room, and telephone to my office for them to send the motor car round here. Will you have a snack, General?" he added. But as the General was intent upon the procession and did not hear him, Mr. Jorkle went downstairs.

It was a long procession, neither van nor rear being in sight. The approaching band was now quite close to the club. It was playing "There is a Happy Land."[117] The General, gazing blankly into the street, produced his cigar case and lighted a cigar.

"They are a noble army of martyrs, General," said the hunting man.

The General frowned and said "Hah!"

"How would you like to lead them to victory, General?" asked the doctor.

The General said "Hah!"

"What a crowd of them," the doctor went on; "really they are a public menace. It is a horrible mistake to coddle and foster these swarms of the unfit."

The General said nothing.

The miserable army tramped on. They were, for the most part, the ill-clothed, rough spun men of the labouring class, with here and there a better-dressed artisan. Their boots were down at heel, their hands were coarse, their faces grimy and weather-beaten. They tramped on silently, looking straight before them, or on the ground. They seemed dull and dispirited, but not angry nor ashamed. With a strange stolidity of endurance, worthy of Oriental fatalists, they trudged along upon their hungry march through the wealth and ostentation of the indifferent West.

"If I'd my way with them –" the hunting man began, addressing the General.

"Hah!" said the General, and, turning sharply on his heel, he left the club.

Directly he reached the street he was accosted by a short, sturdy, grey-haired man in patched moleskin clothes, who rattled a collecting box before him.

The General looked him hard in the eyes for a moment, then produced his purse, took out several sovereigns, and dropped them one by one into the box.

The workman's jaw dropped, his pale blue eyes dilated, he touched his old cap, but did not speak. The General walked slowly on and left him staring.

At the corner the General stopped and gazed dubiously at the grim regiment tramping past. Still gazing, he signalled a hansom.[118] The man drove up and the General got in. "Go to the Rag,"[119] he said, and sat back smoking.

For some minutes he smoked and thought, paying no heed to the traffic. Then he threw away his cigar, curled his moustaches, and said, "Hah! Dammit! Hah! What a devilish odd dream. Hah! by Jove! The – the unemployed. Hah! the unemployed! Hah! Damn!"[120]

The End.

A Few Explanatory Remarks by the Author.

I have written this story for propagandist purposes, and because I thought it might be easier to write and to read than a revised edition of "Merrie England." This explains why "The Sorcery Shop" is more of a Socialist tract than a story.

The Utopian romance may at first sight appear to be an easy form of political exposition, but it has many difficulties.

To begin with minor details. How is one to forecast the fashions of Utopia in the matter of architecture and costume? To invent a new architecture and a new dress one needs be a genius indeed. And I notice that in "News from Nowhere"[121] *even William Morris takes refuge in generalisations.*

And then there is the larger question of the development of machinery. Would the Utopians use more machinery, or less? Who can tell! At any rate, I did not judge it wise to introduce flying machines and motor boats and wonderful inventions for saving labour and annihilating distance.

It is only reasonable to suppose that in a wisely-ordered commonwealth the best energies of a highly-trained and intelligent people would be directed towards the improvement of all the conditions of national, civic, and domestic life; but I have left all that to the imagination of the reader, and have tried to show the possibility of organising and carrying on a prosperous and healthy commune without calling in any other mechanical aids than those of which we are already the masters.

To indicate the possibilities of communal efforts, to show what might be done with England by a united and cultured English people, and to meet the common arguments brought against Socialism by the Storms and Jorkles was the purpose I had in view.

To a divided, ignorant, and antagonistic people, such as Carlyle compares to "a pitcher of Egyptian vipers, each struggling to get his head above the rest,"[122] the problem of life must seem bewildering, terrible – hopeless.

But to an ordered and wise nation that problem would be simple and easy. For our country is by nature opulent. We have a favourable climate, and an almost unlimited endowment of natural wealth. Our people are, or would be under proper conditions, hardy, industrious, placable, and inventive. The labour of one man, properly directed, and with the mechanical aids we now possess, would suffice to supply the needs of many.

Poverty, crime, disease, war, drunkenness, and ignorance, are all preventable evils. Were it not for the ignorance of the many, and the foolish greed and vanity of the few we might have a happy, healthy, and beautiful England now.

In conclusion, I beg to tender my thanks to the any readers to whom I am indebted for very many letters of encouragement and advice.

I wish "The Sorcery Shop" were a thousand times better than it is. But in the nature of things it can only be as good as I have been able to make it.

McGinnis, 'An Idyll of the Dover Road. A True Story' (1907)

It was a handsome, well-washed, bright-eyed English March morning – the kind of morning when one steps as if to the tap of the drum, leaving douce old Daddy Care at the first lap, and dropping years at every milestone. The milestones on the Dover Road. Yes. Spake Blades, the curate, thus:

"The goatherd, when he marks the young goats at their pastime, looks on with yearning eyes, and fain would be as they. And thou, when thou hearest the laughter of maidens, dost gaze with yearning eyes, and fain would join their dances. *Begin, ye uses dear, begin the pastoral song.*"

"Nay, then, shepherd," quoth I, "assuredly thou will be damned. For 'tis not meet that one of thy cloth should chant the pagan songs of Arcady."[1]

But Blades cut capers and responded: "Goats of mine, keep clear of that notorious shepherd of Sibyrtas, that McGinnis: he stole my goat-skin yesterday."

Then said I, "The muses love me better than the minstrel, Blades; but a little while ago I sacrificed to the muses."

"Hurroo!" cried Blades, with a Limerick skip, "Let Himera flow with milk instead of water, and Crathis run red with wine, and all thy reeds bear apples."

"Bad luck to yez, Blades," said I clicking my heels. "My goats eat cytisus and goats-wort, and tread the letisk shoots, and lie at ease among the artintus."[2]

"Bedad, then," answered Blades, "if it comes to lying – what's that?"

We were nearing a village, and from its quiet street came a sound as of some one reading or preaching, in measured and sonorous tones.

"We have a rival, Blades," said I.

"Hark!' said Blades, "it is a crier surely."

Faintly, with a buzzing, as of a phonograph, came to us some intermittent words: "reforms – important - 'rish Coun – cils!"

We turned a corner, and the chanting voice was blurred beyond coherence. But after a good deal of rumbling, we thought we heard the words: "Save the King."

Now our road made a fork, and we took the way to the left, intending to loop round the village, election cries being, in our then mood, and upon that so auspicious morning, foreign to our desires.

The left-hand road swerved again to the right, and we came clean across the village green, and, as the lawyers say, "heard something to our advantage."

On the green, and over against the tavern door, stood the crier, a stubby little man, in a bottle-green tail coat, and a cocked hat, not to mention his striped trousers, who, with his bell tucked under one arm, was uttering in a loud staccato to the surprised delight of the village children, the conclusion of his harangue, which took the following startling form:

"Our army – of paid officials – wants reducing – not – increasing. Let us keep – our own poor – cure our own sick – empty our own cesspools – inspect our own – nuisances – or – better still – create none.

"Pay your own – rates – direct – live in your – own – houses – work your – own – land!

"We deserve as good – treatment – as Ireland – ("Not a bit of it!" quoth Blades). Let us see that we get it!

"God – save – the King!"

Finishing with a loud and defiant note, the bellman shambled off, and left us staring.

"Man alive," said Blades, "these be weird happenings." Thereupon, mocking the port and delivery of the crier, the amazing curate stood forth and gave joy and admiration to the souls of the gaping children, by the following recitation:

"When Britain – first – at heaven's command – arose from out – the azure – main – and gun – powder – treason was plot – confound their knavish – tricks[3] – God – save – the King."

And as he ceased came from the corner of the green the voice of the legitimate crier:

"Above all – if possible – they should be men – who fear God – and hate –covetousness!"

"Well! Stap my vitals!" cried Blades, "is this a wild and feverish dream?"

But it was not. It was sober fact. It was the Kentish method of bill posting – by word of mouth. And, to my mind, it has many beauties, and of blemishes none that I could discover.

So, giving thanks, as true men should, we went upon our way rejoicing.

Glanville Maidstone, 'His Sister. A Little Spangle of Real Life' (1907)

London was a wintry horror. The streets were ankle-deep in snow broth; the sleet came down in slanting sheets; there was no sky, no distance, no atmosphere; nothing but a blur and scour of fog and snow and darkness, whirled by the gusty north-east wind.

"It's wicked," growled the strong man, driving his gloved hands deep into the pockets of his heavy overcoat, "it's simply devilish. Hullo! What's that?"

He had passed a shrinking, shivering figure – a woman: a girl. She was thinly clad, sopping wet.

"The devil!" said the strong man.

He overtook the woman by Whitehall Gardens, and spoke to her. But she could not answer, because of the chattering of her teeth. The man looked her over. She was small and thin; quite young. She was cold to the heart, and leaned against the railings shuddering and sobbing.

"Come," said the strong man, and took her by the wrist.

They moved on in silence to the coffee stall at the corner by the bridge. There the girl was taken in by the fire and plied with hot coffee and soaked biscuits, until she could speak well enough to give her address. Then the stranger hailed a hansom.

"It is here," said the girl, as the cab drew up, "but she will not let me in."

"Hah! I think she will, though," said the strong man.

After a few moments a shuffle of footsteps was heard, and a hoarse voice asked, "Who's there?"

"Open the door, please," said the stranger in his deep, firm voice.

There was silence for a little. Then the key turned in the lock, and the door opened cautiously, and revealed a blowsy woman holding a candle in her hand, and scowling darkly.

"By your leave, madam," said the strong man, and he strode in, holding the girl by the arm, and closed the door.

"What's this? Who are you?" the woman demanded, in a threatening way.

"This girl is your lodger, I think," said the stranger.

"Not when she don't pay, she ain't," said the woman, "not by no bloomin' possibility."

The strong man stood and looked the woman in the eyes. "All right," he said with quiet decision, "I'll attend to that. Kindly show us in."

"And who the – who might *you* be?" the woman asked, "and what right have you to come 'ere givin' orders."

The stranger held her with his steady gaze. "In the first place," he said, "she is my sister. In the second place, look at this." He held up a sovereign.

"Oh, well; that's another pair o' shoes," said the woman, "if you're a gentleman, and 'll pay."

"All right," said the man, again. "Now go to work, like the sensible motherly woman you are. Put a fire in the best bedroom –"

"What! The best bedroom? I'll see her –"

"Steady," said the strong man. "I pay, and I pay well. And I see that I get what I pay for. Please don't waste time."

"You – you ain't too modest, mister," the woman began, but there was something so sane and resolute in the stranger's face and manner that she was afraid. "Well," she concluded, "the best room, begod, what else?"

"Please be quick," said the stranger, "light a fire in the best room, take the sheets off the bed, put this child some dry things on, and tuck her up in the blankets. While you do that I'll make some hot grog. You have whisky, I know. I'll trouble you to get it for me. The kettle, I see, is on the hob."

"And how do I know –" the woman began. But the stranger cut her short. "You *do* know, so don't waste words," said he.

The woman took another long look at him, then obeyed. The strong man was used to having his own way, and nobody ever doubted his word.

When the arrangements were all completed the elderly woman came back into the kitchen and reported to that effect. The man took up the candle and said, quietly, "Please to bring the toddy; I will go and see that the child is all snug."

The woman made no objection. This was not a man to be bullied nor agued with. The two went to the side of the bed where the girl lay, still shaken by occasional convulsive shudders.

"Drink this," said the strong man. The girl drank. "I will call tomorrow, early," he said. "Good night."

When he and the woman were back in the kitchen he gave her the sovereign. "Now," he said, with quiet sternness, "If I find everything all right when I come to-morrow, I will give you another pound. Be good to the child, and see that she has a real fine breakfast. Good night."

He walked out calmly into the storm, and the woman closed and locked the door. The she stood and stared at the sovereign. "If anybody 'ad told me as a man could walk into my drum, an walk over me like that," she said, "come it high-'anded over Betsy Hardman like that" – she glanced sidelong at the stairs – "I'd put the cat out into the yard, money or no money, only" – here she sipped on a glass of hot toddy – "only I'm *afraid*," said Betsy Hardman.

Grace Potter, 'He Was a Valuable Dog' (1907)

She wore a black dress, carefully made. Dainty white collar and cuffs, and a fluffy chou of chiffon[1] in her hair, proclaimed her a maid servant in a wealthy family.

She was out on Park Avenue in the fashionable Murray Hill district,[2] airing a dog. A stout chain stretched taut between the young woman and the dog in front of her showed that she was holding him by main force.

There were anxious lines about her mouth, and she seemed to be expecting someone as she neared the corner of the street. Standing still, she looked down East Thirty-sixth Street with the greatest concern. She was holding the dog with much effort. She could only restrain him a second and then in evident disappointment had to go on. As she was crossing the street, however a little girl appeared, seemingly from nowhere, and eagerly grasped her skirt.

The child's dress, stockings, and shoes, careworn, unchldish face, and thin, grimy little hands, might all be summed up by saying she was unmistakably a "poor" child. Just as the maid turned in hurried eagerness to her the little girl gasped out: "Mother said to tell you he's worse to-day – oh, much worse, Nell! Mother said to say that first." There were tears coming fast which she tried bravely to dash away.

"Jennie," cried the maid, "tell me" – then she had to stop a minute and give some attention to the dog; he was pulling so hard he nearly got away; he was a valuable dog – "tell me at once! Is Jim dead?"

Jim was the young woman's husband.

"Yes," sobbed the child, "he died this morning at eight."

They were both walking fast to keep up with the dog. A hard grey mask seemed to have suddenly slipped over the face of the young woman. Before, despite her anxiety, her face had been mobile. Now it seemed set in lines that would never change.

They had walked down the block together, and at the corner of Thirty-fifth Street the dog was pleased to stop and graciously survey his surroundings.

"I was giving Prince his bath this morning at eight o'clock," said the maid.

"Mother was afraid if we sent for you again you would lose your place. You've come home so much lately. And Jim wasn't conscious."

"Tell me about it, Jennie. Did he wake up after I left last night?"

"Yes. Once he woke up. Mother went to him. It was near morning. He was coughing, and I woke up, too. When he could speak he said: 'I want Nellie.' Mother said: 'Why, Jim, Nellie had to go. It's nearly morning now. She might lose her place.' He coughed bad again, and mother gave him his medicine. 'I forgot,' he said, 'Of course she couldn't stay.' Then he was so tired he didn't say any more. He went to sleep after a time. He didn't wake up at all." The child picked up her faded apron and wiped away her fast-flowing tears.

The dog was ready to go on.

"Tell mother we can have the funeral Thursday, when I have my afternoon off."

"Yes, mother said that, too. And she said to tell you you better not try to come over home till to-night."

"All right. Yes. Now, run home, Jennie. We've talked too long already. She's out driving this morning and She might see you. So be quick!"

As Jennie turned east on Thirty-fifth Street a carriage came from the opposite direction and went up Park Avenue. A luxurious lady lolled on the cushions. It was She. At a signal the coachman stopped. The maid brought her charge to the curb so that his mistress might look at him.

"His coat doesn't look quite as white as it should, Ellen," said the mistress. "Did you scrub him carefully this morning?"

"Yes, ma'am," responded the maid.

The dog was pulling so at the chain the maid could hardly hold him.

"Be a little more careful tomorrow, Ellen. And he seems so restless, perhaps you'd better stay out an extra half hour with him. Remember, he's a valuable dog. Drive on Thompson."

As the maid turned away her mistress reflected that Ellen seemed less polite than usual. "Her face had a queer set look," said the lady to herself. "I hope she's not getting sullen."

R. B. Suthers, 'The Peasants and the Parasites. A Fable' (1908)

Once upon a time there was a Peasant, who by diligence and industry wrung from the earth a decent living. And one day, while he was at work in the fields, he suddenly felt a weight descend on his shoulders. Without looking up he asked "What may this be?"

And a voice answered, "I am thy King."

"My King?" quoth the Peasant. "Whence and what are thou?"

And the King answered, "I come from the gods, and I have been sent to rule thy goings and comings, and to defend thee from enemies."

And the Peasant knelt and gave thanks to the gods.

Thereafter the Peasant was the slave of the King, and did his bidding in all things. And many times the burden was grievous to bear, but the Peasant complained not, for so he would have flouted the gods.

And it came to pass that one day, as the Peasant toiled, there came another stranger, and when he saw the King, he stopped and looked and a light came into his eyes. And he said to the King, "Who art thou?"

And the King answered, "I am the King of this Peasant."

"Thou a King," cried the stranger. "Who made thee a King over this man?"

"The gods sent me," replied the King. "And who art thou to question me? Go thy ways, or it may be worse for thee."

But the stranger stirred not. "If thou art indeed a King," said he, "show me the sign."

"What sign?" asked the King.

"Ah!" cried the stranger. "So thou knowest not the Sign. Thou art no King. Thou art an impostor. Thou has deceived this poor Peasant. – Thou –"

"H'sh!" whispered the King in terror.

"How if I denounce thy villainy to the Peasant," said the stranger. "Then would he cast thee down and throw thy body to the wild beasts."

And the King trembled with fear, and looked piteously at the stranger. And the stranger smiled a cunning smile and said, "Make room."

And the stranger climbed on the back of the Peasant, and the King made room, and the colour came back into his cheeks.

And the Peasant felt the new burden, and he said, "What may this be?"

And the stranger answered, "I am thy Priest."

"My Priest," said the Peasant. "What and whence art thou?"

"I come from the gods," replied the Priest, "and I have been sent to teach thee to love and obey thy King, and to guide thy King aright, peradventure he stray from the path the gods would have him follow."

And the Priest winked at the King, and the King was comforted.

And the Peasant knelt and thanked the gods for their great kindness to one so lowly.

So he had now to bear a double burden, and often his poor back ached. And the King and the Priest were as brothers, howbeit sometimes they quarrelled as to who should be first. And one day, when they had nigh appeared to come to blows, a stranger appeared.

"Why revilest thou one the other?" he asked.

And the Priest was wroth and answered, "This impostor would fain rob me of my Priestly dues. Let him beware, lest I inform the Peasant that his King is no King, and carries not the sign of the god-sent."

And the stranger pondered for a time, and then turned to the Priest and said, "Hast *thou* a sign?"

And the Priest was covered with confusion, and spake not.

"Oho!" cried the stranger.

"Villain," raged the King. "Hi! Peasant – I will denounce thee –"

"H'sh!" said the stranger. "Make room for me."

So they made room and the stranger climbed up beside them on to the back of the Peasant.

And the Peasant felt the new burden and said, "What may this be?"

And the stranger answered, "I am thy Lawyer."

"My Lawyer! What and whence art thou?"

"I come from the gods," said the Lawyer, "and I have been sent to be a Judge between thee and thy King and Priest, to the end that they may not thoughtlessly deprive thee of thy just rights."

And the Lawyer winked at the King and the Priest, and once more they breathed freely.

And the Peasant knelt and thanked the gods for their gift.

So now the burden of the Peasant was still more heavy, and his eyes were always turned to the earth. And the years rolled on, and the King and the Priest and the Lawyer began to be afraid that the Peasant might sink under their weight.

And one day there came by a stranger, and when he saw the Peasant with his load he exclaimed, "Friend, thou art sick."

"Aye," said the Peasant, "I grow old, and my limbs are stiff –"

"Old! Thou old?" cried the stranger. "I will soon cure *thee* of old age. Wilt thou take my advice?"

"Nay, I follow no advice but that of my Lawyer, my Priest, and my King," replied the Peasant.

And the Lawyer said to the stranger, "Come up higher, friend."

So the stranger climbed on to the back of the Peasant beside the King, the Priest, and the Lawyer.

And the Peasant felt the new burden and said, "What may this be?"

And the stranger answered, "I am thy Doctor."

"My Doctor!" said the Peasant. "What and whence art thou?"

And the Doctor answered, "I come from the gods, and I have been sent to teach thee the laws of health, and to cure thy body of pain and disease." And the Doctor winked at the King, the Priest, and the Lawyer. And they smiled, and the anxious looks left their eyes.

And the Peasant knelt and thanked the gods for their goodness and loving kindness.

So now his burden was heavier than ever, but still he toiled on and never murmured. And the years rolled by. And in turn there came a Poet, to sing to the Peasant, and a Politician, to orate to him, and an Actor, to amuse him, and a Scientist, to bemuse him. And they all clomb on the back of the Peasant beside the King, the Priest, the Lawyer, and the Doctor.

And one day a MAN appeared, and when he saw the Peasant and his terrible load, he was moved to anger. And he heaped scorn on the King and the Priest and the Lawyer, and the other riders, thinking to shame them out of their cruelty. But they heeded him not, and reviled him, and called him "Infidel."

So he turned to the Peasant and prayed him to stand up and be a man and cast off the cunning scoundrels who oppressed him.

And the King and the Priest and the Lawyer and the rest trembled and were afraid.

"If he should look up," they said.

But the Peasant heeded not the voice of the MAN.

And the Lawyer said to the MAN, "climb up."

And the MAN looked at him, and the Lawyer quailed before the MAN's eyes.

And when the others knew that the MAN would not climb up, their hearts sank within them.

And the Politician said, "Let *us* climb down."

And again and again the MAN urged the Peasant to stretch himself and to stand up, and assert his manhood. But for a long time the Peasant heeded him not at all. And at length, the MAN angered the Peasant, and he, too, reviled the

MAN, and called him "infidel." And the King and the Priest and the Lawyer and the others jeered at him, and said, "We are safe again."

But the MAN clung to his task, and at last the Peasant began to listen.

And the Priest said, "I also think it is time to climb down."

And they quarrelled amongst themselves, and could not agree what to do.

And the Peasant has not yet stood up, nor have the Parasites climbed down.

But the Peasant is listening to the MAN with both ears.

A. Neil Lyons, 'Little Reggie Writes Home. A Childish Document, Edited' (1908)

MY DEAR MATER, – Many thanks for the cough lozenges and chest protector which I have now eaten. My cold is better although I still have to be very careful about washing and etc. so as not to catch a chill. Thanks for the cake which was smaller than last time. Five shillings will do.

There is no news except I've got to equations and old Seppie says I am the only boy in the form that really sees the principle of it. Don't forget to tell what Seppie says to the Pater. A chap in my dormitory has got a pair of pads[1] with pneumatic tubes all up the front and they only cost his mother eight and sixpence. But five shillings will do.

I have done so jolly well over my equations that I got chosen on Shakespeare Day to go with Seppie and Missus. Seppie and young Dora to the Demonstration. Have you heard about the Demonstration? It is an idea of old Seppie's for keeping up Shakespeare's memory. I went to carry Seppie's wreath because of my equations and because my hands were cleaner than Willson II's. It was rather lucky really because all I had done to them was putting them down the waste pipe to fish up Jackson's door mouse or two. Their habits are very interesting to watch. I think I could make five shillings do for the pads.

The Demonstration took place at Westminster Abbey. It was got up by the National Shakespeare Circle of Streatham which Seppie is President of. Seppie has written a long poem about it in the Streatham Sentinal and Tooting Tribune. Did you see it?

When we got to Westminster Abbey, Seppie and Mrs. Seppie and young Dora and me, it was half an hour too soon for the demonstration and we went to an Alphabet Cake Shop[2] for tea. And I had coffee and sponge cakes, which came to ninepence which Seppie paid; but of course it wasn't the sort of lunch I'd rather of had if I could have had what I would rather of had. But Seppie said I ought to choose a more substantial dinner than vanilla wafers: and he said that chicken patties were the thing but it wasn't even chicken patties because Seppie had some words with the lady who waiting at our table and she brought us coffee instead of tea and sponge cakes in mistake for patties. It makes a chap feel rather juvenile to be fed on sponge cakes.

There is a shop here where they sell a rather decent sort of cake, which I like because you can digest it so easily. Has got cocoanut inside it and split almonds and preserved cherries. Some of the biggest chaps in the school are not up to equations yet.

When I had finished my sponge-cakes, we walked across to the Abbey and asked a bobby whether he had seen anything of the Demonstration and he said what Demonstration. Seppie looked hurt but he kept his temper and was polite to the bobby and the bobby woke up and said that now he come to think of it he had seen something of the sort and he thought we should find it going strong at the back of the Abbey. So we crawled round into a pretty big street and thought we heard a noise and thought we'd found it but it was only some girls and ladies out for a walk with dinner-bells and flags.[3] So we went back to the Abbey again and we were just in time to meet the Demonstration getting out of a bus.

It wasn't as big as you might expect because the rain had kept old Mrs. Pott away and Mr. Pott's little boy has got a gum boil: but Mr. Pott had come and Mrs. Pott and a girl Pott and the two long-haired chaps who belong to the Shakespeare Circle and they had a wreath wrapped up in the "Daily Mail" and Mr. Pott was wearing a read silk pen wiper thing in his button-hole and he had brought a lot more of them and we all had to put one on. Mr. Pott is a funny man and he is Seppie's greatest friend and looks like it. He stood still and took off his hat whenever we came to any of the statues outside the Abbey. I couldn't help smiling and young Dora saw me smiling and told her father. What a pity she's a girl. All the girls are out of place nowadays. If anybody could have the magic power to turn them into boys for five minutes, I would teach them to be decent. Seppie did a long rebuke and said he was disappointed in me and he said that Mr. Potts' proceedings did not call for laughter because he was honouring the memory of the departed great. The statues round this part of London have mostly got trousers on and it looks funny: but I suppose they didn't leave soon enough to do without clothes like the ancient peoples who we read of in our studies. I am trying to think of what you said and be careful of my clothes this term. The Sunday trousers are hardly spoilt at all and my everyday's are very good considering: but Mrs. Seppie says they are past doing anything else for. Perhaps I can make them do for some time yet. They don't show when you are sitting down and anyhow I think the pads are more important because you can break your leg with a cricket ball. The five shilling ones are quite strong although the eight and six are much more comfortable but you can tell the Pater that I daresay I can manage with the five shillings. I would rather have the money than the pads because then I can get an exact fit.

There was some trouble about getting in to the Abbey at first. The bobby at the door thought we were out for a lark until Mr. Potts came up and you could see that nobody with that sort of face would go out for a lark. But the bobby followed us in and when we got to Shakespeare's statue, he stood on one side and watched us. I suppose he still didn't trust us and thought we had come to steal the pews.

We all stood in front of the statue and looked at it. Mr. Potts went close up and stared at it for about five minutes, as if he was going to do some mesmerism. Then he made a noise like gargling your throat and put the wreath round Shakespeare's head, but it fell onto his neck, so he looked like dog Toby. Everybody else put flowers round the bottom of the statue and Seppie put his wreath on Shakespeare's feet: and he was very ratty because I'd lost the ribbon, a pale blue affair, with red writing done by young Dora: "To the undying memory of the Bard of Avon from the Rev. Septimus Pink, M.A. And Seppie made a speech. And Potts made a speech, all about Milton being blind. He said this was the fifteenth band of grateful Miltonites which he had led up to the shrine: and Mrs. Pott got very red and nudged him and he apologized for calling Shakespeare Milton. *I* didn't mind. To a chap who has to parse the beggars viva voce there isn't much to choose, but everybody else looked very shocked. I suppose it happened because Mr. Potts belongs to so many circles.

When we got outside, everybody shook hands and Seppie said it was a record Demonstration. And Mr. Potts said he must hurry off to write to the papers about it. And Mrs. Potts kissed me: which was pretty cool. And the Potts girl told young Dora that she didn't like her hat. So I did another smile as close up to young Dora as I could. There were no more sponge-cakes or anything.

I think these Demonstrations are a very good thing because they help to keep the memory of these people alive. I wonder if Shakespeare was good at equations. If I can keep it up I ought to get a prize at the end of the term. I hope the Pater will remember what he said about giving me another for every one I get. I hope he won't think it ought to be a book. If he lets me choose I shall choose something more useful – a blow pipe I think for making glass balls.

I must now close as preparation time is approaching and I have a lot of quotations to do. If the Pater is very pleased you could tell him to look in the window at Gummidge's in Cheapside, and he can see what good pads are being made nowadays. But I daresay I can make the five shillings do. With love. Your affectionate son,

REGGIE

Victor Grayson, 'The Myopian's Muddle' (1909)

In the land of Coma[1] dwelt the Myopians[2] – a strange people. Able and industrious were they, and the earth did yield abundance to their labours.

The sun sent forth his genial rays to arm and gladden the earth, and grateful showers did gratify its thirst. Thews and sinewa[3] of iron had the Myopians, and no task was too onerous for their enterprise. Yet were they not happy, for their vision was clouded. A few there were – yclpet[4] Panopians – whose sights were whole. And by reason of this they directed the labour of the others.

When the harvest was reaped, they of clear vision did appropriate the major portion. For the Myopians held their seeing brethren in humble fear and reverence. There was one among them, strangely garbed, deprived of physical vision; yet could he see with his soul. Him they called the Fakir. But, being a defective offshoot of the Panopions, he lived after their fashion and slept in their halls. When discontentment moved the Myopians to sighings and complainings, when they did whine of hard labour and small fare, he did endeavour to assuage their grief with hopeful prophecies. He told them of a happy land far, far away, where everyone would see; and those who saw least in Coma would see most in Utopia. He urged that the sight of the soul was better than the sight of the eyes, and taught them by precept, if not by example that frugal fare was best for the soul's vision.

The people heard his message with gladness, and the Panopians did pamper him in that he soothed the people. But it so happened in the inscrutable ways of Providence, and because of the considerable appetites of its favoured ones, that there came a great drought.

* * *

And the Myopians began to murmur moodily. They said there was plenty to eat, as they had produced abundance. But the Panopians and the Fakir said that was an illusion due to myopia. They were short of bread because they were short of sight, and they could not see how that could be remedied until they reached Utopia. However, the matter had been receiving their consideration, and they had decided to construct, or at least to direct the construction of, a railway that would lead them to the happy land. And the poor people worked hard with little food, heartened by the hope of better things. At last the railway was completed. The Panopians charged them a goodly price for he journey; and one of them in a blue uniform drove the train, while another in a red uniform collected the cash as conductor. With hearts full of joy and hope the Myopians embarked. They could not see where they were going, but they could feel the motion of the train, and that did them good. For many, many days they rode in the train. The air became foul and noisome. The food was stale and inadequate. But they were buoyed up with faith in the knowledge and skill of the blue Panopian who drove and the red Panopian who conducted.

At last the train pulled up, and the Myopians sent up a cheer, thinking they had arrived at their destination. But the red conductor merely shouted, "All change here!" Then they dismounted, but owing to defective vision could not recognize that they were in Coma again. They had built their railroad in a circle. Then the conductor led them round into the same train, but from another platform. Yet they recked not. The blue man went to the back of the train, and the red man to the front. And off they started again for the land of Utopia. They again rode for many dreary days. And they were cold and hungry, for they had paid their money to the Panopians for the journey. In due course, however, they stopped again. And this time the blue man shouted, "All change!" They were then led round the platform and entered the other side of the train. The blue man drove this time and the red man conducted the train. But some of the Myopians grew impatient and suspicious and some grew very angry. One said he did not think that either the driver or the conductor knew where Utopia was. And another said he thought they knew were it was, but for some reason or other did not want to go there.

* * *

In the end they sent a deputation of the Myopians to the driver to make inquiries. The driver, as was his wont, received them kindly and heard their complaints. They must not, he said, be led away by ill-disposed men of their class. They must learn to be patient. Utopia was along way off, and the roads were very steep, and the train must of necessity move very slowly. Meanwhile, however, he was very, very sorry for them, and would be be most pleased to pull up at Palliativo, where there was some fairly clean water to drink and a bit of grass to eat. He would give them some of his own stores gladly, but he needed all he had to feed the nerve necessary to his responsible position. So they returned encouraged to their unwholesome carriages.

So it fell out, however, that one of the younger Myopians suddenly recovered his full vision; and he bored a hole through the side of the carriage and watched the track. To his surprise and disgust he soon discovered that the train was travelling in a circle. Twice they passed through the land of Coma before he opened his mouth to inform his brethren. But, behold! When he told them, they called him "liar" and "malcontent" and "dreamer." And it came to the ears of he driver and guard that the young Myopian had recovered his sight and was spreading malicious rumours. So the Fakir was sent again to soothe the pilgrims, who were beginning to believe that there was something in what the young man said. The Fakir was replete with righteous indignation. He assured them that progress was being made, though very slowly. They had set out for Utopia. What was it and where was it? Utopia, he said, with touching solemnity, is not a place: it is a state of mind. If only they would see that truth, they would not care if they never reached Utopia at all. Life consisted in striving. Man never is, but always to be, blessed.

And the young man, being refined and courteous, was overheard to murmur, "Rodents!" And the Fakir, having taken a little collection for his stomach's sake, blessed them and departed.

* * *

The young man, however, persisted in his statement that the train was travelling in a circle. And he converted some. These went to the driver again, and he promised them that he would inquire into the matter. Day followed day, and they still went round and round. The young man grew impatient and angry. He even went the length of applying the brake and refusing to release his hold. And the Myopians had a meeting and dissociated themselves from his action. The proper way to solve the difficulty was to use moral suasion on the driver and conductor. They admitted they were going in a circle, but they contended it was better to travel in a circle than not to travel at all.

The young man was seized by the driver and dropped off the train amidst the applause of the Myopians. They were last seen in a compromising position approaching the brake.

Victor Grayson, 'A Dead Man's Story' (1909)

Once the Editor held converse with a human skull. Last night I talked with a skeleton.

It was a in a dream, of course – a silly, horrible, convincing sort of dream. I can see it now – and I feel an eerie chill. Last night it seemed quite natural, and usual, as things do in dreams. It seems just as real to-day; in fact, *more* real than waking experiences and living acquaintances.

It is a ghastly thought but I think everyone should have at least one conversation dreaming or otherwise, with the dead. It shakes one's thoughts loose and the sensation reacts so vividly on life.

Before I dozed I had been reading the statistics of suicide. And these set me thinking of the history of self-murder.[1] How Socrates had taken his own life, calmly remembering as he held the hemlock that he "owed a cock to Esculapius"; how Pliny and other Romans had eulogized suicide and counted it among the virtues; and how smug jurymen in our times value so highly their mean, grasping worrying little existence that they deem a man insane who cuts the cord. And I wondered myself into a realm of dreams.

* * *

"Were you insane?" I asked him, "or are we?" He sat silent in the opposite chair, his eyeless sockets turned towards the red glow of the fire.

"Insane? Yes up to the point of my decision to die," he answered. "Ay! Stark mad. That decision was my moment of temporary sanity. Your sleek jurymen and wise coroners know nothing about it. Nothing! I've learned all I know about life since I left it. I've met my father and grandfather and we've talked over things. They both died what you humorous folk call *natural* deaths, at the end of hideously unnatural lives. And they would hardly recognize me when they saw me. They said I had disgraced the family record. My grandfather boasted that he has worked for forty years under one family, and never got more than sixteen shillings a week. And although he was buried by charity, he said, everyone agreed that poverty and destitution was no crime. My father was the most intelligent and best educated of the family. So he drifted to the town and obtained work as a clerk at twenty-five shillings a week. He married below his station as my mother was a 'hand' in the factory. She died of blood poisoning, caused by chemical fumes, when I was four years of age. 'We'd a genteel funeral,' said my father, proudly, 'and the coffin was old oak.'

"My father died naturally on a seat on the Thames Embankment. His death was due to hunger and exposure, and the reduction of the cost of production. I died –, but let me first tell you how I lived.

"My father, as I have already observed, left the working classes to be a clerk. His weekly income was of such a magnitude that he very often had to decide between a clean collar or a rasher of bacon; usually the collar had it. My mother, prior to her marriage, had been earning an average of fifteen shillings per week. But as the class to which my pater had attained could not brook the idea of a wife *working*, she left and divided her time between cleaning up the band-box in which we lived and keeping my face clean. I don't remember her, of course. But I've heard my father say that 'there wasn't a woman breathing that had a better grip of the genealogical trees of the titled families than she had.'

"I was a feeble and ill-nourished lad, and barely missed dying before the age of one. That accident has been the subject of many a bitter hour of remorse since. After my mother died, my life could not have been very prosperous or comfortable, for at the age of 16 I was driving a team of horses for a timber merchant.

"I got married, too. Blood will tell, somehow. Marriage only increased my misery. Without realising what it involved I'd soon two little human lives to sustain. Then came the ghastly climax to a life of aching slavery. One day I drew my wages and found a strip of paper in the tin box. It was the usual damnably polite formula of dismissal.

"I swallowed the lump of bitterness, pocketed my money and my pride and started to walk home. This thing had dazed and stunned me. I don't know how long I walked, but it was dark when I reached my home. My wife grew hysterical when I told her the news. I went into my bedroom and locked myself in. For an hour or so I lay stupefied.

"Then I listened at the door and could hear my wife crooning sadly as she rocked the cradle, 'Daddy's sacked, my angel, poor daddy's got the sack.' It's a silly thing to remember, but somehow it's just those silly little things that stick to a chap.

"The hideous misery I endured for the next four months can't properly be put into words. Day after day I trudged the weary round – a thing unwanted, an ugly intrusion on men's peace of mind. It's wonderful how much you see in human faces when you've reached that stage. I saw lines of greed and low cunning in faces that had previously seemed benevolent.

"One day I was standing over the grid of a baker's shop trying to dry the wet rags that served me for boots. A little girl came out of the shop, and the make-weight or 'jockey'[2] fell from the loaf she was carrying. I picked it up and was about to hand it to her when I was seized from behind. In vain I pleaded and explained. The burly constable had 'been spotting me for over half an hour.' I shall never forget the ride in Black Maria, handcuffed to a Norwegian sailor who sat dazed, looking straight into space. Then the dreary wait in the noisome cell till it pleased His Worship to open the court. We were a strange gang of humans and we exchanged confidences and craftily advised one another on the best attitude to adopt in court.

I got off and was released in the afternoon. It was a biting cold, dark, foggy day in November. As the great gate closed behind me I had a horrible sense of guilt. The stain of the gaol was on me, and I hurried nervously away. I took to a long, deserted road by the docks and kept to the shade of the warehouses. As I passed the corner of a narrow court, a woman, standing in the narrow entry, said 'Good night duckie, won't you take me with you?'

"I stood still with a feeling of horror. I knew the voice. It was the same that crooned 'Daddy's got the sack.'

"I began to run, madly. I don't know how far I ran. All I remember was the delicious sensation of coolness and rest that I felt when the water closed over me.

"Temporarily insane? Who shall say? But what is the use of sanity in this crazy labyrinth of a world? You have it all there, my young friend. All the shame and horror that tracks the lives of thousands of my class. We don't take our own lives they were taken before we were born. Insanity is life's sedative to the spiritually sick."

* * *

I woke with a shudder, and stared hard at the opposite chair. My dream companion had departed. The fire had gone out and the room was cold. I shivered. Skeletons are morbid and nasty companions. They sour the soul and darken the outlook. This morning I heard the birds singing. And a crowd of boys and girls were happily gamboling in the streets. Their laughter disperses the morbid vapours.

Life must be made worth keeping. It must be as free as the sun and as dignified as the stars.

A. Neil Lyons, 'My Lady's Chariot' (1910)

I met it, first of all, on the sun-baked slopes of our local Everest, which is called Chalk Hill, and which is well called, being composed entirely of large white holes which are separated, one from the other, by small, lopsided, melancholy specimens of the ever-grey juniper shrub. It was a two-wheeled chariot, constructed chiefly of old chicken-cooping and propelled on the primogenial or push system.

He who pushed it was a native-born man named Smithers: a brown-skinned, uncleanly fellow, of mirthful habit, whom the people of this neighbourhood call Jack o' Clubs. He is, by public profession a buyer and vendor of rabbit skins, but he really lives by his wits – a method of living which is practiced by hardly anybody in Sussex. Therefore, they despise him and call him Jack o' Clubs. He steals old iron from their dust-heaps every evening, and sells it to them, newly burnished, every morning. Also he sells to me at extremely reasonable prices teal and woodcock, which are specially raised for him by Major-General Tinker, of Bishops Bury Hall.[1]

The chariot, when I met it on the wind-smitten slopes of our local Everest, contained much that properly pertains to the midnight dustbin. Also, it contained a full-grown girl. She lay in a sort of hollow amid the sardine tins and kettle spouts and furs and spices, with her shamefully public legs dependent from the dash-board – or, rather, from that part of the chariot which presented an acceptable site for a dash-board. She had small eyes, crimped hair, red lips, a smut on each cheek, and an expression of quiet happiness. When Jack o' Clubs pulled up the chariot her head rolled here and there amid the furs and tins and spices.

"Good marnin' to *you*, sir!" shouted Jack o' Clubs. "Can I sell you a very curious l'el old iron hook, sir? 'Tis a verry curious, antikew l'el piece. 'Pon my word, sir, 'tis a beauty."

I did not want an iron hook. Nor did I want a spoutless teapot, a second-hand dog-collar, a leaden clock-weight, a broken garden ornament, or a bag of stolen golf balls.

"Then what about this here ole-fashioned l'el bread-pan, me gentleman?" persisted Jack o' Clubs, holding up an ill-shaped bowl of brown earthen ware. "'Pon me word, 'tis a splendid thing: one o' the old sort. Do to bake *anything* in. I on'y want a shillin' for it. 'Pon me word, sir, 'tis a bargain."

"Your sister?" I inquired, smiling the bright smile of intelligent friendship at the lady in the chariot.

"My mate," responded Jack o' Clubs. "I fetched 'er from down below there. She belong to a reg'lar 'ard-working family, but I fetched 'er away. Shall we say a shillin'?"

I looked again at the lady in the chariot, who did not speak or move, but whose big red lips were parted in a smile, whose little eyes showed forth contentment. "Did you steal her?" I demanded. Jack o' Clubs said, quietly:

"I fetched 'er away.

"And," he added, "seeun as there be two on us now, and 'tis so 'ard to make a livin', I'll say tenpence 'apenny." Again he held up the little brown pot.

"It's value is tuppence," I informed him.

"Not to-day, sir," he answered, gravely ... "The clay be got so dear. Shall we say fourpence, then, me gentleman? 'Pon me word, sir, 'tis a bargain."

"Where do you keep her?" I inquired.

"I got some l'el premises be'ind they furzes there," said Jack o' Clubs. "Would you care to look at a couple of very rare old anderions,[2] me gentleman? 'Tis only a step to where I keep 'em. They be a wonderful uncommon l'el pair, 'pon me word, sir. Worked out in the shape o' two young naked females, sir, which I'll take me oath, young gentleman, if you wasn't a bachelor, I dursn't recommend them."

I had seen some of Mr. Smithers' valuable antiques before that day, and therefore did not care a great deal whether I saw the shameless iron females or not; but I did want to see the premises. So I permitted Mr. Smithers and the chariot and the lady to head a procession round the chalk pits – which procession came to a sudden halt before a stretch of canvas which was spread upon sticks behind a gorse bush.

"This be our villa," said Jack o' Clubs. "And that," he added, pointing in the direction of a powerful smell, "is where I keep the surplus."

Before I could ask him to refrain from disturbing the surplus, Jack o' Clubs had ascended a precipitous monument of his nightly labours, and had extracted therefrom the andirons. They were exceedingly old and beautiful andirons. "Where did you get them?" I inquired of Mr. Smithers.

"I fetched 'em away, sir," said that gentleman ... "Six shillin'."

"Three," I replied. "Aren't you afraid that she'll catch cold or get fever up here on the hillside?"

"Five, then," said Jack o' Clubs. "No fear. She be one o' the roving sort. That's why I fetched 'er away."

The girl sat up and threw a rabbit-skin at him. Then she lay back again among the tins – and smiled.

"These evening mists –?" I hinted: "the rain; this wet chalk, the – er – rigours of summer? Let's say three-and-six."

"Four-and-six," said Jack o' Clubs. "We don't trouble naarthun, 'er and me. She be one o' the moonlight sort."

So we struck it at "Four" (with threepence for the moonlight sort thrown in), and I said good-bye to them. Jack o' Clubs said, "Good-bye," too, and the red-lips widened lazily.

Now, we keep late lights in the cottage where I live, and sometimes people come, when it is dark, and ask for straw and shelter. Being Christian folk, we often give then ha'pennies or cheese. I therefore was not surprised to hear a tapping at the gate two nights ago; but I was surprised, on going to the gate, to find there – Jack o' Clubs, and the chariot, and the legs; but no red lips: no smiles.

"I brought you the l'el earthenware pan, sir," said Jack o' Clubs. "'Pon me word, sir, 'tis a wunnerful good l'el pan. I don't arst naarthun for it, sir – on'y – on'y –"

"Only what?" I demanded.

"A l'el drop o' whiskey, sir, or gin, me gentleman, or wine. 'Pon me word, I wouldn't arst it, on'y … I think the chill 'ave took 'er. And now – this last minute – I think … I think … Begod, I dursn't look.

"You see, sir," said Jack o' Clubs, "I becarryin' 'er back again, carryin' 'er 'ome." He peered at me with eyes from which the cunning had departed, and plucked at the rough sacking which covered her (all save the legs) like a pall.

Glanville Maidstone, 'Nightmare Bridge' (1910)

I knew in my dream that I was lost. Weary and cold, with aching feet and heavy eyes, I plodded along that silent and solitary thoroughfare of a great city. The vista seemed endless; the winking lamps stretched on as far as one could see. Far as I walked I had met no one, not even a policeman. Stay! There is a constable standing in the shadow of a gateway. I stop before him; I ask him whither does this road lead. He looks at me with strange eyes; he does not speak, he whispers: "To the bridge." He is very pale, the constable, and very lean. His face – his face is like a skull: it *is* a skull. No; but how hollow are his eyes! How sharp and prominent are his cheekbones! And as I turn away he laughs. His laugh puts fear into my heart. I turn cold with fear. I try to walk rapidly away from him, but my feet are like lead. And he follows me. I hear the sound of his feet, and the echo of his measured step comes back from the dark and silent houses. Will this road never end? Do those glimmering lamp-lights stretch on, an avenue of stars, to the edge of the world? Where is this bridge? Why did he call it *the* Bridge? I tramp on, the constable following without a word. Then – then I see the Bridge. I am on the Bridge. It is a wide bridge, brilliantly lighted, exquisitely paved. There is a broad footpath on either side, and lines of gilded railings. Overhead stretch festoons of beautiful flowers. The road is used by motor cars and handsome equipages drawn by noble horses. In the carriages and cars are men and women dressed luxuriantly. I can see the sparkle of gems and hear the sound of conversation – conversation gay and witty, carried on in high-pitched aristocratic voices. The traffic in the roadway is not dense: there is ample room. On the footpaths there are but few people; they are the counterparts of those in the carriages: men and women, handsomely dressed lounging easily, laughing and talking: a picture of wealth and happiness. Outside the railings? – outside the railings it is dark. There seems to be partly visible through the shadowy obscurity a moving crowd, a dense traffic. There is a great deal of noise: the noise of tramping horses, heavy wheels, cracking whips; the noise of angry voices, or curses, sobs, and groans. What goes on there in the semi-darkness? Is it a riot? Is it a battle? Hark! a scream!

What bridge is this, then? What does it span: a river? I look for the terrible constable. He is at my side. He shrugs his shoulders and says, in his horrid whisper: "You do well to choose the middle of the Bridge. You would not enjoy the outer roads. I know: I used to be among it."

"What does it mean?" I asked. "What is it? Let us go there, where the noise is. Let us go and see. Come, come, come; let us go to the side of the road, where the crowd is."

"Come," said the constable, "I don't care. I'm safe enough – unless I lose my feet or my head."

"Lose your feet? What do you mean?" I asked.

"Come and see," says the constable, with a grim smile. "If a man goes down in that crush he gets no quarter: not from *them*."

"From whom?"

"From his fellow creatures." The constable leads me back towards the entrance to the bridge. "If you fall," he says, "do you know what they will do to you?"

"Tell me," I ask him.

"Well," he says, "you be careful. If you fall they will kick you; they will trample on you; they will hustle you over the edge, into the river."

We are on the Bridge – on the outer road. What dense traffic! what a terrible crowd! There is not room. There are no footways, and the heavy traffic is mixed with the struggling pedestrians. On the outer side, next the river, there is no parapet. The people fight frantically to keep away from that edge. But they cannot. Hark! another scream! "What is that?"

"Another one gone over," says the constable, "a woman. She's too old and weak to fight. Many of the weak ones go: men and women, and children, too – very many children."

In appearance this crowd resembles an ordinary London crowd – of poor people. The crush is so severe that at every few yards distance we see groups fighting – fighting like animals – fighting as I have seen women and men fighting round the tram cars and the motor omnibuses. And the constable spoke the truth. When a pedestrian – man or woman, yes, or child – goes down, the case is desperate. A girl falls close by us. Another woman kicks her, a man treads upon her; when she screams a second woman strikes her in the face. Then – oh, a huge wagon laden with iron crashes through the crowd. A man is down – down under the wheels!

"In the name of Heaven," I cry, turning to my sardonic guide, "what does this mean? Why do they not widen the Bridge? Why do they not put a parapet on the outer side?"

"No money," says the constable. "Who's to do it?"

"Do it!" I exclaim. "What kind of city is this? Is there no government – no authority?"

"Of course," the constable answers. "This is a civilized country: a Christian country. Government? What are you thinking about?"

"Then," I say, "tell me, who governs this city? Who is responsible for this bridge?"

The constable nods his head towards the wide and beautiful central roadway. "Those," he answers; "those ladies and gentlemen, there."

"But," I cry, "those people take no heed. They are lounging, talking, trifling, laughing. Do they know that men and women are being crushed to death? Do they know that little children are being hurled into the river or crushed under foot? Why do they not stop these horrors? Why do they not widen the bridge?"

The constable shook his head. "I told you," he said, "you would be better in the middle – seeing you'd had the luck to get there. They cannot widen the bridge, do you understand, outwards; they could only relieve the crush by throwing down the railings and throwing open the wide middle road. That's the difficulty."

"But," I said, "in the presence of this awful crush and struggle, this terrible suffering and loss of life, surely they could do as you say! There is room on the bridge for all and to spare."

"True," the constable nodded. "But," he said, "the middle way is *theirs*, do you see? Naturally they will not give up any of their room; that is why they have put up those gilded railings. There are very few can climb those railings."

"But the crowd," I said, "will the crowd endure this? They are so many. They could pull the railings down."

"They are very strong," said the constable.

"If they are made of steel –" I began.

"Steel?" The constable laughed his horrible laugh. "They are made of something stronger than steel," he said.

"Of what are they made?" I asked.

"Of lies," said the constable, and kicked a fallen man out of his way.

"But," I cried, "Lies can be broken with truth. I will speak to the people. I will appeal to them for the sake of their women and children. I will give them the truth so break these lies."

The constable shook his head. "Do nothing of the kind," said he. "Go back to the middle way. You will hardly be heard in all this noise; and how can men listen or understand when they are fighting for dear life? They will pay no attention to you; or they may throw you down, and then they will trample on you. Go back to the middle way."

"Then," I said, "I will appeal to the ladies and gentlemen of the middle way. I will tell them what I have seen."

"No use," said the constable, "those people on the middle way like a lot of air and space; they like to be grand, and they like to be happy. They keep their eyes away from the side road, and talk beautifully about all kinds of noble ideas and pleasant things. But they'll see you damned before they will give up an inch of their room. Try them. Nice, polite, refined, well-spoken ladies and gentlemen they are; but try to take a foot of their road, and you'll think you have been thrown to the lions."

"But," I said, "it is horrible. It is infamous. These people are worse than savages. This city is a disgrace to humanity."

"Steady, steady," said the constable. "What city do *you* come from?"

"I? I come from London."

The constable laid a bony hand on my shoulder. His pale face grew redder, his smile became more human, his baleful eyes twinkled humorously, and his whisper rose to a firm, deep voice. "Why," he said, "London? Bless our two souls! London! Don't I know London? Don't I know that London is just exactly like this? Why, governor, this *is* London. What part is it you want to go to? Now then, wake up, mister; you must not sleep here."

"Good heavens! Why – fancy my falling asleep in a railway station! In the refreshment bar –"

"Well," said the constable, "the bars are closed, sure enough. Not," he added, "but what there might be ways of getting something if you really feel the want of it, sir."

And there were.

JUSTICE

Anon., '"Happy Valley." A Fairy Tale', *Justice*, 20 July 1907, p. 5.

C. L. Everard, 'The Eternal Feminine', *Justice*, 7 March 1908, p. 5.

Charles Allen Clarke, 'The Red Flag', *Justice*, I, 2 May 1908, p. 5; I (continued) and II, 9 May 1908, p. 5; III, 16 May 1908, p. 5; III (continued) and IV, 23 May 1908, p. 5; IV (continued) and V, 30 May 1908, p. 5; V (continued) and VI, 6 June 1908, p. 5; VI (continued), 13 June 1908, p. 5; VI (continued) and VII, 20 June 1908, p. 5; VI (continued), 27 June 1908, p. 5; VI (continued) and VIII, 4 July 1908, p. 5; VIII (continued), 11 July 1908, p. 5; VIII (continued) and IX, 18 July 1908, p. 5; IX (continued) and X, 25 July 1908, p. 5; X (continued) and XI, 1 August 1908, p. 5; X (continued), 8 August 1908, p. 5; XII, 15 August 1908, p. 5; XIII, 22 August 1908, p. 5; XIV, 29 August 1908, p. 5; XIV (continued) and XV, 5 September 1908, p. 5; XV (continued) and XVI, 12 September 1908, p. 5; XV (continued) and XVII, 19 September 1908, p. 5; XVII (continued) and XVIII, 26 September 1908, p. 5; XVIII (continued), 3 October 1908, p. 5; XVIII (continued) and XIX, 10 October 1908, p. 5; XIX (continued) and XX, 17 October 1908, p. 5; XX (continued) and XXI, 24 October 1908, p. 5; XXI (continued), 31 October 1908, p. 5; XXI (continued) and XXII, 7 November 1908, p. 5; XXII (continued) and XXIII, 14 November 1908, p. 5; XXII (continued) and XXIV, 21 November 1908, p. 5; XXV, 28 November 1908, p. 5; XXV (continued), 5 December 1908, p. 5; XXV (continued), 12 December 1908, p. 5.[1]

Edward Hartley, 'The Man in the Street. High Rates, Officialism and Socialism', *Justice*, 20 November 1909, p. 8.

W. Anderson, 'The Fool and the Wise Man', *Justice*, 13 August, 1910, p. 6.

In 1907 *Justice* (1884–1925), which continued to be edited by Harry Quelch (1858–1913), was enlarged from eight to twelve pages, and in October of the same year the SDF changed its name to the Social-Democratic Party. In 1908 Henry Hyndman, despite his associations with European socialists through the International Socialist Congress, joined Robert Blatchford in his warnings about potential German invasion and control of the seas. Hyndman argued in his second autobiography that 'being dependent for six-sevenths of our food on foreign countries, we could be starved out even by a chance superiority at sea',[2] and he called for a strengthened navy in 1910.[3] Divisions between the SDP and the Labour Party, as the latter worked to distance themselves from socialism in order to maintain good relations with trade unions and the Liberal Party, were not helped by some of the articles published in *Justice* under such titles as 'The Liberal Labour Alliance' (17 October 1908), 'The Labour Party and its Wreckers' (23 January 1909) and, even stronger, 'Keir Hardie as a Pacifist War-Monger' (22 August 1908). In 1908 *Justice* launched what it called the 'Red Vans', a scheme along the lines of the Clarion vans that began in the 1890s and were revived in 1907, to take the message of socialism across the country.

There was a revived interest in fiction as a vehicle for the socialist message, particularly in *Justice*; during this period the final two serial stories were published in *Justice*, making a total of four in its first thirty years. The first of these two serializations, Charles Allen Clarke's 'The Red Flag', was published in *Justice* between 2 May and 12 December 1908; it was originally serialized in his own periodical, *Teddy Ashton's Fellowship*, between 9 November 1907 and 15 February 1908, under the pseudonym Vernon Harvey Franklin. (See the headnote for the *Bolton Trotter* in Volume 1, pp. 1–2, for Clarke's biographical details.) The second, Henry Baxter's 'David Dexter, Socialist', was serialized between 28 August 1909 and 28 May 1910. Both deal realistically with the male protagonist's involvement with socialism, but Clarke's fiction was selected for this volume because of its interesting use of genre. The serial draws directly from social investigation, specifically Mary Higgs's undercover investigations into workhouse life, weaving it into the fiction.

C. L. Everard (n.d.) and E. R. Hartley (1855–1918) were the authors of much of the short fiction published in *Justice* during this period. Everard published a number of short stories in *Justice* in 1907 and also published under the pseudonym 'Gadfly'. He went on to write for the *Daily Herald*, the first socialist daily newspaper, and for the *British Worker* during the 1926 general strike. Edward Robertshaw Hartley published in *Justice* his didactic 'Train Talk' series, which centred on the narrator's discussions of socialism carried out on train journeys. These stories were later collected and published by the Twentieth Century Press and sold for a shilling. Born to a Bradford family of woollen and worsted spinners, Hartley was drawn into the socialist movement through his membership of both the SDF and the ILP in the 1890s, when unemployment in Bradford was high. He worked as a journalist, was briefly the editor of the *Bradford Labour Echo*, and was involved in both the Clarion van project and the 1902 Dewsbury by-election when Harry Quelch stood for office. He stood as a 'Socialist Unity' candidate in the 1906 election as a protest against the close association of the LRC with the Liberal Party.

William Crawford Anderson (1877–1919) was not as prolific as Everard or Hartley, 'The Fool and the Wise Man' being his single contribution to *Jus-*

tice fiction during this period. Anderson was born in Findon, Banffshire, to a blacksmith in a community of crofters; he encountered socialism during his apprenticeship as an industrial chemist. He attended meetings of the local SDF group and a lecture by Caroline Martyn (1867–96), and he joined the Shop Assistants' Union when he worked as an assistant in a grocery store in Glasgow, before leaving to join the ILP in 1907. He was elected to the National Administrative Council of the ILP in 1908 and supported himself by writing and speaking engagements, until he became a member of the board of directors and lead writer for *Daily Citizen*, the daily socialist paper. He successfully stood as Labour MP for Attercliffe, Sheffield, in 1915. Lastly, the identity of the anonymous author has not been discovered, but this is the only unattributed story published in *Justice* during the period covered by this volume.

Notes

1. The frequent continuation of chapters across issues of *Justice* continues Clarke's refusal to be bound by the periodical page when writing and publishing long fiction. He would often divide chapters between issues of his own periodical, *Teddy Ashton's Journal*; for instance, the second instalment of his serialization 'A Daughter of the Factory', published in the issue of 26 February 1898, opened with a continuation of Chapter II from the previous week, gave the complete Chapter III, and ended with the first twelve paragraphs of Chapter IV, which then continued in the following issue of 5 March 1898. The layout of *Justice* was generally more rigid than Clarke's fluid style, and when publishing long fiction, it would usually separate the fiction from the surrounding journalism by a thick, dark line. Nevertheless, *Justice* accommodated Clarke's fluidity, giving between half and three-quarters of a page to the instalments depending on their length, but not at the expense of 'serious' journalism. Clarke's 'The Red Flag' generally shared a page with 'A Woman's Point of View' by 'Jill', which was expanded or contracted accordingly.
2. H. M. Hyndman, *Further Reminiscences* (London, 1912), transcribed by E. O'Callaghan, *Marxist Internet Archive*, at http://www.marxists.org/archive/hyndman/1912/further/index.html [accessed 6 April 2013].
3. M. Crick, *The History of the Social-Democratic Federation* (Keele: Keele University Press, 1994), p. 233.

Anon., '"Happy Valley." A Fairy Tale' (1907)

Once upon a time – when the world was still beautiful, and, instead of ugly factory chimneys belching forth hideous smoke, fair gardens and orchards made the air sweet and fragrant, and the sun shone golden on the corn; when good fairies flew from home to home in the broad daylight, and were not afraid, and men and women welcomed them and were glad the live-long day – far away, in the heart of the country, there lay a pretty valley.

Poppies nodded amongst the corn, and grew rosy when a bold ear stooped and tickled them. The children never wanted to steal apples, for they could always pick them for the asking. No notice-boards, saying "Trespassers will be prosecuted," were to be seen, so there were no naughty little elves to run round and whisper into children's ears how nice it would be to trespass. But then there were no fences to climb over, although there were plenty of trees to climb up, and I daresay the children tore their clothes sometimes, and gave their mothers plenty of trouble in this way. Still, on the whole, children and grown people, too, were very happy, and the good fairies grew fat and lazy through having no work to do.

One day the people were startled to hear a curious, rumbling sound, and the whole earth seemed to shake. If they had even heard of such a thing they would have thought it was an earthquake – but they never had.

The noise grew louder and louder, until a crowd of people, with scared faces and eyes and mouths wide open with fright, came running into Happy Valley. When they had recovered themselves they were able to tell what they had seen.

A terrible monster – a giant, they said, was coming, and with him two horrible dwarfs, who seemed to be his servants, as they were carrying his baggage, consisting of two enormous sacks, upon their shoulders.

Sure enough, they had no sooner finished their story than the rumbling grew louder, and the people saw a hideous giant, with the two misshapen dwarfs on either side.

When the giant saw the prosperous little valley his eyes began to sparkle, until the country-side was lit up, as though with lightning; but seeing the men and women running from him in fear, he stopped short in his descent, and sent one of his servants on in front to speak to them.

Seeing that the giant appeared inclined to be friendly, the people gathered round the dwarf to hear what he had to say.

"My good people," said he, "I come from my master, Monopoly, who, seeing that you are unnecessarily frightened of him, bids me tell you to be of good cheer. For, though he could easily crush you with one stamp of his foot, he has no such unkind intention; but, indeed only wishes to be your very good friend and to render you all the service in his power."

At this the people began to pluck up courage, and although a few still had some misgivings (for the dwarf was so terribly ugly) yet most of them began to feel ashamed of their fears.

"My name," continued the dwarf, "is Capital, and I and my fellow-servant, Competition, have worked many years for our master, who is the best of all possible masters, and treats us exceedingly well. Seeing your poor little valley, with its miserable orchards, and knowing how hard you have to work to make your corn grow and how few nice things you get in return for your work – my master (with his usual kindness of heart) has taken pity on you, and will show you how, by working for him, you can have a great deal more comfort. Indeed, if you are industrious you may become rich as he – look!"

With that the dwarf opened the sack he was carrying, and poured out its contents – a number of glittering gold pieces, which came tumbling out before the astonished gaze of the people.

Now a curious thing happened – at the sound of the tinkling gold all the good fairies spread their wings and flew right away.

It was not long before the dazzled people were persuaded to accompany the dwarf to his master; and, following the servant's instructions, knelt at the feet of the giant to receive his blessing and words of advice. First he flattered them by telling them how sensible they were to come to him as they had done; and the people were just beginning to think that they were very wise indeed, when he began to call them fools.

"See here!" he said, "have you not been spending all the best years of your life in growing a little corn and fruit for yourselves, when under your cornfields there lies a gold-mine, which would make you and your children rich for ever?"

At this the people looked at each other in astonishment, and some were for running to dig at once to see if it were true. But the giant roared with laughing. "Do you think with your foolish, little spades that you can unearth the gold which lies deep hidden in the earth?" he said. "No, no! my friends." Then, seeing their disappointment, he added, "But I will tell you what I will do. I will give you spades with which to dig all the gold you want, but I shall expect you to give me a share in return."

At this the people were delighted and cried out how good and generous kind Giant Monopoly was, and they set to work to build him a great palace to live in; for none of their homes were large enough for him.

* * *

If you could have seen Happy Valley a year after the giant came you would have been surprised at the change which had come over it – surprised, and sorry, too, I think. For instead of the laughing cornfields and orchards, great ugly pits yawned everywhere; even the sparkling rivulets were turned to dirty, muddy streams, as the people threw the earth into them and washed their gold in them. Oh, yes! There was gold, plenty of it. The giant's spades (each of which took 100 men to dig with) tore up the whole cornfield with one spadeful, and there it lay – a great glittering mass.

But now, see how cunning old Monopoly was! He took a great sack and held it out before the people. "When this sack is full," he said, "the rest of the gold shall be yours, and I will only take this for my share."

"Very reasonable," said everyone; "of course there will be plenty left for us." So they shoveled up the gold with a will, and poured it into the sack.

But (poor, silly things!) they could not see the hole in the other end of the sack, and that as fast as they filled it the gold ran out, and was gathered up by Monopoly and carried off to his palace.

Soon, however, the people grew very weary of trying to fill a sack that was never full. They began to want food, but no one had any time to get it, and their orchards and cornfields had all been dug up. The giant, seeing that they were likely to die from hunger, and that he might have to turn to and dig up his own gold, called his servant Competition, and bade him throw a handful of gold amongst them. This the people scrambled for, and some were knocked over and killed in the tussle, and some who got a few lumps gave it away to their fellows in exchange for the food they were so sorely needing.

So this went on for years, and the people grew more and more afraid of the giant, and many hated him because they had seen the hole in the sack, but they dared say nothing about it.

One day, a young man called Fairplay, instead of going to work in the gold-mines, sat down to think. Now everyone knows that if you want to do more work than you can manage in a day, it is no use to sit down and think about it, or you will not do any at all. And this is what happened to Fairplay. The more he thought, the more disinclined he was to work, and the end of it was that, instead of going to work at the gold-mines he went wandering away and away, until at last he lost sight of Happy Valley altogether, and found himself in the heart of the country.

What beautiful fields and woods," thought he; "why should I not stay here, and live on berries and mushrooms!" So he set to work, and built himself a little home of wood, and here for a short time he lived very happily.

But he had not been long in his little wooden hut when he began to feel very, very sorry for his fellowmen toiling so miserably without enough to eat.

"How can I free them," thought he, "from that terrible tyrant, Monopoly? We must kill him; but I, alone, cannot do it. I must get others to join me."

So back he went to the Valley, but when his fellow saw him they all began to jeer. "Here is a lazy fellow, who won't work," said they; and they threw stones at him. "Better stone Monopoly," cried Fairplay, "for not only will he not work, but he grabs all the gold for which *you* work so hard for himself."

But they hooted and stoned him all the more for that; only some went home and thought over what he had said.

These few sought out Fairplay afterwards, and asked him what he meant.

"Have you seen the hole in the sack?" said he. And they nodded silently.

Then he told them his plan, of how they must free themselves from the giant and his servants, and they agreed to help him.

Lo! one night, when the giant was asleep, a long procession wound round the valley. First came Fariplay, with his followers; after them the women and children; and after them quite an army of fairies, each with a glittering sword in his hand. They knocked at the door of the palace, and killed the terrible giant, and his servant, Competition, ran away and was seen no more in Happy Valley.

"But what about Capital?" you ask.

Well, I'm coming to that. When they tried to find him they could not see the ugly old dwarf anywhere, but, instead, found a beautiful princess, whose long, golden hair reached to the floor.

"The giant wanted to marry me," she told them; "and when I would have nothing to do with him he turned me into an ugly dwarf, and made me work for him. Dear people, you have made me free! To show you my gratitude I will work for you all my life."

So Princess Capital married Fairplay, and they worked for the people, and were happy ever after.

C. L. Everard, 'The Eternal Feminine' (1908)

"The country's going to the dogs!" said the Colonel, throwing down the "Times" in disgust.

"I wish I could say you surprised me," said the Doctor.

"Those wretched women, sir, have captured the House of Commons," said the Colonel.

"I wish them joy of their conquest," said the Doctor cynically. "But 'dogs' was hardly the word."

"What's the trouble?" asked the Barrister, who had just come away from a dreary debate at St. Stephen's.[1]

"Two hundred and seventy-one members in favour of Woman's Suffrage," said the irate Colonel, "and only ninety-two against."

"Majority, one-seven-nine," said the Barrister.

"Correct," said the Doctor, admiringly. "The whole ninety-two, to Prejudice were true."

"If you'll abstain from your flippant doggerel," said the Colonel, "I will proceed."

The Doctor's apologies were numerous.

"As I was about to remark," continued the Colonel, "this resolution will ruin the country."

"The road to Hell is paved with Parliamentary resolutions," commented the Doctor.

"There must be a permanent Paving Scandal in the infernal regions," said the Barrister.

"If the resolution means nothing else," said the Colonel, "it means that the government of the country will soon be handed over to the women – the shrieking sisterhood."[2]

"Rome was saved by the cackling of her geese,"[3] said the Doctor.

"The point we are dealing with," said the Barrister reprovingly, "is the question of the new political faith, I take it, of those members who voted for the resolution."

"Political faith be hanged!" said the Colonel.

"Can you hang what doesn't exist?" asked the Doctor. "The resolution was supported, not by faith, but funk. It only confirms my estimate of the House of Commons – a collection of fourth-rate politicians, with fifth-rate ideas."

"I'm inclined to agree with you," said the Colonel.

"I can't help that," replied the Doctor. "You condemn the Commons for being too advanced; I condemn them because they are not advanced enough – that's all."

"They represent the intelligence of the nation," protested the Barrister.

"I can quite believe it," said the Doctor, "since the British nation is principally composed of individuals who have lost all individuality."

"Yet you believe in the democracy," said the Colonel.

"The definition of terms is the Achilles' heel of philosophy," replied the Doctor. "I believe in Democracy as a principle of government. For 'the democracy' of which you speak – meaning the mob; for 'the democracy' which exults over a Boer War and whines when called upon to foot the bill;[4] which sheds crocodile tears over Chinese Slavery,[5] and is content to remain in a state of slavery itself – for this democracy I have little admiration."

"There is not much political difference between us," said the Colonel.

"As befits an old politician," replied the Doctor, "you do not study politics. 'Party politics is your forte. You believe – I do not impugn your sincerity – in Toryism, and beneficent feudalism, governed by a hereditary aristocracy; you stand for the party of yesterday."

"Quite true," said the Barrister, cheerfully.

"Our legal friend here," continued the Doctor, "as becomes a prospective Liberal member for Slumton-cum-Jerriville, was mis-educated in the Manchester school.[6] He believes in the Divine Right of the Captains of Industry – the plutocracy of to-day – to govern us. He ably represents the party of to-day."

"And what of your noble self?" asked the Colonel, with a smile.

"As a Socialist," said the Doctor, "I believe in government by an *educated* democracy – not a mobocracy, mark you. I am content to support the party of to-morrow."

"To-morrow never comes," said the Colonel triumphantly.

"Your originality is almost startling," said the Doctor; "but your party has not yet arrived at to-day. I stand by my definition, nevertheless."

"What of the party of the day after to-morrow?" queried the Barrister.

"On the day after to-morrow," replied the Doctor, "there will be no parties."

"We are apt to wander from the point in these discussions," said the Colonel. "We were discussing Woman's Suffrage originally."

"The Eternal Feminine is the Eternal Question," sighed the Doctor.

"Are you in favour of Woman's Suffrage?" asked the Barrister.

"I support the enfranchisement of women, certainly," replied the Doctor; "but I do not believe that the franchise should apply only to certain amiable females, who labour under the delusion – a woman without a delusion is like a fish without sauce – that a woman who pays rates is a lady. I think the vote must be given to all women."

"I hardly expected you to take up that position," said the Colonel, "after the opinions I have heard you express on the subject of Sex Equality."

"It is not a question of one's personal predilections," replied the Doctor.

"It is a question of sentiment," said the Barrister gallantly.

"It is a question of economics – a subject of which you, fortunately, know nothing," said the Doctor. "As a matter of fact, my position is logically consistent. I admit this with trepidation. The mind of the man who is constantly striving to be consistent is apt to attain to the consistency of mud."

"Joking apart," said the Barrister, who hails from Stirling Burghs,[7] "do you think it is desirable that women should have votes?"

"Plautus says, 'there are some things which are admirable and desirable; there are more things which are necessary and inevitable,'" replied the Doctor. "The enfranchisement of the woman is, at any rate, economically necessary and inevitable."

"I doubt if Plautus said that," said the Colonel suspiciously.

"It may have been Herbert Spencer," replied the Doctor, "Or Machiavelli.[8] It doesn't matter much."

Charles Allen Clarke, 'The Red Flag' (1908)

[2 May 2008]

I. In A Common Lodging-House.*

In the dreary dusk of a chill November afternoon, in the northern manufacturing town of Blakeham, just when the factory folks, after their day's labour amid spindles and shuttles, were, with clattering clogs, hastening home to their "tay,"[2] or evening meal, two women – one aged about forty and the other not more than twenty-four or five – stood talking at the door of one of those Christian temples called a "Citadel" to a black-bearded and kindly Salvation Army captain.[3]

The two women were apparently of the "tramp" class, for they were shabbily clad, wearing old shawls on their heads, and their boots were cracked, leaking and dilapidated. The face of the elder was plain, but compassionate; the countenance of the younger had elements of beauty that not even the dress of poverty could wholly hide.

"In this town there are no common cheap lodging-houses[4] for females only," the Salvation Army captain was saying.

"Are you sure? Not one anywhere in all the town?" asked the elder woman.

"Not one, I'm sorry to say," said the captain, "and I speak from full knowledge. We get many tramps, women and men, coming to ask us where they can get shelter; and so I have searched the whole town and made inquiry as to such places. There is no common lodging-house in Blakeham for women only. For any destitute woman, tramping into this town, unable to beg or earn the few pence for a bed, there are only three lodging-houses, and these take mixed lodgers."

"It's a shame," said the elder woman, "for you know what mixed lodgings mean. It means debauchery and vice."

"I know but too well," said the captain. "Would to God things were different for the sake of our poor sisters of the road and the fallen and the weak."

"Then which is the best of the three houses? Which would you advise us to go to?" inquired the elder woman.

---

* For much of the raw material woven in this chapter I am indebted to Mrs. Higgs' graphic book on tramp life, "Glimpses into the Abyss."[1] – AUTHOR

"Well," said the captain, thoughtfully, "there's one in Water Street, but I couldn't recommend that. It's patronised by 'gay girls.'[5] There's another in Bank Street, kept by a woman, but there the single men have to pass through the sitting-room to bed, and though the proprietress does her best to prevent any 'carryings-on,' the conditions are not conducive to decency. The third is in Moor Street, and I think you'll find it the best, as far as there can be any best in such places."

Thanking the Salvation Army captain for his information and advice, the two women, after receiving directions as to the route, set off for the common lodging-house in Moor Street.

"Isn't it scandalous, May?" said the elder woman, as the two walked along through the crowd of factory operatives and artisans, many of whom stared at them, "isn't it scandalous that in a big town like this there is no provision made for homeless women, apart from men? No town lacking in such accommodation is doing its duty. There are widows and friendless girls and outcast women everywhere, and it is most important that every town should provide a place of refuge for such – it would arrest many a poor lassie in her downward career and save many a poor soul from destruction. I hope we shall find this place satisfactory to which we are going. I almost wish you were not with me – though I am thankful for the encouragement of your company; I fear it will be no fit place for you."

"I shall take no harm, Mrs. Wilkinson," said May; "and I want to learn the worst, that I may do my best."

"You are a brave girl, May," said Mrs. Wilkinson. "If only all good women would come and see for themselves how badly their unfortunate sisters fare in our present civilisation there would soon be something done."

The dark of a damp, starless night was now on the town; and after passing along several shop-keeping thoroughfares, brilliantly lit up, and through which electric tramcars were gliding, the two women, taking a turn past a church, grey and cold in the gloom, entered a narrow street, whose style of dwelling showed it to be one of the oldest parts of the town, as well as one of the most squalid.

A few doors on the right they came to a sign bearing the words, "Brown's Lodging House – Beds, 4d." On the footpath and in the road in front of this house stood half-a-dozen men, "tramps" – the weak, glimmering light of a lamp partly revealing the evidence of their forlorn plight.

"Is this the way into the lodging-house?" asked Mrs. Wilkinson of one of the men.

"No," said the man. "The office is up that alley there to the right. If you don't mind, I'll show you the way," he added, obligingly and respectfully.

"Thank you," said Mrs. Wilkinson. The man, with a short, keen glance at the elder woman, and a longer look at the younger one, led the way up the main entry, or passage left between two houses, till they came to a lighted room, in the window of which was a small square of glass which, when opened, made an aperture as in the booking-office at a railway station.

"You pay here," said the guide, who was a man of about thirty years of age, sturdy, with broad shoulders, and a pale face with a dark moustache.

"Thank you," said Mrs. Wilkinson, "it's good of you to take the trouble to show us."

"Not at all," said the man, quietly, "my duty to all who are of the sex of my mother," and off he went back down the alley, while Mrs. Wilkinson knocked at the window, and paid sixpence for a double bed.

"When you go up to bed," said the man in charge – he was in his shirt sleeves, and untidy – "you'll have to pass through this room, and up a stair to the right. The room up that short stair to the left is where you can sit and have your supper – if you've got any," and with these words the man slammed the window down and disappeared.

Going up the short stair, Mrs. Wilkinson and May found themselves in a big room, with a large fireplace. On the mantelpiece was a little board on which some humorist tramp had drawn a clock face, and underneath these words – "No tick here.[6] Stopped." Hanging on the wall to the right of the mantelpiece was a big frying-pan, on which somebody had chalked this droll inscription – "Out of work," while to the left of the fireplace, on the back of a big piece of cardboard (which was the back of a mineral-water manufacturer's advertisement), some poet of the road had written this couplet –

"If you've nought else to chew, you may chew your gums;

If you can't find a chair, then sit on your thumbs."

There were five or six tables in the room, with well-used wooden forms alongside them, and at one of these tables, in a corner near a slopstone or sink, Mrs. Wilkinson and May took their seats. Over the slopstone was a card informing the lodgers that they must wash any "pots" they used. The crockery consisted of a few old enameled basins, plates, and tea-pots, all of which looked as if they had seen long served and even been "in the wars,"[7] for they were mostly cracked and snipped.

On the wall near the door were hooks on which the lodgers hung their hats and caps and shawls.

"The room is lofty and airy," said Mrs. Wilkinson, "and would not be bad if it were clean. I wonder how long it is since it was beautified? And the floor – it must be months since it felt a scrubbing-brush. Still, it's not bad, and perhaps when one considers the kind of folk who use this place we can't expect it to be much different."

On the other side of the table at which May and Mrs. Wilkinson sat was a man with a profusion of black hair "cobbling" his wife's – or anyhow, his female companion's – boots.

At the next table some men and women were eating and smoking – they had got some fried chips. On the forms near the fire sat other men and women and children. In a corner stood two dirty and rickety perambulators, belonging to two of the families on tramp. There was one young couple, husband and wife, the woman rather good-looking, with three small children, one a babe at the breast, the eldest not being more than four years old, yet, due to the misfortune and experience that sharpen the wits and make children prematurely adult, quite a little woman in her way, looking after her own requirements, and doing shopping errands for the family.

One pretty child, with golden curls, and a black velvet dress, had got a bowl at the sink, and was, with the air of one who is an authority and an expert, washing some pocket-handkerchiefs, which certainly needed the operation. One man and woman were steadily engaged in making paper mats – they kept their stock-in-trade in a tin box.

The mender of shoes, like most followers of St Crispin,[8] was somewhat of a student and philosopher, and, as his talk showed, had evidently been a considerable reader of books.[9]

"We were nearly run over by a motor-car, to-day," he said. "Drat the fume-pots on wheels – the highways are no longer safe for honest tramps, poor pilgrims of the pad. There's a passage in Shelley that describes the motor-car very graphically and prophetically. Listen to it –

> 'Iron wings that clang the wind,
> Vapours steaming up behind:
> Clanging loud, an endless crowd: –
> These are Jove's tempest-walking hounds
> Whom he gluts with groans and blood!'

That's in 'Prometheus Unbound'[10] – a magnificent poem."

"You've read the poets, then?" said Mrs. Wilkinson, addressing the cobbler across the table.

His wife answered for him. "He's read everything. He's read too much. If he'd read less he might have done more – and we not have been in this place to-night."

"Rail not at reading," said the cobbler. "Books are my kingdom that not even princes can take from me. There I wander with 'shapes that haunt thought's wildernesses.' That's from 'Prometheus Unbound', too. But the finest bit is at the finish – this –"

"Oh, let's have more work and less talk," said the cobbler's wife.

"At this job a man can talk while he works," said the husband, driving a nail into the leather sole, "shoe-making and tailoring are the only two thinking crafts. Cobblers and snips are always advanced men – men to the front –"

"With their trousers out behind,"[11] said the wife; and May and Mrs. Wilkinson smiled at the vulgar summarization of the fate of the men who dream and lead; but the imperturbable cobbler went on serenely talking about the poets, and delivering extracts from their books.

"There's Burns too, and Byron,"[12] he said. "I like 'em both. Burns was only a shade above us tramps – he was just as poor, and he mingled among us. Read his 'Beggar's Cantata.' That's true to life. Describes such a scene as may often be witnessed in these common lodging-houses, where all the failures among men, the broken-down, the gutter-bound, the luckless, the weak, the bottom dogs,[13] are to be found; and of all ranks, too, parsons, lawyers, scions of the aristocracy, schoolmasters, college men, as well as common labourers, mouchers,[14] and vagabonds."

"And what brings them to this degradation?" asked Mrs. Wilkinson. "Isn't it drink?"

[9 May 1908]

I. In a Common Lodging-House. (*Continued.*)

"No, not drink – not always; very seldom. It is chiefly Human Nature and Fate, and, what's worst of all, as Burns says, 'man's inhumanity to man!'[15] The rascals and thieves at the top are largely responsible for the rogues and tramps at the bottom. Did you ever read 'Venice Preserved' – Otway's play?[16] He lived in the time of Charles the Second, and a gay[17] king among the girls was that same Charles, as history tells us. I don't know how many thousands of pounds we pay every year to the descendants of his bastards, but I've calculated it would be enough to feed all the starving in the British Isles."

"I haven't read 'Venice Preserved,'" said Mrs. Wilkinson. "I have not had time to rummage amongst the old dramatists – except Shakespeare. But you seem to have read everything, as your wife says. You are quite a scholar."

Modestly proud of this praise, the cobbler said, "Well, in 'Venice Preserved' occurs this passage –

'I'm thinking how that damned starving quality
Called honesty got footing in the world.

* * *

Why, powerful villainy first set it up
For its own ease and safety: honest men
Are the soft, easy cushions on which knaves
Repose and fatten. Were all mankind villains
They'd starve each other: lawyers would want practice,
Cut-throats rewards; each man would kill his brother
Himself; none would be paid or hanged for murder.
Honesty was a cheat, invented first

> To bind the hands of bold deserving rogues
> That fools and cowards might sit safe in power,
> And lord it uncontrolled above their betters.'"[18]

"That's like the talk of a wild Anarchist or an extreme Socialist," said Mrs. Wilkinson.

"I'm no Anarchist, nor Socialist either," said the cobbler, "but I believe in right and liberty for all. If there were justice in the world, there would be few vagabonds and criminals. And, if I may say it – without blasphemy, for I mean none – Christ Himself was a tramp, for He had nowhere to lay His head."

"That is true," said Mrs. Wilkinson, "and I wish Christians would bear that fact more in mind."

"There was Oliver Goldsmith,[19] too," said the cobbler, "he was a poet and a tramp – the vagrant genius who played a begging flute for bread. He wrote the glorious 'Deserted Village,' in which come these lines –

> 'Ill fares the land, to hastening ills a prey,
> Where wealth accumulates and men decay.'

"Most of the poets," he continued, "show how the wolves prey on the sheep. Have you read Byron's satire in 'Don Juan'? I know that 'Don Juan' is not reckoned a respectable poem for ladies – but it's good for men and women; and we are not ladies and gentlemen here – we're men and women. Those who judge us and condemn us are no better than we.

> 'Now justices of peace must judge all pieces
>   Of mischief of all kinds, and keep the game
> And morals of the country for caprices
>   Of those who've not a licence for the same;
> And of all these excepting tithes and leases
>   Perhaps these are most difficult to tame:
> Preserving partridges and pretty wenches
>   Are puzzles to the most precautious benches!'[20]

"Well, Well, it's a rum world; and what does it matter as long as we muddle through it? As Byron says –

> 'It's all a mystery. Here we are,
>   And there we go – but *where*. – Five bits of lead,
> Or three, or two, or one, send very far!
>   And is this blood, then, formed but to be shed?
> Can every element our elements mar?
>   And air – earth – water – fire live – and we dead?
> *We* whose minds comprehend all things? No more:
>   But let us to the story as before.'"[21]

II. The "Swell"[22] on Tramp.

While the cobbler was in the midst of his quotations and declamations there entered the room a man of about twenty-seven years of age. He was tall, dark, slender, and handsome, with a pear-shaped head, his chin being his weakest feature – it was slightly receding. There were signs of refinement and culture about his face and person, though he was very shabbily attired. He wore a white collar and tie – the only man in the place possessing such outward distinctions of respectability. He had a little moustache, and his chin was in need of a shave. Regarding Mrs. Wilkinson and May inquisitively, and rather boldly, this newcomer sat down at the end of the form near the cobbler. Pulling a sandwich out of his pocket, he began to eat.

"I'd have had a drink, too," he said, speaking into the back of the neck of the cobbler, "if I had had any money. But with the fourpence for the bed went the last cent, and I can't have even a common gill of ale – I, who have in my time drunk wine and champagne in the great cities of the Continent – in Paris, Vienna, Berlin, Rome, St. Petersburg, and even Constantinople."

The cobbler half-turned his head round. "You have travelled, then?" he said.

"Travelled? Ay;" answered the young man, "and on important diplomatic missions, too. But I'm down on my luck now. Everything's against me."

"It sometimes happens that way," said the cobbler. "What the cabalists and mystics call the Wheel of Fate[23] brings strange vicissitudes. But, as Shelley says –

'Though the future is dark and the present is spread
Like a pillow of thorns for thy slumberless head,'[24]

Nil desperandum,[25] my boy; never give up."

"Don't talk rot," said the young man. "There is no hope. Life's hell, and there is no God. The best thing to do is to end it by a jump into some water. I was on the point of doing that to-night, when a man gave me sixpence, and I almost wish he hadn't. I should have been at rest now. Life's all right if you've money; but if you've no money you're better dead. And I, by rights, ought to be rolling in wealth. My father is a millionaire."

"Then what are you doing here?" said the cobbler.

"Because my father, though a millionaire, doesn't happen to be my mother's husband."

"Ah!" said the cobbler. "That's the tale, is it? Still the man ought to help you – by nature, if not by law, you are his son."

"He's a swine – yet a most respectable swine!" said the young man. "And he has some legal sons who are surrounded with money, and have big houses and carriages and servants, while I am a tramp on the road. It's not good enough, and by G—, if he doesn't do fair, I'll do for him."

"Don't talk like that," said the cobbler. "You'd only get hanged if you killed him."

"Well, what does it matter? He's given me a life I don't want, so I'll take his and call it quits."

The young man felt in his pockets.

"Not even a cig.[26] to console me," he said.

Then he turned to May, whom he had been scrutinising intently even while he was talking to the cobbler, and said: "Pardon me, but haven't I met you before?"

"No," said May curtly.

He looked keenly into her face, and said: "Well, perhaps as you are now also down in the world you don't wish to let on. But weren't you at Morecambe[27] three – yes, I think it's three – years ago."

"No," said May.

"Strange," said the young man. "I could swear you were the same girl – anyhow, you have a remarkable resemblance; the same eyes and mouth. I don't forget pretty faces in a hurry."

May averted her head.

"I don't mean to be rude," said the young man. "But she, who was so much like you – indeed, I can't believe you are not the same – was at Morecambe on a summer holiday. We got to know each other and had a jolly time together. She promised to write, but she never did. I guess she thought it was only a seaside flirtation, and had to end at that. But to me it meant much more, and might have meant more if she had only corresponded as she promised. Ah! it is cruel to think of those bright days in such a time and scene as this. Have you nothing to say? Don't you wish to speak to me?"

May made no answer. Mrs. Wilkinson looked angry.

"Very well," said the young man, with a glance at Mrs. Wilkinson. "Is this your mother?"

"Just you mind your own business," said Mrs. Wilkinson.

"Oh, all right," said the young man, rising, and striding across the room to the fire, where a bedraggled woman, who had just come in, was putting the kettle on. "Is it raining?" he said to the woman with the kettle.

"Cats and dogs," said the woman.

Meanwhile, the little girl with the golden hair, having completed her washing, came to Mrs. Wilkinson, and said, displaying the handkerchiefs, "Now, haven't I made a good job of 'em?"

"Very good indeed," said Mrs. Wilkinson, patting the girl on the head, and wondering what would become of this child in this horrible life.

"If you've anything to wash I'll do it for you," said the little girl.

"I'm sorry, but I haven't anything," said Mrs. Wilkinson.

"You've a pocket-handkerchief, haven't you? Let me look at it."

Mrs. Wilkinson smilingly pulled out the handkerchief.

"There," said the child, "I knew it wanted washing. It's really disgraceful – don't you think so?" And Mrs. Wilkinson and May laughed as the child went on, turning to May, "and you give me yours; I'm sure that wants washing, too."

May had to pull out her handkerchief, and the child merrily took it to the sink along with Mrs. Wilkinson's.

"We'd better get a little supper, May, and then go to bed," said Mrs. Wilkinson. "Shall we have some milk and bread? There's a shop outside. These pans don't look very enticing to boil milk in, but we shall have to put up with 'em."

"All right, I'll just run out for the milk and bread," said May.

"I think I'd better go," said Mrs. Wilkinson. "This is a low quarter, and there are rough, vile men about."

"Nonsense," said May, "what is there to be afraid of? I'll go. What is it we want?"

"A small loaf and a pennyworth of milk. But you stay here; I'd rather go."

"No, let me," said May, rising as she spoke. "I want a breath of fresh air after sitting in this foul room. I'll be back in a few minutes," and she picked up one of the enamel basins, crossed the room, and began descending the stairs to the street.

She was hardly half-way down the stairs when the "swell" young man who claimed previous acquaintance with her, hurried after her, to Mrs. Wilkinson's alarm, who was undecided whether to get up and follow.

[16 May 1908]

III. The "Piecer"[28] on Tramp.

May had just stepped off the stairs and entered the grimy, gloomy entry when the young man touched her on the shoulder.

"Now, what's the use of pretending you don't know me?" he said. "You are the girl I had a jolly time with at Morecambe."

"I am not," said May. "I have never met you before. Please leave me alone. I don't wish to talk to you."

"Oh, none of this nonsense," said he, impetuously, "I don't know why you should repudiate the old acquaintance. I'm sorry you've come down in the world since then. However, there's one sweet thing in a bitter world – give me a kiss for the sake of the jolly old time."

"Go away," said May, feeling a little frightened. "I don't know you, and I don't want to know you."

"Do you really mean to say you are not the girl I had many a lover's walk with at Morecambe?"

"I do really mean to say it. I have never seen you before. If you are a gentleman – please let me alone."

He laughed. "Gentleman!" he repeated.

Then he said, "Well, if you are not the same girl, you are a pretty girl, and one pretty girl's as good to kiss as another. It's long since I had a kiss – pretty girls and women are not for poor devils like me – but now here's my opportunity" – and he slipped his left arm round her waist and tried to draw her face towards him.

"Let me go!" cried May, as she struck him on the head with the enamel basin.

"No, I will not let you go," he said. "I'll have a kiss for the blow."

May struggled to release herself; but he was stronger than she.

"Help!" she shouted, and a man came running up the passage from the street. This man, whom even in the dim light May recognised as the man who had shown her and Mrs. Wilkinson to the lodging-house office, seized May's assailant and shook him off.

"Let the girl be," he said, "or I'll break you neck."

"What's it got to do with you?" said the other man.

"Clear off before I let you see," said May's defender. "I'm not going to argue with you. But if you don't get away I'll kick you away."

The shabby "swell" regarded the other man with a look of contempt. "I don't fight with such refuse as you," he said. Then, turning to May, he made an insulting remark about her character. In an instant the other man struck the "swell" in the face, and followed up the attack by vigorously pushing him and kicking him out of the passage.

Returning, he said to May, "You were going on an errand, weren't you? May I go with you? I don't think that fellow will molest you again – but it's best to be on the safe side."

"I thank you for your protection," said May; and then she went to the uninviting little grocer's shop across the street. Here May purchased a loaf and some milk, and she then crossed back to the lodging-house.

"You've not been in this life long?" asked the man.

"No," said May.

"I guessed not. I hope you'll soon have the good luck to get out of it."

"And I pray the same for you," said May, "indeed, for all – and especially the children. What chance can they have brought up in such surroundings?"

"You talk like one who has known far better days."

"I am only a working-class woman," said May.

They ascended the stairs to the room where Mrs. Wilkinson was waiting.

She said, "You've been a long time, May. Somebody said there was a fight outside. You've not been watching it, have you?"

"I couldn't help seeing it," said May, smiling. "But I've taken no harm. This young man was good enough to look after me."

"Oh, it's our friend who showed us the way to the lodging-house office," said Mrs. Wilkinson. "You seem to be different from the ordinary run of tramps – I suppose you are a labouring man out of employment."

"I'm only common clay, same as the ruck," replied the man. "It's true that I'm not a professional tramp. I'm out of work and hard up, that's the tale; and a common tale, too, in these times."

"Put the milk on," said Mrs. Wilkinson to May, who poured the milk into one of the old pans and set the vessel on the fire.

Other rovers of the road, male and female, haunters of the highway, slouchers of the streets, came into the lodging-house. They were all wet, for the rain had set in steadily for the night, and mostly weary. Some of them had children and babes in arms. One woman had an infant which was very weak and ill; the poor little thing looked pathetic in its silent suffering.

Mrs. Wilkinson looked very serious as she saw this child. "Give it some of this warm milk," she said to the mother, adding quietly to May, "though I am afraid it won't be any use – the child's dying."

They had to force the milk into the child; it was too weak to desire food; it was already half in the arms of death.

"We ought to have a doctor to it," said Mrs. Wilkinson. "Have you had any medicine for the child?"

"No," said the woman, speaking as a statue would speak if it could talk, "How can I pay a doctor?"

"You oughtn't to be tramping the road in this weather with that child," said Mrs. Wilkinson, "it's murder."

"I can't help it," said the woman, "life's murder; it's all murder. I've walked twenty miles to-day, carrying the child, and begging bread. It's a murderous world, and we're all best out of it."

The woman was frozen into an apathy deeper than despair. She had got into the state of one who has lost all effort, who simply submits and slowly rots into extinction.

"Why, the child's dying now!" cried Mrs. Wilkinson, gazing horror-stricken on the little mite gasping on the mother's knee. "Run for a doctor, somebody!"

Too late. The child sighed – and passed out of all sighing. The mother stared at it stolidly as it lay stiffening on her knee. She had no tears; she made no moan. She had sunk below weeping and lamentation. One would have felt relieved had she cried or moaned; she would have looked human then. But the ways of civilisation had turned her into something less than human.

The proprietor of the lodging-house was angry about the affair. He was for turning the woman and her dead babe out. He didn't want any corpses on the premises.

But Mrs. Wilkinson prevailed upon him not to take this course. She pointed out that he would get into trouble with the authorities if he did; for there would have to be an inquest.

So he grudgingly allowed the mother to take the dead child to her bedroom. As the woman carried the child out Mrs. Wilkinson said, "Come back and have a talk with me. Perhaps I shall be able to help you."

The woman made no answer; not even a "Thank you"; but, in a silence that struck one with nameless horror, passed out of the room bearing her little dead burden.

"It's hellish," said Mrs. Wilkinson. "There are hundreds of babies die like that every year on the road – in this great civilised country, this great Christian land. Herod's swift slaughter of the innocents was merciful compared with our system. What are we doing – what is the nation doing – to prevent this terrible infantile massacre? Surely the curse of God will fall upon us for our neglect. Think of the suffering that poor little child must have gone through – hungry – starving – on the cold wet roads. And we permit it. We take no steps to alter such a state of things. We look on it as inevitable. My God! are we monsters, or are we mad?"

The cobbler spread out some of his philosophy and quotations from the poets about life and death.

"Little children who thus die are well off," he said. "Death's nothing. It's the end of us all. What do a few years, more or less, matter?"

[23 May 1908]

III. The "Piecer" on Tramp. (*Continued.*)

"It's not death, so much as the slow suffering that I protest against," said Mrs. Wilkinson. "Death we are unable to abolish; it's got to come to all, though we ought to see that it does not come cruelly and prematurely to anybody, but all this suffering we can prevent, and ought to."

The cobbler looked at her curiously. "You have the talk of an educated person," he said. "You are a strange bird."

Mrs. Wilkinson flushed, then smiled. "There are all sorts of ups and downs in a life," she said.

"Life is all a variorum,"[29] began the cobbler, and quoted on, while Mrs. Wilkinson turned to the young man who had brought the loaf and milk in with May and said, "You, too, seem somewhat different from the rest here."

"You've said that before," said the young man. "We're pretty well all of a bunch," and he and Mrs. Wilkinson and May got so sympathetically into conversation that he told them his history, while others of the vagrants were drinking and singing songs, and passing jokes – some of them very vulgar, and most of them not clean.

"My name's Jim Campbell," he said, "and I am a factory operative. At the age of eleven I went to work in the spinning-room as a piecer, and put in fourteen years or so at that job, eventually becoming what is called a big piecer and waiting my chance for a man's work and a man's wage at a pair of mules. But promotion in the cotton factories largely goes by favouritism, and even if it didn't there are not openings for all the piecers, as you may readily reckon up, when you are told that every spinner is continuously training two or three piecers. Thus I got to the age of twenty-seven, with not much prospect of ever being anything more than a piecer, with a wage of fifteen shillings a week, which is clearly no wage for a man to marry on, is it? And I was courting at this time" – (May looked shyly at him, as if this news was somewhat of a surprise) – "in fact, I had been courting for years, courting a good and bonnie lassie. Anyhow, tired of waiting, and thinking that we might as well marry poor at the age of thirty as at fifty, we got married" – (May looked more quiet astonishment) – "and were as happy as our poverty would permit. Then some of us piecers got talking together, and wondered if nothing could be done to get our wages raised. There were many of us who were married men – some with children – on fifteen to seventeen shillings a week. This meant that the wife had to go out working, too, as well as bearing children –"

"A shameful thing," said Mrs. Wilkinson.

"Well, we piecers talked and talked," said Jim Campbell, "and decided to follow the example of our employers, the operative cotton-spinners, by forming a trade union. I should say we were in a sense compulsory members of the Spinners' Union. We paid a small contribution, but had no voice or vote, which is clearly unfair. So we resolved we would have a union of our own. I should tell you that the operative cotton-spinner is really a middleman betwixt the factory-master and the piecer. The operative spinner, or minder, pays the piecer out of the money made by the spinning-mules of which he is in charge. The factory-master has nothing whatever to do with the piecer; he neither engages him nor discharges him, nor pays his wages. The employers of the piecers are the operative spinners; and, like most middlemen, they look after themselves. The have for themselves anything from two pounds to four pounds a week, while paying the piecers a paltry fifteen or sixteen shillings."

"But the minder has all the responsibility, hasn't he?" asked Mrs. Wilkinson.

"Not much more than the big piecer," replied Campbell, "and the big piecer certainly does as much work as the minder. But we didn't want the minders to divide their earnings with us, we only wanted then to pay us a fair wage – a few shillings more a week."

"And did they object?"

"Rather!" said Jim Campbell, grimly. "Though terrible trade unionists themselves, they objected to their piecers forming a trade union. They smashed our little union up by intimidating the members, and sacking the leading spirits.[30] I was one. And I got the sack – not for wanting to form a trade union, oh no! – my boss was too wily to say that – but for some faults in some cops,[31] common flaws which nothing had ever been said about before. But I know that really I was dismissed for daring to be secretary of the piecers' union. Not only was I dismissed by a trade unionist, instigated by a society of trade unionists, for no more offence than seeking to promulgate trade unionism, but I was also boycotted by the same noble army of trade unionists, who are merely trade unionists so long as it profits themselves, but quite as tyrannic as any other employer when it comes to parting with brass.[32] Not only was I sacked and boycotted, but half a dozen other chaps had the same fate. Two or three listed;[33] some went to Canada; the rest drifted into labouring jobs. That was my barrow. I got occasional employment at foundry-yards, railways, gas-works, and other places, but nothing regular. With the clemming and the worry my wife fell ill, and the baby too."

The narrator paused a moment; mournful memories were at work; there was the sound of a sob in is voice. May looked at him, compassionately, strangely.

"I had had nothing to do for weeks," he said, "nothing at all coming in. We pawned all we could, though we hadn't much to pawn; it was a poor little house, with only the barest necessary cheap furniture – but, poor as it was, it was a happy place to the wife and me and the babe – I would be content with no other heaven – but even that had to know death and destruction. The baby – poor little chap –"

He gulped, then went on bravely: – "Well – he – was very ill – pneumonia – he might have been saved if I had had any money – if we could have afforded – but, well – he died – he died – I thought of him as that woman's baby died on her knee. It's a hell of a world is this for the babies of the poor."

"The woman's not come back yet," said Mrs. Wilkinson. "Perhaps she wishes to be alone with her dead child. But we'll go and see what she's doing if she does not return shortly."

"And then my wife died," said Jim Campbell. "She never got over the loss of the bairn; she fretted a deal about it; but, for all that, I say she was clemmed to death in this rich and Christian land."

He clenched his fist and bowed his head.

"Well," he said at last. "That's a year ago. All that's over. Since then I have been on the road, searching work; I've been through all the filthy horrors of the tramp wards, struggling, starving, not caring very much whether I lived or joined my wife and child in the grave.

IV. In The Bedroom.

At this juncture there came in the "swell" whom Campbell had struck when molesting May. His eye was discoloured. With a stealthy glance at May and Mrs. Wilkinson and the man who had given him the black eye, he went and sat down beside the cobbler, who began to pour poetry upon him, ere long quoting Shelley –

> To suffer woes which Hope thinks infinite;
> To forgive wrongs darker than death or night,
> To defy Power which seems omnipotent;
> To love and bear; to hope till Hope creates
> From its own wreck the thing it contemplates;
> Neither to change nor falter, nor repent;
> This, like thy glory, Titan! is to be
> Good, great, and joyful, beautiful and free;
> This is alone Life, Joy, Empire, and Victory.[34]

"To the divvel wid Poethry!" cried a voice in the Irish brogue, and a gay, blue-eyed man who had just entered, in dripping, ragged clothes, stood up near the fire and addressed the cobbler merrily, "An' are ye still quotin' the classic rhymesters, Matthew Brundy? Begorra, but the last time I saw ye, an' that was in Yorkshire somewhere – wasn't it at ould Gorman's lodgin'-house in Sheffield – ye were slingin' out Shelley or some other wordy wastrel?"

"Why, it's Denny Doolan!" roared half a dozen voices.

"Shure an' it's Denny Doolan, an' who else should it be?" said the Irishman, "just arrived here from goin' up an' down the earth, like the party in Scripter[35] – God save us all from bein' blasfamous – my repecks to th' Pope, an' all the holy tribe – I wouldn't say a word against the saints an' prophets, though I do say, an' mane it, wid regard to religion – may its shadow never grow less – that we could manage to put up wid a bit less of it inside the churches an' a good dale more of it outside."

"Hear, hear," said the cobbler.

"Whist, ye famished echo!" said Denny. "Ye cry 'hear, hear' to everythin' except the tramp-ward skilly an' stone-breakin'.[36] The curse of the snakes of Egypt on yer poethry, Matthew. Poethry's all very swate to sing about, but it's a poor thing to make a supper of. Begorra, an' it's just now I could say grace over somethin' to ait. For the night is wetter than any drink I've had this blessed day, an rawer than any beefsteak that will go into the ould fryin'-pan for me this evenin.'"

[30 May 1908]

IV. In The Bedroom. (*Continued.*)

"Have you been working lately?" inquired a big man, who, from his garb, was evidently a navvy.

"Workin', begorra?" said Denny. "Is it workin' ye remarked? By jabers, I have had neither work nor wages for a month, an' it's perishin' of idleness – not to mention lack of somethin' to digest – that I am this very minute. Look at my togs[37] – a scarecrow would blush at 'em; look at my boots – enough to drive any man off his understandin'. Well, boys, anyhow, we'll have a jolly night. Where's the liquor-jug, an' who's any brass?"

"Will you sing 'Father O'Fynn'?"[38] asked somebody.

"Give me somethin' to sing off," said Denny, "an' I'll sing anything' ye want. Hello!" as he caught sight of the "swell" with his black eye, "there's one man here earned somethin' to-day, though I suspect he'd rather have gone widout the pay. 'Tis a lovely black eye ye have, mate."

"Mind your own business," said the "swell."

"Oh, very well," said Denny. "I was merely prompted by neighbourly civility to take an interest in ye. However, if ye don't like it, it's all one to me. I was only thinkin' that as ye might be purchasin' a lump of steak to doctor the abrasion we might have had it for supper after ye had done wid it."

Amid the laughter raised by this sally, Denny went on, "I'm wonderin' where I have seen ye before – or somebody terribly like ye, young man. Oh, I recollect now: 'Twas when I was coachman for Mr. Landgon – we all know him, the millionaire – has a big house at the sayside – an' I could tell ye some fine tales if I would of the girls that go there – for he's been parted from his wife a long time" – (the "swell" suddenly looked up and listened intently) – "an' his son is marvelously like this young fellow here. But, of course –"

"Why aren't you coachman there now?" asked somebody.

"Ah, there's yer inquisitiveness," said Denny, good-humouredly, "but I don't mind relavin' yer suspense. The raison why I am not now coachmanin' for Mr. Langdon – an' if I am not tellin' ye the sober truth may I never blow the froth off a pint again. Well, one night the horse got drunk –"

"Oh, that'll do, Denny," said somebody.

"Very well – make the tale yerself," said Denny. "I will now take a sate, an' refresh myself."

He sat down by the "swell," who said to him, "So you have worked for Mr. Langdon?"

"Oh, yes – at Sandunes, near Brightpool,[39] ye know," said Denny. "Are ye any relation of his? Begorra, but there's an awful resemblance."

"Well, I may be a relation, but I don't want a din making about it – not now and here, anyhow. You understand?"

"Oh, yes, I'm a divvle to understand," said Denny. "But it's hard luck that ye should be in this state an' Mr. Langdon tumblin' over money every time he lifts his foot."

"We'll alter that," said the young man. "How long is it since you were in his employ?"

"Oh, a couple of years now. I consider he trated me very unfairly. 'Twas but a modest little spree. There were some friends of mine down at Brightpool, an' I went to have an hour or two wid 'em. 'Tis not enough cause to dispense wid the services of a tried an' faithful servant. That I incidentally got locked up for throwin' a base and solemn policeman wid no sense of a joke into the say has very little to do wid the case, though it made a case for me an' got me the sack. Since then I have been on the rocks. I daresay I have taken a glass or two to drown my sorrow, but what's a bottle of ale or two in this vale of tears? If I could only rake up a little capital I would become a donkey proprietor on the sands –"

"I suppose Mr. Langdon carries on in the old style at Sandunes?"

"Oh, yes. What a boy he is for the girls. Solomon in all his glory could not count more concubines.[40] He's got a new un now – a reglar charmer."

"How do you know? You've not been in his employ for a while."

"That's thrue, but I was round there last week. I called to see if he could help an ould sarvant. I saw her in the grounds, an' she would have helped me – she had a swate, kindly face – but for his comin' up. He ordered the servants to kick me out, to set the dogs on me – the ungrateful ould divvle. But she would have helped me, would have given me a dollar, I am sure. She had the givin' face. Ah! she was very much like that young woman sittin' over there. I could almost swear 'twas the same," and he looked towards May.

"What!" said the "swell," rather excitedly.

"'Tis as I say – the very image of that young woman. And you are the very spit of Langdon's eldest son. 'Tis evidently the night for a crop of resemblances."

"May," said Mrs. Wilkinson, "let us go to bed. Those men keep staring at us. The place is getting rowdy; some of 'em are half-drunk, and their talk is foul and coarse."

Bidding good-night to Jim Campbell, who was reading a dirty fragment of old newspaper in which some fried chips had been wrapped, Mrs. Wilkinson and May went to the lodging-house office, where a slatternly young woman lit a small candle-end and said she would show them their room.

"It's time the whole lot was shapin' for bed," she said, as she led the way up a narrow stair, "it's gone ten o'clock. But they'd sit boozin' and campin' all night if we'd let 'em."

Reaching a small room, the young woman who was leading the way opened the door, and shot the dim light of the candle into the dark, cold chamber.

She took a step forward – suddenly stopped – and shrieked.

Peering over her shoulder, Mrs. Wilkinson and May saw, spectral in the uncanny flicker of the candlelight, the mother of the dead baby hanging lifeless against the bed-rail; clasped to her bosom, clutched in the death-grip, was her dead babe.

V. To Bed Again.

Instantly there was a commotion in the lodging-house. A doctor was sent for, and after a considerable time he appeared. The suicide had been left hanging till his arrival, the denizens of the place all declaring, in accord with common notion, that it was against the law to cut down the body till the doctor and the police came.[41] But for this absurd idea the woman's life might have been saved, little as she desired it.

However, when the doctor came, almost simultaneously with a policeman, life was extinct. The woman had hanged herself with her garter – a long piece of thick string.[42] Her baby was so tightly clutched to her bosom that great force had to be used to take the little corpse from the dead mother.

"All Christendom ought to be compelled to see this sad spectacle," said Mrs. Wilkinson. "All those who in their own selfish prosperity assert that all is well with the world ought to see this sight. Perhaps it would touch their hearts and awake their consciences."

Of the dead woman's history little could be gleaned. Some who knew her said she was parted from her husband, and took too much drink.

"Let us not judge her," said Mrs. Wilkinson. "Whatever she was she was a woman and our sister, and the world has not dealt kindly with her and her child."

The lodging-house population remained up later than ever that night; the tragedy gave them an excuse, and a theme for talk. Not that they thought much about death; suffering and death were so common amongst them that they had come to regard all calamities with a philosophic indifference, if not callousness. Some few, however, showed in their subdued demeanour a respectful sympathy towards the event; the end that sooner or later, in one fashion or another, comes to all human clay, whether it be tramp on the road or king on a throne.

[6 June 1909]

V. To Bed Again. (*Continued.*)

The cobbler trotted his inevitable quotations out, giving some lines from Shelley's "Adonais": –

"Peace, peace! he is not dead, he doth not sleep –
He hath awakened from the dream of life –

'Tis we who, lost in stormy visions, keep
With phantoms an unprofitable strife.[43]

Whence are we, and why are we? Of what scene
The actors and spectators? Great and mean
Meet massed in death, who lends what life must borrow.
As long as skies are blue and fields are green,
Evening must usher night, night urge the morrow,
Month follow month with care, and year wake year to sorrow."[44]

Then he spoke a couplet from "The Sensitive Plant": –

"Death itself may be
Like all the rest a mockery."[45]

One man, evidently well educated – some of the others whispered that he had been a clergyman, brought to beggary and disgrace by drink – said he hoped not. When he died he trusted that it would be dreamless sleep for ever. He had had enough of life.

The cobbler began to gabble on the great problem of, Is there a hereafter or not? and Mrs. Wilkinson noted that, despite their oaths and blasphemy, most of the vagrants had a faith in some Almighty Power, whom they regarded with awe, presiding over the universe; and what is perhaps more surprising, though they occasionally growled at their hard luck, they seemed to have some vague, instinctive sense of the justice of their fate, feeling, though they could not tell why, that somehow they had brought it on themselves and deserved it.

Mrs. Wilkinson began to sing the hymn, "Light After Darkness," May helping her. Some of the women joined in; then a few of the men. Other hymns followed; the company starting them themselves. Their favourites were "Jesus, Lover of My Soul," "Lead, Kindly Light," and "Abide with Me,"[46] the last being the most loved. One can easily understand why these two song-poems, with the pictures of forlornness conjured up by the words, appeal to the social outcasts who rove the road and "nightly pitch their moving tent"[47] in tramp wards, workhouses, and dosshouses[48] –

"Lead kindly Light, amid the encircling gloom.
    Lead thou me on:
The night is dark, and I am far from home –
    Lead thou me on."

Mrs. Wilkinson saw that the members of this strange congregation – yet such a gathering as Jesus would have loved, and compassionately moved amongst – were singing with all their souls. They felt what they sang.

"O'er moor and fen, o'er crag and torrent, till
   The night be gone;
And with the morn those angel faces smile
Which I have loved long since and lost awhile."

There were tears trickling down some of the women's faces as they sang these lines. They were thinking of – even now they beheld in vision – the faces of their parents, brothers, sisters, perhaps little children, who had been with them in the long ago, ere they fell into this skulking life of hard ways. May, glancing at Jim Campbell, saw him brush his hand across his eyes; he, too, was musing down the mourning paths of memory, longing for "the touch of a vanished hand, and the sound of a voice that is still."[49]

Then they sang –

"Abide with me, fast falls the eventide;
The darkness deepens – Lord, with me abide.
When other helpers fail, and comforts flee,
Help of the helpless ! O abide with me."

But not all were joining in the hymns. One group was telling experiences and stories, some merely droll, and others lewd and indecent, as well as talking about current crimes, murders, and executions (there had been one that morning), over an ale-jug; another quartette was playing cards for money.

"Begorra, but 'tis doleful we are," said Denny Doolan, "an' the same is a curse to any man, be he rich or poor. If we cannot have money, let us be millionaires of merriment. 'Tis no good saddlin' ourselves wid the dead – God rest their sowls an' all good luck to 'em – but the livin' have to think about life. I only wish I'd got some shekels,[50] begorra I'd invite all the world to a drink. But the grabbin' landlords an' all the other rascals kape us wid empty pockets. I think I'll start a league for the gentle extermination of landlords an' get myself appointed treasurer. However, I'll sing ye a good ould Irish song to be goin' on wid," and he trilled "The Cruiskeen Lawn,"[51] his cronies joining in the chorus.

"But on the whole," said Mrs. Wilkinson to May, "making allowance for their lack of opportunity and environment, these people are no worse than any average batch of human beings in any sphere of life." Then she talked with Jim Campbell, asking him many questions about his experiences in tramp wards and workhouses.

"The tramp wards are terrible," he said. "Gaol is heaven to most of 'em. Convicted criminals get better treatment than genuine working men on the road, in search of work. Our law makes it pleasanter to be a thief than an honest labourer. The prison lodgings and beds are better; the prison fare is better, far more nourishing. I tell you it is impossible for a man, after having a few days of tramp ward diet, to be fit for work. It makes men ill. It weakens them with diarrhoea. If it had been specially designed to kill men off it could not have been worse."

"Are the tramp wards clean?" asked Mrs. Wilkinson.

"Swarming with vermin," said Campbell. "It's impossible to keep clean in them – you need fumigating after you've been in one. How it must be for the women, heaven knows, but it's bad for the men. Dirt! The tramp wards, whether so meant or not, spread dirt and disease, and the country pays in fever and epidemics. It is notorious that epidemics can generally be traced to tramps. But don't blame the tramps so much. The chief blame lies on the authorities, who do not keep the tramp wards clean. I remember going to the tramp ward at Colborough.[52] Of course, we are compelled to have a wash, which would be all right if you really got it as it should be. There were three or four of us in the bath-room together, and one hot water had to do for the lot. There was one man – he was stripped – covered with foul, festering sores. I did not object to him having a bath; but I declined to bathe in the same water. The attendant sent him off, without his bath, and he was given the usual rugs to sleep in. These rugs, without any stoving,[53] were mixed with the other rugs next morning. That's the way to spread disease, isn't it? This man had been on tramp from place to place and could not get to see the doctor. You don't find a tramp ward doctor putting himself out to attend to the inmates. I could tell you worse things of horrible dirt – but that's enough."

"It's more than enough," said Mrs. Wilkinson. "It's too much."

"One can understand the starvation and neglect of tramps, and the heavy, unjust tasks," said Campbell, "when one knows that it's only by such methods that a tramp ward master can keep down his returns. Tramp wards don't help tramps; they punish them. You get only bread and water, and sometimes a bit of cheese, for meals. How can we expect men, generally clemmed to begin with, to keep their strength on such a diet? Tramp wards rob the ratepayer and ill-treat the tramp, who, often enough – though I grant some tramps are born loafers and never mean to work – are bona fide workmen in search of a job. Instead of helping them the tramp wards drive them further down."

Mrs. Wilkinson agreed with him. Then Campbell said, "Well, I'll be getting off to bed. I want to be off soon in the morning for Friartown, on my way to Churcham.[54] They're building a big new workhouse there, and I may get a job."

"We'll pack off to bed, too," said Mrs. Wilkinson.

The young woman in charge of the sleeping arrangements took them upstairs again to another room, the one they were to have at first being occupied by the body of the woman who had committed suicide and her child.

Mrs. Wilkinson and May were put into the room next to the chamber of the dead.

"It's rather gruesome," said Mrs. Wilkinson, "but we shall have to put up with it; and the dead can do us no harm. God grant the poor soul and her bairn are in peace."

While they were undressing a woman of about fifty came into the room, which contained two beds, each bed to accommodate two persons.

"I wonder who's to sleep with me to-night," said the woman. "I hope it's somebody clean." She was not communicative, but Mrs. Wilkinson elicited that her trade was begging. She grumbled that times were bad – never worse; it was hard to pick up one's meat and drink.

Before Mrs. Wilkinson and May were fully undressed the candle-end went out, and they could not make any investigation of the bed.

However, they got in, and soon discovered, very uncomfortably, that they were not the only tenants of the bed – by dozens![55]

VI. On The Way To The Workhouse.

In the morning, after a "plagued" and restless night, Mrs. Wilkinson and May got up as soon as the dull day broke, and set about freeing themselves from the insect pests that had crawled and bit themselves into intimate acquaintance. It took them a long half-hour to get moderately free of the entomological specimens, which were as diverse as numerous, big and little, all sorts and sizes.

"Well, May," said Mrs. Wilkinson, "we shall never get wholly free of these things till we can have a bath, plenty of carbolic soap, and privacy for decency's sake. It's a shame that our civilisation does not see that better bedding is provided for those on tramp, even if only for cleanliness, let alone Christianity. It's impossible for any tramp woman to get clean again after sleeping in such a bed. Anyhow, we must make the best of it."

Having dressed, the descended, not without scratching on the way, to the dining and living room, which, unswept, untidied, was repulsive in the light of day. There was the refuse of a week, dirty paper, fragments of food, dust-heaps, and worse, lying on the floor.

Mrs. Wilkinson and May had small appetites for breakfast. They desired to get out of the place as soon as they could.

While they were having a cup of tea in the old uninviting enamel cups, Jim Campbell came to them.

"I'll bid you good morning," he said. "I've had my breakfast, and I'm off. I've a long tramp in front of me to-day. It looks like more rain, too."

"We hope you'll have good luck," said Mrs. Wilkinson.

"The same to you, and twice as much," said Jim Campbell. "Good morning."

And he was off, rather hurriedly, it seemed to May.

[13 June 1908]
VI. On The Way To The Workhouse. (*Continued.*)

"He's no a bad man, that," said Mrs. Wilkinson. "I wonder if we shall ever see him again. Perhaps not. Never. I feel interested in him. I like him. Yet fate may bear him down, and down, and with all his striving he may perish in the gutter. This is no state of things for a Christian land."

The young "swell" tramp who had sought to be familiar with May the evening before, took his departure soon after Jim Campbell. As he was going he looked at May and Mrs. Wilkinson, but said nothing.

Shortly afterwards Mrs. Wilkinson said: "We'd better be going, too, May."

* * *

In the twilight of the same day Mrs. Wilkinson and May were walking along the paved highroad to the manufacturing town of Rackington, whose lights lay before them, almost close at hand, the great lit-up cotton factories showing conspicuously.

"I wonder if we shall find the workhouse at Rackington any better than the lodging-house we were in last night," said Mrs. Wilkinson. "God help our poor sisters of the road!"

Presently they overtook a middle-aged woman hobbling laboriously and painfully along. In reply to Mrs. Wilkinson's inquiry as to the location of the workhouse, the woman said, "I'm going there myself, and I'll show you the way if you don't mind going slow. I'm awful troubled with the rheumatism in my legs."

"All right, we'll go together," said Mrs. Wilkinson. "How long have you been on the road?"

"Me? Years. But I wasn't always so. I was respectable once, and had fine times of it. But that's got nothing to do with anybody but me, has it?" And the woman relapsed into silence, broken only by grumblings at her pains, till they came to a public-house, when she said: "I could just do with a drink of whiskey. I should feel all right then. Whiskey's good for rheumatism. Are you absolutely hard up? You couldn't lend me twopence, could you? I'll pay you back someday, as sure as there's a God in Heaven. If I'd only the least drop of whiskey I could get along ever so much better.

"You may have this twopence," said Mrs. Wilkinson.

"Thank you, thank you," said the woman greedily taking the coppers, and Mrs. Wilkinson and May noticed, in the light from the window of the inn, that, though bedraggled and fouled and debased to ugliness now, this woman must once have been beautiful. But her face was loathsome now; the eyes were bleary, bloodshot; she looked a hideous old hag.

"Won't you come in and have a drink, too?" she said.

"No, that's all the money we have," said Mrs. Wilkinson. "Be sharp and get your whiskey, and the we'll get along to the workhouse."

In a couple of minutes the woman rejoined Mrs. Wilkinson and May.

"The landlord wasn't for letting me have it at first," she said. "He said they didn't serve the likes of me. But I told him my money was as good as anybody else's, and let him have some of my tongue; so he let me have the whiskey to get rid of me. Ah, there was a day when such upstarts would have gone on their knees to me, when I walked into their pubs flinging five-pound notes about. Ah, those were the days!"

The liquor had loosened her tongue, for she continued, as they walked along, "Yes, you may not believe it, but I was a handsome young woman once –"

"We can well believe it," said Mrs. Wilkinson. "'Tis a pity you should fall to this."

"Pity, ay! That comes of being a beauty – that was the mischief of it. Do you know? – he was a rich gentleman that took me up. He was downright in love with me; he'd do anything for me. No; I'll not tell you his name, that wouldn't do; but if I can only manage to walk the distance I'll go to see him, for he's alive yet, respectable and married, though he lives apart from his wife now. Ah! I'll warrant he never found one to suit him as I did. Yes, and I'll go to see him – he lives at Sandunes by the sea, and I've got the address all right, but it's a long way, a very long way, and my feet are so slow. If somebody would only give me the railway fare now, it's only a few shillings – but when on earth shall I ever have a few shillings in my pocket again, I who used to have pounds, and dresses that cost a mint of money? But I'll get to see him if I can, for it's only fair that he should do something for me – the one who ruined me, as they say. Sometimes I feel I could curse him – ay, I will curse him, for he is as selfish as the devil! – he thinks of nothing but himself and his damned respectability! But I'll let him see if he doesn't do the decent thing – I'll raise a row at his very door, even if I get locked up for it – that would be nothing new; I'm well used to the gaol now; and he'd think no more of sending me to prison than of throwing a burnt match away. For he sent me to gaol once – that's years ago. I called on him, and he ordered me out. His servants put me out, and because I resisted, and sent a stone through his drawing-room window they fetched the police and had me locked up, and I got seven days for being drunk and disorderly, though I was no more drunk than I am now. But I have been drunk often enough since; drunk all day – drunk all the night, if I can get it, drunk year in, year out, for one forgets when one is drunk. But it's all his fault – curse him, curse him!" and her voice became a shriek.

Mrs. Wilkinson almost wished she had not given the woman the money for the whiskey.

"Calm yourself," she said. "Don't shout."

"I'm not shouting, but I will shout if I want. Haven't I cause to shout? Curse him, and curse my mother, too, she sold me to him. My mother knew what it meant, and I didn't. Yes, my mother, although she knew when he came and gave her fifty pounds to let me go into his service, jumped at the offer, and sold her virgin daughter for filthy gold. She thought it a fine thing, something to be proud of, that such a gentleman should take a lustful fancy to her daughter – she bowed and abased herself before him as if it was the proper thing for rich gentlemen to buy the girls of the poor as one buys horses and cows – she thought it was an honour! Good God! and she was my own mother! Curse him, and curse her, too! May she never rest in her grave; may she have to haunt the earth unable to get a minute's ease; may –"

"Nay, don't curse your mother," said Mrs. Wilkinson.

"Why shouldn't I? She has cursed me. If I had known; if I had only known – but when I knew it was too late to do anything except keep on this path to hell."

"It is never too late," said Mrs. Wilkinson.

"None of your parson cant," said the woman. "Let the parsons talk of what they know, and then we might listen to them. Parsons, bless you; they're as bad as the rest, and worse. I could tell you some tales about the parsons. Curse 'em and their preaching, and all their humbug! Parsons are no different from all other men, and all men only look at a woman in one way. That's all they think about. There's not the odd one that doesn't! Curse the parsons; they toady to such as him my mother sold me to, because of the money. Where money and women are concerned your parson's just the same hog as other men – curse 'em all!"

Mrs. Wilkinson thought she might pacify the woman by turning the theme.

"Have you no children?" she asked.

"Children!" said the woman, "ha, ha! – children, yes; I had two by him – curse him! – a girl and a boy. The girl died – lucky kid – but the boy lived – he grew up – worse for him!' – but what's become of him I don't know! A fine boy, too; a bonny boy. He deserved a different father – my boy! – I wonder where he is this night – perhaps houseless on the road as I am."

"Hope for the best," said Mrs. Wilkinson. "Perhaps he's all right."

[20 June 1908]

VI. On The Way To The Workhouse. (*Continued.*)

"I doubt it. His father never did much for him – curse his father! – he insulted me over the child! – declared that he wasn't the father! – curse the wretch! There was his friend – no, I'll not mention names; but he was another rich man, and played the same game. I'll admit he was fond of me, for I was a woman to be fond of in those days, and the two men quarreled about me; broke a lifelong friendship and have never spoken since. It's rum what men will do about women, isn't it? – curse 'em all, all the men – they're all alike! The men are beasts, and we women are fools – that's the top and the bottom of it!"

The three were now close upon the workhouse gates; the lamp at the entrance shone dingily on the iron bars, damp with the November night-mist.

"Here we are," said the whiskeyed woman. "I wonder if old Gubble's in charge of the door to-night."

"Who is Gubble?" asked Mrs. Wilkinson.

"One of the inmates. Just a pauper like ourselves. But a pauper put in authority is just like all other men with power – looks on women as prey. Pauper or prince, they're all alike when they sniff a woman, and if they can force her to their way they will. Gubble tries his tricks on with all the women who seek admission – especially if they are young. Ay, they're all alike, tramp or duke; give 'em a chance and they'd have a harem. It's not only so at this workhouse, but at most of 'em. At Wagginden Workhouse the portress leaves the women entirely at the mercy of one of the men, and he does just what he likes with 'em."

"They ought to defy and expose him," said Mrs. Wilkinson, indignantly.

"Oh, talk's all very nice," said the woman, "but when you're desperate and dead-beat, and hungry, and run down by the workhouse diet, and are dying for a shelter and a bite, how much resistance can you muster up? You'd be inclined to say to yourself, 'What does it matter?' and give in, and join the swine like all the rest."

"It's a horrible state of things," said Mrs. Wilkinson.

It was nearly six o'clock when they rang the bell at the workhouse lodge. A middle-aged man, with a sensual face, admitted them – "it's Gubble," said the woman who knew – and, staring hard at May, began to ask the usual questions – name, where they had come from, where they had slept last night, etc.

This lonely gate-office, superintended by this man, was some distance from the workhouse buildings; and, as Mrs. Wilkinson said to herself, any female tramp coming to this place was entirely at the mercy of this fellow, or who else was in charge; there ought to be a woman to admit and interrogate women.

While Gubble was questioning the trio an aged man in rags, clearly very destitute and very ill, came in.

"Clear off," said Gubble, "you were here three weeks ago."

"Let me in," pleaded the poor fellow. "Don't turn me out."

"Pack off," said Gubble, domineeringly – and Mrs. Wilkinson noted, with pain, how one pauper in authority can lord it over another pauper in his power, when one would think that a fellow-feeling and memory of similar experience would stir to sympathy. "Be off," said Gubble. "You were here three weeks ago, and you know The Law." (He uttered the words The Law with all the impressive emphasis he could.) "The Law ways you can't sleep at the same workhouse twice in one month."

"I know, I know," said the outcast, piteously, "but what am I to do? Where am I to go? If I stop out to-night it will kill me!"

"Good job, too," said Gubble. "You'll be no more cost to the rates then."

May, try as hard as she could to restrain herself, could not help saying to Gubble, "Remember that you are on the rates, too."

"Oh!" said Gubble. "Who asked you to speak, madam? I'll deal with you presently. So I'm on the rates, too, am I? Well, I do earn my keep, and that's more than this fellow can say." He tuned to the old applicant again. "Clear off, now. You're not coming in here."

"Oh, let me in," said the old man. "I can't reach another workhouse to-night."

"That's nothing to do with me. Out you go!"

The forlorn old man limped away – out into the night and the cold – nowhere to lay his head.

"Somebody's father – somebody's baby once," said Mrs. Wilkinson to herself. "And this is the way we treat our fellow men in a Christian land!"

"And now," said Gubble to Mrs. Wilkinson and the other woman, "you two may go – across the yard there, to the Tramp Ward. I've a few words to say to this person," glancing at May.

"She'll come along with us," said Mrs. Wilkinson.

"Didn't I tell you?" whispered the other woman to Mrs. Wilkinson. "He's a pig."

"None of your whisperin'," said Gubble, savagely. "Off you go – or else I'll turn you out."

"I shan't go unless she goes," said Mrs. Wilkinson, stepping alongside May.

"And I say you shall!" stormed Gubble. "I'll let you see who's master here."

"Why do you want her remain behind?" asked Mrs. Wilkinson, looking Gubble full in the eyes.

"That's my business," said Gubble, avoiding her gaze.

"Unless you tell me, and give me a satisfactory answer," said Mrs. Wilkinson, "she goes with us."

"And who are you?" roared Gubble, "to put questions to me?"

"I am a woman," said Mrs. Wilkinson, "and I will be treated as such."

Gubble sneered. "You're a female tramp," he said, "and we all know what female tramps are."

Mrs. Wilkinson was wrathful now. She strode up to Gubble. He shrank before her. Something in her mien, her eyes – something of the majesty of the pure woman – frightened him.

"Say another word," she said, "and my companion and I will instantly quit this place. We will go straight to the nearest police station and report your conduct. For I know your foul purpose – I know how you have taken base advantage of other women who have come here. Now stand aside and let us pass."

Like the cur and the coward he was, Gubble was silent, though full of rage at being baulked.

Mrs. Wilkinson and May walked out of the office into the workhouse yard. There they waited for the other woman, and they heard Gubble say to her as she stepped away from the door, "Two terrors those – but I can see you are of different stuff. You're just the right age for a bit of fun. Come down later on, and I'll get you a cup of tea, and we'll have a talk," and he slipped his arm round her and tried to kiss her.

She broke away with a coarse joke, and joined Mrs. Wilkinson and May, saying, "My word! how you did flare up at Gubble! It's a wonder he didn't turn you out."

"He's have known about it if he had," said Mrs. Wilkinson. "In fact, he may as it is."

"It's no use bothering," said the woman. "The poor can do nothing. His bosses would believe him against you any day. Now, didn't I tell you what he was? He fancied this young woman – your daughter, I suppose – as a nice morsel. Didn't I tell you. All the men are alike – from pauper to prince – all alike! curse 'em! It's best to pretend to humour 'em – and fool 'em! I know what the men are! – I know what men are! Curse 'em!"

VII. In The Workhouse And The Tramp Ward.

The tramp ward in the workhouse was an oblong room. There were six bedsteads, with wire mattresses and pillows of dirty straw. There was also a wooden table. On the wall was a notice-board – "Regulations for Tramps."

The windows on one side overlooked the yard where the male tramps did their tasks. These windows were painted, but one had been broken and replaced with plain glass. Perhaps the authorities had found it necessary to leave one window through which the women could see the men; it was better to do this than have the frame constantly broken on the sly. For male and female seek each other everywhere, even in workhouses and tramp wards, as Mrs. Wilkinson and May had discovered. On quitting the tramp ward in Bolborough one morning a few weeks ago, they had found a couple of men from the male ward awaiting them. The males are turned out before the females; but they usually hang about till the women are released. The two men wanted to "pick up" with Mrs. Wilkinson and May, and it was only with difficulty that they shook them off.

[27 June 1908]
VI. On The Way To The Workhouse. (*Continued.*)

But not only was it male tramps who regarded tramp women with eyes of lust; workmen, and others they met on the road, were just as guilty of the same insult. It is almost impossible for a destitute woman to keep her virtue. As one female tramp had said to Mrs. Wilkinson, "You've got to pick up with a man in order to protect yourself from the other men."

The matron, a motherly-looking woman, now came into the room, and Mrs. Wilkinson and May said they would like a bath. They had the bath-room to themselves.

Then they were given blue nightgowns, which, though they had been used before, were tolerably clean, though rather dirty about the neck and stained in places. Mrs. Wilkinson hoped they had been "stoved",[56] but found that such is not the daily custom in all workhouses, though the Government regulations say that a clean garment may be demanded.

For supper they were given a small can of hot gruel and a piece of dry bread. They were hungry enough to eat almost anything, but this was not very palatable.

Then at eight o'clock, the room-door was locked by a man, and the five female inmates of the room were left alone – to go to bed.

Mrs. Wilkinson was disturbed by the fact that a man had the key of the room, and could not get to sleep for a long time.

"Well, May, are you asleep?" she asked of her young companion.

"Not yet," replied May. "I'm cold, and I can't get rid of an impression of uncleanliness."

"It's as good as we may expect in these places," said Mrs. Wilkinson. "Tramp wards and workhouses do not make for cleanliness."

However, they got to sleep at last.

In the morning, after breakfast – thin gruel and dry bread again – Mrs. Wilkinson and May, in departing, asked the matron to accompany them to the gate, because there might be insolence from Gubble. Mrs. Wilkinson informed the matron of Gubble's conduct, and that lady said she would report it to the authorities – the Workhouse Committee.[57]

Rain was falling in a chilly drizzle as they walked away from the workhouse. They walked on alone, having left the other three women behind; indeed, to Mrs. Wilkinson's disgust, their companion of the night before, the woman who cursed all the men, was chatting familiarly with Gubble, though, no doubt, only to wheedle something out of him.

"Well, May," said Mrs. Wilkinson, as they went along, "I feel that a few weeks of this life, with the starving diet and the filthy surroundings, will reduce me to the level of the veriest tramp slut. There is no opportunity for cleanliness, and the food is enough to take all the vitality out of anyone. No wonder the tramps sink and sink, too feeble ever to rise again, especially the women. Oh, want an awful world this is for the woman who has no home!"

* * *

In the afternoon, Mrs. Wilkinson and May approached the manufacturing town of Waddiham. It was still raining. It had rained all day – that deadly, dismal downpour characteristic of the moist shire of shuttles and spindles.

The highway was lonesome. On the moor-sides were scattered farms, but only here and there a few little clusters of cottages by the roadside. The dull November afternoon, wet, misty, concealed the adjacent mountains behind a great grey veil.

Occasionally they met a vehicle, and once a postman; but for the most part the two women had the path and the prospect to themselves.

"How can any, except the very strongest, fail to become an utter failure in this tramp life?" said Mrs. Wilkinson. "How can any man help but drop to reckless despair, when he is foodless, ill-clad, and nothing but the workhouse bed and fare before him? Our present workhouse and tramp ward system does nothing but manufacture tramps – grind unfortunate workingmen into helpless vagrants and vagabonds. As for the women – oh, the insults the women get!" and she recalled her experience in a workhouse the week before, where, on seeking admission, the porter had been familiar and objectionable, asking where her husband was, and then insinuating that she led an immoral life.

It was quite dark, when, weary and wet through, Mrs. Wilkinson and May reached Waddiham Casual Ward, after being directed there by a policeman.

The Casual Ward was situated in a low neighbourhood. There were five or six men and two or three women waiting for admission, and as the gate would not be opened for a quarter of an hour, Mrs. Wilkinson and May took a short stroll, looking longingly at some poor but cosy working-class houses they passed, for these, howsoever humble they were, possessed the beauty and the glory of home. Mean though they were, what a contrast they were too the forbidding Tramp Ward.

When they returned the gates were opened, but the waiting was not all over. They had to stand outside in an old, dilapidated shed, the rain coming through the roof. There were four or five women now, and a number of men, about a dozen. Most of them were in their prime, clearly genuine working-men in search of labour. Only two or three seemed to be of the irreclaimable "moucher" brand.

Presently the office window opened, and a man in uniform proceeded to catechize the tramps. Married couples were to give name and address, and age; also whence they came and where they were going.

The official was curt and cold, and addicted to bullying.

"Have you been here before?" he would demand.

"No."

"Then see you don't come again." Or

"Where have you come from?"

"Raddington."

"Why didn't you stop there, then? What do you come here for, sponging on the rates?"

"I've a right, haven't I?" said the man thus addressed. "I've paid rates in my time."

"Shut up! No cheek! or you'll get put in your place."

"Why doesn't somebody put bullyragging officials into their place?" wondered Mrs. Wilkinson.

This official – whose name was Slamdrop – was exceedingly sharp with all the casuals. There was one poor woman with a bandaged head he ordered to get away quick or he would have her in gaol as an impostor. "And all you women will have to stay two nights and pick three pounds of oakum,"[58] he said.

Mrs. Wilkinson felt her heart sink as she listened to Slamdrop's volleys of abuse. Then came her turn and May's.

"Have you been here before?" snapped Slamdrop.

"No."

"What are you doing here, then?"

"I am on my way to join my husband."

"Well, you've no right to be here imposing on the rates. Do you know I could give you three months for it? I've a good mind to send you off tramping in search of your husband to-night instead of letting you sleep here to burden the rates. Have you any children?"

"Yes."

"Is this one?" pointing to May.

"No."

"Where are your children?"

"I don't know."

"You're evidently a bad character, deserting your children and tramping the country."

"Oh, no, I'm not."

"How dare you speak back? See you don't come here again."

"I won't."

"Well, if you do," said Slamdrop, "it will be the worse for you. I shall remember your face."

And Mrs. Wilkinson felt sure she would never forget Slamdrop's face, with the sharp, cruel eyes, the low forehead, the thin lips, and the heavy-bearded jaw.

Turning to May, Slamdrop said, "And what are you, a young woman, doing, going about the country with a reprobate like this? You must be no better. I know your game – don't think you can deceive me. You are two street-walkers.

Mrs. Wilkinson and May flushed, the former having hard work to keep back an indignant denial; but that would only have made matters worse; probably have meant ejection from the tramp ward – out into the bleak and bitter night.

"Oh, Mrs. Wilkinson," said May, feeling distressed at the foul charge, as they passed on into the trap ward, "do I look like a prostitute?"

"No, no, my dear," said Mrs. Wilkinson. "Don't worry about that man's words. He judges all tramps alike. But somebody ought to check him, and he shall be told of this some day."

The tramp ward was a big room, furnished with a table and a few forms. It was one of the rooms of a little old factory, which had been economically converted to use for casuals. There was no fire, and the building was draughty.

The female tramps were given a bowl of gruel with a slice of bread.

The table and floor were clean.

The meal finished, the female tramps were taken to the bathroom, two at a time, and there was water to the depth of about six inches in the bath. A notice said this was the regulation supply.

[4 July 1908]

VI. On The Way To The Workhouse. (*Continued.*)

The woman attendant hurried them through the bath, and then gave each woman a coarse garment of dark blue bathing flannel,[59] which just covered the elbows and hardly came down to the knees.

Then the women were marched into the dormitory of plank beds, being given three blankets, one for underneath and two for cover. A small gas-jet was left burning, and in the dim light the rafters above looked gaunt and spectral. Mrs. Wilkinson and May soon found out that the human body was not made to accommodate itself to a plank bed, even when eased by a few blankets.

"You can't get to rest on this thing," she said to May. "It's not a bed, but an instrument of torture. If you lie on your back your hips suffer, and you have to raise your knees, and then the air comes under the blanket; if you lie on your side you soon feel sore and cramped in the shoulder and hips. If you put more blanket under you you've none to cover you, and suffer from the cold – it's awful whatever way you do."

May felt exactly the same. She turned this way and that way to rest, but in vain.

The other inmates were in the same plight. They could not sleep. Some were squirming and groaning and complaining; all were uttering exclamations of discomfort and misery.

"My God, what a hell-hole!" said one woman who had started up for the fifth or sixth time out of troubled slumber.

"I've never been used to this," said an old woman of over sixty. "I'd sooner be in my grave! I wish I'd died ere ever I came to this! I've never been in a tramp ward before, and only in the workhouse to sleep twice. If I could only find my son I should be all right. I've tramped to Bolborough – he worked in the factory there – to find that he was out of work and his wife and child dead, and so he had gone on tramp."

Both Mrs. Wilkinson and May instantly thought of the piecer, Jim Campbell, whom they had met in the common lodging-house at Blakeham – was this poor white-haired old soul his mother?

"I'm not used to this," the old woman went on, querulously, pathetically. "I'd a good home till my husband died a few months ago. Lord, who'd ever ha' thought this would have happened to me? We never know what we shall come to before the end. I wish I were in my grave and at rest, though I don't want a pauper's grave. It's not fair after working hard all my days. And I should have been well off if my husband had had his rights. He used to work for Mr. Langdon, who's a millionaire now, I am told; but Landgon didn't do right by him – got all his ideas, sucked his brains and then threw him aside. A clever man was my husband, and so is my lad Jim, too, wherever he is. He left Brunborough to go working in the factory at Bolborough, and settled there, and married. But now it's all over; his wife dead, and he gone, perhaps dead, too."

"No, I don't think he's dead," said Mrs. Wilkinson.

"Why, have you seen him?" cried the old woman. "No, he must be dead. He wouldn't let me be in this plight if he were alive. For he was a good lad, was Jim, always good to his mother."

"I'm sure he was," said Mrs. Wilkinson, "and perhaps he'll find you, and be good to you again."

Mrs. Wilkinson prayed so, for she was sure that this old woman's son was Jim Campbell. Should she tell the old woman she had met him? What if she did, giving her a hope and then the poor fellow, never getting any chance to help his mother, was unable to get out of the tramp's rut? For certainly the odds were against him. What a wickedly unjust world it was to keep a man down so that he could not make his living and help his mother. What were the rulers and lords and bishops doing to let such a state of things exist?

"Ah, no!" said the old woman, "I fear he must be dead. Something must have happened to him, or I should have heard from him. Ah, me, my Jim! my poor Jim! Husband gone – son gone. I am a poor old woman left all alone on the brink of the grave."

Mrs. Wilkinson could hold back no longer. She felt that she must give this solitary old soul a bit of comfort.

"Your son is alive," she said.

"Alive! How do you know?" cried the old creature.

"I have seen him. We met him in a common lodging-house at Blakeham. He said his name was Jim Campbell, he was a piecer, and had lost his wife and child."

"That's my son," said the old woman excitedly. "But where is he now? Perhaps gone to Brunborough to seek me, and I not there. Perhaps he's been there while I was seeking him, and now we may never find each other again. What did he say? How did he look?"

"He looked in fairly good health, and was going to Churcham to seek work," said Mrs. Wilkinson.

"Churcham? Where's that?"

"Through Friartown – on the way to Brightpool. They are building a new workhouse there, and he thought he might get on as a labourer."

"Churcham – it's a long way off, then. And if I follow him and he has not got work there, I should not know where to seek him. Oh, what must I do?"

"I should advise you to go to Brunborough and stay there," said Mrs. Wilkinson; "for he is sure to go there again in search of you. If he gets work at Churcham he is certain to seek you out. He would slip over some week-end to find you. For I am sure he is not the sort of son to forget his old mother."

"He is not," said the old woman, whimpering. "He was always good to me. It would break his heart if he knew my plight – no home, and nothing before me but the workhouse. Ay, he would be in a way if he knew I had been on tramp, and putting up in tramp wards, where one gets nothing but insults. The man who let me in here to-night called me an old cadger, and said I ought to be put in gaol, and I have never begged in my life, nor asked anybody for help till lately. And what could I do? Must poor old folks lie down in a ditch and die? Ay, ay, that would be better – then we should be no bother to anybody."

"Don't worry about what the man said here," said Mrs. Wilkinson. "He's a bully."

"If my Jim had been here he would have knocked him down for talking so to me," said the old woman. "But when one's poor, one's to submit to everything – to put up with impudence, and cruel words, and insults. But it's not good enough that an old woman, who has worked hard all her life, and always paid her way, and doesn't owe anything to anybody – I've gone short of food and clothes to pay my way – should be treated so. It's not good enough, is it?"

"It certainly isn't good enough," said Mrs. Wilkinson, "and some day there will be a change for the better. Some day all men and women who have worked hard during their youth and prime will not be thrown out on the roads and into the workhouses when they are old, but will be given justice and treated with respect."

"Ah, that will be all right," said the old woman, "but I fear that 'some day' will never come – not in this world. We shall have to wait for it till we get to heaven, where there are no tramp wards and workhouses. I can't forget what that man in the office said to me. Called me a lazy old loafer – me who has slaved hard all my life, and brought up my children decent, and always paid my way. Lazy old loafer, he said, and looked on me as a dog. Has he never had a mother of his own – and how would he like somebody to talk to her like that?"

'Have you no other children besides Jim?" asked Mrs. Wilkinson.

"A girl in Canada," said the old woman. "She's married – went out there many years ago. She wanted me to go to her, and I wish I had gone now. If I find Jim we'll both go out to Canada to our Lucy. She'll welcome us, I know. Yes, we'll go if we can only raise the money; but Jane[60] will help us with that, if she can. Yes, I think we'll go to Canada, Jim and I. It can't be a worse place than this, can it?"

"Are Jim and Lucy all your children?"

"Yes, all that's alive. There were five others, but they died young. The poor bury a deal of babies, you know. It's got to be a tough baby that lives to grow up amongst the poor. Well, well! There was Willie, and Sarah, and Harry, and Maggie – fine young men and women they'd have been now if they'd lived. Willie would have been twenty-three – a bonny baby was Willie – I wish he'd lived. The scarlet fever took him off, and Sarah, too; both in one week. Ah, that was a sad week. Well, well, they're better off, better off; and Harry and Maggie, too. Harry died of pneumonia, and Maggie of croup.[61] I remember Maggie as if it was but last night. How the poor little thing choked. Ah, it was awful! Why does God punish little innocent children so? Well, well, they're all in the grave, long ago, and I would I were with them. For the sooner we die the more trouble we miss. Ah, my babies, my bonny babies. I am old and weary, and I wish I were with you; at rest! at rest!"

VIII. The Dreary Pauper Day – And Night Again.

There was little sleep in the tramp ward. The plank beds would not permit it.

"It's better in the grave," said the old woman – whom the others began to address as "Grannie" – "one can find rest there."

But the night passed, as all things must, even of torture, and in the morning, after the thin breakfast, the women tramps were set to work – to do something for the keep and lodgings they had had at the expense of the rates.

Grannie was too ill and weak to do anything. She was allowed to lie on a form while the others scrubbed the floor.

"Well, May," said Mrs. Wilkinson, "I don't feel much like singing; but let's see if a hymn will do us any good," and she started "Rock of Ages."[62]

Grannie lay listening then she said: "This life makes one think there cannot be a God. What have I done that I should come to this? Can you tell me that? Can God answer it?"

"Never mind, Grannie," said Mrs. Wilkinson, "all this world and its ways is a mystery. You'll not be in it long, perhaps, but in a better place."

"You mean heaven," said Grannie. "Well, there ought to be a heaven, anyhow, for the likes of us that's suffered here. But I begin think that if there's a heaven they'll not allow tramps – it'll be kept select for the rich, same as this world is."

[11 July 1908]
VIII. The Dreary Pauper Day – And Night Again. (*Continued.*)

"Nay, Grannie," said Mrs. Wilkinson, "God is sure to give you a good place in the kingdom."

"I don't know," said Grannie. "I'm no great sinner that I know of, and I think I'm entitled to some heaven; only I'm not making sure of anything now. Anyhow, if I go to hell –"

"Nay, never, Grannie," said May.

"As I was saying," said Grannie, "if I go to hell I'm sure I shall meet my tormentors there – all them workhouse chaps – and then I'll throw bricks at 'em for all eternity."

"Hot bricks," said Mrs. Wilkinson, with a smile; but Grannie was in no joking mood.

"You ought to forgive 'em, Grannie," said Mrs. Wilkinson. "We are told to love our enemies, you know."

"That doesn't work in this world," said Grannie, "nor in any other, I'm thinking. For if it does, why doesn't God forgive his enemies instead of sending 'em to hell?"

This was a poser for Mrs. Wilkinson.

"I can't help hating the workhouse bullies," said Grannie. "It's nature, and I can't help it. Even if it keeps me out of heaven I hate 'em – hate 'em all!"

Mrs. Wilkinson was not surprised. It is easy to love our enemies theoretically, especially if we are comfortable and they cannot harm us; but in practice, and when the enemies are harassing and hurting us every day, it is another matter.

There was a woman of about fifty years of age, with a pleasant face and manner, scrubbing steadily away.

May and Mrs. Wilkinson got talking with her as they worked together.

"It's hard work isn't it?" said May.

"Hard it is, sure enough," said the woman with a tired smile, "but it's a hard world, and we can't expect anything else. I wonder how my husband's going on. He's in the men's ward. He's not well; got an awful cough. I know him by that cough. Soon as we get out of the tramp ward, where he'll wait or me, and I hear that cough, I know it's him."

"Have you been long on the road?" asked May.

"No; I came out of the Brunborough Workhouse, me an' my old man are going back there."

"Why did you come out? Weren't you comfortable?"

"Oh, yes; as comfortable as one can be in a workhouse. Why did we come out? Well, I heard that my sister in Chorham was dying, so we thought we'd like to see her before she passed away. But we were only in time for the funeral. It's nearly a forty mile tramp from Brunborough, and we had to walk all the way, and we've walked all the way back."

"Was there nobody to give you the fare?"

"Ah, well, you see, my sister's husband has enough to do, I dare say, though he keeps a grocer's shop and seems flourishing. He did lend me and my husband some things to attend the funeral, seeing that we'd tramped forty miles to show our respects to the dead. I would have walked there if it had been a hundred miles, for she was my sister, and we were very fond of each other, though our ways parted when we married – marrying does scatter a family and bring strange changes, doesn't it? Well, she was luckier than I – and I'm glad of it. I was the black sheep of the family. I married a man my parents didn't like, because he had poor prospects; but we've been very happy together, and I wouldn't swap him for any other husband in the world. If he'd only had luck he'd have got on, for he's plenty of talent; but the luck's always been against him. Perhaps you don't believe in luck, but what else is it? Why does everything one man does turn out a failure, while everything another does brings prosperity? No, it's not drink or idleness. My man is neither drunken nor lazy, and yet he's at the bottom, while many who are neither sober nor industrious are at the top. No, it's all luck, and what we're born to. If a man's born to get on he'll get on, and nothing can stop him. He may make mistakes, and be careless, but he'll get on all the same, while if a man's born not to get on he'll go down, not matter how thrifty and careful he may be. Misfortune will pounce on him at every unexpected corner. For it's so, though heaven knows why it should be so. Now, I've finished my scrubbing; shall I help you with yours?"

"No thank you," said May, "though it's very kind of you to offer," and she felt an affection for this woman, who, though beaten to the ground by the fates, yet kept a cheerful countenance and a kindly word and a helping hand for others.

"So you are resigned to your lot – to die in the workhouse?" said May.

"What else is there for us?" said the woman. "I'd rather have it otherwise, if it could be; but as not, then I must make the best of it. But what can be done? My husband can do nothing now; he's a perpetual invalid. Ah! and he was so clever, and is so clever still. But he never had a chance. Perhaps God won't let a man have both money and brains and it's a mercy he lets the others have the money, as they've nothing else to comfort 'em. But, as my husband says, a man with a mind had a glorious kingdom that no millionaire can buy and no landlord take from him."

"May I ask what your husband's line is?" asked May.

"Oh, yes, an inventor; but he can also draw and paint. He can do a lot of things. He's invented all sorts of ingenious contrivances, some of them now making money for others. You've perhaps heard of Mr. Langdon, the millionaire; he comes from these parts. He owns the big Empire Emporium, you'll have heard of it, in Manchester – where you can get anything, if you've the money, from a packet of pins to an ironclad,[63] they say. He's also a big shareholder in several Brunborough factories. Well, my husband designed a lot of things for him, and Mr. Langdon has made a pile of money out of them. A cute man is Mr. Langdon, and, my word, but how he has got on. But, as I've heard him say himself, the secret of getting on is knowing how to use and pick other men's brains, and he's a good 'un at that game. He used my husband's for one, and then cast him off when he thought there was nothing more to be got out of him. However, Mr. Langdon is welcome to all his wealth; for I hear he's not happy with it – or anyhow, it's brought him trouble and scandal. He's been parted from his wife for years, and they say he carried on a rake's racket in his big house by the sea. I'd rather be my hardup husband's wife than his. And – but what's the use of telling that?"

"Telling what?" said May.

"Never mind; but I might have been Langdon's wife. My parents often reproached me – that's after Langdon got on – for not taking the chance. But I'm glad I chose as I did. I never liked Langdon. If he'd married me, I should most likely have had to leave him, as his wife has done. Of course, he allows her a fine income, and I suppose that covers a deal of things, even if it doesn't make up for misery. But rather than have Langdon with all his money, I'd sooner have my husband without a penny, and share a workhouse life and a pauper's grave with him."

Grannie asked Mrs. Wilkinson and May to sing again, so they sang "Pilgrims of the night."[64]

"You'll make a good living on the road by your voices," said a tall, shapely, handsome woman, and Mrs. Wilkinson and May smiled. "My husband has a fine voice," she went on. "He was once a singer in a church choir, but his trade failed – it began to leave the district – we had to seek work elsewhere, and then our woes began. There's nothing for us up in the North, so we're tramping back to the South, to our old neighbourhood, to see if things are now any better there. For I'm tired of this trudging up and down the land."

She looked weary indeed, and was ill with a severe cold. But she made very little murmur.

There was another woman, Molly, a flare-up kind of character, evidently well used to the vagrant life, for the officials knew her. She had been left stranded by her husband at another tramp ward, she said. "It's not fair to let the men out so long before the women," she complained. "It gives a husband every chance to slope his wife if he's so inclined – as mine must have been that morning. He'd be miles on the road before I was let out. But I'll catch him yet, and when I do, let him look out. I'll give him running away from his responsibilities."

Mrs. Wilkinson asked Molly not to swear.

"One must let steam off," said Molly. You'd swear if you'd been in all the workhouses I have, and tussled with the tyrants. I've been in gaol, too, for throwing my bread and cheese at a matron. I'd do it again, too, for the officials have no feelings for us poor road-bugs, as they call us. Well, I'll have my fling, for I suppose I'll live and die on the road now."

"Nay, never give up hope," said a Scotch woman, who was tramping with her husband in search of work. "Surely my man will get a job somewhere, and then we'll get a chance of being clean again. I wish they'd let me wash my clothes. It's a horrible rule that forces you to have a bath for your body in the workhouse and tramp Ward, yet won't allow you to wash your clothes. But I managed the other day in Bolborough's Tramp Ward. I was told off to do the washing, and I got some of my own clothes washed and dried before the officer came and told me I'd to wash none of my own things."

Having finished the scrubbing, Mrs. Wilkinson and May were taken to do some oakum picking,[65] at which task they were kept two hours. It gave May a headache. Then Mrs. Wilkinson was sent to scrub the lavatories.

[18 July 1908]

VIII. The Dreary Pauper Day – And Night Again. (*Continued.*)

Then came the dinner – bread and cheese, and water. But Mrs. Wilkinson and some of the other women had little treasured packets of tea, and these they produced. But they wanted hot water. The woman in charge of the room saw and pitied. "I will get you some hot water," she said. Mr. Slamdrop, the office man, when he saw what she was about said, "What, taking the trouble to get these beggars hot water. You are soft."

"I can't help it," said the woman.

"God bless you!" said Grannie. "I feel I should die if I hadn't a cup of tea."

The tea somewhat relieved May's headache, and there was an hour's rest allowed after dinner. Then other tasks had to be tackled – more scrubbing and cleaning – till supper-time and bed at seven o'clock.

When came the evening meal – gruel and dry bread – Mrs. Wilkinson and May, like most of the others, were too jaded to eat. The gruel was slightly sour, too.

Then they went to their plank bed for another night of tossing and uneasiness. A newcomer, a respectable woman, well dressed, growing grey – she was a waitress, she said, in quest of a situation – came in rather late, and Mrs. Wilkinson showed her how to make the best of her bed. She showed horrified amazement at the tramp ward accommodation. It was her first time in such a place. She could not rest on the plank bed. She sat up, then lay down, sat up again – but to no use. "My God," she groaned, "one cannot sleep in this place."

Grannie was moaning, too. Her rheumatic limbs almost caused her to scream.

"Oh, I wish I was dead," she said. "Jim must be dead, too, or he would have found me."

"Now, be brave, Grannie," said Mrs. Wilkinson. "And see here – to-morrow, when you go out of this place, go to see the Reverend Arthur Milnthorp, the Primitive Methodist minister, in Brunborough, and I think he'll help you – I think he'll help to keep you out of the workhouse till such time as your son turns up. Say Mrs. Wilkinson, of Alderham, sent you. Can you remember?"

"Yes, I can remember – Mr. Milnthorp; I've heard him preach once or twice, I think; they say he's a friend to the poor; but what use will it be to say you sent me, for you are only a tramp like me?"

"Never mind that. Do as I've told you, and you'll find it all right," said Mrs. Wilkinson. "I have – never mind how – some influence with Mr. Milnthorp."

"Very well," said Grannie, "one can't understand everything in this world, and I'm getting too old to bother about it. It's only the young that are always wanting to know everything. So I'll ask no questions; but I'll go to Mr. Milnthorp and see if he'll save me from the workhouse. Oh, how my arm hurts; I can hardly abide!"

"Bear up, you'll be better in the morning," said Mrs. Wilkinson.

Under the grim, ghostly roof the female outcasts tried to sleep – to rest – but in vain. No creatures more needed rest than these road-rambling wretches. Yet everything was designed to keep slumber from them, to sicken them, to torment them.

IX. The Millionaire's Will.

In the afternoon of one of those genial autumn days of sun, which even in November, month of misty misery in smoky towns and cities, brighten the green Fylde coast, Mr. Samuel Langdon and another gentleman sat in the library of the former's mansion at Sandunes.

Mr. Langdon, a man of about sixty ears of age, tall, neat, and good-looking, occupied a chair near the fire, from which, through the big window, there was a view of extensive gardens and grounds, and the border of willow trees with tops inclined inland by the western gales, which fringed the highway – the road from Friartown, by way of Leythorpe-on-the-Sea, to Brightpool, the popular holiday resort of the manufacturing North.

The other gentleman, whiteheaded, tall, thin, with a foxy face, was Mr. Croston Screwm, solicitor, of the firm of Screwm, Croston, and Co., Manchester. He lived at Leythorpe, the little garden watering-place two miles away from Sandunes, and connected with it by electric tram as well as railway.[66]

Mr. Screwm was dressed in black, Mr. Langdon wore a grey suit.

On a little table close to their hands were a bottle of wine and a box of cigars. They had just filled their glasses.

"A day like this makes one feel young again," said Mr. Langdon.

"Yes; we don't get any November days like this in Manchester," said Screwm. "Not that I go often now. I keep away from the city as much as I can. I'm getting old, and inclined to leave the work to the younger ones. It's much better in my bungalow on the beach than in my office in the city."

"You should take to golf," said Mr. Langdon. "I should have been on the course[67] to-day but for my appointment with you."

"I fear I'm too old for golf," said Screwm.

"Nonsense; a man's never too old for anything he resolves on."

"An, yes, he is," said Screwm. "An octogenarian is too old for a sweetheart of twenty. Nature has a say in these things as well as we."

"I won't have even that," said Mr. Langdon, with a smile on his sensual heavy jaws. "If a man only takes care of himself he's young enough for anything – even for a bride," and he laughed. "Didn't Sims Reeves – who used to be very fond of Sandunes; he always put up at the hotel here when coming to fulfil engagements at the Brightpool concerts – well, don't you recollect that Sims Reeves[68] at seventy or over married a young woman and had a son?"

"I fancy you're confusing the great tenor with Blondin,[69] the tight-rope walker. I believe he married a young girl while performing on the high rope at Brightpool."

"No, I don't think I'm mistaken, Screwm. It's no doubt true of both the veterans. So here we have two cases of old men who retained the vigour of their youth to the end of the span; and probably there are may more instances. No; it's nonsense to say that a man must debilitate as he puts years on. As I said, a man's always young enough to do anything he wills."

"I must beg leave to doubt it," said Screwm. "I submit that under the laws of nature –"

"That'll do, Screwm. You may be an authority on the laws of England, but you don't know much about the laws of nature. If I had not always believed that where there's a will there's a way, I should not have been the man I am to-day, whether in body or pocket, and you'll grant that I've got on, I think."

"Yes, you've certainly got on, marvellously," said Screwm.

"And started with nothing," said Mr. Langdon, proudly. "It's organisation, tact, and knack that do it. I've always had one special and supreme ability – the ability to utilise other men and their brains. I don't mind confessing – between ourselves – that I've no particular talent of my own. But I've always had the talent of getting other men's talent at my service, and that's the thing that pays – that's how the money's made. I've turned to profit the talents of men who didn't know how to make a ha'penny out of their gifts themselves. A million and a quarter in thirty years is a pretty pile, isn't it?"

"It's an achievement," said Screwm.

"Now to that will. I suppose you're getting it into ship-shape?"

"You shall have the rough draft in a day or two," said Screwm. "I came to-day to see if there are any more particulars about the almshouses you are going to endow – any special conditions."

"Oh, yes," said Mr. Langdon. "There must be conditions. Certainly. We can't let everybody and anybody run into my almshouses. I will have no riff-raff. The recipients of my charity must be respectable persons, moral, religious. No poor persons who have had illicit relations, who have not been legally married, must be admitted – no woman who has had illegitimate children. We must insist on morality and religion."

"Just so," said Screwm. "If morality and religion are not upheld the foundations of the State are sapped."

"Exactly," said Langdon. "Poor people, above all things, ought to be virtuous. Seeing that they have no money or possessions to help the State in any other way, it is the least they can do to be virtuous. Virtue should be their contribution to the State. They should make that the object of their lives. For, however poor a man may be he may at least indulge in virtue."

"Excellent reasons for the practice of virtue amongst the populace," said Screwm. "There is also the monetary point of view. The poor can't afford vices. They can't find the necessary legal expenses in case their aberrations lead them into law trouble."

"Don't wander, Screwm," said Langdon. "Anything else about the will?"

"Er – yes," said Screwm. "Excuse me, but when wills are being made it is sometimes necessary to refer to past matters that may not be altogether pleasant. In case Mrs. Langdon survives you, the settlement allowed her still goes on; that's all right. But supposing she married again?"

"In that event it ceases, of course," said Langdon. "For if she marries again I expect she'll marry somebody able to provide well for her. She'd be a fool if she didn't. Is she still living at Leamington?"

"Yes; leads a quiet, and, I am told, charitable life there."

"She's welcome to it. Let's see; how long is it since she and I parted by mutual agreement?"

"Nearly thirty years."

"H'm. She was fool. Most women would have had sense to see nothing and say nothing. So long as I let her have all she wanted, and kept her in style, I don't see why she should kick up a fuss about my – er – kindness in taking a girl a little holiday. By the way, what's become of the girl – of Milly Fordham? Heard anything of her lately?"

[25 July 1908]

IX. The Millionaire's Will. (*Continued.*)

"Last I heard she was on tramp – a common vagabond of the roads."

"Ah! Pity," said Langdon. "She was a fine girl. But she was a fool, too. All women are – if not in one way, in another. You're never sure of them. She might have been living in affluence under my protection still if she'd only known how to behave herself."

"Do you really think," said Screwm, "that there was anything between her and Mr. Wangton?"

"There was too much for me, and that's enough," said Langdon, frowning at the memory of an incident of years ago – his bitter quarrel with his friend Wangton on account of this beautiful reckless girl, Milly Fordham.

"She had a son, you know," said Screwm.

"Well, I'm doing nothing for him," said Langdon. "Her son he may be, but mine – well, that's more than a question. Why did the jade play me false? She was a pretty girl, with such glorious ways – ah – and I was very fond of her. What's become of her son?"

"The last I heard he was on tramp, too," said Screwm.

"Dirt always gravitates to the gutter, said Langdon. "The fellow had his chances. Wangton helped him considerably – as I suppose he had every duty to. He's had good berths, under the Government, travelling abroad in the diplomatic service, and lost 'em all. Drink, I guess. Well, a man should learn to keep sober. Nobody but teetotalers must be admitted to my almshouses. Make a memorandum of that, Screwm. So the young fellow's on tramp, is he? He's married, too, isn't he? Of course, he will be – he's just the sort to drag a wife and family down with him."

"Yes, he has a wife and two children."

"Are they on tramp with him?"

"No. My information – and it may be relied upon – says he left them in Birmingham."

"In short, deserted them?"

"I suppose it amounts to that. He'll have the authorities on his track; for I reckon the wife and children will have to go on the parish."

"Life's a queer affair, isn't it, Screwm?" said Langdon. "Now, about those others – that boy I have apprenticed to the veterinary surgeon in Friartown, and the girl who is in service in Yorkshire. You can put a hundred pounds each down for them. I'd better do a bit for them. A hundred pounds will be a little fortune to them, though the boy will most likely go to the devil with it, and the girl, too. Girls always do, in one way or other. Some of then even through matrimony. There's nothing else you wish to ask in regard to the will, is there?"

"No, I think that concludes the business."

"Then fill your glass and take another cigar. Ah, I'd forgotten one thing. The almshouses must be called the Langdon Charity. There must be a stone inscription to that effect in the front centre of the buildings."

"I'll make a note of it," said Screwm, "and it shall be done."

"Right. Now to the wine and the smoke. Ha! who's coming?" and Langdon, hearing footsteps, glanced towards the room door.

X. The Millionaire's Outcast Son.

There was a soft knock, the door opened, and a handsome young woman, azure-eyed and fair-haired, neatly attired as a servant, yet with something of the air of mistress, entered the room, pausing as she saw the two men.

"I thought you were alone, Mr. Langdon," she said.

"Oh, it's all right, Gertie," said Langdon, gazing on her with an old man's greedy amorousness. "What is it?"

"I thought I'd just run down to the sands with Fido."

"Well, I daresay the dog needs a run. You'll not be long?"

"Oh, no, only about half an hour," and she departed, closing the door behind her.

"Ah, I mustn't forget Gertie," said Langdon, tenderly. "But I'll not bother putting her in the will. I'll give her a lump sum to put in the bank in her own name."

For ten minutes Langdon and Screwm sat sipping, smoking, and chatting. Then Screwm rose to go, and there was a knock at the door.

"Come in," said Langdon, and, as a pretty maidservant entered, "What is it?"

"There's a man at the door wishes to see you, sir."

"Who is he?"

"I don't know, sir. He didn't give me any card," and the girl smiled.

"Is he begging?"

"I don't know, sir. He doesn't look well off, and yet he doesn't look like a beggar."

"Some shabby genteel cadger. I'll soon get rid of him," said Langdon. "Excuse me a moment," to Screwm, and he went to the door, where on the top of the two steps stood the "swell" tramp whom Mrs. Wilkinson and May had met in the common lodging-house at Blakeham. His eye was still slightly discoloured – though hardly discernible now – from the blow Jim Campbell had given him for molesting May, but there was a considerable improvement in his attire, though the clothes were second-hand and "shiny." But he was clean and shaved, wore a collar and tie, and polished, though old boots.

"Well, sir," said Langdon, "what's your business with me?"

"I would rather discuss it indoors," said the young man.

"I don't take strangers indoors," said Langdon.

The young man put on a smile. "I oughtn't to be a stranger," he said. "If you know your own features, and will look at me, I think you'll trace a resemblance. My name is Ronald Fordham."

"Fordham? What do you mean?" demanded Langdon.

"I mean that Milly Fordham is my mother, and that I am your son."

Sudden anger showed on the face of Langdon.

"Who told you that tale? It's nonsense. You're no son of mine," and he turned to end the interview.

"I didn't know myself that I was till recently," said the young man. "And I'm sure my information is correct. My aunt, who brought me up – you knew her, she lived with you once – told me the secret as she lay dying."

"Dead or alive, she is a liar!" cried Mr. Langton. "A wild, drunken creature – her word is nought."

"Even wild drunken creatures tell the truth on their deathbeds," said Ronald Fordham.

"Blather! Be off with you!"

The young man looked disappointed, desperate.

"I am your son, and I want you to help me," he said. "I've had hard luck."

"It's no affair of mine," said Langdon, raising his hand dismissively and turning round. "I say you are not my son, and I won't be blackmailed."

"So you won't help me, then! I don't want alms. Set me on my feet. Help me to get a situation, or give me enough to go abroad."

"I shall give you nothing!" said Langdon hotly. "You've no claim on me whatever!"

"Your conscience – if you have any – tells you better," said Fordham. "Simply because my mother hadn't the sense to make you buy her a wedding ring, I am to be a penniless outcast, while your other sons are living in luxury. Is that fair? Is it my fault that I'm an illegitimate child? Why should I suffer for your lust and my mother's weakness?"

Langdon turned away and shut he inner door in the young man's face.

Fordham laughed grimly. "He shall pay for this!" he said bitterly. "He shall pay for this."

He stepped along the gravel path.

As he reached the open gates he started at sight of the young woman, Gertie, returning with her dog. As she saw him she, too, stared in surprise, and blushed.

"Surely I'm not mistaken this time," he said, raising his hat. "You are Gertie, whom I met at Morecambe, aren't you?"

"I think I am," she replied. "But Morecambe's a long way off, and that's long years ago, and all dead and done with now."

"Where sweethearts' souls are concerned," he said, "there is no distance and there is no time; but everywhere and every time is always here and now."

"Oh, yes," she said, "that's the romantic sort you talked at Morecambe. But let holiday flirtations be bygones."

"Why did you cease writing to me?"

"Did I? I thought it was you who stopped first."

"If I did I am sorry. Perhaps I did. I have had worries and troubles since that time at Morecambe."

"Do you mean you are married?" said Gertie, archly.

He flushed, and laughed.

"The world's full of silly little tragedies," he said. "Do you know, I met a girl a few days ago, and I could have sworn she was you. In fact, I spoke to her, but she denied any acquaintanceship. Have you a sister who is much like you?"

"I suspect it's my cousin May. She is said to be he very image of me."

"And so she is, if that were she."

"Where did you meet her?"

"Ah, never mind where – that's what I couldn't understand. But I wanted to kiss her, and got into a row over it."

"Serve you right. I guess you're not slow at kissing whenever there's opportunity."

"I would like to kiss you now, Gertie," he said, "just as in that happy time at Morecambe. I was feeling awfully down and dejected just as I met you – to tell you the truth, I was thinking of suicide, for – but that's nothing to do with you – anyhow, as soon as I saw your face I felt cheered up, and life was bright again, and I believe I'd kiss you now if you weren't standing at this gate in the daylight. Ah," as the idea flashed on him, "what are you doing here? Are you going to this house?"

"Yes; why not?"

"Into this house?" he repeated.

"Yes; why not? I live here."

"You – live – here!" he gasped. "You live here!"

"Yes; what's there alarming about that?"

"You are in Mr. Langdon's employ?"

"Yes."

"What as? Servant?"

"Ye-es," she drawled.

"And what else?" he asked fiercely.

[1 August 1908]

X. The Millionaire's Outcast Son. (*Continued.*)

"I think you'd better be going," she said, gently.

"I will go; but I want us to go together, Gertie," he said, stepping to her side, and putting his hand on her arm.

"Don't," she said, with a glance towards the house, where she saw Langdon and Screwm at the door together, and she saw that Langdon had seen her.

"Gertie, you know I love you – come away from this house with me. It means ruin if you stay here. Come away with me. I am poor, but I'll work for you as only a man can work for the lass he loves. It's a pity we were ever sundered. But with you by my side I could rise again. You are just the woman to make me a man – the one woman in all the world who would be my salvation."

"Hush!" she said rather sadly, "it is too late!"

"What!" and his voice was a shriek. "Too late! My God! Has the villain who has robbed me of the rights of heirship also robbed me of my sweetheart? I'll kill the beast!"

As he excitedly turned to run to the house he saw Mr. Langdon, with rage in his face, and Mr. Screwm, coming down the garden path.

"You swine!" he yelled, and, rushing upon the old merchant, threw him to the ground, and seized him by the throat, to strangle him.

Screwm feebly tried to push the young man off Langdon. Gertie called for help, and presently the coachman and the gardener hurried up. They dragged Fordham off and held him fast, he struggling madly to get free and fly at his foe, who now lay unconscious. Another minute and he would have been past help.

"Shall we send for the police, sir?" said the coachman to Screwm.

Screwm reflected a minute before he answered. "No," he said; "put him outside and lock the gates."

The two men hauled the kicking Fordham to the gates and flung him out into the road.

He sprang to his feet, bruised, bleeding, and ran at the gates with a kick, and struck them with his fists.

A man in coarse, working-class garb, seemingly of the "navvy"[70] type, coming along the road at this moment, said, "Now, mate, what's the game? Been getting the chuck-out? Here's your hat," and he picked it up. "Come, you'll do no good by fighting the gate. You'll only get locked up."

"I don't care; I'll kill him!" said Fordham. "Let me get at him."

"Better come away," said the man. "Hello!" as he caught sight of Fordham's face. "Why, you're the chap I gave a black eye. You do seem to have the knack of getting into trouble. Come on, now. Come away before you land in gaol. I don't bear you any ill-will, and I hope you bear me none. Come, now," and he took

Fordham kindly by the arm, whereupon the young man broke down into sobs, almost like a hysterical woman, and said, "Oh, it's too cruel! Treated me like a dog, and seduced the girl I love – and yet he is my father."

"Well, that's a rum tale if it's true," said Jim Campbell. "But come on. You'll do no good by staying here; come along," and he led Fordham along the highway towards Leythorpe.

The red sun was sinking over the sea; a white mist was creeping over the meadows.

"It looks like frost," said Jim Campbell. "We'd better get along towards some shelter before the dark. You can come with me if you don't object to my company. I'm on tramp. Been to Churcham after a job; but no luck. Then I went on to Brightpool; but there's nothing doing there now the season's over. In fact, many of the poor lodging-house keepers are in a bad plight. So I'm making my way to Brunborough to see if I can drop across my old mother there. What's your direction, mate?"

Fordham, who was now somewhat composed, answered wearily, "I don't know, and I don't care. I have nowhere to go. The best thing I can do is to throw myself into the sea."

"I don't think that would do you any good, or anybody else," said Jim Campbell.

Fordham was gloomily silent. When they reached a turn of the road just entering Leythorpe he broke away from Campbell and ran towards the shore. Jim Campbell caught him as he was rushing into the water.

"Now, this won't do at all," said Jim, sticking to Fordham's arm. "Come on," and he forced him away.

"You'd better have let me go," moaned Fordham. "It would be by far the best, by far the best?"

XI. The Open-Air Meeting.

On a dark, starless Sunday night, in a chill, damp November air, from a corner of the old Brunborough Market Place, surrounded with shops and warehouses closed and silent in the Sabbath custom, rose the sound of singing, a singing about which there was something unusual, for neither the words nor the tune were of the kind usually associated with orthodox hymnology. Jim Campbell, who had just trudged into the town – he had parted from Fordham, the man who claimed to be the millionaire's son, at Friartown, Fordham saying he thought he would find some friends of his in the ancient borough on the River Ripple[71] – drew towards the group who were singing. He might as well stand here as elsewhere. He had nowhere to go. He had been through the street where his mother lived, to find her gone in search of him to Bolborough, since when the neighbours had heard nothing of her. And Jim Campbell felt sad, and more than sad; he was full of a sullen rage against the world that drove poor men's mothers to the workhouse or into the life of the tramp. Also, he was hungry; he had had nothing to eat all day, but he did not think about that, though he did think bitterly about the well-dressed people he had met going to places of worship. They had, like the priest and the Levite of old,[72] passed him by, though it needed nothing but a glance at him to reveal his starvation and destitution.

He had paused at one church porch – it was the place his grandmother used to go to – and where she had taken him when a boy; he believed he had been christened there; and a churchwarden, fat and rosy with the righteousness of getting on,[73] had, after staring at him rater rudely for a moment, said, "What do you want?"

"Nothing," said Jim.

"Then be off; this is no place for the likes of you."

"I guess not," said Jim, and walked on, saying to himself, "By God, if Christ on tramp, as He used to be, came to that Christian Church, that man at the door would order Him away."

It wasn't often Jim Campbell thought of theological matters, but the sight of the cosy, well-lit church had recalled the story of the Gospels he had heard when a boy; and, as he had never done before, he could not help contrasting preaching with practice, and felt full of atheistic antagonism towards the Church that was such an awful humbug.[74]

So he came to the Market Square just as the group at the corner were starting their singing, under the leadership of a white-faced, clean-shaven man, with brilliant, dark eyes, who stood on a chair and read out the verses of the poem. He wore the distinguishing "Trilby" hat[75] of the Socialists and a red tie. The tune was the old German folk-song melody, "Tannenbaum," and the words were these: –

> The People's flag is deepest red.
> It shrouded oft our martyred dead,
> And ere their limbs grew stiff and cold
> Their hearts' blood dyed its every fold.
>
> > Chorus:
> > Then raise the scarlet standard high;
> > Within its shade we'll live or die,
> > Though cowards flinch and traitor's sneer,
> > We'll keep the Red Flag flying here.
>
> It waved above our infant might
> When all ahead seemed dark as night;
> It witnessed many a deed and vow –
> We must not change its colour now.

It well recalls the triumphs past,
It gives the hope of peace at last;
The banner bright, the symbol plain
Of human right and human gain.

It suits to-day the weak and base,
Whose minds are fixed on pelf and place,
To cringe before the rich man's frown,
And haul the sacred emblem down.

With heads uncoverd swear we all
To bear it onward till we fall;
Come dungeon dark or gallows rim,
This song shall be our parting hymn.

> Then wave the scarlet standard high,
> Within its shade we'll live or die.
> Though cowards flinch and traitors sneer,
> We'll keep the red flag flying here.[76]

At the other end of the square, some distance away, underneath another red flag – the Banner of Blood and Fire – the Salvation Army,[77] with a loud cornet and a great deal of drum, was holding a meeting, but it was sufficiently distant not to interfere with the hearty singing of the men and women who were giving their voices to the Red Flag.

The pathos of the air, suggesting loved ones lost and happy days gone, touched Jim Campbell; the vigour of the chorus, as of a man suddenly springing to his feet and defying the powers that punished him, roused him; his heart leapt up, ready for war.

[8 August 1908]

X. The Millionaire's Outcast Son. (*Continued*.)

Then the speaker gave an address on "Thieves and Toilers." He showed how, from his Socialist point of view, the capitalists robbed the workers "all ends up," as he put it. They swindled them out of their wages. They fleeced them by means of rent, they cheated them by the shoddying of clothes and the adulteration of food – the workers did not even get honest value for their money when they went to spend their little wages – they made laws to enforce and perpetuate their exploitation, they kept soldiers and police to defend the interests of the idlers and parasites against the workers, and they bribed "religion" to wheedle the poor folks and take their eyes off this world by setting 'em on a purely hypothetical next world.

As Jim Campbell listened to the oration – for the speaker had eloquence – he saw his own life passing before him, his hard struggle for bread, his willingness to work and no opportunity to get it, he saw his starving wife and child, he realised that all his misery and the death of his darlings had been brought about by this foul, murderous capitalist competitive system which the speaker was so tremendously denouncing. He felt a wild anger against the rulers and authorities and employers, his soul rose in revolt, and he shouted out in his excitement, "By God, you're right!"

The audience glanced round at Jim's vehement comment on the address, and the speaker went on, "I know I'm right, for it is not I who speak, but the facts of our life – the hideous and pitiful facts of our everyday existence. I am glad to find that somebody else sees I am right. Would that all the workers could only have their eyes opened in the same way to-night – it would be a joyful day for England to-morrow."

There were a few questions asked from the audience which had increased to about a hundred while the lecture was in progress.

"You Socialists would divide everything up, wouldn't you?" inquired one man. "Well, if you did, we should all be as bad as ever in a few days. Some would have sold their share for drink, and others lost it through idleness or thriftlessness, while the active and diligent ones would have got hold of a big lot again."

The lecturer answered, "No man who has studied Socialist literature would ever put a question like that, and the best thing to do and the fairest, I may add, before asking such questions is to make yourselves familiar with our Socialist pamphlets. No socialist ever advocates dividing-up – it would be nonsensical. What we do propose is this – by law to make all the land, factories, railways, workshops, etc. national property – a sort of co-operative ownership by all the nation and then to give every man, woman, and child their keep – food, clothes, shelter, education, and whatever recreations and amusements it will run to – out of the produce instead of, as at present, letting a few landowners and capitalists – who never made the land, and have no right to it, and who never made their capital, for it is the result of the efforts of thousands of workers of this generation and past generations – take the lion's share, to which they have no title, either in reason, humanity, or religion, while leaving the donkey's share to – well, the people. And the people are asses to stand it. Therefore, friend, you see that what we propose to do is not to divide up the land and the machinery and tools, for that would not be much good, but to distribute fairly amongst the people. I see nothing unjust or irrational about that."

"But is it practical?" cried a man. "What we want is practical politics, not dreams."

"Well, if what we see around us to-day is the result of practical politics," was the reply, "the sooner we try some impracticable politics the better. But, in my opinion, Socialism is perfectly practicable. If trade-unionism is practical, if co-operation is practical, then Socialism is practical, for it is only a combination of the two with logical developments added."

"What about our savings under Socialism?" said somebody.

"What about those who own their own house of a bit of property?" asked another.

"One answer will do for those two questions," said the lecturer. "What do you save for? Why do you acquire your own house – which is only another form of saving? To provide something for old age, isn't it? or to give your children a start with something behind 'em? Well, now, if house, shelter, and food are sure for you as long as you live – as they would be under socialism – what need to save or get a house of your own? Further, if your children are all sure of work and wages – as they would be under Socialism – what need to save to give them a start? While theoretically having no private property or savings of your own, you would have more – you would be an equal partner in all the property and wealth of the nation, a far solider and safer thing than anything you could do by your own individual effort."

"But that would do away with thrift and incentive, wouldn't it?"

"It would do away with selfish thrift and selfish incentive," said the lecturer, "but these are not so desirable that we need bother about them – we see the consequences of them in the misery about us – every man trying to 'get on,' even at his neighbour's expense. But there would come in their place a wider thrift and higher incentive, born of the good fellowship that would want to see all the nation prosperous and happy."

"Then the diligent and thrifty would have to work to keep the idle and careless?"

"Oh, no – but what if you did? You do it now, don't you? How many rich parasites, as well as wandering vagrants, do you keep now? Far more than you would have to keep under Socialism. For under Socialism every man in health and strength would have to do his share in the work of the nation, or – have nothing to eat till he came to his senses."

"Isn't Socialism against religion?" queried a man, attired in silk hat and black suit, who stepped up to the group as he was passing, evidently from some orthodox place of worship.

"I just depends what you mean by religion," said the lecturer. "If by religion you mean forms and ceremonies and blind acceptance of theological tales and superstitions, then Socialism is against religion. But if by religion you mean doing our duty to our neighbour, pitying the poor and oppressed, and doing all we can to help them – which, I take it, is the true religion according to Christ's own teaching – then Socialism is not against religion. A man may be a Socialist and a member of any creed or sect he believes in, just as a man may be a Liberal and a Churchman or a Nonconformist, or an agnostic[78] as many Liberal (as well as Conservatives) are. Personally, I am an agnostic, but I sink my agnosticism to work with Churchmen, Catholics, and others, for that in which we believe in common – Socialism."

"Does Socialism believe in God and hereafter?" asked the last questioner.

"Socialists as a body have nothing to do with that question. Individual Socialists may answer it as they like. God and hereafter are matters no man can prove or disprove, therefore best left out of the argument. But I do say that is if there be a God, and evolution is His work, that God is on the side of Socialism."

"Rubbish," said the man in the silk hat, walking away.

"It's funny how every bigot fancies that God thinks just as he does," said the lecturer, stepping down from his chair, and rubbing his hands together to warm them. "It's cold," he added, "too cold to stand arguing here. We are now going to the Socialist Room. If any of you wish to come and talk things over with us, then you are very welcome."

The lecturer saw Jim Campbell. "Ha," he said, with a smile, "you're the man who shouted out. You look starved."

"I am starved," said Jim.

"Hard up?"

Jim Campbell looked at his interlocutor, and hesitated. Then he said, "Some folks don't want the truth, but I believe you're a man to tell the truth to. Yes, I'm hard up."

The lecturer looked keenly at Jim's face. "Have you had anything to eat today?" he asked.

"Ne'er a bite," said Jim.

The lecturer put his arm in Jim's. "Come along," he said. And Jim Campbell suppressed the sob with which this unexpected and surprising comradeship touched him."

[15 August 1908]

XII. The Socialist Room.

Heedless of the passing people, who, in the light of the street lamp, stared to see a well-dressed man arm-in-arm with a tramp – for fellowship is such a rare thing in a Christian country – the lecturer led Jim Campbell to a street off one of the main thoroughfares, followed by a dozen or two of the men and women who had been the nucleus of the audience in the Market Place.

Just when turning off from the main street, at a corner where a public-house glittered in the night, a wretchedly-clad woman begged for a copper.

"I'm hard up, sir, or I wouldn't ask," she said, addressing the lecturer, "and I'd no need to beg once – I had all I wanted till the villain that ruined me grew tired of me –"

"All right, Milly," said the lecturer, "we know your tale."

"Then you know it's true," said the woman. "Oh, it's you, Mr. Summerfield, is it? Well, you know my tale, as you say, and you've always been good to me. If all the men were like you I shouldn't curse 'em."

"Why don't you go to the old rascal and make him pay you something?" said Summerfield. "He's rich enough."

"Ay, he's rich enough, but he'll not give me anything."

"Go and smash his windows, then."

"You told me that before. I did it, and he had me put in prison – curse him."

"He's a beast!"

"Beast," said Milly, "a beast is an angel to him."

"Well, he ought to do something for you," said Summerfield. "He owns half-a-dozen factories here, and that big place in Manchester."

"He'll do nothing. He says I've no legal claim on him."

"More's the pity. Anyhow, here – that will help you for to-night," and he handed the woman a coin.

"Thank you, Mr. Summerfield, you're a gentleman; and though there's some runs you down, and calls you a wicked Socialist and atheist, I sticks up for you, and tells 'em I always speaks as I finds, and if you're a wicked Socialist and atheist, then I only wish all the world was wicked Socialists and atheists – for that villain I won't name, he's no Socialist, and no atheist neither, and yet look how he's treated me. Good-night, Mr. Summerfield, and God bless you," and away she hobbled.

"She'll spend the money on drink," said Summerfield, as he and Jim passed on, "and yet – who shall judge her or blame her? Her story – well, a rich man's plaything for a time, and then cast out on the streets. He one of your self-made men, too – the great Langdon, of the Empire Emporium, Manchester, millionaire and hell-maker."

"I've hear of him before," said Jim. "In fact, only a few days ago I met his son – well, a fellow who says he's his son – he told me his name was Fordham –"

"Then Milly's his mother," said Summerfield. "Where was he?"

"At Sandunes – on tramp. Been to ask Langdon for assistance. Got kicked out."

"That's Langdon's way. Every man ought to be made to keep his children, legitimate or not."

"You think this young fellow is Langdon's son, then?"

"There's no reason to doubt it. When did you see him last?"

"I left him at Friartown."

"And he was hard up, you say? I heard he was doing well."

"He had done well once, I should think. He had education and style; but he's come down now. Ah –"

"What's up?" said Summerfield, gently.

"I feel faint – but it's nothing."

"No wonder. But we'll soon fix you up, and take the faintness away. We're there now."

They turned up a street and, entering by the side door of a big building, ascended some old stairs, which led into a fairly big room – an old warehouse of some sort – on one side of which was a kind of refreshment-bar and a door leading to another room, from which came a sound like the click of billiard balls. The lecturer, whom some of those present, seated in front of a pleasant fire, greeted as Joe, led Jim to the bar, and said to the shirt-sleeved man in charge – a jolly-faced man of about forty – "What have you got to eat, Ned?"

"Nothing, only some pies and cakes."

"They'll do. Put some on a plate." Turning to Jim, "Now, mate, what'll you have to drink? Have you any tea on, Ned?"

"No, but I can soon make some."

"You can have a glass of beer, or tea," said Joe to Jim, "which is it?"

"I'll take tea," said Jim.

"Teetotal?" asked Joe, but without any criticism in the enquiry.

"No, but tea's warmer than ale."

"And you are cold. Well, I'm glad to meet a man with sense and will. Though nobody could reasonably blame a chap in your plight for taking to beer. Here, sit down and tackle the pies. Now, Ned, how long will that tea be?"

"As soon as I can," said Ned, who was attending to another customer.

"Here, let me get at the tea-pot," said a woman, stepping forward. She was one of those who had been at the meeting in the Market Place, along with her husband – "Ned's busy."

"That's it, Mrs. Greenley," said Joe, with a smile. "This poor fellow's famishing."

Mrs. Greenley, with no words, but a nod to signify that she understood – her kind, motherly heart grasped the story of the tramp's plight at a glance – had the kettle on the fire, and a cup of tea brewed in a few minutes. She brought it to Jim, who was having a little talk near the bar with Joe.

"You're a brick, Mrs. Greenley," said Joe.

"Somebody's got to be brick in a world of stones," said Mrs. Greenley, a woman of about thirty, with a flush, but whether at Joe's praise or indignation at the society that permitted starvation is in doubt; perhaps it was both.

"Now, then," said Joe, to Jim, "shift that stuff, and if there's not enough you shall have more."

"There's plenty," said Jim. "I thank you very much."

"Has your faintness gone?" asked Joe.

"I feel a lot better now, said Jim.

While eating, Jim told his story to Joe, who listened sympathetically.

"You've had hard luck," said Joe. "And so the spinner trade-unionists stopped the piecers from forming a trade union, did they? It almost looks as if Lord Salisbury was about the bull's-eye when he described trade-unionism as selfish.[79] Anyhow, trade-unionism's not the remedy for our ills. Socialism is the only cure."

Jim looked round the room. In one corner was a book-shelf – filled with progressive literature, though there were also some of the poets and the world's great novels. Over the mantelpiece were Socialist cartoons and photographs of Socialist leaders. In the centre of the wall, over the fireplace, was a great red flag, folded.

The occupants of the room were smoking and chatting, except, of course, the ladies, of whom there were a few. At a little table in the corner were a few men playing cards.

"This would shock the orthodox," said Joe, "especially those fellows playing billiards in that room – all on a Sunday."

"It seems to me there are worse things than playing billiards on a Sunday." said Jim. "For instance, to go to church well fed and pass starving tramps."

"You're about right," said Joe. "Still, not all our comrades approve of billiards and cards on a Sunday – not from any silly scruples about Sabbath-breaking but because they say we should respect the genuine religion of others, and we should rather conciliate the narrow goody-goody than get their backs up. There's some weight in that argument, but we'll not discuss these things. Have you had enough to eat?"

"Quite," said Jim. "Enough to last me a week."

"Now, have you got anywhere to sleep to-night?"

"No – I –"

"All right, just wait a minute," and Joe went to talk with some of the comrades.

When he came back to Jim, he said, "I'm sorry none of us have a spare bed, but you can sleep here. You'll have a roof and fire at any rate. Do you think you'll be comfortable?"

"It'll be like heaven to me," said Jim.

So, after all the Socialist comrades had left, and Joe Summerfield had bade him a hearty good-night, Jim Campbell drew a big chair up to the fire, and, blessing the good luck that brought him amongst these brotherly folk, settled to sleep under the Red Flag.

[22 August 1908]

XIII. The Vision Of The Red Flag.

After a little doze, Jim Campbell wakened, and put more coal on the fire. Except the light from the grate the room was in gloom. The remote corners were deep in shadow. The firelight flickered on the walls and ceilings; occasionally, a fitful flash of flame made ghostly streaks on the dark. Over the mantelpiece the Red Flag lay folded, like a warrior taking is rest before the morrow's fight.

There was silence all around – the great hush of night. No sounds came from the street. All traffic was at rest; all the world was in slumber, or, at least, in bed – except, thought Jim, who, having been amongst these facts, could not help remembering them, such luckless wanderers of the road as had not been able to secure shelter in casual ward or workhouse.

He wondered uneasily about his mother. He must find her. Perhaps she had gone into the workhouse. He must make inquiry in the morning. He must find her and help her; yet, he reflected bitterly, how could he help her? He had no home to which to take her – he was a penniless, houseless out-of-work.

Then Jim Campbell stood up, paced the floor in front of the fire, and felt like cursing the universe.

He thought of his dead wife and child; and his thoughts were as the swords of rebels, seeking slaughter and vengeance. No matter what good luck befell him now, that tragedy could not be undone, never, never, never in this world. Even if he got work and wages to keep himself and family, he could not bring the dead ones back again. But he could help his mother, if he could only find her.

Then he thought of Mrs. Wilkinson and May, and wondered how they were faring. They were, he was sure, not of the usual order of tramps; there was something mysterious about them. But that was true of many of the outcasts he had met; there were strange, romantic tales behind them.

He felt he would like to meet these two – Mrs. Wilkinson and May – again. He liked May greatly – somehow, she reminded him much of his dead wife; there was the same sweet look about the eyes and the mouth. He felt a desire to see May – to go in quest of her on the road; and at this he smiled sadly. Even if he found her – what then? He was a tramp, and she was a tramp, in the kingdom of the damned; there was no hope for them.

Yet, though despairingly, he felt that if ever he had a home of his own again he would like to see May abiding there as well as his mother.

And then he felt he could laugh madly at such an impossible idea.

He looked up, musingly, at the Red Flag; and, as he looked, he remembered the Socialist lecture. He realised what the gospel of the Red Flag meant. It meant salvation for such as he – nay, it meant much more than salvation. It meant actively lifting them out of hell, and, if not putting them in heaven, at least setting them on the happy earthly road thereto – the road to all that was goodly and glorious.

Sitting in the chair by the fire, there opened unto him a vision. He saw the life of the drudging poor as if he were a spectator, apart from it; yet, having known it, he felt in his heart all that he saw. He saw his own father and mother in the struggle of the days and the anxieties of the nights. They had worked and worried in the dreary hand-to-mouth existence of the ill-paid toilers – never certain of the morrow's bread, the cupboard always threatening emptiness. No man ever slaved harder than his father, no woman ever bore so many burdens as his mother; yet, with all their labour, their end was pauperism. Surely something was wrong where such a state of things could be.

He saw in detail his father's life. He was a worker in a goods yard on the railway; he was off early in the morning, long before the children got up, to his task; he was away all day, as their house was too distant to permit him to come home in the brief dinner hour. He worked hard, amid the danger of shunting wagons. Many men got maimed or killed. He forgot exactly how much wage his father got, but it was not much – nineteen shillings or a pound. Out of that there was five shillings for rent for a start – fifteen shillings left to feed and clothe the family of four or five. Holidays were out of the tale; they could not even afford medical attendance when necessary – a doctor's bill was a terrible thing. Did he not remember his mother wailing, even as his little brother and sister lay dying of fever, "However shall we pay the doctor's bill?" For she loved to pay her way; she had a hatred of debt.

He saw the little house where they lived – four small rooms in all – one of many similar cottages in a district thick with them; a district full of narrow streets, that shut the daylight out, and great spinning factories, and ironworks, and the corporation gasworks. There was always a distinctive smell about the neighbourhood. But those who did not live there said it was healthy – it was a sort of iron tonic in the air. There was also a deal of smoke, and fumes of all sorts and plenty of dirt – quite different from the west end of the town, where there were trees along the roads, and the rich lived in houses with gardens.

He saw his mother at her daily work – up early, too, to make the breakfast, generally porridge and milk: not bad stuff, no doubt, but monotonous. Their bill of fare had not much variety in it. When they had tea it was very weak, and they had to be careful of the sugar; and his mother had to butter the bread very thin when they had bread and butter, and there was always an ominous clattering of the knife against the sides of the butter-basin – doleful hints that there was far more vacuum than butter. Indeed, he rarely had buttered bread without hearing the awful boding of the knife touching the sides of the pot; and often enough there had to be so much scraping round the sides of the dish that it was a wonder the dish wasn't scraped as thin as paper. What a pleasure it would have been to have seen the knife put into a dish so full of butter that there could not have been any possibility of it clashing against the sides!

The reminiscent butter basin loomed large and typical of the poor working-class life – never full, as a rule more empty than full, with always the dread that there wouldn't be enough in it, even with the most pinching distribution to go round. Indeed, in a grotesque fantasy, he saw a huge butter dish, as big as a gasometer,[80] with thousands of ragged wretches scrambling up its sides to get a lick, while two or three mocking demons, with great iron claws and gilded tails, scooped huge chunks of the yellow food and bore them off – the hungry horde being so busy fighting each other up to the sides of the dish that they hadn't time to think of stopping the big plunderers.

And he saw, as it had been sometimes, the butter dish in the little cottage quite empty, as bare as the landlord's shiny bald head – but even then the landlord said he must have his rent; and they went without butter – and other things – to pay it. Yet the landlord must have been a good man; he went to chapel and was quite respectable; he only insisted on his rent. Perhaps Christ wouldn't have done that – but then people didn't live in the New Testament; they lived in Clankyshire, which was a very different place.

He saw his mother mending and patching the clothes, to make the worn-out last a little longer; he remembered one day when he couldn't go to school while his clogs were mended – and it was a hard job to pay the clogger; he recalled incidents about this mother's apparel – he had never seen her in a new dress for years, and one time she got an awful cold through her old boots letting water in; he saw her standing over the wash-tub, washing for others as well as herself, in order to make a little money, standing over the washtub – all day and moaning with headache – he remembered these things, and clenched his fists at the memory.

He remembered much more. He saw a Christmas Eve, when he was longing for a little toy "puffer"[81] – he lingered long at the shop window; he asked his mother to buy it, she said they could not afford – he wondered how it was; other children could have toys, but he couldn't. He cried for that "puffer" – cried all Christmas night, and much of Christmas Day.

He saw thousands, tens of thousands, of other mothers and fathers in the same coll[82] and plight as his parents – some worse off, some slightly better off, all struggling hard and yet never getting anything but the merest and poorest necessaries, and not always those; he saw all the workers in factory and mine and foundry yard and railway, and worse off even than these, the wretched who did "home employment" in miserable dens and hovels; and, worst off of all, those desolate ones who were, often with wives and children, trudging the highways in search of work.

All these he saw, a mighty host clemmed, suffering, shorn – he saw them forming into a great procession, men thin, pale, stunted; women weary, white, worn-down; little children pitiful to see, with sickly, famished faces – and, suddenly, up in front of the throng, was raised the Red Flag; and there was a great shout, and then the procession marched on, singing –

> "Raise the Scarlet Standard high,
> Within its shade we'll live or die."

Wither where they marching? Against the oppressors and the robbers – the luxurious ones who swindled and wheedled their victims out of their due of life.

Then he saw a strange, horrifying spectacle. Hovering behind the marching crowd was an army of ghosts – ghosts of men, women and children; those who had perished of hunger, of famine, of disease caused by an unrighteous and unclean social system – ghosts of men and woman who had killed themselves in their despair; ghosts of little children who had been murdered by want and starvation; ghosts of old men and women who had died in workhouses, and in the streets, and on the roads – and all these with spectral hands pointed to the Red Flag; and it seemed as if they were singing too, and urging the living men and women on.

His soul took fire from the Red Flag. He resolved to march with that procession. He shouted –

> "Raise the Scarlet Standard high,
> Within its shade we'll live or die."

He saw men of all classes and conditions joining the army of the Red Flag – not only working folks ground down and skinned by the capitalists – but clergymen, writers, physicians, clerks – even lawyers – all those who saw that the present state of things was ill and unjust, and made misery amongst men. And he saw a wonderful sight: the heavens above these people were in mystic motion, and the stars marched with them.

And then he saw a picture of the land of good fellowship, towards which the Red Flag was being borne – he saw industry and trade so arranged that there was food for all, clothes for all, shelter for all – no pauperism, no unemployed, no starvation; everybody had a butter-dish where the knife didn't clatter sadly against the inside – a land, not of human beings who allowed a few money-maniacs to make trouble for all the rest, but a land where all that the co-operative nation produced was shared out equitably amongst all – and over this happy land of healthy men and fair women and joyous children, the Red Flag waved triumphantly.

[29 August 1908]

XIV. The Primitive Methodist Minister.

Next morning, about ten o'clock, the caretaker, a round-faced, jolly, intelligent man, came up the stairs, and greeted Jim with a kindly "Hello! Well, what sort of a night have you had? Were you comfortable?"

"I've been all right," replied Jim. "I think I'm giving you a deal of trouble."

"Trouble's nothing if we can only get justice for everybody," said the caretaker. "Have you had any breakfast?"

"No," said Jim.

"You ought to have helped yourself," said the caretaker. "There's plenty of stuff in the bar."

"I'm taking no harm," said Jim. "I'd a good supper last night."

"One good supper won't last a chap for a life-time" said the caretaker. "I'll boil some water, and you can have a drink of coffee, and some bread and butter, unless you prefer another pie. But twopenny pies get monotonous, don't they?"

"It all depends whether you are hungry or not," said Jim.

"Let's get the kettle on," said the caretaker. "I'm glad you kept the fire in."

"At the expense of your coal," said Jim.

"Well, it's got to be burnt; and who's more right to burn it than the class that toils? Yet there are thousands of workers can't afford a fire – even in this weather; and the price of coal is going up. The colliery proprietors always pick their time to raise the price when coal is most necessary – always in the winter. Oh, they're the most damnable rascals!"

"You're against all the men that make things dear?" said Jim, seeking for information as to the aims of this movement, whose members, anyhow, though evidently shunned and denounced by the orthodox in creed and politics, had received him as a fellow-man, and treated him as a brother.

"Certainly we're against 'em – the plunderers!" exclaimed the caretaker. "Under a proper system of Government all the necessaries of life could be made cheap enough to supply everybody. It's these capitalists with their rents and royalties, and general all-round cop, that makes things dear. The miner doesn't get the price we pay for the coal; the mine-owner and the owner of the land take shillings where the poor collier gets pence. And it's the same with everything, and we say it's not right, and we'll put an end to it. Could put an end to it this very day if the workers themselves had only the sense to see how they are gulled and robbed. But they seem to think – as far as they can think, which isn't much – that that which always has been always must be, world without end, Amen!"[83]

Jim smiled, while the caretaker rattled on for a few moment, jumping up eventually and saying, "The kettle's boiling. Now for coffee. The man that got the idea of the steam engine from watching a kettle boil is the man that made the fortunes of the capitalists. Then they talk of what *they* have done! All they have done is to grab every invention that's come up, and use it for their own aggrandisement.[84]

He spoke the big word as if it were a pet of his – one that he had found, and gathered with a special affection.

"Yes, all for their own aggrandisement," he said. "All inventions should be owned by the Government, for the benefit of the whole community – not for the aggrandisement of a few. Now here's your coffee. I'll get some bread and butter. Whack in, and let the hungry dog in the kennel enjoy himself."[85]

He got a plate of bread and butter, and, lighting his pipe, smoked and chatted while Jim ate.

"You slept well, eh?"

"Oh, yes," said Jim.

"Didn't the clatter of the clogs wake you up between five and six? There's a lot of workers pass this way in the early morning – off to factory and weaving-shed in the cold and the dark. Mugs! There's no need to get up at that unearthly hour – especially to make money for the fellows who are in bed. From six o'clock to breakfast time the workers work for themselves – the rest of the day they are piling it up for their masters. Two hours' pay for the man – eight hours to the master.[86] That's rich, isn't it? Yet the mugs can't see it even if they got the eight hours work for themselves, and gave the master the two hours, it would still be unfair – but it would be far better than it is at present; and we Socialists won't rest till there's a change."

"This place is a Socialist branch?" asked Jim.

"Yes; do you know anything about Socialism?"

"A little; but I mean to know more. From last night I am a Socialist."

"Then last night – the good Sunday evening," and the caretaker smiled – "if you didn't find salvation you found sense; which is a better thing. For sense means salvation in the true sense of the word – not the little Bethel selfish notion of salvation – a man saving his own soul and securing a Jew's harp,[87] while everybody else may go to the blazes."

"What do you call this branch or club?"

"Brunborough Branch of the S.D.F. – which means Social-Democratic Federation."

"Is the S.D.F. the only Socialist body?"

"Well, it's the only thorough one. There's the I.L.P. – Independent Labour Party – trying to coax people with the word 'labour,' which isn't so dreadful to the donkeys as the word 'Socialism.' But there are good Socialists in the I.L.P. There's also the Labour Church[88] – gives a bit of religion as a sop.[89]

After he had finished his breakfast, Jim said he'd better be going to see if he could find work. He asked the caretaker if he knew any place where he might have a chance at labouring.

"I don't," said the caretaker. "There are hundreds of unemployed in this town, as in all other towns. Rum state of affairs, that – men willing to work and can't have it; can't even go on the land. They're a pack of cowards or they wouldn't stand it. Seeing so much unemployment, and men working for wages that won't keep 'em decently alive, and pauperism for their reward in their old age – its these things that make us Socialists. Our present system breeds nothing but paupers, loafers, criminals, hypocrites, lunatics, cowards and grabbers. Let's try some system that will produce 'gradely' men and women, as we say in Lancashire – honest, clean, and brave. It's a rare thing to meet a real man – a man who dare be what he thinks, who dare speak his true mind, and stand erect under the sun and stars – in old England nowadays. We all lie, and fawn, and cajole, and pretend, and deceive, and dupe one another in order to get a living."

"Are you one of the Socialist speakers?" inquired Jim.

The caretaker laughed. "It's my gas that made you put that question. Well, I don't reckon to be any orator, but I do my bit at times, when there's nobody better to mount the tub. – Oh, if you are going out, call in again this afternoon and let us know how you go on. Joe Summerfield wants to see you. He'll be here after dinner."

Jim had no luck in his quest for work. None to be got anywhere. He tramped about till he was weary and disheartened.

Then, passing along a street on his way back to the Socialist Club, he saw, outside a brick chapel, a noticeboard, which started a train of memories and hope. On the black board, in gilt letters, was this inscription –

PRIMITIVE METHODIST CHAPEL
Preacher: The Rev. Arthur Milnthorp
Residence: 14, Pendle Street.

I'll go to see him," said Jim. "He'll perhaps be able to tell me something about my mother."

His mother had occasionally attended the chapel. Jim had been one of the scholars in the Young Men's Class at the Sunday School. Even if Mr. Milnthorp himself could give no information about Mrs. Wilkinson,[90] he would be able to put Jim on the track of somebody who could.

[5 September 1908]
XIV. The Primitive Methodist Minister. (*Continued.*)

When Jim reached Pendle Street, and was just knocking at the door of No. 14, the minister, hat on, evidently setting forth on some errand or visit, came out. He was a small, slender man, with a benevolent face and intellectual forehead, grey-eyed, and bearded.

"Mr. Milnthorpe?" said Jim.

"Yes, that's me, my friend" – peering at Jim to see if he knew him.

"I think you've forgotten me," said Jim.

"I'm afraid I have – but, no, I remember you now. Jim Campbell, isn't it?"

"Yes, sir."

"Who went away to Bulborough to work – let me see – it's only three years ago. You are greatly changed, Jim; you look as if you had been through the mill."[91]

"I have been through the mill," said Jim. "A good deal can happen in three years. But I came to see if you could tell me anything about my mother."

"Now, that's curious; yes, I can."

"She's alive, then?" asked Jim.

"Oh, yes; she's alive, Jim, and fairly well, all things considered."

Jim said nothing, but he looked his joy.

"She came to me three or four days ago – yes, it was Friday," continued Mr. Milnthrop, "recommended by an old friend of mine, Mrs. Wilkinson, of Alderham."

"Wilkinson," said Jim to himself, and remembered the elderly woman, who, along with the sweet young woman called May, he had met in the common lodging-house at Blakeham.

But what could this Mrs. Wilkinson have to do with his mother – and how could she be an acquaintance of the minister? Of course, it must be some other Mrs. Wilkinson; it was a common name.

"And where is my mother now?" asked Jim.

"I put her to lodge with an old couple in Ogden Street."

"And who is paying for her?" asked Jim.

"Now, Jim –, don't be too inquisitive," said Mr. Milnthorp, with a smile.

"I know; it's you!" said Jim. "I am very grateful – I –"

"That'll do, Jim. Come along – I'm going in the direction of Ogden Street. I daresay you're eager to see your mother."

XV. A Son Finds His Mother.

On the way, Jim, in answer to the reverend gentleman's questions, told his story to Mr. Milnthorp.

"Well, you've fairly been in it, my lad," said Mr. Milnthorp. "No wonder I didn't recognise you. But then, even before you went away I hadn't seen you for some time. You kept away from the school. Why was that?"

"I told our teacher I couldn't believe in eternal punishment – hell-fire – and after that he was always calling me an atheist in the class; so it wasn't nice, and I stayed away."

"You ought to have come and told me, Jim. Between you and me, I no more believe in everlasting damnation than you do. Of course I don't tell my congregation so. One has to lead people gradually out of these old superstitions. Where did you sleep last night? Not outside?"

"No, I was lucky. I got amongst the Socialists, and they let me sleep at their club."

"That was good of them. There are some fine chaps amongst the Socialists. I know some of them."

"I mean to be a Socialist henceforth," said Jim.

"I would like to hear every workingman in the land say the same thing, Jim. To a great extent I'm a Socialist myself. Any man who truly follows Christ as the Divine Teacher must be a Socialist. God's a Socialist, Jim; for the whole plan of evolution and the purpose of the universe is to develop brotherhood. Ah! I can see what you're thinking, Jim," and the minister smiled. "You are wondering why, if I am a Socialist, I don't say so in the pulpit. Well, if I did, I should pretty soon have no pulpit – the bulk of my flock would turn me out. So I've got to teach them step by step; give them Socialism in small doses and without label, and even that startles them sometimes. Yesterday in my sermon I spoke in favour of a great Socialistic writer who has done excellent work for humanity and is now opposing Christianity because he honestly thinks it blocks the path to progress.[92] I said the man was our brother, and even if he opposed our theological beliefs, he was a good man, and a man more after God's own heart than many who attended chapel regularly. That rather shocked some of them, I can tell you. Ah, Jim, very ignorant and narrow-minded are most men yet; and we shall have to be careful how we deal with them."

"Well, I daresay you understand these things better than I do," said Jim. "I don't know what's the best way to lead people, nor to put the world right. But I do know that there's terrible suffering amongst the poor."

When they reached Ogden Street, and entered the house of the good people with whom Mrs. Campbell was in haven, Jim's mother, as soon as she saw her son, started up from her chair. "It's Jim! Jim, my lad!" she cried.

"Ay, it's Jim," said her son, "and I'm glad to find you've dropped amongst friends, mother."

"Ay, ay," said Mrs. Campbell, "I'm among friends now, Jim, but I've had some awful times. I've tramped, and slept in the workhouse, and in the casual wards. I never thought I should come to that. And the men in charge of those places are cruel and insulting. There's the man at Waddiham Tramp Ward –"

"I know him," said Jim, "and I'd like to give him a jolly good hiding."

"Don't get savage, Jim," said Mr. Milnthorpe, smiling.

"You'd be worse than savage if you'd to submit to that man – Slamdrop's his name," said Jim. "But I'll look after you now, mother."

"I know you will," said the old woman. "You were always a good lad, Jim. But you've had hard luck yourself. They told my your wife and child were dead, and you out of work."

"Ay, ay," said Jim, moodily, remembering that he was out of work still, and wondering how he would be able to keep his mother. For he had neither house nor wage, nor any prospect of work.

"I shouldn't have been here, and kindly helped by Mr. Milnthorp," said Mrs. Campbell, "but for a woman I met on tramp – Mrs. Wilkinson her name is, and she has a young woman with her called May. She gave me a note to bring to Mr. Milnthorp, and she said he would help me. And she was right. He's a good man is Mr. Milnthorp."

"Now, no praise, Grannie," said the minister. "I only try to do my duty."

"Mrs. Wilkinson also said she had met you, Jim," continued Mrs. Campbell, "and she said you would be sure to find me. She's proved right, too; though, not hearing anything of you, I had given you up for dead. You've been tramping about, too, in search of work. It's an awful world for the poor, isn't it, Jim?"

"Who is this Mrs. Wilkinson?" said Jim, turning to the minister. "You must know her, of course. I met her in a common lodging-house at Blakeham."

"Oh, yes, I know her," said Mr. Milnthorp.

"Excuse me," said Jim, "but why don't you help her, then? She is a good woman, I am sure."

"She is most certainly a good woman," said Mr. Milnthorp.

"And yet she is on tramp," said Jim. "How comes she to have such influence and such friends, and yet on tramp?"

Mr. Milnthorp smiled, and said: "There's a time to ask questions, Jim, and a time for answering them. But the time of asking is not always the time for answering."

Jim was sure there was some mystery about Mrs. Wilkinson and May, but perceived that Mr. Milnthorp would not – even if he could – help him to solve it; not at present, anyhow.

After another minute's chat, Mr. Milnthorp went away and Jim was left talking with his mother, who interrogated him about his troubles and his trampings. But, not wishing to upset her any more than could be helped, Jim told her as little as possible of this hardships, and said he thought he would be able to get work in Brunborough – though he hadn't the least idea how or where – and then he would get a little cottage, where he and his mother would live cosily together.

Presently, promising his mother to come back in the evening, Jim set off for the Socialist Club, where Joe Summerfield was waiting for him.

[12 September 1908]

XV. A Son Finds His Mother. (*Continued.*)

"I've been hunting for work," said Jim, "and not got any. But I've found my mother. She's been having a rough time of it, and I must get something to do now to keep her, or she'll have to go to the workhouse, and I don't want that."

"I don't approve of the workhouse system myself," said Summerfield, "but in the present condition of things I should advise the unemployed and destitute to go in a body to the workhouse, and thus compel the authorities to do something. If two or three thousand people all marched to the workhouse demanding admission they would stir things up. And I know that at this very moment in Brunborough there are two or three thousand people who don't know where the next meal is to come from. But come along, we'll go to see Dick Blythe; perhaps he will be able to find a job for you. I don't know – so don't hope extravagantly – but there'll be no harm in seeing him. He's one of us, and he'll help you if he can."

Quitting the club, where a few members were busy at the billiard-table, and others reading or playing cards, Joe and Jim crossed the centre of the town till they came to a street of warehouses near the railway and the canal.

"Dick Blythe is a cotton waste dealer," said Joe. "Here's his place; there's the name-plate on the door."

They found Dick Blythe, a genial, fresh-faced man of about forty, with a Roman nose and jolly blue eyes, in his office. He was garbed as an ordinary businessman, in a light-grey suit, cuffed and collared, a gold watch-chain across his waistcoat, a ring on the little finger of his left hand. He seemed quite a flourishing gentleman. Jim was surprised to find such a man connected with the Socialist movement. He had thought that only the hungry and the hard-up would rally round The Red Flag.

"Well, Joe, what is it?" said Blythe to Summerfield.

"Doesn't the tale tell itself?" said Joe, with a glance at Jim. "Comrade here on the rocks. Wants a berth. Have you any opening, Dick?"

Blythe grinned, and it was a treat to see that indescribable, good-natured grin; it expressed the whole droll, happy character of the man; and, scratching his head in comic bewilderment, said: "Well, Joe, if I could find work for everybody that wanted it, I should be the biggest employer on earth. But I would if I could. Had you a good meeting last night? I meant to get down, but the missus wanted me to take her to church – she's quite orthodox and respectable, though I'm nobbut a wastrel" (he sometimes dropped a dialect word into his speech), "so I took her, for when a chap's got a wife he can't always go his own way, not if he wants peace at home, anyhow, and peace is a pretty thing, especially for a man that likes to be comfortable as I do. There was a cycling club meeting, too. I should have been at that to get out a programme of runs for next season, and arrange what Socialist literature to take with us and scatter about among the benighted villages and heathen places of Britain."[93]

"Well, have you any opening for this man, Dick?" asked Joe.

"How can I tell till I've thought a bit?" said Blythe, rubbing his right hand up the side of his head – it was a little habit of his. "Dang it all! a chap can't do a thing without considering, unless it's tumbling off a house, or some lumber of that sort. I was listening to Job Bullock's tales last night. I went in the King's Arms after I'd been to church – it was really necessary cause and effect, after such a sermon as I heard – and Job Bullock was telling his tales. And he has a merry stock of 'em, too. That man and his tales ought to be put into a book. If I could only write like some of our Socialist scribes I'd make a fortune out of Job Bullock's yarns. Well, now, about this young fellow that's after a job." Turning to Jim: "Where do you come from? What can you do?"

Jim briefly related his story.

"Miserable devils, them spinners," said Blythe. "Some of 'em, anyhow. There are one or two decent chaps in the spinning factory – we've two or three among our members, haven't we? But the bulk of 'em – God scrape their selfish souls!"[94]

After some more chat, and a few questions to Jim, Blythe said, grinning, and rubbing his right fist up his head, as if bothered out of his life; "Well, I'll give Campbell – that's the name, isn't it? – a start at a pound a week, just to labour at anything that's knocking about, and do odd jobs, though the lord knows I haven't the slightest idea of what I can find him to do. There's not enough work to go round for the men I have now. But I like to help a chap if I can."

And Jim rejoiced as if he had come into a fortune, as a miner suddenly coming across a diamond or a big gold nugget. For he had got work! With twenty shillings a week he could do wonders! He would get a little cot for himself and mother, and once more know what home was. To the rich, to those who have never known want, a pound a week is but a trifle, a nothing; but the poor know that miracles can be wrought with twenty shillings a week. Significant is it that, in their extensive hope that is satisfied with so narrow a realisation, they generally think of the pound as twenty shillings – not as a one pound unit – for twenty, even though it be in silver, looks and feels more than one in gold. So Jim Campbell's heart was uplifted, and he was in glory. He had got work and that meant wages; and that meant he was no longer a helpless, drifting boat, but a vessel with a rudder to steer his course.

Only those who have known what it is to be unemployed and in despair can realise the joy of Jim Campbell as his heart sang, "Work, work – I have got work!"

XVI. Explosive Proposals.

Ere Christmas, Jim Campbell and his mother were comfortably established in a little cottage. They had only the most necessary and cheapest furniture as yet, for one cannot do everything on a pound a week, but they were gradually acquiring more and more; and Mr. Milnthorp had helped by giving them a bed and table and a few chairs, while, Mr. Blythe, Jim's employer, had given Jim an old sofa. Altogether they looked very snug in the little cot, which lay on the edge of the town, on the road to Thornfield and Pendlcham.

Jim had become a member of Brunborough S.D.F., and was finding out the ramifications of the Socialist movement. He discovered there were various sections. There was the Independent Labour Party, which, though based on the Socialist programme – that is, the socialisation of the instruments and means of production and distribution – allied itself, for political purposes, with Trade Unionism.[95] Also there was a Labour Church, dealing more with the ethical and spiritual side of the movement. The strongest and most numerous body by far was the I.L.P. The S.D.F., the more militant and uncompromising body had nothing like the membership of the I.L.P. The Labour Church was but in a struggling way, too, most Socialists having no inclination for things spiritual. The I.L.P. and

S.D.F. were in most towns tacitly, if not openly, antagonistic, or, at least, walked separate ways, though in some cases they combined at election times.[96] The S.D.F. claimed to be the only true and genuine Socialist organisation.

Jim was rather surprised to find difference and jealousy in the Socialist movement. He thought that men holding the same ideas would march together. But he saw and understood how different temperaments would seek different methods of attaining the goal.

Most of the Socialists belonged to the working-class, though there were a few tradesmen and professional men amongst then, including doctors and journalists, and a solicitor. But the bulk belonged to the workers – the middles class, as a whole, held aloof, as also did the lowest working classes, and the great army of unemployed was outside the movement. Most of the Socialists were so from a sense of injustice and a spirit of rebellion against the capitalist-competitive system. Some were Socialists from sympathy with the poor and oppressed.

Socialism was a natural reaction against the government and social system which caused cruel poverty, uncertainty of employment, and insufficient wages.

As Dick Blythe said, "If everybody had three good meals a day and a bob to spend there'd be no Socialism. If the capitalists and aristocrats want to stop socialism, let 'em take that tip – see that the multitude's well fed, and there'll be no revolutions. That's what Ben Brierley said – he's a very funny sketch were he brings that philosophy in."[97]

In the first week of the new year there came into Brunborough Ronald Fordham, the swell tramp, the millionaire's son, and Jim was surprised to see him one evening playing billiards in the S.D.F. Club. He greeted Jim cordially, and treated him to a drink.

"I'm doing well now," he said. "Fell amongst friends. I've a tidy berth at travelling. I'm thinking of settling in Brunborough for a while, as I'm working this district."

[19 September 1908]

XV. A Son Finds His Mother. (*Continued*.)

"Then you'll be glad I didn't let you chuck yourself in the sea?" said Jim, with a smile.

Fordham laughed uneasily. "I'm not sure about that," he said. "I was mad that night. I think I'm mad now sometimes. When I think of that old villain, and the money that ought to be mine, and when, worst of all, I think of that girl there – the girl I love – I feel mad and desperate."

"Oh, you mustn't think of that," said Jim. "You've got enough to be happy – money isn't everything."

"No, but when you're cheated out of your rights and properties that's something, isn't it?" said Fordham. "But I'll be even with the old wretch some day."

"I shouldn't trouble about him if I were you," said Jim.

"Well, perhaps it would be best not to, but I can't help it. Anyhow, I'll see how I go on here. I think I'll find a house and send for the wife and kiddy."

"You're married, then?" asked Jim, rather astonished.

"Oh yes; been married a couple of years."

Jim was silent a moment. Then he said, "Why should you bother about that girl, then? You can't marry her now."

"No, curse it, I can't. But you don't understand. It's a tragedy."

"I understand this," said Jim, "that it's silly to go after another girl when you've already got a wife."

"Well, I can't help it. And, knowing out of what I was born – the wild lust of that fellow and my mother – is it any wonder that I am what I am? What can you expect the child of debauchery to be? Sometimes I feel mad; I wish to be better, and can't. I feel like taking my own life, and I'm afraid I shall do so some day."

"Nay, don't talk like that," said Jim. "Pull up, and keep a hold of yourself."

"All right. Have another drink," said Fordham. "Let's be gay while we can!"

Fordham came to the club nightly, talking with the more extreme and impulsive members.

"Look here," he said, "we Socialists shall never do anything by being quiet and peaceful. We've got to scare the world. Why not make some bombs and blow a factory or two up? Take old Langdon's for a start. I know a fellow that will give us all the instructions for the manufacture of infernal machines[98] and bombs. We're too tame. Let's make a stir!"

Some of the members of the club only smiled at this as a nonsensical outburst, but two or three listened seriously. Joe Summerfield, however, hearing of it, and hearing that Fordham was continually on this string, privately warned his fellow-members to pay no heed to such proposals. "Fordham's either cracked, or is a spy," he said. "He may be a spy in the pay of the police. You know how a few years ago the Birmingham police entangled some of our comrades in a plot which was really a trap laid by the police themselves.[99] Those in power, and those behind 'em, are ready to resort to any baseness to cast discredit on our growing movement. Socialism is growing rapidly, and they're beginning to fear that the day of the blood-suckers and money-grabbers is at an end. Just be careful of Fordham, and have nothing to do with his schemes for violence. Our weapon is the ballot-box and no other."

But some of the younger Socialists who had read of the Paris Commune, dreamed of revolution and barricades.

XVII. Surprises.

Jim Campbell found his work pleasant under Dick Blythe, and soon got an increase of wages, for his employer, finding Jim capable of doing a little bookkeeping and clerical work, gave him jobs to do in the office.

One day Blythe asked Jim if he had ever been to the Sunday night meetings at the Labour Church, and, on Jim answering in the negative, said. "Well, I should have a look in sometime if I were you. You'd better see all sides and phases of the movement."

"Some of our chaps at the pub sneer at the Labour Church," said Jim.

"Well, we'll let 'em off; it's their way," said Blythe. "Some of our chaps are a bit narrow and intolerant, you know – they think there's only one point of view, and that's the one they hold. Too materialistic, some of 'em, too; can't stand anything that savours of religion. We can hardly blame 'em for that, for religion's mostly holy humbugs nowadays. Then, again, some of our chaps are at loggerheads with old Tommy Winder, the president of the Labour Church, and I must admit, to be fair, that Tommy doesn't keep the gloves on when he's dealing this those who object to his policy. But, all the same, he's a fine old chap, and if I had to choose between our club and the Labour Church I should give myself to the latter. But, as it is, I'm the connecting-link, and the peace-keeper. For the various sections of the movement sometimes forget the brotherhood they preach and get cross with one another. The hot extremists have no patience with the compromisers and the trimmers, as they call them – with those Socialists who, for political ends, are prepared to give and take with the merely Labour men. Anyhow, have a look in the Labour Church sometime."

Jim went to the Labour Church the next Sunday evening, liked the service, and became a frequent attender, though still retaining his membership of the Red Flag Club. No matter what happened, he would never forsake that; he owed it too much gratitude.

But he found that other members of the club went to the Labour Church – some often, some frequently, and most of them on any occasion when some prominent Socialist or Labour leader occupied the platform.

One Sunday night, his mother not being well, Jim stayed with her, and missed the Labour Church, so did not hear the unusual announcement of the next Sunday's speaker. But, glancing through the advertisements in the Socialist paper he took in weekly, he started as he read this: –

BRUNBOROUGH LABOUR CHURCH.
Sunday Evening, March 15th.
SPEAKER: MRS. WILKINSON, of Alderham,
on
"TRAMP LIFE."

"What's this mean?" wondered Jim. "Can it be the same? If so, she's got out of the tramp life, and if she has, her companion, May, will be with her, I am sure. This is the best news I've seen for a long time."

He read the notice again and again; he could hardly believe it.

Then he had a doubt. It might be some other Mrs. Wilkinson. But – tramp life. There could not be a lot of Mrs. Wilkinsons who had had experience of tramp life. No, it must be she.

"Mother," he said, – she was just clearing the tea-things away after the evening meal – "just listen to this," and he read the Labour Church announcement.

"Well, what about that?" said Mrs. Campbell. "What are you botherin' me about your Labour Church for? What new sort o' church shall we be havin' next? There never was but one church, and Catholics and Methodists, when I went to such places."

"Never mind that, mother," said Jim. "What I wanted you to notice was the name of the speaker – the lady's name."

"Ay, women preachin', too," said Mrs. Campbell. "I'm sure that's again' the Scripture."

"But the name," said Jim, smiling, "the name – Mrs. Wilkinson! Don't you remember Mrs. Wilkinson? The woman who sent you to Mr. Milnthorp?"

"Oh, yes; but what's she got to do with this?"

"Well, I fancy it's the same woman."

"Nay; she was on tramp."

"Well, may she not have had good luck, like we have, and be a tramp no longer?"

"I hope she has," said Mrs. Campbell, "for she deserves it. She was a kind woman, and did me a good turn, and she didn't look like a tramp. I'm puzzled about that woman, Jim."

"So am I. But I'll go to hear her, and then we'll solve the mystery. Do you think you could manage to come, too?"

"Nay, nay. I'm best by th' fire i' this weather. I mustn't give my rheumatism any chance to be worse, it's bad enough as it is. If I could go I'd like to see her an' thank her for she was very good to me. But if it turns out to be her, you thank her for me, Jim, and tell her that Mr. Milnthorp helped me, and that you an' me have found one another, an' are all right."

On the Sunday evening, Jim, full of expectation, was down at the Labour Church early; he was the first there. He got a seat near the front, and presently the chairman came out of the ante-room near the platform, followed by a lady, at sight of whom Jim's eyes filled with astonishment.

It was not Mrs. Wilkinson. It was May.

Jim was more perplexed than ever.

How could Mrs. Wilkinson be May? Was the notice a mistake – should it be Miss Wilkinson?

Yet that only made more confusion. For Mrs. Wilkinson had said May was not her daughter.

[26 September 1908]
XVII. Surprises. (*Continued.*)

While these puzzled thoughts were jumping up in Jim's mind May had seated herself on the right of the chairman, and how beautiful she looked, thought Jim. She was simply robed in a dark-blue dress, with white lace about the bosom.

After the singing of a hymn, and the saying of the Lord's Prayer by the chairman, the old veteran, Tommy Winder, the chairman, said: – "Friends, I have to make an apology and explanation. Mrs. Wilkinson cannot come to-night, and she greatly regrets to have to break her engagement, but she is indisposed. However, she has sent in her stead one who, for all I hear, will prove an excellent substitute, and who will address us on the same subject, "Tramp Life." This is Miss May Marsden, whom, I am sure, we are pleased to welcome here to-night. This is her first appearance on a platform in Brunsboruough. As you know, Mrs. Wilkinson, a lady of courage as well as sympathy, resolving to find out what tramp life really was, took the best method there is of studying anything – that is, experience. Disguised as a beggar, a tramp, she has visited various workhouses, casual wards, and common 'doss-houses' in towns of the north. She has known and suffered all that the outcasts of the road know and suffer, and I believe she will ere long publish the result of her investigations in a book. We cannot help but admire such a noble woman – would there were many more such women in the world. Women who resolve to see for themselves how their poor, wretched, penniless, homeless sisters fare. There is, I am proud to say, another such woman – young though she is – sitting by me. I refer to Miss Marsden. For Mrs. Wilkinson in most of her journeys, feeling that two would be safer than one, did not go alone. Her companion was Miss Marsden. This young lady, sitting here, looking, if I may say so, so trim and pretty" – the audience had a smile, in which May blushingly joined – "this young lady, little as you would suppose so, has tramped the roads as one of the destitute, has slept on the plank bed in the tramp ward, has sampled the workhouse diet and routine, and to-night will tell us of some of the things she has seen and heard in her strange travels in that submerged world of humanity which is part of our own world, yet of which, to our shame, we know so little. I am proud to know such a brave young lady, a young woman who has such a heart to feel for others, and a soul to dare to speak in their behalf, and I am sure you will all give her a thorough rousing welcome."

The audience cheered enthusiastically, while Jim Campbell sat staring at May. The mystery was solved now. And who would ever have dreamed of this explanation?

While the chairman was speaking, May's eyes, roving round, had hit on Jim Campbell; she seemed surprised, puzzled, as if she could hardly credit her sight.

But when she rose to address the meeting she was quite composed. "My friends," she began, "our fine old chairman, whom I fear is too complimentary, said that my friend, Mrs. Wilkinson, and myself had tramped the roads as the destitute, known for their troubles and woes. That is not exactly correct. For though it is true that we have known, for a time, the tramp life, with all its hardships and injustices, we had one thing that our unfortunate sisters of the road had not – we had the joy of the knowledge that our tramping was but for a time, that it was by choice, not compulsion, and that, most blessed consolation of all, we could end it when we would. But for that I fear we could not have endured the horrors – they would have driven us to drink, or madness, or suicide. What, then, must the tramp life be to those who have not our sustaining knowledge that it was only for a few days, after which we should return to our home comforts?"

Miss Marsden then went on to detail the experiences of Mrs. Wilkinson and herself, while Jim Campbell, as he listened to the sweet, pleading voice, thought of May as he had last seen her, in the low squalor of the common lodging-house at Blakeham, and wondered was that the dream, or this?

Well, he had his desire; he had met May again, and learned who she was. And he felt even further from her than he had done in the common lodging-house, and this feeling was not a glad one. For Jim Campbell had also made another discovery this evening. He had found out that he loved May Marsden.

XVIII. Jim and May.

When the address was over, and the assembly dispersing, Jim rose to go with the rest. Had Mrs. Wilkinson been the lecturer he would have spoken to her, and given her, as commissioned, his mother's grateful thanks. But, well, it was all different now. He would have liked to speak to May, but – well, he did not know what to do, and was walking out of the room when Miss Marsden, who had been chatting with a group, hurried after him, and, touching him on the shoulder, said. "I'm not mistaken, am I? You're Jim Campbell. Don't you know me again?"

Jim felt like answering, "Shall I ever forget you any more for ever?" but he only blushed, and said; "Yes, I am Jim Campbell."

"I am pleased to meet you again," said Miss Marsden, "and so pleased to see" – she glanced at his clothes and collar, the indications of at least some certain income – " to see that you have got work. Isn't that so?"

"It is," said Jim. "I'm glad to say I've been working here some months now, and it's a good shop – I work for Mr. Blythe."

"Oh, Dick Blythe! I know him. Jolly fellow! The life and soul of a cycle ride. I've met him many a time. And you're living in Brumborough now?"

"Yes."

"Oh, how shocking of me!" cried May. "I ought to have asked you that first of all. Have you found your mother?"

"Yes; we're living together."

"That's grand. The dear old lady. You know Mrs. Wilkinson and I dropped across her in Waddiham Tramp Ward – poor, dear old soul! She wasn't used to it, just as we were not, and it punished her. I'm so glad you found her. We guessed you were her son. She told us that she'd tramped to Bolborough in search of you. You ought to have let her know your whereabouts, you know."

"Yes, I know that," said Jim, guiltily, "but I was in trouble and desperate – and –"

"Anyhow, it's all right now," said Miss Marsden.

"My mother told me to thank Mrs. Wilkinson – and that means you, too – for being so kind to her. I told her I thought Mrs. Wilkinson was lecturing here. I wasn't sure it was the same, you know."

"And, then, through her not turning up, you've had a disappointment," said May, with a smile.

"Oh, no!" said Jim, smiling too, "not a disappointment, but a bigger treat than ever I expected."

"Ah, you're flattering," said Miss Marsden.

"My mother would have come down to the hall but for her rheumatism," said Jim.

"Give her my best regards," said Miss Marsden. "Poor, dear old grannie. I should like to see her and have a talk with her. I've half a mind to run up to your home with you. Is it far?"

"We can go in ten minutes on the tram," said Jim, who, as a rule, spent nothing on electric cars, but, with bliss at the thought of riding with May for ten minutes, was prepared to do reckless things in the way of expenditure.

"Well, it's not late," said May. "It's only just eight o'clock. I promised Mrs. Blythe to have supper with her, but there's plenty of time for that. I'm staying with the Blythes overnight, you know. I don't go back to Alderham till Monday afternoon. I've to see Mr. Milnthorp in the morning. Just wait a moment while I tell my friends to tell Mrs. Blythe – I see Dick's not here to-night – why, hello! here he is. This is a nice time to come to a meeting, Mr. Blythe."

"Very sorry," said Blythe, with his own droll grin. "I intended to come to the lecture, but – well, I didn't get. Anyhow, I'm in time to escort you up to our house."

"Well, I'm not coming yet," said May. "I'm just running up to Mr. Campbell's to see his mother, an old acquaintance of mine."

"Oh, you know Jim, then?" said Blythe. "Very well, if Jim's no objection, I'll go up with you."

"Jim may not have any objection," said May, "but I have. This is a private affair" – she smiled, archly – "Mr. Dick Blythe."

"Very well," said Blythe, scratching his head. "I'm jiggered if I understand, but if a chap had no more sense than waste time in trying to get round all the ununderstandable – how's that for a word? – things in the world he'd soon be in the lunatic asylum. Well, get off, but see you're back in time for supper at ten. I'll tell Mrs. Blythe."

"That's a good fellow," said May. "And now," to Jim, "I think we'll be getting along, eh?"

[3 October 1908]

XVIII. Jim and May. (*Continued.*)

Bidding good-night to the chairman and other friends, and a few people who wanted to have the honour of shaking hands with her, May and Jim quitted the Labour Church Hall – an upstairs room in a building in the centre of the town – and were soon in the tramcar, speeding towards Jim Campbell's home. And Jim felt glorious and happy. Even to have the lady of his heart by his side for a few moments – then, perhaps, never again as long as he lived – was bliss.

"Do you know," said May, "when I looked at the audience and saw you I never was more surprised in my life. But I was pleased, too. And I'll warrant you were amazed, too, when you saw me step on to the platform, were you not?" and she laughed.

"I was almost startled," said Jim. "It was so strange, so unexpected, and yet I was glad, too. I had thought I should never meet you again."

"So you have thought about me?"

"Oh, yes," said Jim, saying so little because he dare not say the much that was in his mind. "Somehow, when I saw you and Mrs. Wilkinson in the lodging-house I couldn't believe you were ordinary tramps."

"Was our make-up so bad, then?" asked May, smiling.

"No, it wasn't that. It was your ways, your manner. I thought you must be something far above the usual run of tramps."

"Oh, not much," said May. "I'm only a factory lass – a weaver."

Jim rejoiced at his news. It brought the angel so much nearer his own sphere.[100]

"Whatever you are," he said, "you are learned and eloquent. You pictured the tramp life well. As you talked, I saw myself back in the common lodging-house in Blakeham, where I first met you."

"Ah, that was because you had been in it. You'd been through all I said. I'm very glad to find you have risen."

"I've been lucky," said Jim. "I fell amongst good friends."

"Well, if Dick Blythe's one of 'em, you did. But tell me about it."

Jim told his tale, and May said, "I'm pleased Dick Blythe found you work. He's a good jolly soul. He's the life and heart of our Socialist cycle meets."

"So you're a Socialist, then?" asked Jim.

"Of course. Everybody ought to be Socialists. Aren't you one?"

"Yes, and a red-hot 'un," said Jim, and May laughed a his vehemence. "Is Mrs. Wilkinson a Socialist, too? Who is she? – or am I too inquisitive?"

"Not at all," answered May. "Mrs. Wilkinson is not an avowed Socialist, but she's as good as one. All her sympathy is with the down-trodden and fallen. Her husband is a Primitive Methodist minister at Alderham. That's how she knows Mr. Milnthorp. He and her husband are old friends – were students together."

"Now I begin to understand a few things," said Jim. "I see why Mrs. Wilkinson sent my mother to Mr. Milnthorp. And she goes on tramp, and you with her?"

"She has been many more tramp journeys than I,"[101] said May. "I've only been two – that was my second when I met you. The first was in my summer holidays – the second time, our weaving-shed was stopped for a week, so I took the opportunity to see what tramp life was in the winter."

"You're a plucky one," said Jim.

"Well, it's best to see for oneself what things are, and then you know what you're talking about, you know. Mrs. Wilkinson is a member of the Alderham Board of Guardians.[102] When first she suggested ameliorations and reforms the gentlemen guardians said the workhouse inmates and tramps were all right – were exceedingly well done to – what did Mrs. Wilkinson know about it? So she resolved to find out from actual personal experience and confront the guardians with facts. They don't twit[103] her now – they listen to her with great respect."

"She's a grand woman," said Jim. "Here's where we get off."

They were soon at Jim's little house. His mother was delighted to see May.

"Bless your bonnie face," she said. "I am so fain to see you again – and in my own home, not in an awful tramp ward. Have you got off the road, too – you look like it – you are nicely dressed?"

"Oh, yes," said May. "Tell your mother all about it," and she turned to Jim.

"Well, mother," said Jim "it's quite a tale. Mrs. Wilkinson and M – Miss –"

"Oh, call me May," said May, smiling, "for we are chums, are we not?" – and Jim was delighted.

"Well, mother," said Jim. "Mrs. Wilkinson and May were not tramps at all," and then he detailed the reason of their going on tramp.

"Well, I never!" said Mrs. Campbell. "It's just like a book – and I thought so all along. But it's no use worrying about mysteries. Best keep quiet and be patient, and things will come out in their own time."

"Oh, grannie, I'm so glad that you are all right – out of those hateful casual wards and workhouses," said May. "I wish we could only rescue all the other poor old creatures, and the young women, too. Mrs. Wilkinson will never rest till they are at least better treated."

"Where is Mrs. Wilkinson?" asked grannie.

"At home in Alderham; she's not well. No, you needn't be alarmed; it's nothing serious, though it's a very bad cold, the result of getting wet through on our last tramp."

"Give her my kind regards," said Mrs. Campbell, "and tell her how grateful I am. Mr. Milnthorp has been very good to me. Tell her she must be sure to call and see me whenever she comes this way."

"I am sure she will, grannie; she often talks about you."

"You'll stay and have a bit of supper with us, won't you? Jim, put the kettle on," and, as Jim rose to carry out the order: "You've no idea how good Jim is, and how handy he is about the house. He makes the fire, and can cook, and do everything like a woman, and it's well he can, for my rheumatism prevents me from doing as much as I would."

"But never mind making any supper for me," said May. "I promised to have it with Mrs. Blythe."

"Oh, but she'll excuse you for once," said grannie. "It won't be five minutes. I'd like you to have a bit with us. We've nothing much. But you can have a drink of cocoa and a slice of warm toast. It's a cold night. Jim toast a slice of bread for the young lady."

"Well, I'll just have a cup of cocoa with you," said May, "but never mind the toast."

"Oh, but you must have it," said grannie. "Surely you'll never run away without having a bit of something to eat."

"Very well," said May, "but I can't stay long. My friends are expecting me. Here" – taking the toast from Jim – "I'll do the toast," and she knelt down on the little iron fender in front of the fire.

Jim was in glory. There was an angel come to the house, and this was heaven.

It was a jolly little supper. The outward and visible viands were the poorest earthly trifles, but the heart and soul of it, and the invisible nourishment, were divine. May beamed, and chatted, and laughed, and filled the place with delightful enchantment.

"I wish you were at our table always," said Mrs. Campbell, and Jim silently and prayerfully echoed his mother's wish.

But May had to go.

"I really must get off now," she said; "it's nearly ten o'clock. The Blythes will wonder wherever I have got, and blow me up terrible. You'll take me to the tram!" and she turned to Jim, who was gloriously eager to be escort.

"Well, good-night, grannie," said May, stooping over the old woman, and kissing her, "I'll see you again sometime."

On the way to the car May said to Jim: "I'm glad to see you so snug in your little home. How sad it is that your wife and child are not sharing it with you. You remember telling Mrs. Wilkinson and me how they – passed away when you were out of work. If they had only had justice they might have been alive with you now."

"Yes," said Jim, softly.

[10 October 1908]

XVIII. Jim and May. (*Continued.*)

"You must do all you can to help the Labour and Socialist movement forward, that other mothers and children shall not perish as they did."

"As long as life I shall work for this cause," said Jim, earnestly.

"That's good. Ah, there is so much to do, and so few of us to do it; so great an array of evil to fight, and so little a force against it. Have you ever tried to speak on a platform?"

"No," said Jim. "That's too much for me."

"Nothing is too much for a man who is sincere and resolute," said May. "If you stood up and told the story of your experiences as you told it to Mrs. Wilkinson and me I think it would move an audience and set 'em thinking. You can speak from hard and cruel experience; you can tell from your own case the bitter woe of the workers; it is such men as you who are needed to tell the tale that shall transform the world."

"I shall do my best, in every way I can," said Jim, "to help forward the movement. This is your tram."

"Well – good night –" she hesitated a moment, as she held out her hand, then said: "Jim – it sounds so far-off saying Mr. Campbell. Good-night Jim."

"Good-night, May," and Jim felt a thrill as he spoke the word.

The next instant the tramcar was bearing May away through the darkness. Jim watched it till it went out of sight round a corner.

Then he walked home, dreaming as lovers dream.

When May reached the home of the Blythes, Dick, who opened the door for her, cried: "Now, Miss Rambler, where have you been? Here's supper been waiting for you over half-an-hour. Where did you run off to?"

"Let me get my things off, and I'll explain," said May. "I'm sorry I've kept you waiting, Mrs. Blythe, but I know you'll forgive me."

Then she told them where she had been.

"Um!" said Dick, with a grin. "Ah, this needs thinking about. Is it the old lady or the young man, now, that you are most interested in?"

"Don't be silly, Dick," said May.

"Well, he's not a bad-looking fellow, is Campbell," said Dick, quizzingly, "and he's as straight and honest as they make 'em. But I understand that he's a widower. I never dreamt that you'd go in for a widower, May."

"Don't talk rubbish, Dick," said May, laughing. "Can't one go to visit an old woman without being accused of – of –" and then she blushed.

"Oh, it's all right," said Dick. "But I thought you were already engaged. What about that young man in Alderham – that clerk – let's see, what's his name?" and Dick rubbed his right hand up into his hair – "Oh, Herbert Malden; you once brought him to one of our cycle meets, where he looked like a fish in a florist's. You know who I mean – that superior, sniffing young man, who rode his bike in collars and cuffs, while we heathens wore sweaters, and who also regarded us as if from a pedestal of perfect piety."

"Oh, Dick, shut up with your chaff," said May.

"Yes, let us get to our supper," said Mrs. Blythe, adding to her husband, "and stop your nonsense." Then, turning to May, "You only have to endure Dick's foolish talk now and then, but I have to live with him."

"Good shot from the missus!" cried Dick, greatly tickled.

XIX. To The Station.

On the Monday morning May Marsden went to see the Rev. Arthur Milnthorp. He wished to arrange with her to give a lecture in his chapel some night.

"Oh, hadn't you better get Mrs. Wilkinson?" said May.

"No, I'd rather have you for this occasion. I want our young women, and your young men, too, to see how one young woman is doing her duty in the world."

"It's very nice of you to say so," said May, "and I daresay I am doing a bit – I'll not put any mock-modesty on, for really I am trying to do a bit, and I know I'm trying, even if I don't do much. But let's not make a song about it."

"Then you'll come?"

"Yes, I'll come if you want me," said May.

"Thank you very much," said Mr. Milnthorp.

"You've a fine view of the hills from your window," said May. "Isn't that old Pendle[104] over there? You can tell its big long whale-back shape as soon as you see it."

'Yes, that's Pendle. It looks fine on a clear day like this. But many days of the year our Brunborough smoke and rain and fog shut Pendle Hill from the view. Have you ever been to the top?"

"Never," said May. "But I think I shall go this summer. There is to be a Labour and Socialist gathering there some Sunday."

"Sabbath breaker," and Mr. Milnthorp smiled. "But you'll enjoy the outing and the climb. The ascent of Pendle is made through some pretty scenery. Brunborough, grimly old town thought it is, is set in a glorious frame of bonny moorland. There are also places of historic and literary interest on the way to Pendle – the old house of Mrs. Nutter, who was burnt to death as one of the

Lancashire witches two hundred years ago – I daresay you'll have read Harrison Ainsworth's romance.[105] He tells all about it. I've been up Pendle and all over the district with our Co-operative Rambling Club. There's a delicious well on the hillside; it's delightful to be up there and have a picnic with spirit-kettles.[106] It's called Robin Hood's Well, though whether the bold Robin ever drank there or not is a question."

"Oh, I must go to Pendle, then," said May.

"On favourable days there's a splendid view from the top. The Irish Sea can sometimes be seen," said Mr. Milnthorp.

"All this idle land lying about, and yet so many unemployed," said May, surveying the extensive prospect of moorland. "How are things going on in Brunborough?"

"As everywhere else under the present system," said Mr. Milnthorp. "It's been a bad winter; a great many men out of work; a great deal of poverty. And it's almost as bad yet. The trouble is always with us;[107] always will be with us now till there is revolution – or some more equitable system of trade and industry. Our Socialist friends have pushed the unemployed to the front – they have had their processioning through the streets this winter, trying to force the authorities – the Town Council or the Guardians – to do something. But nothing was done except talk. The poor are very patient."

"Too patient, I sometimes think," said May.

Mr. Milnthorp smiled. "Yes, evolution does seem a long, slow job," he said. "But, after all, patience is better than violence. Things done violently have generally to be done over again, though I daresay even in matters political social, or physiographical, earthquakes have their time and place, and are necessary."

"Surely you don't mean to say that earthquakes are necessary?" asked May. "I never could see any reason for earthquakes."

"There are a great many things in this world for which we mortals cannot see any reason, but that does not prove there is no reason; it only shows our ignorance. Earthquakes, I should think, are necessary to effect certain geographical changes required in the programme of evolution."

"But couldn't the change be effected in a gentler and less destructive fashion?" asked May.

"Only one who knows the whole tale and purpose of evolution can answer that question," replied Mr. Milnthorp, "and I believe that the ultimate outcome of all things – of all tragedies, of all catastrophes – is good."

Then he quoted Tennyson, his favourite poet, about good being the final goal of ill, and the "one far-off divine event toward which the whole creation moves."[108]

After a little more chat with Mr. Milnthorp and his wife, a little pleasant woman, who, having disposed of some household affairs in which she was engaged when May called, May set off back for the Blythes, with whom she was to have mid-day dinner before setting off back for Alderham. Dick Blythe was not present at this meal, having had to go away to Manchester on business.

May set off in good time for the station. Mrs. Blythe would have accompanied her, but May begged her not to trouble. The road was straight and easy.

Somehow, on the way to the station, May caught herself thinking about Jim Campbell, and thinking how – how – no, she could not find the exactly suitable adjective – it would be if she should meet him; there would be nothing strange in it; he was in the same town; he might be going to his work; yet the chances were she would not.

And she did not – and, quite extravagantly irrationally for so sensible a young woman, felt a little disappointed.

But she met somebody she knew; and somebody she was not thinking of, and did not want to meet – Ronald Fordham.

[17 October 1908]
XIX. To The Station. (*Continued*.)

He raised his hat, smiled, and stopped. But May walked on. He turned about and followed her.

"Excuse me," he said. "I don't seek to pester you in any way. I want to apologise for insulting you that night at Blakeham. I was mistaken – you are not the girl I thought you were. I beg your pardon; I am very sorry."

May was a tender-hearted maid. "Oh, it's all right," she said. "But I've no time to talk with you."

"I hardly knew you," continued Fordham, walking by her side. "Then you were in rags; now you are dressed like a lady. You are a creature of mystery and change."

May could not help smiling. "I suppose all women are naturally that," she said. "But I'm nothing unusual in that line."

"I should like to be favoured with your explanations," said Fordham.

"I've no time to talk. I'm off to the station to catch a train."

"Well, I've nothing particular to do," said Fordham. "I'll walk along with you if you don't object. For I'm dying to solve the puzzle."

"It's very simple," said May, and told him all.

"Well, I'm blest!" exclaimed Fordham, with a laugh. "I shouldn't have thought you were so eccentric."

May noticed that he didn't call her brave, as Jim Campbell had done, and thought how differently men regard the same thing.

"And what are you doing in Brunborough?" asked Fordham.

So May had to tell that story.

"Well, I'm blest again," said Fordham. "You a Socialist lecturer! I wish Id known you were at the Labour Church, I'd have been there. Do you know, I've joined the Socialists, too? I'm a member of the local S.D.F."

"I'm glad to hear that," said May, "though I don't approve the uncompromising S.D.F. policy. I'm a member of the I.L.P. myself."

"Oh, the diluted Socialism," said Fordham, with the faintest trace of a sneer. "I believe in the red-hot gospel of the Red Flag – the real thing, no watering down."

"But," said May, smiling, "don't you think that the raw spirit may cause intoxication? But, we'll not argue. I suppose you're working now."

"Yes, I'm working," said Fordham, "though I'm not making much at present. Oh, and do you know that other young fellow you met in the lodging-house at Blakeham – Jim Campbell – is at Brunborough?"

"Yes, I have seen him," said May, with a little flush. "I hope you and he are friends."

"Oh, yes; we've forgotten all about that little scuffle on your account," and Fordham laughed. "He served me right. I met him a few days after, and he did me a good turn. I had been to the house of the old rascal who is keeping the girl who is so much like you."

"My cousin Gertie," said May, rather sadly. "It's a pity."

"It's more than a pity," said Fordham, fiercely; "I feel that I shall kill that old villain for it some day. The same old wretch ruined my mother! and he's taken Gertie from me. If I could only have married Gertie, I think it would have been my salvation. And yet, I don't know – for she's evidently not the girl I thought she was. She's for the man who can give her the easiest time and the most luxury. She's not like you – a girl of solid principle. One like you would take the man she loved whatever he was – and the poorer he was and the more down in the world would stand the stronger by him. I don't think Geritie would do that. No, she can't have much ballast, or she wouldn't have stayed at Sandunes a day after she discovered what it meant. And that old rascal's spending in debauchery the money that should be mine – or, anyhow, a lot of it that's mine by every right of nature and justice. You know he owns factories here in Brunborough, and his hands get the worst wages in town. I've advised 'em to set fire to his mills, and they would do if they'd the pluck of a mouse. But they suffer and whine, and dare do nothing."

Fordham talked excitedly, and May was glad when they reached the station.

"You needn't come any further now," she said.

"Oh, so long as I've come so far, I'll finish the job and see you off," said Fordham. "It isn't often I've the luck to escort a charming young lady."

He went on the platform with her, and stayed till the train came in. He stood at the window as the locomotive started, and May saw him waving his hat as she was borne away.

"A very strange man!" she said to herself. "Fancy him, of all the men in the world, being the one to see me off."

She had much rather it had been Dick Blythe, or Mr. Milnthorp, or – or –

She was thinking of Jim Campbell.

XX. Another Son Finds His Mother.

Ronald Fordham went to the S.D.F. Club. There was to be a great Unemployed Demonstration that afternoon, and some of the S.D.F. members, including Joe Summerfield, had it in hand. The unemployed were to assemble in the Market Place and march through the principal streets of the town.

"We'll show the tradesmen and middle classes what misery there is in their midst," said Summerfield. "And may it be a warning to them – to see that justice is done before there is revolution."

"There'll never be revolution in this country!" said Fordham, bitterly. "The English are too tame."

"Or the bulk of 'em are doing too well," said Summerfield, "though how any workingmen can think so in the present state of things is a puzzle to me."

"Give an Englishman eighteen bob a week and Saturday afternoon for a football match and he's satisfied," said Fordham.

"There's a great deal of distress in the town," said Summerfield. "The weaving trade's bad, and there's a lot of growling at Langdon's mills."

"Growling's all they dare do," said Fordham. "If they'd any spirit they'd burn the mills down."

"That wouldn't do any good," said Summerfield.

"It would terrify the tyrants and plunderers," said Fordham.

"We must get out of the muddle by the ballot-box, by Parliament," said Summerfield. "Even the middle classes are beginning to see that there's no remedy but Socialism for bad trade. We have alternating Liberal and Conservative governments, but nobody's any better off except those in office. In Brunborough, as in other manufacturing towns, where the capitalists are trying to make as much as they can out of labour, and the shopkeepers are in fierce competition for a living, the various sections of the community are seeing that they will have to re-arrange things before there is any real progress or stable prosperity."

"Ah, but the folk won't have Socialism," said Fordham.

"They'll have to have it or go to the devil," said Summerfield.

"I'll bet that hundreds of the unemployed won't even turn up to demonstrate," said Fordham.

He was right. They did not. Many of them did not want to make a public parade of their plight. But there was a great muster, nevertheless, gathered in the Market-Place, where Joe Summerfield and others harangued them, telling them they ought to march to the Town Hall and demand work or food.

"You've a perfect right to," said Summerfield. "Every man who has worked, and is willing to work, has a right to be kept. There's quite enough stuff in this country to feed us all, and the workers have a right to it, for they have made it and produced it."

He then demanded, in the name of the people, that the local governing authorities should do something for the unemployed; find them work in road-making or mending; or get them back to the land.

Then the crowd, numbering about a thousand, the bulk being genuine out-of-works, of the lower labouring classes, marched in straggling procession to the Town Hall, collecting provisions from tradesmen on the way, some of the shopkeepers giving out of sympathy, and some out of fear. For at times the mob seemed threatening, and there were many extra police put on duty to guard against any outbreak.

"It's been a fizzle," said Fordham, as he went back to the club, where, after having a meat-pie and some tea, he spent the rest of the evening in playing billiards. He had ill-luck at the game, and, being neither a cheerful nor philosophical loser, became moody.

Jim Campbell called at the club while Fordham was in the middle of his last game, or, at least, the game he said should be his last that night. Fordham, cue in hand, came gloomily to Jim, who was sitting near the table, and whispered, "You couldn't lend me half-a-crown, could you? I've had fearful luck, and I'm hard up. Fact is – though I've told nobody yet but you, not even the wife – I'm out of work again. Got word this morning. I guess the firm's taken on some poor devil who'll do my job at a less commission, and that was small enough, Heaven knows."

[24 October 1908]
XX. Another Son Finds His Mother. (*Continued.*)

Jim knew nothing of Fordham's occupation, but he knew that it was bad to be hard up. "I haven't half-a-crown to spare," he said, "but I can lend you sixpence."

"That will only just pay, with what I have, for the games I've lost," said Fordham.

"Well, I'm sorry, but I've no more on me," said Jim, "and I if were you I would chuck playing after this game – for to-night, anyhow."

"I will," said Fordham. "I've had enough, and lost enough. The luck's dead against me," and he walked round the table to make his shot. Not scoring, he came back to Jim, and said, "Oh, do you know, to-day I saw that girl you quarrelled with me about."

"There was no quarrel," said Jim, smiling. "Yes, I know all about it. I saw her last night."

"And you know she's not a tramp – as we were, then?"

"Yes."

"Curious, isn't it? Hullo, my turn again."

"I'll be off towards home," said Jim. "Good-night."

Jim had not got out of the street in which the club was situated when he heard a moan, and, in the dim light, perceived a woman lying against the wall. He knelt down beside her and raised her head; and at once noticed that the woman's breath smelled strongly of drink. But, drunk or sober, clearly she was ill.

"Who is it?" she wailed. "Let me be! Oh, I am cold! But I was a beauty once, and had rich, warm furs – curse the man that bought 'em me!"

"Who are you? Where do you live?" asked Jim, wondering what he should do with the helpless creature.

"I'm a tramp, and I live nowhere," replied the woman. "Once my name was Milly, and I had a pretty face, and my mother sold it to a man – curse him and her! I had a son, too – a baby boy – oh – oh! –" and Milly Fordham's head fell back as if she were fainting.

Jim wished someone would come to help him, to fetch assistance; the woman needed a doctor. But this side street was very quiet. The woman was moaning, in great pain and Jim was about to leave her while he hurried into the club for help, when he heard footsteps, and Ronald Fordham approached.

"I'm so glad you've come," said Jim; "here's a helpless woman here – very ill, I think."

"Drunk," said Fordham, indifferently; "best let her be, or send for a policeman. Let's have a look at her," and he stooped over the wretched, ragged female.

"Can't you get up?" he said. At his voice the woman started, and raised herself on her left elbow.

"Can it be?" she gasped. "Let me look at your face," and she peered at Fordham's features in the light that fell from the solitary lamp close by – "Why, you are my son, Ronald."

"What!" cried Fordham.

"My son! and I have not seen you for years," and she tried to fondle his face. Fordham shrank in disgust – this foul, loathsome thing was his mother.

"Have you seen your father lately?" she asked, in feeble tones.

"Who is my father?" returned Fordham, almost savagely.

"You know – Langdon – curse him, though he is your father! I went to see him to ask him to find you and do something for you, and – and – he had me locked up! – curse him! – and all the men – except – except – oh – my own little lad! – oh –"

She fell back, as if in a swoon.

"I think I'd better run for a doctor," said Jim. "Let's carry her up into the club; she'll be better there than here – it's a frosty night – and I'll go for a doctor."

But even as they lifted her Jim felt that it would be no use to fetch a medical man. She was dead. Her limbs were stiffening.

As they reached the top of the stairs leading into the club room the members present stared at the strange sight.

"A poor creature we found just outside," said Jim; "let us get her near the fire."

"She'll never be warm again," said Ned, the caretaker, after a glance at the woman's face. "She's dead."

"Lay her down," said Fordham to Jim; and they set the corpse on the floor.

"Comrades," said Fordham, to the score of men who had left their cards and billiards to see what this unusual happening was, "this dead woman – this woman who lies dead of neglect and starvation – is my mother. The rich man who is my father, but not her husband, set her first on the road that has brought her to this. For all he cares, I may go the same way. If this woman was your mother, comrades, what would you do?"

No one spoke.

"I know what I will do," said Ronald Fordham.

XXI. The Respectable Young Man.

The next day, Dick Blythe, being alone in the office with Jim, said, "So you and May Marsden are old friends, Jim?"

"Not exactly that," said Jim. "We have met before, that's all."

"Oh, yes, she told me all about it," said Blythe, "and how you thrashed a fellow who was pestering her. What do you think of her, Jim?"

Jim made no reply.

"She's a fine brave girl," said Dick Blythe, sliding his hand up the side of his head and putting on his droll grin, as he went on, "and, by gow! if I hadn't already a wife and family, and wasn't old enough to be her father, I should be after marrying her myself. Though I guess there'd be little chance of that even if I were free, for she's engaged to a young chap at Alderham – they've been keeping company for a few years, I think. I don't know much about it myself, but the missus does; the women are always big on news of that sort."

Jim Campbell's soul sank to despair. May already had a sweetheart. He had never thought about that. Well, it was his luck, he supposed. He must make the best of it. He only hoped the young man was worthy of her, and would make a good husband.

Dick Blythe observed Jim furtively. He had suspected that Jim "was sweet" on May, and had, in all kindness, given Jim this news to prevent him indulging in hopes that could not be realised. And he saw that Jim was hit, and was very sorry for him.

"Anyhow," said Dick Blythe to himself, "it's best for him to know the truth, and then he won't suffer any more disappointment."

When Jim set off for home in the evening, the rain, which had started in the afternoon, was steadily falling on the drenched world as if it never meant to cease. The male and female weavers, hastening home from the factories, were wet though, and looked miserable, dripping objects. This was the kind of weather which, the operatives emerging into the chilly damp from the artificially greatly-heated mills, sowed the seeds of chest complaints and consumption in the not-too-well-clad bodies of the workers in the manufacturing North.

As he went along the main street, where the rain was running off the crowded trams with their breath-blurred windows, Jim met a couple of tramps, man and woman, each carrying a child. They were all soaking wet. The man's clothes were thin; his boots leaky; the wet was running down his face from his saturated cap.

As they passed, Jim said to himself, "I've seen that man and woman before – where now?" And suddenly remembered. It was in the common lodging-house in Blakeham, where he had also first met May, and these two were the parents of the bright, golden-haired little girl who had offered to wash everybody's handkerchiefs: the child who evidently wanted to keep clean in a dirty world.

[31 October 1908]

XXI. The Respectable Young Man. (*Continued.*)

Jim hastily turned round and overtook the tramp couple.

"Mate," he said, "a word with you."

The man and his wife stopped, and stared at Jim.

"Perhaps you don't remember me," said Jim. "I was in the common lodging-house at Blakeham once, and saw you there. You had a little girl; she wanted to wash all our handkerchiefs."

"She's here," said the man, glancing at the child in his arms.

"Is she asleep?" asked Jim.

"No; she's not well," replied the father in that awful tone of habitual despair used by those who have given up all hope of everything, and trudge like living corpses through the world.

Jim looked at the child, and as he looked he cursed the society that created such tragedies as this. Here lay stricken, perhaps dying, the little innocent soul that wanted to keep clean; crushed, clemmed, begrimed, by the tramp life. What chance had the world given this little one? Nay, not only had it given it no chance, but deprived it of the necessary food and clothes and shelter. Even if the child lived, what chance would it have to grow up clean and fair? And it was such a sweet white little soul; would develop into such a good and useful woman if it only had the opportunity. Oh, the pity of it, and the curse of it!

"Before little children should suffer like this," said Jim to himself, "if men were men they'd turn the world upside down and roast the grabbers on their damned luxuries."

Jim pulled a shilling out of his pocket.

"Here, mate," he said to the tramp, "take that and get something for the kiddies."

The man handed the coin to his wife, and said to Jim, "You're not on the road now, then?"

"No; I've had luck," said Jim; "and I wish all other men could have it as well."

"There's no luck for me," said the man.

"Nay, never give up," said Jim.

"That's what I tell him," said the woman, speaking for the first time. "But it really does look as if we never shall have any good luck again. We have been on the road six months now. We were very hopeful at first, but now we begin to think we're too many in the world.[109] There's no work to be got anywhere."

"What's your job?" asked Jim of the man.

"I'm a general labourer. I was all right till I got my arm broken in the machinery at the factory. I had to go to the hospital, and when I came out the wife and children were in the workhouse; and that was the beginning of it, and it's hell."

"Didn't you claim compensation?"[110] said Jim.

"No, I didn't know about it till too late. The factory-master helped the missus a bit till it got too late to claim, and then he wouldn't give anything more.

"Oh, these damned captialistic rascals!" said Jim. "How they trick us, and dodge the law!"

The little girl wearily opened her eyes.

"Don't you know me?" asked Jim. "When are you going to wash some more pocket handkerchiefs?"

The child stared, but did not even smile; and Jim groaned in his soul.

The little one shivered.

"Get away, and get her something warm at once," said Jim, huskily, "and something for yourselves, too. And if you're knocking about this town to-morrow, come to the S.D.F. Club, near the Market Place – anybody will show it you – and ask for me, Jim Campbell. I'll help you all I can: it's not much I can do; but I'll do my best. But hurry off now, and get something warm for that child, and get her in bed. You've enough to see you through this night, and get a bit of breakfast in the morning."

The tramp husband and wife, carrying their two little ones, hurried off to the nearest common lodging-house, while Jim musingly pursued his homeward way.

"By God!" he said. "I'm fighting this damnable system to the death!"

He could not forget the little child with the golden hair: the little girl who wanted to be clean and helpful, and whom the world was murdering by inches, and driving to dirt and degradation, as it daily murdered and drove its thousands.

"I might have taken 'em home with me," thought Jim, "but we haven't room. The poor haven't even the means to help each other as much as they would."

Besides, Jim's mother was not well, and needed looking after.

On his way home Jim called at a herbal dispensary for a bottle for his mother. Her rheumatism troubled her a deal, and she began to feel ill "all over," as she said. The real matter with her was old age; she was breaking up.

"I'm gettin' to the end, Jim," she said, "though I'm not seventy yet, only sixty-seven; an' I shan't be with you long now. Us workin' folks don't last as long as them that has easy times; we've too much to go through; too much worry an' pinchin' days; an' that makes a mess of the strongest; we grow old before our time, an' die when we ought to be at our best. But I'm content; I'm tired of this world; an' I shan't die in the workhouse, now, an' be buried in a pauper's grave. An' that's a comfort. She – you know who I mean, Jim – said I should be sure to get to heaven; God would be good to a poor old woman like me, she said. That was in Waddiham Casual Ward, when I was racked with rheumatism, and I said I would throw bricks at those who had punished me when I met 'em in the next world. An' I believe I shall, even if I get to heaven. There's that brute Slamdrop for one; if there's no bricks in heaven I'll hit him on th' head with my golden harp, an' I'm sure the good Lord will forgive me, for that man's a demon. However, wherever I'm going to, Jim, I'm going somewhere, sure enough. I shan't be with you long – you'll be left all alone – all alone, my poor lad, with no mother to look after you."

"Nay, don't talk of dying, mother," said Jim; "cheer up. There's years in you yet."

"There isn't weeks, Jim. Do you know, Jim, as I've lain here, I've been thinkin' about that young woman? She'd make a good wife. You an' her might make a match of it, an' she could look after you when I'm gone."

Jim said nothing to this. What could he say, knowing what Dick Blythe had told him?

"Don't you like her, Jim? Don't you want her?"

"Oh, don't bother about that, mother."

"But surely you'll marry again some day? You're only young yet. And a man needs a woman to look after him. It's not nice to be in lodgin's. You ask her, Jim; I think she's fond of you. I should die quite happy if I knew you and her was together."

"Here's your physic," said Jim. "How have you gone on to-day? Has Mrs. Hipper been in?"

Mrs. Hipper was the next-door neighbour, and Jim had asked her to look in and keep an eye on his mother, who was now confined to her bed, while he was out at work.

"Yes; she's been in, though she can't come much. She's her own home an' family to attend to; and a woman with all those children hasn't much time for attending to sick folk next door. Noisy children they are, too; the baby's got awful lungs, an' cries more than any child I ever knew. The woman seems lost amongst the lot. I used to keep my children in better control, I know. Oh, they do make a racket."

"You wouldn't notice it if you weren't ill," said Jim. "I don't think Mrs. Hipper's youngsters make any more din than other children."

"Ah, you're not here to hear them. The youngest lad has been bangin' on the stairs with the shovel all afternoon."

"Well, try and rest a bit," said Jim. "I'll sit beside you; I'm not going out to-night."

While Jim was acting as nurse to his mother, May Marsden, on the outskirts of the factory town of Alderham, was walking along the highway with a trim, neat, delicately-built young man – the Herbert Malden about whom Dick Blythe had chaffed May after she had spent the evening with Jim Campbell and his mother.

Herbert Malden, who on week days was a clerk in the Borough Rate Office at Alderham and on Sundays a teacher at a Wesleyan Sunday School, had known May ever since she and he were children; their parents were old friends, and lived near together, and of late years the two had drifted into a sort of companionship which their acquaintances regarded as courtship. The parents of both sides desired, and looked forward to, a union between the two. May and Herbert had accepted this as their destiny; there was nothing displeasing about the prospect. Herbert Malden was not a man of any strong passion; he would probably never know truly what love meant – the love that makes romance and rapture and tragedy; mating and marrying was a mere matter of routine, and one woman was as suitable as another so long as her character was all right, and her status in society respectable. These were the chief considerations.

[7 November 1908]
XXI. The Respectable Young Man. (*Continued.*)

As for May, she had at first had similar notions, but recently there had come a change in her heart, and she knew that though she might respect Herbert Malden, and though she might marry him, she could never love him. What the difference exactly was she could not tell, but she was sure that she had not the feeling for Herbert Malden that a maid ought to have for the man whom she chooses for husband. His presence awoke no thrill, no stimulus in her; she felt normal. Not as she felt when talking with Jim Campbell – at the sight of his face, the sound of his voice, her whole being rose responsive in bliss and wonder and mystery.

She was thinking of this, perplexed, as she and Herbert Malden walked silently along the highway, where a lamplighter was busy hurrying along in the duskening twilight.

Herbert Malden was thinking of wedding. He had just got a considerable increase of salary; he could afford to marry comfortably now; to have a piano, parloured house, and all the display of orthodox respectability. The whole aim of his life was to be conventional and prosperous. Of course, he might have selected Emma Wright to be his wife. Emma's father owned a row of houses – mortgaged, of course, but he was steadily wiping the debt off – while May's father only owned the house he lived in purchased through the Co-operative Society. Still, he thought magnanimously, he wouldn't mind that; he would say nothing about it; though Emma was a milliner, too, which was rather more respectable than being a factory-girl, as May was. However, he would over look these things; of the two girls he preferred May – that is, if she wouldn't be rather wild at times, and do such freakish things as interesting herself in tramps and low persons. Still, marriage – marriage with him – would take all that out of her.

"I've been thinking we might get married, now, May," said Herbert. "I've enough saved up; we could fix it for Whitsuntide.[111]

May was startled. "Oh, there's plenty of time," she said.

"There's no reason for any further waiting," said Herbert. "We can start housekeeping comfortably. Have you anything saved up?"

"Only a pound or two," said May.

Herbert was disappointed. "I thought you would have had more," he said.

"I give all my wage to my mother," she said, quietly.

"But she ought to allow you something to put by."

"She gives me what I require," said May.

"Well, shall we say Whitsuntide for the wedding?"

"Oh, I don't know," said May. "Don't bother about it."

There was tramp approaching them; he looked undecided whether to beg or not.

May recognised him as Denny Doolan, whom she had seen when she first met Jim Campbell – in the common lodging-house at Blakeham. How odd that she should be reminded of Jim Campbell just now – Jim Campbell, whom she had first known as a tramp – when a successful and properly respectable young man was wanting to arrange matrimony with her.

Denny Doolan halted by the pair. "If ye plase, sir," he said, "could ye help a forlorn fellow-cratur on the road?"

"Be off with you," said Herbert. "Go and work for your living."

"Begorra an' I would," said Denny, "if I could only get the chance. But there's no chance nowadays."

"There would be if you'd keep of the drink," said Herbert. "But clear off, I don't want to talk to you."

May pulled out her purse. "Here, Denny Doolan," she said, handing him a penny.

"God bless ye!" said Denny, "but who are ye that knows me? Well, well, 'tis no matter. I am a notorious man in sundry respects an' known to many."

"How's Brundy, the cobbler, going on?" asked May.

Denny Doolan was surprised. "Begorra, but ye know us all," he exclaimed. "I haven't seen Brundy for a while. The last time I met him was at Friartown, where he was quotin' the ould poets wid avidity, as usual. I've just come up from Manchester, an' there I met another of us – the tramp swell who was at Blakeham. Ah! I have ye now; ye were the young woman I saw there wid another woman, quite respectable both of ye – not like the rest of us. I am mighty plased to see the luck has turned, an' that ye are doin' well an' actually courtin'. I hope ye'll have swate matrimony together, an' never know what it is to be on the rocks as I am."

Herbert Malden stood aside in disgust while his sweetheart talked with the tramp. He said, "When you've done with that low fellow, May, I'm waiting."

Denny Doolan looked as if he were about to flash a hot retort back, but, for May's sake, refrained. "Well, good-night, an' God bless ye," he said. "I'll be gettin' on to Alderham. I've lodgin's to find for the night yet. Good luck to ye, Miss!" and, with a smile for May and a scowl for her lover, Denny went on his way into the gloom.

"May," said Herbert, angrily, as the two resumed their walk. "I'm astonished at you, speaking to such riff-raff. Who is he?"

"A poor tramp Mrs. Wilkinson and I met in our lower-world experiences," said May.

"Yes. I don't approve of your tramp journeys with Mrs. Wilkinson. I've told you so before. I don't approve of 'em, I tell you. They're not respectable. It would look better of Mrs. Wilkinson to stay at home than wandering about in workhouses and tramp wards. No Christian woman would do it."

"Oh," said May, calmly. "I should think such work essentially Christian."

"Nonsense," said Herbert. "See what it leads to; all the wastrels of the road will know you, will recognise you when we are out together – it's disgraceful."

"They are our fellow-men and women," said May, "and God is their father as well as ours."

"Don't talk infidel rubbish. This comes of going to Labour and Socialist meetings. I tell you I don't approve of it. I didn't like you going to lecture at Brunborough, but, as I thought it was only for once and because that misguided Mrs. Wilkinson couldn't go, I said nothing. But you really must stop this kind of thing, or when we are married we shall have all the loafers and rascals in the kingdom on our doorstep; but if any come while I'm about I'll have 'em locked up. When you are my wife you must cease all connection with these Labour and Socialist people and faddist reformers – in fact, you had better begin now. For when you are my wife –"

May's temper was getting up. She interrupted him; and her tone checked him into silence.

"I am not your wife yet," she said, "nor," she added, deliberately, "ever likely to be now."

XXII. As A Man Sows.[112]

There passed a year, full of big events and small; but, if different to anybody else, much the same to the workers in weaving-shed and factory and mine and joiner's-shop, and all the other places where labour does so much for so little. The factory wheels went round and railway trains whistled through the town, and people rose and went to their work in the early morning, and to bed at night after the day's toil, fringed off with a little amusement at the theatre or music-hall, or Sunday-school concert, according to their temperament and taste; and the news-lads shouted out football news – in summer the "latest cricket," – and almost all through the year the racing results; and on the newspaper placards were the usual lines of rumours of events abroad; something threatening the Czar; trouble with the natives of Washybooling, and a pretexts for a protectorate and annexation; crisis in the east, as usual; missionaries in a mess in China; Parliamentary palaver; great speech by the Liberal leader; great speech by the Tory ditto; theatrical defiance of the House of Lords; scandal in high life, Lord Thunderblow marrying a ballet girl; aristocratic divorce; unemployed demonstration; discovery of new sayings of Christ; big strike; General Booth and the workless; discussion on Is life a frost? Are servants getting too cocky?; strained foreign relations – in short, all the old tales. And through it all the masses went on with their drudging and struggling and dying and breeding, never asking was it worth while, or was there no better and happier way of spending their time on this perplexing planet spinning amid the stellar glory of the Milky Way.

[14 November 1908]
XXII. As A Man Sows. (*Continued.*)

With the persons with whom this fragmentary history deals life went on in routine not much different from the ruts of the rest, except for some vision and revolt.

Jim Campbell heard May lecture again, but got little chance to talk with her.

Fordham was out of the town and then back again several times – erratic in his occupation and generally impecunious.

Jim had heard no more of the tramp and the little girl who was so anxious to keep her pocket-handkerchief clean. He expected the man would have turned up at the S.D.F. Club, but he never came.

"Probably the child is dead, and the man's gone under like so many more," said Jim. "And men go on with their heartless buying and selling, thinking only of profit and pleasure, while these things are going on every day, and little children going to the devil, nay, actually enduring hell all the time in this great civilised Empire."

In Brunborough, as in all the manufacturing towns, trade was very bad, and the poverty terrible. One of Jim's neighbours, a willing and steady man, desperate at being long out of work, and his family starving, had hanged himself, and his wife and three children had been taken to the workhouse.

"Then folks wonder why Socialism is spreading," said Jim. "There's got to be some reform or wild revolution before long."

* * *

Early in the New Year, at a meeting at the S.D.F. Club, the "comrades" were pressing Jim Campbell to "stand" for the forthcoming Guardians' election. Jim was bashful, but Dick Blythe and others insisted that he was just the man to be on the Board of Guardians. He knew tramp life and workhouse treatment from experience, and so could see justice done to the poor. Jim protested; but his friends would not hear nay; he must be nominated.

"But I can't talk," said Jim.

"We'll talk for you till you can," said Ned the caretaker. "But we'll soon make you into an orator. You'll be all right when you've had a bit of street-corner practice."

On the same night, Ronald Fordham was pacing the pavement in front of Langdon's Empire Emporium – the colossal building where they sold and supplied everything, from a sausage to a skull, from a pin to a palace. He looked up at the six-storied building, and said bitterly, "Mine by rights – or a big share in it, anyhow. I'd set fire to it if I could. But there is no chance; too many police about."

He looked harassed and wild, but was dressed tidily.

"Old Langdon hasn't been to-day – doesn't come down often now, they say," he said to himself – "prefers to be in his harem by the sea, I suppose" – and a terrible look came on Fordham's face as he thought of the girl at Sandunes. "But they say he'll be here to-morrow, certain. Well, I'll interview him to-morrow."

In the morning, just before noon, Ronald Fordham threaded his way through Manchester's restless throng – through the busy multitude, each unit of which was engrossed in his own little world of toil and trouble, or idle amusement, all seeming together in the crowd, yet every soul so separate in reality, going its own way, with its own thoughts and desires; some full of speculation, some thinking of the money they would make this day, some of the orders they were after, some, perhaps, thinking of lust and carousing, and one, at least, full of despair, intent on murder and suicide.

This one, Ronald Fordham, stepped into Langdon's and asked to see Mr. Langdon. The uniformed attendant said he couldn't see Mr. Langdon unless he has an appointment.

"He is here then?" said Fordham.

"Oh, yes, been here an hour. Have you any appointment with him?"

"No – yes. Take him this note," and Fordham scribbled a line on a card.

The man went off, and up some stairs, with the note, while Fordham surveyed the big shop and the scores of girls behind the counters.

"Nice girls, all of 'em – the old wretch," he said. "But he's rich, and so he's respectable. Money can do pretty well as it likes. Poverty's the crime after all."

The attendant returned. "Mr. Langdon says he will see you. Follow me."

"Thanks," said Fordham, feeling at some solid object in his inside breast pocket, and smiling strangely to himself.

He was ushered into Mr. Langdon's office on the first landing. It was a glass-partitioned structure – from it Mr. Langdon could see all over the room; the book-keepers and clerks and men and woman in charge of various counters.

"Ah," said Langdon, as Fordham stepped into the little glass structure, "I didn't know it was you. What have you come here for? How dare you?"

"To give you another chance to do justice," said Fordham. "I am hard up. Will you help me? I have every claim –"

"I will not be blackmailed," said Langdon, standing up, "you had better go quick. You have no claim on me."

"I am not blackmailing, nor begging either," said Fordham. "I only want work. I've had infernal luck. Give – or lend me – money to get out of the country, and I'll never trouble you again. Surely you can do a little for your son."

"You are not my son," said Langdon, angrily.

"I should almost be glad to think I wasn't," said Fordham. "But son or not, you ruined my mother. She died in the gutter. I picked her up in the streets of Brunborough, dying – and all your doing."

"Her own fault. She should have kept off the drink."

"And who drove her to the drink?" demanded Fordham, fiercely. "Be careful; I don't want to tell you what you are, and quarrel with you – I want to give you a chance to prove yourself a man with some sense of honour –"

"Enough of this!" cried Langdon. "I ask you to retire."

"Not till I have said my say."

"Oh, you defy me. I will have you thrown out" – Mr. Langdon stepped forward as if to touch a bell on a little table. Fordham strode between him and the table, saying, "Will you do justice? Is there no feeling in you – no feeling for your own flesh and blood?"

"Bah!" said Langdon. "Begone!" Fordham stretched his head forward. There was a mad gleam in his eyes. "By God," he said, "I am a desperate man now, and I don't care what happens. I didn't come her to threaten you, but you have driven me to extremes by your callousness and taunts. See here!" – he flashed out a revolver. "Promise to do justice or I'll shoot you and myself."

"Bah! you daren't. Help!" shouted Langdon.

There was the crack of the revolver. Langdon fell, with a bullet in his brain. Another crack – and Fordham lay beside him, bleeding from a wound in the eye, where the bullet had entered.

There was instant alarm and commotion in the place. The women shrieked; the men came rushing up. Some ran for the police.

Langdon was quite dead; but Fordham, though greatly injured, was alive. "Let me be – let me die!" he moaned, as they lifted him up and bore him away in an ambulance, whilst the corpse of the millionaire was laid on the table in his own little office.

What an awful and uncanny transformation one little minute had effected in the fates of Langdon and the young man who claimed to be his illegitimate son. Sixty seconds ago Langdon was superintending a mighty business; hundreds of souls were at his beck and call; thousands depended on his will for their daily bread. And now he lay prone in death – shorn at one stroke of all his power and property.

And the hand that had laid him low had grown out of his own sensual passion or his folly; out of a lustful moment of long ago had grown this hand that was to send the bullet into the millionaire's brain.

Yes, it was all over with Langdon as far as this world was concerned. Gertie Marsden would know his caress no more; no more dalliance in the villa by the sea. Lawyer Screwm could bring forth the will and read its provision. The aged poor – if they were respectable – could now look forward to Langdon's Pauper Homes, the monument that was to perpetuate his memory.

XXIII. The Whisper.

In the Brunborough S.D.F. Club, where the members were having a special meeting to discuss ways and means of Jim Campbell's candidature, the news of Langdon's murder, which was the sensation in all the evening papers, was being discussed.

"Well, let's get on with our business," said Joe Summerfield; "it's waste of time discussing this crime, or whatever you care to call it. It's simply an accident. Hundreds of working men are killed every week at their tasks, on railways, and in factories, and nobody thinks anything about it; but when a rich old rake happens to get a bullet in him the world goes wild with excitement. It's a sad thing for anybody to get shot out of life, but we needn't waste any pity on this millionaire. He's had a good time of it; he's always had plenty to eat and drink – at the expense of those who drudge for him – and now his slate's filled, and broken. There are far more deserving objects of pity than a dead millionaire, who is, in a sense, as criminal as the man who killed him, though I didn't think Fordham was a chap of that sort. Queer he was, I know, but I never dreamt he'd run to homicide. Of course, the fellow's mad, but they'll hang him all the same. He's really more to be pitied than the man he's slain; for all crime is disease. Moreover, he had been deeply wronged by this man – but for whom he would never have existed."

"Ay, it's a curious thing – looks like fate – sowing and reaping," said Dick Blythe. "I think Fordham had a bit of insanity in him."

"No doubt of it," said Jim Campbell. "His talk about bombs and revolution showed an unbalanced mind. And I myself once prevented him committing suicide."

[21 November 1908]
XXII. As A Man Sows. (*Continued*.)

"Tell us about that," said Ned, the caretaker.

So Jim briefly related the circumstances, and Joe Summerfield said, "Well, chaps, this isn't business. It's more important for us to discuss the plan of campaign for the Guardians' contest than to talk about a dead millionaire."

"It seems Fordham's alive, and the doctors have some hope of saving him now," said Ned.

"In order to hang him," said Dick Blythe. "What a farce!"

After the inquest on Langdon – a verdict of "Wilful murder" being returned against Fordham, who was progressing in hospital – there was a great funeral in Brumborough, where Langdon was buried. His wife, who had not lived with him for twenty years, attended the funeral. What must her thoughts have been as she followed to the cemetery the corpse of the man who had been her husband in name only?

While the doctors were healing Fordham for the trial, the Guardians' election contest was making a little stir in Brunborough. Jim Campbell was being opposed by a Liberal and a Conservative. May Marsden, being down in Brunborough to give a lecture stayed a day and addressed a special meeting on Jim Campbell's behalf; and Jim was delighted.

"Oh, I do hope you'll get in," she said. "We want some men like you to attend to the administration of the Poor Law – to teach selfish Guardians their duty to the poor, and to keep insolent officials in their place."

The morning after the meeting Dick Blythe said to May, as she was getting ready to go to the station, "Hadn't you better stop another day and try to help Jim Campbell some more?"

"I would if I could," said May, "but I can't keep stopping off my work. The boss doesn't like it. I shall be getting sacked. He wouldn't have let me off this time, only I found a very good weaver to go 'sick' for me."[113]

"Oh, well, if he sacks you, you can get married," said Dick, grinning. "And by the way – excuse me if I'm presumptuous – but don't you think, though you're doing it quite unconsciously, I believe, that it's not right to be so – so encouraging with Jim Campbell – letting him build up hopes, etc., you know, when there's no earthly chance for him, as you are engaged to another fellow? You know, May, it looks terribly like flirting."

May blushed. "I'm not engaged to marry any other man," she said.

"What!" cried Dick, gaily. "Is it off with that Herbert Malden?"

"Yes, it's off," said May, smiling.

"I'm jolly glad," said Dick. "Shake hands, May. Let me congratulate you. That chap would never have suited you as a husband. So it's off, is it? This is the best news I've heard for weeks."

"I'm a jilted girl," said May. "Mr. Malden has broken the match off. He said he objected to my bothering with the Labour and Socialist movement; and that I should have to stop it when I was his wife. So we had a tiff. I said I should not bind myself to see things as he saw them, and I could never forget nor forsake the poor. At that he declared we had better part; and I said I quite agreed with him."

"Oh, the snob and the cad!" said Dick. "I should like to bash his head! – not for freeing you – for that's a blessing – but for insulting you. Oh, I am so jolly glad you're rid of the little prig! And I guess you're not sorry yourself. You don't look a bit broken-hearted. Ah – um –" and Dick laughed. "Now I guess other things will happen."

Later on in the day, when Dick Blythe went to Jim Campbell in the office he said, "Jim, I think May Marsden takes a great interest in you. Wasn't she up at your house to tea before the meeting last night?"

"Yes – to have tea with my mother," said Jim.

"Well, I suppose you'd be there, too," said Dick, with his special grin.

Of course Jim had been there. He would never forget that tea. May's presence had made his mother very happy – though the old lady had said that she wouldn't last long now, at which both Jim and May had cried "Nonsense." But Mrs. Campbell had called May to her and said, "Bend your ear down, I want to say something private to you – Jim, go and stand at the other end of the room, or go into the back kitchen. Now," and as May inclined her head, the old woman whispered something which caused the young girl's face to blush and shine.

And Jim wondered what it was that his mother had whispered to May. He was thinking of this secret as Dick Blythe stood looking at him.

Then all at once Dick blurted out, "Jim, May Marsden's not engaged to anybody. I thought she was, but I was mistaken. Go in and win both the election and the girl."

And before Jim had got over his astonishment at this outburst, Dick Blythe had vanished out of the office.

XXIV. Fordham's Fate.

Jim won the election, anyhow; and found himself pitted against the ignorance, bigotry, and prejudice of the majority of the Board of Guardians – most men who had got hold of a bit of money, or property, and meant to stick to it, no matter how the rest of the world went. They had no sympathy, no sense of justice. The poor they regarded as a nuisance, to be dealt with sternly and stingily. Jim they looked upon as a wild revolutionist, who was prepared to seize everybody's little possessions, and divide them up amongst the poverty-stricken.

So Jim Campbell had not a sweet time of it amongst the Guardians. But he was a dogged man in the cause of right, and stuck to his guns. He was nearly always in conflict at the Board meetings, but he compelled the Guardians to do some of their duty. He saw, however, that the Poor Law administration was a costly and inefficient affair; and came to the conclusion that what was needed was fewer workhouses and more out-door relief, and old age pensions. The bulk of the money of the ratepayers went in paying officials and the upkeep of Poor Law institutions. For the pauper children he advocated the Cottage Homes system.[114]

Not long after the election his mother died. Before she passed away she said, "Jim, when I am gone, marry May, if you can. She'll make a good wife."

He wrote to May in Alderham, telling her of his mother's death; and she sent back a very sympathetic reply, which concluded thus: "I suppose you'll have to go into lodgings now. But if I were you I wouldn't. Keep the house on yourself a bit, to see how things go on."

"Whatever does the girl mean by that?" wondered Jim.

Meantime, Ronald Fordham, brought back to health by the kindliest nursing, was brought to trial on the charge of murder. The nurses who had had him in their care wept when he left the hospital for the prison, knowing that he was on the way to the scaffold. Also, the papers said, his wife was in a piteous way, expecting a babe, whose father would probably be hanged before it was born.

Fordham's face, too, was disfigured by the bullet he had shot at himself. His left eye was destroyed; had to be taken out, and there was a scar along his cheek. He looked haggard and troubled, and weary of life, as he stood in the dock, where the whole tale of the tragedy was told, and the dark history that had led up to it revealed. Those in court during the trial noticed the distinct resemblance between Fordham and Langdon's eldest legalised son, who gave evidence. There could be little doubt of their common parentage.

"Funny business," said Dick Blythe, commenting on the case, "here's a man's actions come back to him – an inevitable reaping of what's sown. It seems to be a law of the universe. Somewhere, sometime, somehow, we've got to reap what we have planted; if not in this life, in some other. But it's all a bloomin' mystery. Rum thing is human life, and fate. But one thing's clear – that it's best and sweetest for us all to try to be true and just; to do nothing that will injure others, and then we shall be dong nothing that will ever injure ourselves."

Ronald Fordham was sentenced to death; and immediately there was an outcry throughout the country. The strange, sad story of his mother, the belief that the condemned man was really Langdon's son, the feeling that there was a mysterious retribution and destiny in the true tale, the pathetic romance of the tragedy, stirred public sympathy, and there was a great multitudinous demand that the slayer should not be put to death. Petitions for the royal clemency were numerously signed. The newspapers were full of letters pleading for mercy for the poor fellow in the condemned cell. Though, on the other hand, there were a few persons, chiefly lawyers, who in letters to the Press declared that no silly sentiment should be allowed to interfere with the course of the law.

Fordham himself, in an interview with his solicitor, said he preferred the quick death of the rope to the awful imprisonment for life that a commutation of his sentence would mean.

For days there was a terrible suspense over the land. As the time fixed for the execution drew nigh the public ran eagerly after every fresh edition of the daily and evening papers to see if the Home Secretary had granted any respite.

Then one evening, Dick Blythe, just returned from Manchester, came into his office with a paper in his hand, and cried out, "Fordham's reprieved."

"I'm pleased to hear it," said Jim.

"I'm jolly glad," said Blythe. "'Gradely fain,' as we say in these parts. But I hope he won't be imprisoned for life. That would be worse than the gallows. They ought to set him free in a few years."

[28 November 1908]

XXV. May Day.

On the first Sunday in May Jim Campbell joyously made his way to Brunborough Station, where he eagerly awaited a certain train, which presently, a few minutes late, came thundering in.

Jim eagerly scanned the carriages as they clattered past him; from the window of one a white handkerchief was waving.

Hurrying to this particular carriage – from the window of which a maiden's pretty face was now looking – Jim Campbell entered the compartment, and greeted May Marsden with a lover's "Good morning."

"I'm all alone, you see," she said. "Had the carriage all to myself from Rackington. Do you think the day's going to be fine?"

"I think it will clear up," said Jim. "It's rather cloudy, and we'd a drop of rain early on, but I think the sun will break through before noon. It's only eleven o'clock yet."

"I hope it does clear up," said May.

"So do I," said Jim. "Rain on Pendle is no cheerful thing, though it's all right in its way, if you've good shoes on and are well wrapped up; and I like to know the weather in all its moods; they are all good – except," and he smiled, "when you happen to be on tramp or attending a picnic. However, I'm pretty sure we shall have a nice day this time."

At the next station – Pendleham – they got out.

"You've left nothing in the carriage?" said Jim.

"Oh, no! I've only brought my umbrella and a packet of sandwiches. Where's your provender?"[115] asked May.

"In my pocket," answered Jim. "Now for the walk to Pendle. It's a long trudge, you know."

"A tramp like me is used to walking," said May, with a smile.

"We'll go through the wood and over the moors," said Jim. So, after crossing the canal at Pendleham, they turned to the right, along the riverside, where yet remained much woodland beauty that even the adjacent manufacturing town had not been able to blight.

As they passed through the wood, bonny with all the green budding of May, the sun broke through the clouds and poured the merry light of spring upon the world.

"Grand," said Jim. "It's going to be a glorious day. There'll be thousands of folks on Pendle this afternoon. We shall have a great demonstration. If you're feeling hungry you'd better get some of your sandwiches."

"Oh, I can last a little longer," said May, laughing. "This is better tramping than tramping to the workhouse, isn't it?"

"Yet that's the way most of the workers are going," said Jim. "We must make the life of the workers more of a walk through the fields than a trudge to the workhouse."

"Oh, the good time's coming," said May. "We must keep doing our best to help it along. Oh, did you see it in the paper last night about Ronald Fordham, poor fellow? Isn't it horrible to think of him fast in a grim prison, while we are out in all the freedom of the hills?"

"No; I didn't see the papers last night," said Jim. "What's up now?"

"Fordham, it seems, has been trying to commit suicide."

"I'm not surprised," said Jim. "He's that temperament."

"He tried to open a vein in his arm and bleed himself to death, so the visiting justices of the gaol sentenced him to twenty days' solitary confinement. He's to be kept all alone in a cell, and for the first nine days is to be fed only on bread and water."

"It's a d— shame!" exclaimed Jim. "That's just the treatment to drive the poor devil mad and to more attempts at suicide. We've no right to torture a man so. It would have been kinder to hang him. They ought either to kill him or treat him in a manner that will make life tolerable. He oughtn't to be kept alone – to brood – in a cell. He ought to be put to some work. For when all's honestly reckoned up, Fordham is quite as much a victim as the man he slew – nay, more so, for he had less opportunity to help himself. Society is as much to blame as Ronald Fordham – our present society that allows men to heap up huge fortunes at the expense of their fellows and then buy poor girls with the money, the consequence being lust, and drink, and crime, and all the evils that come from such an iniquitous state of things. We create criminals and then punish them. It's monstrous. Good God! – when will men learn fellowship?"

"Bravo, Jim!" said May, admiringly, "When we get ten thousand men thinking and talking like that we'll do something to end this crazy, sad old world, you'll see! Oh, isn't it shameful, in all this sunshine, and the flowers and the music of the birds, to think of the suffering and the struggling for bread, and all the ill that comes of it in the towns over there?" And she glanced behind at the factory chimneys all along the valley. "I'm astonished that men can go on eating and drinking and living only to put money into their own pockets, knowing what misery there is all around them, when a little sense and a little love would turn the hell into heaven."

By-and-bye they came to a stile, near a little green grove of trees and a tiny stream, and here May, unwrapping her package, said she would have something to eat. Jim also pulled some bread and cheese sandwiches out of his pocket.

"Isn't it delightful?" said May. "Much better than being stuffed up in a church or chapel listening to a soulless sermon. There's no church more beautiful or holy than the Tramps' Church – which is the oldest and most sacred of all churches. For Christ and his Apostles were tramps, you know – a fact that most Christians forget."

Over the moors, over meadow and past farms and plantations they went, and along the riverside – the bed of the stream being remarkably strewn with stones – "It's like modern religion," said May; "there's more stones than the water of life" – till they came to the pretty village of Burley, where they took the path up the side of the clear little stream that babbled down from Pendle Hill, which now rose, eminent and enticing, before them.

[5 December 1908]

XXV. May Day. (*Continued.*)

And Jim was in glory. For all the world was beautiful, and she was sweet and fair. The joy of May was everywhere – the May green on the trees, the May flowers in the copse, the May blue in the sky, the May breath and balm from the meadows and the moors, the May music of the lark and the thrush and all the birds; and, best of all, May by his side – May, living in human form, the embodiment of all the poetry and the picture and the vision of the May, walking by his side, with rosy face and shining eyes, talking to him, singing snatches of song, laughing and chatting like the pleasant brook, charming as the earth, wonderful as the heavens, beautiful as the May-day.

Jim could resist no longer. The eternal impulse, the desire of his destiny, enthralled him.

Suddenly, as they walked along, screened by a tall hedge on either side, he put his arm round May's waist, and said, "May, I want you to be my wife."

May thrilled, rapturously responsive, blushed like the hawthorn to the wooing of the sun, and said, softly, "Any time you like, Jim."

And he clasped her in his arms, and their lips met in the bliss that makes two souls one.

"Now, I may tell you a secret," she said. "I dare say you will remember that night when your mother whispered to me."

"Yes. I have often wondered what she said to you," said Jim, smiling happily.

"She said, 'Look after Jim when I am gone – be his wife.'"

"And what did you say?" asked Jim.

"Oh, I don't think it's necessary to tell you that," said May, blushing.

Jim kissed her. "Tell me, sweetheart."

May blushed. "I said – I – said – yes, if ever he asks me."

There was more kissing.

"Now I know what you meant when you advised me not to go in lodgings after my mother's death. 'Keep the home on a bit,' you wrote, 'till you see how things go on.' And this is how they've gone on. Ah, you delightful witch, you knew, you saw this coming."

"Hadn't we better be getting along?" said May, demurely. "We shall never get to the top of the hill."

He kissed her again, and, with his arm around her, they continued, lingeringly, the ascent.

"Oh, there's one thing I should tell you," said May, prettily. "It's my duty to tell you. I have a past."

"Never mind the past," said Jim. "The present – and our future together – is good enough for me."

"But I must tell you," said May, with mock tragedy. "The information I am about to impart may change your views towards me."

"Nothing can do that, May."

"Oh all lovers talk like that – and then the first disagreeable trifle that comes along is generally enough to turn them into icebergs. Do you know that I had another lover before you, and that he cast me off? I am a girl that's been jilted."

"The more fool he! whoever he was," said Jim. "I know that you are pure and true, May, and that you love me, and that's all I want. You couldn't have loved this other man, and he couldn't have loved you, or you would never have given each other up."

"I think you're right, Jim. I never felt towards him as I feel towards you. Our parents wanted the match, and I acquiesced. But after I had met you –"

More kissing.

"How can I get on with my story if you keep interrupting me like this?" said May. "But he wasn't the sort of man I could love; I couldn't even respect him. He told me that when I was his wife I should have to cease all interest in tramps and the poor and the oppressed."

"He was a cad," said Jim.

"And I told him I never would be his wife."

"Lucky for me!" said Jim, and there was more kissing.

"He thinks only of getting on, of acquiring property, and being respectable," said May.

"Poor fellow!" said Jim. "He's let his angel go, and is going to the devil. But let us not talk about him. When shall we be married?"

"You're in a mighty hurry, Jim."

"Well, as you know, I've kept the little house on since my mother died. In fact, she told me to – she gave me a hint as well as you. Poor old mother! how happy she would be if she were here this day!"

"Perhaps she knows all about it, Jim, and is rejoicing," said May, thoughtfully.

"I hope so," said Jim. "I hope there's another world where we shall meet her. But that's all mystery. Our work is in this world, and we must do all we can to make it brighter and better; we shall then be ready for any life that may follow. Oh, I am so glad that you and I shall now be able to work together – to do a bit for the world together – and – but what about the wedding, May?"

"Well," said May, playfully, "seeing your awkward plight, I don't mind, under the circumstances, agreeing to let it take place as soon as it can be arranged –"

More kissing.

They reached the farm at the foot of the hill, and could now see human forms on Pendle.

"There's somebody waving a handkerchief," said May and she fluttered hers in answer.

"Shall we take the roundabout path or go straight up?" asked Jim.

"Straight up," said May.

So they tackled the stiff ascent up the breast of the mountain through the knee-high bracken and whin and heather, sweetest of seats for lovers and comrades, and delightful dream-couch for poets. They overtook groups of twos and threes making the climb. There was an old man, over seventy, very nimble for his years; he had come several miles, and had been up Pendle many a time. He was enthusiastic in the Cause of the People. "I'd climb Pendle Hill every day o' th' week," he said, "if it would help to bring th' brotherhood o' man about."

They paused half-way up the hill to rest and survey the view – the stretch of hill and dale and factory towns in the distance.

On the summit of the hill there were hundreds of men, women, and children – increased, ere the afternoon was over, to thousands. In the sheltered side of a hill, near Robin Hood's Well – which, if it had not been inexhaustible, would have been drunk dry this day – scores were seated on the grass, some eating the refreshments they had brought with them, and being supplied with water from the spring in tin cups, willingly and diligently handed round by the men. Spirit-kettles were also boiling, and some were having a cup of tea or cocoa.

[12 December 1908]

XXV. May Day. (*Continued.*)

"Isn't it a magnificent crowd!" said Dick Blythe, coming forward to greet May and Jim as soon as he perceived them. "What a while you've been! Been dallying on the road, I expect," and he grinned. "Oh, I can see there's summat up, and I guess what's happened! Congratulations! The better the day the better the deed – and you couldn't have a better day than this! When's the wedding coming off?"

"As soon as possible,'" said Jim, while May laughingly exclaimed, "Oh, Jim, you shouldn't give the show away like that!"

"I'm jolly glad to hear it," said Dick. "This will be rare news for the missus – though, of course, we guessed – we hoped – it would come to this all along. By gow, isn't there a lot of folk here, and they're coming up the hill now in droves. They're coming from all parts of the shire, by train and bike. There's a dozen cyclists just landed from Bolborough – and some out of Yorkshire. There's a lot come up from the Chatburn side, too – and a droll climb they've had – dragging the women up the steeps. It's going to be the biggest Labour and Socialist demonstration ever held on owd Pendle Hill."

And so it proved, and it was good and pleasant to see the fellowship of the great throng, and the enthusiasm of all these people, old and young, who were brought together by the ideal of a regenerate and righteous society, wherein all men should have work and wages, all women be treated kindly, and all little children be given every opportunity to grow up in health and honesty.

They were mostly of the working class – weavers, spinners, joiners, miners, engineers, mechanics, though there were a few shopkeepers, clerks, journalists, and doctors, and other professional men amongst them. All were full of good humour – joking, laughing, chatting of past meetings and doings, recounting the tale of their travel to the rendezvous, and any interesting or amusing incidents on the way. All were dressed in their best, though some were pathetically shabby; their garb, their faces, told of the struggle in which they toiled; but their eyes were alight with the hope of the good time coming – the good time of justice and fair play for all – the time they were bringing nearer by this enthusiastic gathering, to proclaim once more the message they were spreading throughout the land, the gospel of salvation for the shorn and enslaved.

Not an ignorant mob, by any means. Most of these men – and women, too – could tell you something of the history of industry and the economic causes that had made the present cruelly competitive condition of society; they knew the truth about labour and capital; they knew how the present state of the workers had been brought about by priestcraft and statecraft, by robbery, fraud, spoliation, tyranny, oppression, and injustice, and they meant to alter it. Moreover, some of them were keen nature students; they could name the trees and wild flowers; give chapters from the wondrous tale of geology bearing on their local surroundings; while others had a considerable knowledge of the poets and general literature. No, not an ignorant mob, but a crowd of people that had begun to think, and found out that the world was made not of the selfish and evil aggrandisement of a few, but of the fellowship and enjoyment of all.

On this theme, in the middle of the afternoon, after singing "England Arise,"[116] and "For all the Little Children" – a labour song set to a popular hymn-tune – ere the assemblage dispersed – those who lived near to go to their homes, those who had a journey before them to get a cup of tea in the village at the foot of the hill – the leaders spoke, Jim Campbell and May Marsden being two of the speakers, along with Joe Summerfield and others – to the thousands sitting on the hillside. One man told his neighbour that this meeting set him thinking of a Man who, two thousand years ago, in far away Palestine, thus spoke to the multitude on a mountain.

And the singing and the cheering floated down the hills and over the vales – a challenge to the tyrants, a message to the toilers. It seemed as if all the world was a-surge with the great hope of a new ideal.

"Oh, friends and comrades," cried May, "shout aloud on the hill-tops the gospel of deliverance. Over there lie the towns we are to save and build anew. Shout to them; call upon the people to arise. For the sake of all the little children that suffer –"

"Hurrah! Hurrah!"

"For the sake of all the men who are robbed and crushed and broken –"

"Hurrah! Hurrah!"

"For the sake of the dead who died for us, for the sake of those who live and fight for us, for the sake of those unborn that shall follow us – let us slacken not and cease not till we have done all that mortals may to make our earth a place of justice and righteousness and good fellowship."

"Hurrah! Hurrah! Hurrah!"

Then, all the people standing, the men with bared heads, they sang – looking across the vale at the manufacturing towns over which in the week time hung the Black Banner of the smoke of suffering – "The Red Flag": –

> The People's Flag is deepest red;
> It shrouded oft our martyred dead,
> And ere their limbs grew stiff and cold.
> Their heart's blood dyed its every fold.
>
> CHORUS:
> Then raise the scarlet standard high;
> Within its shade we'll live or die;
> Though cowards flinch and traitors sneer
> We'll keep the Red Flag flying here.
>
> It well recalls the triumphs past;
> It gives the hope of peace at last –
> The banner bright, the symbol plain
> Of human right and human gain.
>
> With heads uncovered swear we all
> To bear it onward till we fall.
> Come dungeon dark or gallows grim,
> This song shall be our parting hymn.

Then from the vast crowd, amid the stillness of the high moorlands, rose the chorus:

> Then raise the scarlet standard high;
> Within its shade we'll live or die;
> Though cowards flinch and traitors sneer
> We'll keep the Red Flag flying here.

Edward Hartley, 'The Man in the Street. High Rates, Officialism and Socialism' (1909)

I have a friend who has been very successful with a business in a shop in the main shopping street of a northern town. When in the neighbourhood I often call in to see him, and at times go to take supper, when his excellent wife gives a most cordial welcome. She says:

"You'll never convince me; but I do really like to hear you talk. It almost seems as though it could be done."

I live in hope of convincing her.

One evening the conversation turned to the question of successful men. My friend inclined to the opinion that the success of the business men was almost entirely due to their superior brain power.

It was pointed out that, as a rule, the inventors did not get very rich; the financier generally taking the lion's share.

On a discussion as to the quality of brains, as between these two, I took occasion to point out that the inventor used his brains to increase the wealth production, while the financier used his brains to get for himself the largest possible share of the wealth produced.

We might have waited another 1,000 years for the inventions, if it had rested with the lower type of intellect, which could not invent, but could take advantage of another man's cleverness.

There were some other friends present, and two business men were emphatically of the opinion that the financial brains were of an equal, if not superior, type to those of the inventor.

Needless to say, neither of them had ever invented anything.

I generally avoid the personal issue, it grows dangerous at times; but my friend is one of the good ones, and on my asking if we might take his case as an example, said:

"That is just what I should like."

"Very well! You by our ability have built up a good business. That is due to your superior brain power."

"Well! Largely!"

"Very well! The rent of your shop is £200 a year. Now, my shop is only £20, yet it is almost the same size as yours. I will let you my shop at £25, and you will save £175 each year."

"Oh! but I could not do the same business on the outskirts as in the centre!"

"Not if you took your brains with you?"

He was taken aback, and said:

"Oh, dash you! You are always lying in wait to trap someone. The position is bound to make a difference."

"Of course it is. If your brains were twice their present quality you could not do the same business in the suburbs as in the centre. Just so! Now, I'm not a very brainy man, but if my father had been the Duke of Gooseberry, I might have been 'poor, but honest,' and twice as silly as I am now; but I could have drawn the rents all right. If my father had been a great inventor, and myself a regular dunce, I could have looked after the royalties. A good stand is very useful. The man whose father left him a castle in the olden days had a distinct advantage over the man whose father left him a hut. Yet at times they changed hands."

At this point the conversation drifted, and one of the business men began to say: "The great evil of modern times is the growth of officialism. You are somewhat to blame for that, Alderman," he said. "You will go on doing it till we begin to shoot them off in sheer despair, when we may include the whole corporation."

I laughed, and said:

"That's all right! If you do the shooting it will be better to stand still, I think."

"Why?"

"Well, I don't think you would hit very often, while if one ran away he might get in the way of the shot."

This restored our good humour; but he said again:

"We shall be ruined by officialism."

"My dear sir! where ever did you read that?"

"Read what?"

"Why, that nonsense about officialism. If you know anything about it, you know it's nonsense. If you don't know, why do you repeat such rubbish?"

"Oh! but in my lifetime there has been a tremendous growth of officials."

"Perhaps so. But there is only one Town Clerk, only one Water Engineer, one Gas Engineer, one Chief Constable, one Medical Officer."

"Quite true. But there are two inspectors to every one."

"Very true. And the population has grown from less than 100,000 to 300,000."

"Yes; but I object to all these changes."

"Are you sure you object?"

"Why, what a question, Mr. Hartley! He said he objected." This from one of the others.

"Yes; but I don't think he does."

"Surely he knows best."

"We'll see about that."

I then turned to the objector, and said:

"You live at Moorhill, don't you?"

"Yes; and you've put up the rates a pretty penny since we came into the city. They've gone up 1s. 6d. in the £."

"You've got a few improvements, haven't you?"

"Yes; but not eighteenpennyworth."

"Sure?"

"Yes, quite sure!"

"You had your gas reduced when the corporation bought out the gas company."

"Yes, 1s. 9d. per 1,000ft. That was all right. We give you credit when you do *good things*."

"Do you use much gas?"

"About 20,000ft. a year."

"Nearly 23,000ft. last year," said his wife.

"May I ask what your house is rated at?"

"Twenty-four pounds a year."

"Now let us reckon up. Twenty-four times 1s. 6d. is £1 16s. 0d. Twenty-three times 1s. 9d. is £2 0s. 3d. It would seem you are 3s. 9d. in pocket, in spite of the rise of 1s. 6d. in the £ in your rates."

"Well, of course, reckoning it that way."

"But isn't that the proper business way?"

"Oh! I suppose so."

He was a bit huffy, but his education was not yet complete.

"I suppose you will remember that eight years ago a private company ran the tramcars up your way?"

"They stopped at the bottom of the hill, though."

"How long did it take you to walk from the private company's terminus to your house?"

"Nearly half an hour up hill, and a good quarter of an hour down."

"The corporation cars go past your house now?"

"Yes, nearly a mile."

"How much extra do they charge you?"

"Whatever are you driving at? They charge us less."

"How soon can you reach home from the cars now?"

"In two minutes."

"Then the corporation trams save you three-quarters of an hour every time you come into the town. You have two sons and yourself in the business, and you all come to town daily, night and morning."

"My husband comes home to dinner every day, Mr. Hartley," said his wife. "And the boys come home every day except market days."

"Oh! thank you! Now, Mr. Blank, I suppose you and your sons will count yourselves as good as navvies or labourers, and your time will be worth at least 6d. an hour?"

"Rather!" he answered.

A laugh went round, for Mr. Blank is something "in wool." He doesn't make any wool. He doesn't carry it from place to place. He doesn't add any value to it. He only sells it for more than he gives for it, usually, and, of course, to talk of such a man getting only 6d. an hour is ridiculous. Sixpence an hour is quite sufficient for the men who *make* useful things, but ridiculous for the men who sell them.

"Very well, Mr. Blank. Shall we now see if you really object? Since the wicked corporation supplied you with tram riding, instead of the kind, good, generous, private company, and since you were under the rule of the tyrannical official, who manages the trams for the good of the citizens instead of the shareholders, you ride up that awkward hill almost to your own door, saving at least half an hour every journey, and your sons do the same. This means two hours a day, ten hours a week; at 6d. an hour, 5s. each week. Your two sons save two hours on two days of the week, and four hours on the other three; that is, sixteen hours of time at 6d., or 8s. each week. Altogether 13s. a week, only reckoning for you traveling on five days in the week. Remember, I'm putting down nothing for the saving when your wife or your two servants are travelling. That we will count as a set-off against the wickedness of officialism."

"Look here, Edward," said my friend the host. "Don't you be so blooming sarcastic." (He didn't say blooming.)

"Steady! Don't let us get away from the point. Now, Mr. Blank, do you admit the figures?"

"Oh! they are all right, so far as they go, and I'm neither objecting to the saving nor the convenience. What I object to is the great increase in rates and the growth of bureaucracy. There are too many officials!"

'You don't object at all. You read those things, and think you believe them. But you don't."

"Don't I, though? I do, and so do thousands of ratepayers. We are going to put a stop to your little gallop; business men are finding out it is very foolish to divide themselves into Liberals and Tories at election times, when you Socialists and trade unionists slip in on three-cornered fights.[1] We shall unite to stop you."

"What are you going to stop?"

"Oh! your municipal trading, and things like that."

"Let us go back a little. Your house is rated at £24 a year. When the rates get to 10s. in the £, that will mean £12 a year. You admitted to a saving of £2 0s. 3d. on your gas bill. We made out that you save 13s. a week by the trams; altogether this would mean £38 a year, or something which is worth it. It would appear that the corporation and its wicked officialism have done as much for you by the trams and gas alone, as your father would have done if he had left you a house worth £38 a year. What do you really object to?"

"Well, of course, I don't object to that. But I do object to the growth of officials."

"If that is all, you've no reason to object at all. You will remember that before we took over the whole tramway system there were two private companies in the town, in addition to the corporation. There were, of course, three general managers, three secretaries, three engineers, three committees, three sets of books, offices, etc. Now there is one manager, who is also the engineer, one set of books, one committee (unpaid), and while the system is three times as big, it is twice as efficient, and the fares all round have been lowered more than one-half. You don't object to that, do you?"

"Certainly not! Though I'd never seen these things in that light."

"Just a moment. You will remember there were four private gas companies bought out by the corporation? That meant five managers, four secretaries, five committees (four of them paid), and you paid nearly twice as much for your gas. Now we've one manager, no secretary, and one committee (which is not paid.) There are less officials, the things the public need are supplied at half price for a better article, and even the workmen get better times."

"Well, Mr. Hartley, we are all Socialists now,[2] you know; and if you can get us other things of a better quality at half price, we shall be very glad to have them?"

"Yes. There is not a single thing the people need which they could not get in the same manner – that is, a better article at half price – if they were wise enough to begin *to make things for use* instead of profit."

Our hostess said: "Now, didn't I tell you if Mr. Hartley came he'd make it seem as if we could do these things?"

Mr. Blank said he'd never studied the matter; but he thought he'd have to be a Socialist after this.

"Get on, Mr. Hartley. I'll vote for a Socialist if you put one up in our ward. You were right. I don't object at all when I now; but, you know, when one reads Lord Rosebery and Lord Avebury[3] and men like that, you think they should know what they are talking about."

"But do they?"

"Well, it would seem not, from our conversation. No sensible man can object when he understands. Let us have some more Socialsim."

"But municipal gas and trams are not Socialism."

"I thought you said they were."

"No. If you think for a minute I never mentioned Socialism. It was only in answer to what you thought were objections. These things are only Collectivism, but they are leading towards Socialism."

"Well, what is Socialism?"

"Socialism is an extension of this principle of collective ownership, until everything we need is owned for the common good, instead of private profit."

"Everything?" asked one of the ladies.

"Yes. If municipal water, why not municipal food? If gas, why not coal? If trams, why not every other kind of machinery? If we can build libraries to house the people's books, and stables to house the corporation horses, why not houses for the citizens, who, surely, are more important than the books, or even the horses? But, enough. I came here to talk about books, and you beggars have drawn me on to lecture; just as if I were at a street corner. Will no one sing for us?"

We finished with a musical evening; but one of the men there is reading and studying Socialism, and pays his subs. to the branch.

W. Anderson, 'The Fool and the Wise Man' (1910)

Once upon a time two men met. One asked the other, "Who are you?"
He answered, "I am a fool, I am called a worker. Now tell me, who are you?"
"I," replied the former, "am a wise man; men call me a gentleman."
"What do you do?"
"I teach fools like you."
"Will you teach me?"
"With pleasure, come with me."
The fool went with the wise man, who took him to a pile of bricks and a quantity of wood.
"Build me a grand mansion and a small hut," said the wise man.
The fool did so, and when he had finished the wise man gave him some money, saying: "I will live in the mansion because I have earned it by my intellect; you will live in the hut, which will be better for you as you are a fool; you would not appreciate the artistic merit of the mansion, and the nails of your boots would destroy the rich carpets; and as the hut belongs to me (you know you made it for me), it is quite correct you should pay me rent for the right to live there."
The fool lived in the small hut, and paid the rent, saying: "What a clever man; I should never have thought of building a hut for myself if he had not mentioned it, and I could not pay the rent if he did not pay me a daily wage."
The wise man took the fool to the entrance of a mine, saying: "Draw out the coal from the bowels of the earth, and when I have finished with it you may have the cinders to warm yourself."
The fool drew out the coal and said: "This man is not only wise but good, because he gives me the cinders to warm myself when he could easily have thrown them away."
The wise man said to the fool: "I require someone to dress me, to prepare my food, etc.; give me some of your children to wait upon me."
The fool sent his children, saying to himself: "This is good, he will teach them to know as much as he has me, and some day they will become gentlemen like him."

A few days afterwards the wide-awake one said to the other: "When I took your children into my service I was compelled to increase my expenses; such being the case you will have to be content with a lower wage so as to enable me to remunerate them fairly."

The simpleton scratched his head for a while, but said at last: "Oh, yes, my children must be paid for by all means. Very well, we must all live."

The man of brains said to the ignoramus: "Build two schools for my use, a spacious one and the other of smaller dimensions, where our children may be educated."

"Why," said the latter, "should one be larger than the other?"

"The reason is, that my children being gifted gentlefolk, like myself, require a high education in order to develop their intellectual faculties, hence the need of a large school. On the other hand, your children being the issue of a fool will have to do manual labour, the same as you, and therefore the smaller will suffice them. As a matter of course you cannot expect your children to be educated for nothing, so you must pay for the service."

One day the clever one betook himself in a very bad mood into the fool's presence, saying: "You have been thinking?"

"Yes," answered the other.

"I will not allow it; if you do it again I shall punish you."

"Oh!" cried the simpleton, dropping his tools, "you have given yourself away. Were you as intelligent as you imagine you would be aware that it is an impossibility for even fools such as I to forego thinking at some time or other. I know you now, you are a knave!"

The following day the slave hoisted a red flag. Armed himself, and rebelled against his master. Thinking was the beginning of the revolution, the consummation of which has not yet arrived.

LABOUR LEADER

Margaret Holden, 'A Scene in Eden Street', *Labour Leader*, 29 March 1907, p. 716.

Ernest Smith, 'Socialist Red', *Labour Leader*, 22 May 1908, p. 321.

Arthur Laycock, 'The "Retired" Street Sweeper', *Labour Leader*, 19 February 1909, p. 122.

Nellie Best, 'At a Servant's Registry', *Labour Leader*, 14 January 1910, p. 29.

The *Labour Leader* (1893–1987) continued to be edited by John Bruce Glasier, who had assumed editorial control in 1905, until his resignation of the post in 1909. He was replaced by J. T. Mills (n.d.), while Glasier continued to write for the periodical after he ceased editing it, although not as prolifically. He had significantly increased the sales of the *Labour Leader* during his editorship, taking weekly sales figures from 13,000 to 43,000 in 1908; but he, the leadership of the Labour Party (the 'Big Four' of Hardy, MacDonald, Snowden and Glasier) and the periodical were criticized for their pragmatic politics and their close relationship with the Liberal Party. One of the most vociferous critics of the Labour Party and its leaders was Victor Grayson, who publicly challenged the party, both in the press and in Parliament, to strengthen its commitment to socialism. This call was repeated through the national branches, and at the 1909 Labour Party conference, a demand for the freedom of each branch to select its own candidate for elections caused the 'Big Four' to threaten to resign from the party in order to defeat the motion.

The inclusion of fiction was clearly not a priority for Glasier. During his editorship in the period covered by this volume, he published no lengthy serials and only included two pieces of fiction that were longer than a self-contained short story. Both of these relatively longer pieces were by his wife, Katherine Bruce Glasier (1867–1950), and both were published over three weeks: 'Tales from the Derbyshire Hills' (28 December 1906–11 January 1907) and a series of linked stories, 'London Pride' (27 December 1907), 'Saxifrage' (3 January 1908) and 'A Snowstorm and After' (10 January 1908). His inclusion of short stories was a little more numerous, but even these averaged just over one a month. No biographical or publishing details have been found for Margaret Holden, but Ernest Smith might be Ernest Brammah Smith (1868–1942), who also published as Ernest Bramah. This author had worked on the staff of Jerome K. Jerome's periodical *Today* between 1893 and 1897, but there is no suggestion in Smith's entry in the *Oxford Dictionary of National Biography* that he had any involvement in or inclination for socialist politics. His is not an unusual name, and the story may be by another 'Ernest Smith' who is now untraceable.

It is possible that Mills replaced Glasier in the editor's chair at the beginning of April 1909, as the volume of short stories increased significantly from 2 April. After a brief run of short stories published in early January, there was only one story published in February – Arthur Laycock's (n.d.) 'The "Retired" Sweeper', included in this selection – until 2 April, when the periodical began including two short stories a week, settling into a weekly inclusion in July. Arthur Laycock was the author of the novels *Steve, the Outlander: A Romance of South Africa* (1900) and *Warren of Manchester* (1906), a collection of short stories entitled *Christmas Sketches* (1900), and a collection of verse, *A Message of Love, from Blackpool Etc.* (1912). Laycock published a great many stories in Clarke's *Teddy Ashton's Journal* and in the *Yorkshire Factory Times*, and he was the author of the serial fiction 'The Young Gaffer' published in *Teddy Ashton's Journal* in 1898. There is little biographical detail available for Nellie Best (n.d.) except that she was a member of the Women's International League and Sylvia Pankhurst's Worker's Suffrage Federation. She was imprisoned in 1916 under the Defence of the Realm Act for making speeches that might affect recruitment. I have found no evidence that she published any other fiction.

Margaret Holden, 'A Scene in Eden Street' (1907)

"How's the parish?" asked the nurse.

"There is seldom any change in the parish," replied the curate; "but there soon will be, for I am leaving; I am going to work in the East End of London."

"I congratulate you," said the nurse. "You will at least find there is *work* to do. Do you feel nervous about it?"

"I'm afraid I do rather; my vicar tells me that it is not only the vice and the dirt one has to face there, but the *ingratitude* of the people is appalling. He says some of them are like wild beasts, and have not a redeeming trait."

The doctor grunted, but retired behind the cloud of smoke that ascended from his pipe. The curate always irritated the doctor; he was such a mild young man.

"I don't need to interfere," muttered the doctor; "he's safe to catch it," for he could see the nurse's nostrils quiver and her eyes flash.

"Yes," said the nurse in a reflective tone, "they are vicious; they drink, they fight, they swear, they steal, they are dirty; but, pray, *what* have they to be *grateful* for?"

The curate gasped.

"Why, for – for? Don't you think they ought to be grateful to *you* for what you do?"

"No, I don't. I earn my daily bread by attending to them when they are sick. Should I not be grateful to *them* for providing me with that? But it is not true that they are ungrateful or without a redeeming trait. I could tell you –" But she stopped.

"Yes, do tell us, nurse," said the doctor, emerging from his smoke cloud.

"I have been in a house all night where the sole furniture was the bed (composed of several orange boxes, the bedding old coats and skirts), and a box for a seat – a box containing oranges to be sold in the street by-and-by; where there was no food and no fire; where the water ran down the walls in streams, settling in little pools on the already damp floor. And into that den another human being was born. I ask you what he had to be grateful for, and how he could grow up other than vicious and dirty? The husband had come out of prison that day, after 'doing' several months for 'robbery with violence' – a coarse, rough man, who expressed himself mostly by aid of oaths, but who waited outside the room in the draughty passage for hours to hear that 'the missus an' the little 'un were all right, bless 'em,' only he didn't say *bless*; and then he escorted me safely home in the early hours of the morning, the 'streets not bein' very nice for a lady at that time,' said he, doubtless knowing well. And some days later a dozen of the best oranges that my seat had contained were polished and left at my house, 'for the little nuss as comes to us in Paradise Street.'

"I can tell you of another instance. I had to go to a case in Eden Street (I am not inventing the names; they are real; and these streets are off *Christian* Street – a district in a North-country town). I went early in the day. In the middle of the street a crowd was gathered. Two men, stripped to the waist, were fighting; their faces were not recognizable; their flesh was torn and bleeding. I had to push my way through the crowd (there was no other entrance, the street being a *cul de sac*). I was almost knocked down by the mad, rage-blinded, swaying bodies, when a cry arose from the crowd: 'It's the nuss; God bless her,' and they lurched in the opposite direction, still fighting. All efforts to separate them were useless; they must fight it out. All day long groups of people were quarrelling and fighting, partisans of the duelists of the morning. In the afternoon two women began.

"My patient was seriously ill, and I could not leave her; but just under that window they fought. Oh! it was terrible; they tore the clothes off each other, the hair out in handfuls, blood bespattered the stones and the watching crowd. At length one of the women became unconscious, and the other woman dragged her by the hair to the pavement, set her up against the wall, and banged her head against it. Then she was dragged off."

"Where were the police?" asked the horrified curate.

"I don't know. I was told the police never came down that street. I certainly never saw one in it. By this time it had become a faction fight. I had to spend the night in the house, and all night I could hear the screaming and quarrelling continue.

"Next day I took my patient to hospital. As we were about to drive away, a little group of women, among them the two combatants of the day before, put their heads in at the window, and called out. 'God bless ye, nuss, for takin' Katy away wid ye; shure, it's the good heart ye'se have, an' the Holy Mother an' the blessed saints will reward yez'; and bottles of gin were pushed into my patient's willing hands.

"I looked at the two women whose blood still stained the pavement; they were standing close together, evidently quite friendly. One of them became a mother a couple of months later. What chance had that infant of growing up a good man, I ask you?"

"But they *were* like wild beasts," said the curate.

"Yes, but I don't think I could have made friends as they did. And I could tell you many in that same street who are living gently and refinedly, and trying to bring up their children well amongst such scenes, and doing it, too. Friend, when you go into your poor district and see those fœtid dens which reek unspeakably in summer, and into which in winter the snow finds its way through every chink, as well as through the shattered windows; when you see wan skeletons huddling together in their fireless room for warmth; when everywhere you see want, dirt, and promiscuity, ask yourself what these starved, diseased, besotted creatures have to be thankful for, and what you would have been had not accident ordained that you should be born and live under other conditions. I went into my first district, the one I have described, with high notions of my *mission*, forsooth. I came away a revolutionary. I used to pass from my district there to the hospital, through beautiful terraces full of enormous houses, and pleasant gardens, with great trees in front of them, and I have wept to think that justice no longer lived."

Ernest Smith, 'Socialist Red' (1908)

A few days ago I entered a hosier's shop in Croydon with the intention of buying a new red tie. Just inside the doorway I was accosted by a large frock-coat containing a small man with well-oiled hair and complexion to match. This gentleman of the floor was adorned with a massive gold albert,[1] and bore himself generally after the fashion of an hotel boots.[2]

"What can I do for you?" he said, wringing his hands, Uriah Heep-wise.[3]

I stated my wishes, and was asked to "step this way, sir – please, sir, and take a seat, sir; thank you, sir."

"Forward, Mr. Simpson," he commanded, immediately exchanging his servile air for one of studied superciliousness. Mr. Simpson at once came forward and stood at attention, albeit with a languid air. He rejoiced in an excessive expanse of collar and an expression of countenance suggestive of a blissful ignorance, tempered with prejudice, of anything beyond dress and girls. Assistants of this type, the *bête-noir* of the S.A.U. organisers,[4] revel in the refined and gentlemanly nature of their employment, and assure themselves (and others, if possible) that they are the cream of middle-class society. Their chief concern seems to be to impress people with the belief that their calling is not the outcome of economic necessity, but prompted merely by the desire to have some hobby in life. They would rather die than join a trade union, and they believe that the working-man should be kept in his place. Politically, their limited views extend no further than a few vague notions concerning the free and glorious British Empire and the honour to the dear old flag. What horror, pain, and mortification they would suffer if only they knew that in the eyes of the law they are not the middle-class or even working-men, but merely "domestic servants"![5] – surely the "unkindest cut of all"[6] to this eminently respectable section of the community. But, then, we all know that the "law is a hass."[7]

Mr. Simpson proceeded to earn his bread and butter – or margarine, as the living-in system[8] was in vogue at this establishment – by placing numerous boxes of ties on the counter for my inspection.

"What shade of red would you prefer, sir?" he asked, showing me various samples. "This is maroon, and this is cardinal; then there is this one; but that is a 'Socialist red.'"

"Um – a 'Socialist red'?" I commented in a half-inquiring way.

"Yes," he said with a sickly grin. "You know, the sort of thing worn by these fellows you see spouting at the street corners."

"Oh?" I said; and waited to see if he volunteered any more information.

"Lot o' rot, ain't it?" he continued.

"There certainly is a lot of rot talked about Socialism," I said; "but what is this Socialism?"

"W'y, ain't you 'eard? Them Socialists want everybody to share and share alike."

"You've made a study of the subject, I suppose?"

"Oh, no; I wouldn't waste my time over such rubbish. I say if a man saves his money and invests it, and is clever enough to make a fortune, then good luck to 'im, that's w'ot I say. And nobody's got a right to take it from 'im."

"Just so," I remarked. "But" said I, changing the subject, "what is all this agitation against the living-in system?"

"Oh, that's them paid agitators trying to stir up discontent."

"I suppose there's really nothing to be discontented about?" I queried.

"Oh, well, of course it ain't all 'oney living in; but these things always 'ave been, and always will be."

"You don't think the agitators are trying to improve matters?"

"They don't seem to do much, do they, except talk? I wish they would."

"How would it be to help them by joining the Union?" I ventured.

"Me join a trade union? Not me. W'y, they're all in with the Socialists, who want to upset everything."

Closuring the discussion, I said: "I think I'll take the 'Socialist red' after all, if you don't mind."

Mr. Simpson, relapsing into a meditative silence, wrapped up my purchase. When, for the good of his soul, I handed him my well-worn copy of Blatchford's "Britain for the British,"[9] he looked absolutely petrified with astonishment.

Of such are the forces against Socialism.

Arthur Laycock, 'The "Retired" Street Sweeper' (1909)

"Yes, I'm livin' retired, here, as we say in Lancashire – too old to work, a bit too young for peddlin' pension.

"How did I come to get into this workhouse? yo' ax.

"Well, yo' see, it were like this: I were a street sweeper, and I were th' foreman o' my gang, too; there were three of us in it: an' I'd what yo' call a sort of standin' bein' a bit of a boss, for it means summat even to be th' gaffer in a mud-shiftin' gang.

"Well, I tell yo', I were doin' vary weel i' my way for an owd felly until a new manager come to boss all th' lot of us scavengers – th' cleansin' superintendent they called him.

"Of course, a chap with a double-barrelled name like that had to show summat for his salary, for he weren't paid a common 'wage' like us – it were a 'salary,' mind yo'. There's a great deal in a name, yo' know. Yo'll remember th' tale about th' chap 'at agreed t' tak' eighteen bob a week for his work. 'But,' he said to his mestur, 'I want yo' to call this wage o' mine a "salary."' 'All right,' said the mestur, 'but why?' 'Well, yo' see,' said th' chap, 'I've nooaticed 'at salaries are allus goin' up while wages are oft goin' down.'

The New Broom

"But I were tellin' yo' about th' new broom – this new manager o' ours. He were fro' Lunnon or somewhere like that, an' were as full o' new-fanglet notions as workhouse life is full o' woe.

"He started o' makin' his improvements reet off, an' how do yo' think he did it? He introdooced – that's how they put it in th' papers – he introdooced some little hand-barrow wi' cans on 'em for us to wheel about, an' empty our sweepin's in. Before this we'd allus swept th' rubbish into little piles at the roadside, an' then it had been shoveled into th' carts. But now, instead of horses bein' in th' shafts, it were us humin bein's – men such as me, – an' me a foreman o' my gang, too, at that!

Undignified Labour

"We were put between these little truck-shafts like jackasses, an' we lugged th' stuff along like that. It did no' look what yo' call dignified. There's a diff'rence, after all, between sweepin' th' rubbish up at your feet an' luggin' it along behind yo'.

"But we had to put up with it an' say nowt, or run th' risk o' bein' sacked. It were all th' same, though, in th' end. Th' cleansin' superintendent, swaggerin' swell as he were, as looked as if he'd go an' sniff in a middin'[1] with a silk hat on his yed – he come sniffin', sniffin round us at odd times at six o'clock in th' mornin'. Just fancy that! – when all other salaried folk were fast asleep i' bed.

"He come potterin' round, peepin' at th' corners, an' catchin' us suddenly like when our chaps were hardly awake.

"By gow, but he wakened, 'em.

Wakened Up

"He come one pertikler mornin' an' happened to catch owd Billy Brance sweepin' a bit slow. Billy had th' rheumatics a bit, yo' see, an' even a salaried supe.[2] canno' be so frisky at seventy-five, espeshally if he's been fattening most of his days on fifteen bob a week.

"Well, I tell yo', he come an' copped owd Billy sweepin' seven strokes to th' minute – the supe. wanted about seventy to th' second. It were mud an' slush, too, 'at we were sweepin' – heavy, sloppy stuff. Th' supe. took no account o' that.

"'See yo' my man,' said he, 'I'll show yo' how to sweep streets.' An' with that he whapped th' long brush out o' Billy's tremblin' hond an' started o' sweepin' at full bat.

"'Oh, ay, I dar'say,' grunted Billy, as he watched him for a two-three seconds. 'New brooms sweep swift an' clean, mestur.'

"'What do yo' mean?' snapped our swell superintendent.

"'I mean,' said Billy, loudly, ''at if I swapped shops an' salaries with yo' I could happen sweep a two-three more strokes to th' minnit, espeshally if I'd nobbut to try it five minutes i' twelve months.'

"Sacked"!

"'Take your notice,' said th' supe. savagely, 'an' leave on Saturday.'

"'An' tak' thy nooatice an' leave now,' said owd Billy with rare spirit, an' as he spoke he snapped th' muddy brush fro' th' supe. an' fot him a sharp welt with it on th' yed, an' sent th' silk hat flyin'.

"Eh, it were worth summant to see, I can tell yo', though most on us were too feart just then to show our enjoyment, an' we had to pretend not to have seen owt at all.

"After that I were prepared for anything' happenin'; but we were surprised to see 'at the supe. did no' bother us no more. Early risin' an amachure street-sweepin' did no' suit him, seemin'ly, for long.

"He were a 'new broom,' too, as Billy truly said, an' his gen'ral enthewsiasm soon simmered down.

"But while he did no' come nosin' round hissel he seed 'at some'dy else did, an' th' assistant supe. did his dirty work. We were hustled an' bustled about so much 'at we wondered whether life were worth livin' at th' street-sweepin' job.

Preparing a Place

"Owd Billy had gone to this workhouse here, an' as he went he towd us he'd go an' prepare a place for us[3] – reck'nin' to quote Scriptur', as he were religious-like; an' he said 'at he'd pray hard for another dry place to be prepared for th' Lunnon swell 'at had sacked him – a place, he said, where our supe. would be kept sweepin' seven thousand strokes to th' second in a sultry – vary sultry – subterranyan street.

"As I were sayin', th' supe.'s assistant were towd off to speshally watch us, his mestur tellin' him we wer too owd to work, an' he must sack us.

"But th' elections come on about then, an' they dare no' do such a dirty trick. We wouldn't have minded givin' up work if we'd each had but a quarter of his salary to settle on. But they dunno pension weary workers 'at ar worn out; it's nobbut th' idle an' showy shirkers an' queer quirkers 'at get 'em.

"They dare no' sack us just then, I tell yo'; they could no' for shame, or their man might have lost th' election. But after a bit they got shut of all of us, for one reason or another.

"For me th' beginnin' o' th' end were they knocked off my extry pay as forman o' th' gang – it were sixpence a week an' th' dignity o' th' job.

Economising

"Th' economisin' chap had got elected, an' they had to save th' public brass; so they knocked th' sixpences off the scavengers an' street-sweepers' wages, while they added £50 a year to th' supe.'s salary for the 'splendid economies he had effected' – the newspaper tawk again.

"That were th' difference between th' wages an' th' salary. We all owt to have been salaried chaps; then we should have been reet.

"I'm towd that they're never too owd to lose their salaries; some o' th' Parly-ment chaps, if they lose their shops,[4] they still get their salaries; an' th' owder they grow an' th' bigger th' salary grows, an' more often nor not they get double pay after they've stopped doing owt.

"They knocked off my extry pay as foreman, I tell yo', an' it so upset my dig-nity an' lost me my 'locus standi'[5] in th' profession – as th' lawyers say - 'at I had to give up.

"I had no' th' spirit' o' owd Billy, or I'd have chucked another brush at th' supe.'s head. But anyhow, a chance to do it would never have come, for when th' supe.'s salary rose he never rose no more early in th' mornin'. He were happen feared 'at th' early bird might catch another brush steyl.⁶

"He wint livin' into a big house at th' swell end o' th' town at th' same time 'at I came to a bigger house among yo' swells out here."

Nellie Best, 'At a Servant's Registry' (1910)

It was a bitterly cold day. Business was slack, for Xmas was near, and servant girls would rather dine on bread and tea at home on Xmas Day than enjoy the luxurious scraps sent from the "dining room" to the "kitchen."

Slack from the "servant' point of view I (as the proprietress of a Female Labour Bureau) ought to have said, for peal after peal of the door bell heralded the approach of some warmly clad and oftimes harsh-voiced "lady."

"What did you say? Plenty of servants on the books but none who will engage until after Christmas Day! Whatever is the world coming to? It all arises from the education of the working-classes." (This particular "lady" was the wife of a successful jerry builder.) "Fancy servant girls refusing service at Xmas time in order to stop at home and dine on fish and chips! Are you quite sure you cannot persuade anyone to come? I simply cannot manage with just one servant. I have had to do all the dusting myself to-day. I am simply worn out. Lazy lot, my last girl was – never got out of bed until 6 a.m., and always retired at 10 p.m., except when we had 'company.' Then she had 'one evening' out per week and every other Sunday evening. And yet – would you believe it? – she had the impertinence to come to me yesterday and say, 'I beg your pardon, ma'am, but I have felt so run down lately that I want to ask you if I can have one hour each day to myself. (Between 6 a.m. and 10 p.m.) My legs get so tired, and my head aches so frequently, that I think I could do my work better if I had one hour in which to lie down or have a "run out" if the weather was fine."

"I do not know what else she would have said; but I peremptorily cut her short by telling her to pack her box at once, and never darken my doors again.

"I don't know what the working-classes are coming to. What with education and Socialism, we will have a revolution soon."

I, with the becoming meekness and modesty of a "registry-keeper," somewhat calmed her ruffled nerves by here interjecting that I was in perfect agreement with her last statement – education and Socialism hastening the revolution.

After wasting another half-hour of my time airing her imaginary woes, another quarter-of-an-hour's discussion took place upon whether I was justified in asking her to pay the shilling registry fee (inclusive) before the engagement of servant took place.

I gently intimated the fact to her that correspondence could not be carried on without stamps, and that the Post Office did not carry my letters free.

I also timidly hinted that even such social worms as "registry-keepers" have to live, and that, being dependent upon my labour, a financial adjunct is essential to procure the necessaries of life to enable me to go on "placing" mistresses and maids.

Whilst she was deliberating whether she would lighten her purse by the sum of one shilling, another peal of the bell preceded the entrance of a girl, about nineteen years of age, tall, slight, and fair in complexion, with that pretty pink flush which is so often the accompaniment of consumptive tendencies. Her attire was very shabby and worn, her boots hardly possessed any sole, and her appearance betokened absolute dejection. Her query, "Have you got anything for me yet?" was entirely hopeless, but without the slightest trace of bitterness.

She had been coming for a fortnight. She was an orphan. She had left her last place because of illness. Some poor friend had given her a crust and a shelter; but before strength had returned her scanty wardrobe had become almost depleted.

I had tried hard to "place" her with the last fortnight; but none of the "ladies' wanted "lag rags" without proper wardrobes.

I returned to the jerry builder's wife and pathetically told my tale, point out that, as she was hard pressed, she could take her temporarily.

Indignantly and loudly, so that it penetrated to my little "unemployed charge," came the answer: "Mrs. Best, have I not told you before not to bring your dirty, trashy, slummy creatures into your business, if you want that business to prosper? I want a smart girl, about twenty years of age, preferably tall, nicely spoken, so that the children won't deteriorate by contact; print dresses for mornings, black dress for afternoon, and plenty of caps and aprons. To a really nice girl I do not mind giving 5s. per week. But I really must have someone for Xmas Day. There is so much to cook, so many visitors to attend to, so many extra things to do to make Xmas happy and joyful, as it should be, that I simply cannot manage."

And the "she" went, or rather sailed, out. Swish, swish, went her silken skirts. Click, click went the silver chain, at one end of which was a little, white, fluffy dog, almost covered with a beautiful fur coat.

And I turned to greet the other "she" – she of the soleless boots, she of the soulless voice; she the homeless, motherless, friendless, and workless. Yet, whilst I hesitated for words to express to her my disgust of the other's vulgarity, without a word she slipped past me and was gone.

And I – I returned to my room and opened the windows.

Vain hope! Psychic influences of selfishness and vulgarity, coupled with those of deep sorrow and misery, refused to be dissipated by material outlets.

A feeling of awful depression seized me. I lay back on my chair. All the articles of furniture seemed to disappear. My room is filled with cold, shivering, haggard men, women, and children. They are all repeating, parrot-like, the words of my previous "mistress" visitor – Xmas should be happy and joyful; Xmas should be happy and joyful.

The rhythmic repetition exercises upon me a curious mesmeric influence, and I enter the land of dreams, and in the land of dreams a Christ-like face dawned upon my vision, and a voice spoke: –

"Piteous plaints reach me year after year. That poor girl who came to your house for work to-day: her cries have reached me, and still echo in my ears."

"Well," answered I, endeavouring to free myself from all blame, "I have done my best. I have so many in distress, and my own means are so small, that, try as I may, I cannot alleviate all their misery."

"Oh!" said the voice, "I am not blaming you. Before many hours are over your own conscience will accuse you without my censuring you."

These remarks were coming a little too near home, and I – I woke up.

How wretched I feel! Wherever I turn I can see that girl's anguished face. I try to get rid of it by partaking of a cup of tea.

On goes the kettle. It begins to sing. What a long time it is in boiling! Why does it seem to sing, "Xmas should be happy and joyful; Xmas should be happy and joyful"? That girl's face rises up again. Her Xmas won't be happy and joyful.

"Yes," I say to myself – half aloud – "when she comes tomorrow I will make a special effort to try and get her somewhere for Xmas."

To-morrow comes. Morning passes, she has not come; afternoon gone, she is not here; evening, 9 p.m. I have given her up, yet cannot get her out of my mind.

The door bell rings. How I start! I must be getting nervous.

It is she. How relieved I feel!

"Come in; I have been wondering about you all day."

"No, thank you, Mrs. Best. I thought you would be worrying; that is why I just called to thank you for trying to get me work. Don't try any more. I – went – on – to – the – streets – last – night."

SOCIAL DEMOCRAT

Frank Rosamund, 'For the Syndicate', *Social Democrat*, August 1907, pp. 500–2.

Prosper Mérimée, 'The Capture of the Redoubt', trans. Jacques Bonhomme, *Social Democrat*, December 1908, pp. 574–6.

M. L. Pitcairn, 'Because They Understood Not', *Social Democrat*, September 1909, pp. 426–32.

F. J. Maynard, 'Unemployment: A Tragedy in Little', *Social Democrat*, 15 February 1910, pp. 93–6.

The *Social Democrat* (1897–1913) continued to be edited by Harry Quelch, who was also a prolific contributor to the content. The periodical maintained its interest in international socialism, and Quelch included articles by Edward (Eduard) Bernstein (1850–1932) of the German Social Democratic Party, Theodore Rothstein (1871–1953), the Russian socialist who had joined the SDF on his emigration to Britain in 1890 and who supported the Bolsheviks and Lenin, and the Polish-born socialist theoretician Karl Kautsky (1854–1938), as well as by British socialists, including Quelch's son, Tom (n.d.).

There was a renewed interest in fiction during this period, and Quelch included two (albeit brief) serials: Theophile Gautier's (1811–72) 'The Dead Mistress', published in the April and May editions of 1907, and an abridged version or synopsis of Victor Hugo's (1802–85) *Notre Dame de Paris* between July and November of the same year. During 1907 and 1908 the *Social Democrat* regularly included fiction in its issues, but this tailed away in 1909 and 1910, when only three stories were published in both years. No biographical or publication details have been found for the authors Frank Rosamund or M. L. Pitcairn, but the story attributed to F. J. Maynard (n.d.) may be by the American trade unionist and leader of the Transport Workers' Federation. Prosper Mérimée (1830–70) was a French dramatist, historian and short story writer who is best remembered as the author of the novella *Carmen*, the basis for Bizet's opera. Mérimée was a friend of Ivan Turgenev and translated much of his work, including Turgenev's short story 'The Dog', which is featured in Volume 1 of this collection under the title 'Only a Dog'; the version featured is not Mérimée's translation but was translated by Jacques Bonhomme, who also translated Mérimée's own story below.

Frank Rosamund, 'For the Syndicate' (1907)

The day was exceedingly hot. The road was parched and dusty. The corn was shriveling in the glaring sunshine.

A cloud cast a shadow on the distant hillside, and crept steadily towards us as a token of promise. The corn rustled as if whispering of the inevitable falling of refreshing raindrops. And so men also whisper among each other of the coming of a something which will make life worth living; which will help them on their way; which will lead them to higher and brighter thoughts of their fellowmen, and of life.

I lingered under the walnut trees to rest; the walnut trees where I played when a child; where I hulled their nuts and stained my fingers green; where I stopped to rest on my way to school.

Ten years had elapsed since I last saw the spot – not that I cared particularly for the spot – for the spot I really wished to see was the old farm and farmhouse. I wished to once more roam through the orchard. I wish to once more drink in the beauty of the garden. I wished to once more draw a cool drink from the well with the old-fashioned windlass.[1]

I was thus meditating when a faint breeze bore to my ears the creaking of a cultivator. I looked around. A man and team were steadily approaching up one of the long corn-rows. The team was wet with sweat; and water could have been wrung from the man's clothing – what little he had on. He turned the team half round where what breath of air there was might cool their heads.

I spoke to the man when he looked in my direction.

His response was inarticulate, owing to his parching thirst.

He stepped to one of the trees and lifted a jug to his lips; it was water.

"Have a smile, stranger?" he asked kindly.

"Don't care if I do," I answered only too gladly.

I lifted the jug to my lips. The water was almost boiling.

And then I thought – thought that the pleasures of life are sometimes drank – the same becoming distasteful, unbearable in their increasing hotness.

"Rather tough working out here in the heat," I said by way of remark.

"Gotter stand it," he answered. "That's what we vote fur."

"Don't you own the farm you're on?" I asked.

"No," he replied, bitterly.

"Who does?" I asked.

"Syndicate."[2]

"Who owns the farm adjoining?"

"Syndicate."

"And the next?" I inquired eagerly; for it was my old home.

"Syndicate," he answered promptly.

"Any one working it?" I asked.

"Renter."

"Does he live there?"

"No – lives next place – runs two places."

"Must make a barrel of money?"

"Does – for the syndicate."

There was brief silence.

"Well, got to keep up mi lick – won't get mi rent paid," he said as he took up the lines.[3] "Hope you'll think over this syndicate business, stranger." And, with a meaning glance, he bid me good-day.

As I approached my old home – the home where my brothers and sisters were born, and since cast out upon the struggling sea of life; where my father and mother died – I was overtaken by indescribable wretchedness.

The weather-beaten house stood conscience-haunting in its conspicuous barrenness. Tall weeds grew close around as if trying to hide from mortal eye the memories of the old home – the happiness of the long ago.

I dared not enter. I was haunted by an awful misery.

The corn grew close by the house. Only leaving room for the teams to turn. Several tall weeds that had grown by the house were lying prostrate – they who had tried to drown or hide the memory.

The dear old well was covered with boards, whereon were poled stones – a grave of the gift of the immortal.

The orchard was gone, save two old trees that had fallen into one another's arms, their limbs embracing one another in their sorrow.

A portion of the garden fence remained, whereon, and covering it, were matted vines of the morning-glory. I lifted up a portion of the vines. What remained of the fence was decayed and rotten. And then I thought and thought – thought that the old fence was as humanity – a thing lost amid splendor, covered, refused the light of beauty; a thing lost in the darkness caused by one of the flower-bearing vines of the world's ornaments. They are the vines of materialism.

Looking down over the cornfield I could see where the old stable formerly stood. 'Twas where the corn grew tallest. It seemed to flourish over the spot – the ruins of part of our old home. And so man flourishes over the ruin caused by sad misfortune born of the monster of man's creation.

Oh, how sad it all was. How sad were the thoughts of living in such a world and trying to make the best of it.

Standing there with the thoughts of a lost life, of all that has been and will continue to be, unless people arouse to social and political action, I pitied humanity, I cursed greed and the profit system.

I thought of an enslaved people. I thought of liberty – not the liberty our forefathers fought for, but industrial freedom. I thought of once more making a defence for rights, for a mighty and just cause, though not with life-taking explosives,[4] but with more practical warfare – the ballot-box.

And then I went on my way realising my environment had made me a Socialist – or was it my friend of the plough? – and that, a Socialist, I could help reconstruct the environment.

Prosper Mérimée, 'The Capture of the Redoubt', trans. Jacques Bonhomme (1908)

An officer who was a friend of mine, and who died a few years ago in Greece, gave an account to me of his first experience under fire. Here is his story as I wrote it down soon afterwards: –

"I joined the regiment on September 4. The Colonel received me rather cavalierly at first, but having read a letter of recommendation from General B. he became more affable, and was even polite.

"He introduced me to my captain, who was just coming back from a reconnaissance. That officer, whom I had hardly time to know, was a tall man with a very hard face. He had risen from the ranks, and his voice, which was husky and feeble, was in strange contrast to his height. It was said this was due to a wound which he had received at Ilna.[1] Hearing that I had left the Academy at Fontainebleau, he made a wry face and said: 'My lieutenant died yesterday.' I understood that he meant to say, 'You must take his place and you are not equal to it.' I was going to reply sarcastically, but refrained from doing so.

"The moon rose behind the redoubt[2] of Cheverino,* which was near our bivouac. She was big and red, as she generally is at her rising, but that evening she seemed extraordinarily large. For a moment the redoubt was seen on the dazzling disk of the moon; it looked like the cone of a volcano just before an eruption.

"An old soldier, near whom I was standing, noticed the colour of the moon. 'She is very red,' he said, 'it is a sign we shall lose many men in taking that redoubt.' I have always been superstitious, and that remark struck me. I lay down, but could not sleep. I rose, and walked for some time looking at the long line of watch fires on the heights above Cheverino. When I thought that the fresh and piercing air of the night had sufficiently cooled my blood I came back to the fire. I folded my cloak round me, and shut my eyes, hoping not to re-open them till daybreak. But sleep would not come. My thoughts took a sad turn: I said to my self that I had not a single friend among the 100,000 men in the plain. If I were wounded I should be in a hospital, treated without care by ignorant sur-

---

* 'a garbled form of the name Shvardinó.' *Carmen*, p. 345.[3]

geons. All that I had heard of surgical operations came into my mind. My heart beat violently and mechanically. I placed my handkerchief and pocket-book as a kind of cuirass[4] over my heart. Fatigue oppressed me, and though I was dozing at intervals, yet each moment a gloomy thought arose with me and awoke me with a start.

"Yet I did fall asleep, and the morning drum awoke me. We drew up, the roll-call was taken, then the guns were loaded, and we thought we should have a quiet day. About three o'clock an aide-de-camp came with an order. We advanced in skirmishing order,[5] and in about twenty minutes we saw the advance guard of the Russians falling back towards the redoubt.

"A battery of artillery was on our right, and one on our left, but in front of us. They began to fire vigorously at the enemy, who replied eagerly, and soon the redoubt of Cheverino was obscured by dense clouds of smoke.

"Our regiment was behind a hill and hardly felt the effects of the Russian fire. Their guns were aimed at our artillery and the shots passed over our head, only occasionally were we struck by earth and stones.

"When the order to advance was given, my captain looked at me attentively, and I touched my moustache with indifference two or three times. Really, I was not afraid, and my only fear was that I might be thought to be afraid. Those inoffensive shots made me heroically calm, because my pride told me I was in danger. I was delighted at being so calm, and I felt how pleased I should be to talk about the capture of the redoubt of Cheverino in the drawing-room of Madame B. in the Rue de Provence.

"The Colonel passed in front of our company and spoke to me, saying, 'You will see some strange things!' I smiled in a marital way, brushing the sleeve of my coat, on which there was a little dust from a shot which had fallen 30 paces off.

"The Russians must have noticed that they were not doing enough execution, for they took to using shells, which were more effective. A portion of a shell took my shako[6] off and killed a man near me.

"'I compliment you,' said the captain to me as I had just picked up my shako, 'you are safe for to-day.' I put my shako on proudly and said as joyfully as I could, 'That is a strange way of forcing men to take their hats off.' This bad joke made a great effect. 'I congratulate you,' said the captain, 'you will not be wounded and you will have my company, for I feel sure that it is all over with me, for I have always been wounded when the officer near me has been hit by a spent ball.'

"In about half an hour the Russian fire diminished, and we started to march on the redoubt. Our regiment consisted of three battalions – one had to tour the redoubt; the others, in one of which I was, had to assault it.

"As we came out in the open we were greeted by a discharge of musketry which did not do much execution, and I could not help turning my head as the balls whistled by. 'After all,' I said to myself, 'a battle is nothing so terrible.'

"We advanced at a run, throwing out skirmishers;[7] suddenly the Russians gave three cheers, then there was a dead silence. 'I do not like that,' said the captain, 'it will be bad for us.' I thought our men were too noisy, and I could not help comparing their tumultuous clamour with the solemn silence of the enemy.

"We soon came to the redoubt. The stakes had been shattered, and the earth scattered by our guns. The soldiers rushed on to the ruins, shouting, 'Long live the Emperor!' and made more noise than one would have expected, as they had already been shouting.

"I raised my eyes, and I never shall forget the sight I saw. The greater part of the smoke had lifted, and was just over the redoubt. Through a blue vapour we could see the Russian grenadiers, motionless as statues, with their muskets levelled at us. I seem to see again each soldier fixing us with his left eye, his right being against his uplifted musket. At each corner a gunner had a lighted torch near a gun. I shuddered, and I thought my last hour had come. 'Now the dance will begin,' said my captain, 'Good night.' There were the last words I heard him say.

"The drums beat on the redoubt, the muskets were lowered, I shut my eyes, and I heard a terrible crash, followed by cries and groans. I opened my eyes, wondering that I was still alive. The redoubt was again surrounded by smoke, and I had round me wounded and dead men. My captain was stretched at my feet; his head had been crushed by a cannon shot, and his brains and blood splashed over me. I and six men were all that was left of the company.

"After this carnage there was a lull. The Colonel rushed over the parapet sword in hand, crying, 'Long live the Emperor!' We all followed him – I do not remember what took place – we fought hand-in-hand – I know I struck, because my sword was all bloody. I heard a cry of victory, the smoke cleared, and I saw the redoubt covered with the dead and dying. There were about 200 men standing in French uniforms, some reloading their muskets, some wiping their bayonets. There were eleven Russian prisoners. The Colonel was on the ground bleeding from a wound in his throat. Some soldiers were raising him from the ground. I came near, 'Where is the senior captain?' he asked a sergeant. The man shrugged his shoulders in an expressive manner. 'And the senior lieutenant?' 'This gentleman who joined yesterday.' The Colonel smiled bitterly. 'Well, sir,' he said, 'you are in command, entrench yourself with these carts, for the enemy is very strong, but General C. will support you.' 'Colonel,' I said, 'are you seriously wounded?' 'I am done for, my good friend, but the redoubt is taken.'"

M. L. Pitcairn, 'Because They Understood Not' (1909)

They were a man and a maid who loved each other, and the moon was shining. They had found for themselves a desolate place, for, with all the refinement of intense natures, they dreaded that others should know their secret of love, nor would they vulgarise their thrice-holy Eucharist of Nature by celebrating it in a shrine trod but by holy feet. Holy feet trod here, indeed, by day – feet worn with over-much toil for over-little purpose; feet which when coffined cold and still showed that the road to heaven had been rough and hard. Well indeed it were that men cast off their robe of flesh when they cease to labour, for surely God would weep to see his handiwork so exceeding marred. "Make us bricks without straw," went forth the Pharaoh's edict generations ago, and even now when men and women laboured to fulfil his word, when Cook's tourists broke ginger-beer bottles round the Pyramids, and said it was "awf'ly funny" how well the mummies were preserved after six thousand years.[1]

And now, day in, day out, men and women shaped the bricks, thinking, when bodily exhaustion allowed them to think, and wondering whether they would crumble to nothing, these strawless bricks, some day. Yet, strange to say, when at last the hardened hands and feet were resting, the Master looked on the bricks of the building, and they pleased him well.

Nor, for a space the workers were at rest, and one was there save the man and the maid. Huge kilns rose on every side, squat and ugly, yet grand as they glowed and reddened with the unconsuming fire. By their side were piled masses of the bricks they disgorged, both kiln and brick-pile ugly and formless, like the tenets of some man-made creed, and like man himself, incomprehensible, yet, at the heart, beautiful, for in each was the fire prisoned. Now they were bathed in the pale moon-glow, and in the ruddy furnace-glare which flushed the sky in a medley of gold and silver, and gleamed in the brown turgid waters of the canal below, which swirled slowly about with a solid motion, towards the lock lower in its course. It was very quiet everywhere.

The man and the maid stood, still and silent, drinking in the beauty-draught – soon they stood closer, and, almost unconsciously, their lips met. Then she sighed with pure delight.

"There are no half-measures between us, Rolf, and I am glad – we drink deep of the wine of life, and it – it – is – sweet."

"And intoxicating, too," he said slowly.

"Intoxicating, perhaps. No, I think not – it makes *me* see more clearly. You have interpreted everything for me now, Rolf."

They were silent for some moments, then Rolf said, "Joan, do you trust me – completely, and in all things?"

"As much as I love you," she answered quietly. "If I didn't trust you, I should have nothing to trust – you are my creed. I want no other."

The quiet dignity with which she spoke redeemed her words from melodrama.

"O, God," he said bitterly, "it is always so. Joan, I'm a cad. I'll go away from you. I'm not fit to speak to you. O, don't ask me why. I'll go at once, and curse myself because you love me."

She clutched his hand in hers as though afraid he would go at that moment, and said faintly,

"Rolf, what do you mean? Don't you love me now?"

"Love you?" he said fiercely. "Do you need to ask? That's the very reason I'll go. No, listen. I'll tell you a story."

He stood gazing into the water, where the red light gleamed – far away they could hear the steady plod, plod of a heavily shod horse, and the lapping of the water round the side of an approaching barge. Joan's one hand was resting on his shoulder, and the other was holding his hand – she dreaded she knew not what revelations. Would he go away? Yet she trusted him; O, yes, she trusted him.

"Yes, tell me your story, Rolf, if it won't hurt. You needn't. You know I trust you, though your words frighten me. I shall love you as much, whatever you tell me."

"Listen, and then judge. But I know now your verdict. I'll speak it as a parable – it doesn't sound so bald. There was once a boy, lonely and miserable in his childhood, and the bricks of which he built his life never pleased him; he could make them so well that he must make them better. They were heavy, and the hard, jagged edges hurt his hands, and his feet were weary with plodding on, each day and all the days, and his eyes were dull and lustreless, for there were no other eyes from which they reflected the lovelight. The boy pondered much as he went about his work, and after weighing all the chances carefully, though he was no coward, he thought it would be well to lie down, and the let the tide of life ebb from him, for he was very tired. Then a woman came, and they loved each other. In their kisses it seemed to him that a thousand generations withal their throbbing endeavour dumbly cried for birth from him and her.

"Now they worked together, and their work was very sweet to them, as they sang together about it. People called them mad that they could find beauty and joy in making bricks; but the Master smiled. 'This work is well done,' he said. 'They work for love now. It is well.'

"All the days of a long summer and a sweet autumn they worked together and played together, and then one day the maid told the boy a strange new secret, he had little known, about the bricks they were building. Then he was afraid, for he knew that his fellow-workers would blame this work, though the Master would, perchance, smile on it, and use it for the building of His own house. Yet the Master's praise sufficed not, and he went away, to work elsewhere. Then once more he grew weary, and would have lain down, for he wearied for his woman helper, and for the work they had begun. Yet he dared not go back. Then there came another woman to help him, and the old sweet love returned. Yes, he loved her better than the first one, and once more, with her help, he built his bricks well, and once more the Master was well pleased.

"Then the woman knew he loved her as she loved him, and one night he loved her so well that he told her of the other. How must I finish the tale, Joan?"

He spoke the last words in a whisper, and she felt his hand quiver in hers, for the love of her was strong upon him. She was silent for a long while, and stood away from him (she had gently withdrawn her hand), looking into the dark water. The lapping of the water was louder now – the barge was coming nearer. Then she spoke.

"The story of the second woman before the man came was like *his* story – one of hopelessness, of toil without a purpose. Then he came and crowned her queen of his love; in return she gave him herself, with all her love for life and death. Then, when the woman, proudest among women by right of the queenship he had given her, lived only for love of him who had crowned her queen, he came and told her that the crown was not hers, and belonged to another. She knew she owed it to him to answer as a queen should answer. Yet she loved, and was weak."

Joan stopped speaking. She saw all the lonely, weary years to which she must condemn herself. She thought how weak she was, and how strong he seemed to her when he folded her in his arms, and said that together they could do things. She thought of those strange, unutterable stirrings of her soul when he pressed his lips upon hers, and the windows of Heaven were opened for her to see all the glories that should be. He could see that she was trembling on the verge of her decision, and taking her hand in his, raised it unresisting to his lips.

"Rolf, I can't – O, I can't! I'm only a woman, and I love you too much – too selfishly. I can't do without you – it's worse than death. I'm not ashamed that you should see how well I love you – it's natural and right. But, then, *she* does, too."

"Yes, Joan, *she* does."

"She suffers, as much as I, perhaps, and is nobler than I, because she was willing to let you go, if going could make you happy. *She* suffers," she repeated musingly, "and I suffer – and you? – if you went back?"

"Joan, I can't – don't ask me."

"But you love her?"

"Yes, I think – yes, I love her; but not as I love you."

"The one who loves is happier than the one who is loved," she said slowly, as if speaking to herself. "There is much suffering in the world. Why shouldn't I bear it instead of her? The Master will look upon the work and it will appear the same – you will forget in time, and I – shall – be – happy – I think."

"Joan, I can't. Now you know, take me for what I am, and let me stay with you – and love me."

She looked into his eyes, and seemed to read his soul; then her own sank, and she looked out into the dark water again.

"I thought perhaps you were afraid to go back, but – are you, Rolf, afraid of what they'll say about ---"

"By heaven, no, Joan!"

"I knew it; you wish to stay because you love me?"

"I *must* stay because I love you."

Joan's courage was fast failing. She felt that she must yield, and let the other woman suffer. For what? Sin? No, a thousand times, no – for love and for the law of man. And she? With the thought of escape came the sweet ecstasy of life again – the song-laden gales of Paradise-to-be seemed to waft before and around her. She would forget this woman and her sorrow, and forget this unworthy thing to which love prompted her. But – was it love?

"O, Rolf, I don't love you well enough. I love myself best. No, I will be worthy of the crown you gave me. Take it; go back to her, and ask her to forgive me, for I did not know. Go – go, before I forget, and call you back. You have my love as long as life parts us – and then perhaps we shall belong to each other."

"Joan, I can't."

"Go," she cried. "Do you think I have no pride? You cannot give me love, when it is hers. Good-bye! You may kiss me once, and then – until you crown me anew in our kingdom, no more." He never guessed what it cost her to give this last token of her love and her sacrifice and then resign him to another's kisses. Women, the best of them, are feverishly, tigerishly jealous when they love. But, enough of this – doubtless the Master smiles on these bricks, made, perhaps, or marred, by love.

"I shall never see you again; at least, not unless *she* wishes – if she doesn't, when we're dead, the eternal parts of us can love without wrong or fear – or –" She broke off suddenly, for the canal barge they had heard in the distance was approaching quickly.

"Hast' got a pipe o' 'baccy about thee, mester?" bawled a hoarse voice from the barge. "I've got a nasty bit o' business on 'ere, and I'm goin' fetch the pleece."

"Here you are – what's the matter?" said Rolf shortly.

"A wench been an' drowned hersel' and' her kiddie, as fur as I can see – I'd stopped for the night up to Bakewell Wood, there, an' all of a sudden I heard a splash, but I didn't think nothin' of it, and' then her drifted down, and bumped in to the boat. This is good 'baccy, mester – wunnerful how it comforts you. Her give me such a turn. I got her in – better not let the young lady see her, her's quite drownded. I'll fetch pleece. W'ut stop here while I go?"

"Do you mind, Joan?" He was really thankful. It gave him a few minutes still with her.

"No – let's see if we can do anything."

"No use, I'm afeared. We'll lift her into the light o' them furnaces. Lend us a hand."

Gently he lifted her, her thin, scanty, soaked garments clinging closely to her, and showing the moulding of the form they only half hid – a slight girlish form, and a sweet, almost childish face, thin and sunken, but flushed now with the rosy fire glow. The dress was opened at the back, and the light gleamed through the strands of dark, sodden hair, which had come unbound and floated over to hide the whiteness beneath. Cold and still, now – but perhaps in that last despairing moment, when she went before her time to ask the Master's judgment on her building, she had stilled the aching mother-heart, and the wailing baby-voice at once, and had forgotten in the divinest of joys, the supreme sorrow. Perhaps –

They had laid her down, and turned away to find the child. Joan knelt at her side, and, knowing nothing better to do, lifted the poor thin hand. Even then, she noticed that it bore not the sign-manual which would win her the world's pity instead of its scorn; then she blushed with shame of herself thinking –

She stroked the hand tenderly, then sprang back in horror – the wrist was broken! She could but surmise how, but tears started to her eyes. Strange that a broken limb should seem more terrible to her than Death itself – but Death was the touch of the Master; and the broken hand? Poor child, the pity of it all! that love should exact so heavy a toll from love's victims! And herself? Suppose *she* were left thus, unprotected, the scorn of the righteous, the virtuous, the unloving – the victim of the world's inexorable law of expediency!

The two men returned to the centre of the circle of light; the bargee puffing at his pipe as he carried a pile of doubtful looking clothing, Rolf bearing a dripping bundle which he shewed to Joan. "Joan," he said simply, "the child may live. It was only in the water a few instants. I expect the mother was exhausted by despair and want, and died almost immediately. Let's get it to the fire – we'll try to save it."

The boatman threw down the clothing, and tramped off to the police-station; together they knelt down to take off the baby's wet garments. Rolf's hand was trembling, and Joan gently pushed it away – of what was he thinking? Joan too, as the tiny form lay naked in her arms, shuddered ... She realised at that moment *another* page of life which her renunciation of Rolf had closed unread. But she dared not think, she could not trust herself, and the minutes were speeding on to the last, last minute of all.

"Rolf," she whispered, "go away for a moment. I'm such a coward. Look at her – her hand is broken, and she's died of starvation, nearly – and this child. Oh, go away Rolf, till that man comes back, or I shall forget – my duty – and my love."

Rolf understood. He almost thought he would stay and win her, yet he felt she was right, and walked away to where the woman lay, while Joan wrapped the child, which was stirring feebly in the warmth of the furnace, in the clothing the boatman had brought her, and her own jacket.

She sat down on the ground, her back turned to Rolf, as she caressed the child, and gazed on its face, thinking of – Suddenly a hand was laid on her shoulder – a hand that trembled She turned quickly, and met Rolf's eyes.

"Joan," he whispered, "it's she. She's come to find me – Oh, it's too terrible. Joan, my punishment is more than I can bear. Joan ... Winnie, forgive me."

He sank on his knees beside her – in an instant she had grasped what he meant, and her woman's wit or her love told her what to do. The child was pillowed on one arm, the other she flung round Rolf's neck, and drawing him close to her, kissed him as in the days before the horror of to-night. Then she gently drew the tiny child nearer to him, until he could feel its body, and hers, against his own.

"Rolf, then there's no need to go – this child is mine – ours – it shall be our master-building – our only master-building." She spoke very slowly, and in a strained voice; but looking again into her eyes, he wondered once more why she should suffer – why *any* should suffer, because he had been too cowardly to face the outraged sycophants of method and established law.

Moved by a sudden impulse, she laid the child in his arms, and weeping, turned towards where Winnie lay, and knelt by her side.

"Winnie, Winnie," she sobbed, "I took him from you, but I didn't know – I'm sure I didn't. Oh, why should we all suffer so much? Yet if you hadn't suffered, I should never have seen Rolf, and loved him. You have suffered, and, not knowing it, given me perfect happiness. Now, I will suffer too. I can love him now without wronging you, and the world will never pry into our secret – but I will never, never usurp that crown of glory – that crown he gave to you to wear."

She sobbed for a moment, then, kissing the pale, troubled face, returned to Rolf, who had heard the words, and understood ... Then, with a kiss, they entered on their kingdom – with a little child to lead them[2] and remind them. And the building went on apace, and the Master smiled and wondered at their childishness, because they had said, "Someone must suffer," and thought how far they were from understanding his will for them. Yet, because of their weakness and misunderstanding they suffered much; but to which woman was meted the heavier dole of woe?

* * *

A month later, a man and woman stood on the deck of a steamer, southward bound, and the woman held a baby girl in her arms, and loved and mothered her for that she was his. Together in the islands of the south, they built well, and made a dwelling-house, stately and beautiful, for the Master. Yet sometimes, in the night watched, he thought of a long dream-summer, and a sweet autumn, when he and another had trod the love-path. Sometimes he longed just a little for her, and wondered if she still loved, and if Joan would ever discover *the lie he had told her* – for love's sake. And underneath the glaring gas-lamps of the Embankment, a girl who wandered faint and weary at night, thought of him who had taught her to write her life, for a long summer and a sweet autumn, in the lovescript, on the history – book of the world. Sometimes she thought of the little child who had died – but most she thought of him. She did not think long or often, though, for others came –

F. J. Maynard, 'Unemployment: A Tragedy in Little' (1910)

Franklin Murdock crossed the threshold of the room. He was an agile man of forty or thereabouts, erect, a trifle pale, with dark hair just turning to grey. His well-worn suit of blue serge was dusty from his day's tramp, but it had that morning been well brushed. He had started in the morning, alert and eager, to look for work. Now, at six in the evening, he was tired, anxious, and hungry. He looked round the room with despair.

It was a dull, comfortless apartment; the furniture consisting of a table, a couple of chairs, and a veteran sofa that could not be pawned. The mantelshelf boasted only a cheap alarum-clock by way of ornament, and a paraffin lamp afforded just light enough to lay bare the crudities of the only picture: a badly-got-up lithograph[1] with a calendar printed beneath, the gift of the local grocer, which served the double purpose of reminding the household of the flight of time and their debt to him. The dismal apology for a fire fitfully smouldered in the grate, spreading neither cheerfulness nor warmth. Still, in spite of its bareness and ugliness, in spite of the semi-darkness and the carpetless floor, an air of domestic pride pervaded the place, for it was spotlessly clean. His wife, a dull, listless little woman, rendered so by the months of struggle against poverty, looked eagerly at Murdock as he hung his coat behind the door.

"Well?" she said, "what luck?"

He drew a chair towards the fire, and, having sat down, answered the woman's query.

"None," he said, bitterly. "I'm beginning to think I'm not wanted. Have you got anything to eat?"

"Yes;" replied the woman, "Mrs. Roberts sent us in a loaf and a bit of cheese."

He looked up with appreciation.

"That's kind of her. He hasn't too much herself, I know. Let's have it, Mary. I'm hungry. Haven't had a bit all day. It's maddening, I tell you, to tramp about all day with nothing in your stomach, willing to work, praying almost for work, and not getting it. They don't want 'em over forty. I met Joe Rogers. He's doing next to nothing. He offered to buy me a drink. I've never touched the stuff, thank God. I told him I'd rather have the money. Here it is."

He threw three pennies on the table.

"Take it, it'll buy a bit of food."

"Did you go to see Mr. Alcott?" asked the woman after a pause.

"Yes, I went to him, the swine, and he laughed at me! He was warm, strong, and well-fed. 'Why, my good man,' he said, 'we can't employ *you*. Why, you're unemployable, that's what you are.' Then he leaned back in his chair and laughed and said: 'You couldn't earn your keep; you haven't an ounce of strength left in you.' I could have strangled him."

He swallowed a mouthful of food viciously.

"Don't lose heart, Frank," said the woman, "all will be well in time. Trust in God, and all will be well."

"I begin to lose trust in everything," rejoined the man. "Eight months to-day. Every day of those eight months I've spent in looking for work. As I've tramped the streets the wealth of the city has mocked my hunger. I've felt an outcast, a stranger. I go into a shop and ask for work, and it is denied me. I walk on through the pitiless rain, and go through the same thing again, with the same result, every day for eight months, till I feel that it's all hopeless, and there's nothing for me but the workhouse – or the grave."

"No, Frank," his wife said, pleadingly, "keep on trying. 'Never say die' was your old watchword."

"The watchword has been beaten out of me," he replied. "Eight months! In that eight months I've seen the home I toiled for go bit by bit to the pawnshop. I've begged for work, and been told I'm unemployable! I'm a skilled mechanic, a tee-totaller, I've been thrifty and careful all my life – but I'm forty-two! Don't you know," he shouted at her; "there's no room for a man that's over forty! *He's* only fit for the scrap-heap. I'm sick of it all."

"It's a shame," said the woman, "a shame. There's one thing to be thankful for: there are no little ones to share our misery."

"That's a blessing. But we can't go on as we are, in spite of that. I see no hope. We owe for everything. The sick-club insurance, the grocer, the coalman – *everything*. And, why it must be five months since we paid any rent. It *is* five months, isn't it Mary? How much do we owe the landlord?"

"You're eating nothing," said the woman, nervously. "Don't worry about anything till you've had something to eat."

"Don't lose heart, the clouds will soon roll by," she added in a dull tone.

"I *can't* eat, somehow. I'm hungry, but I can't eat. The worry of it all takes my appetite away. How long is it since the rent was paid?"

She did not answer for a moment, and then peering out of the window she said:

"It's raining harder than ever."

He was carried adrift by this, and said: "Yes, it's a beast of a night."

The woman looked relieved at the turn of the conversation, but he returned to the old question at once.

"How long is it since the rent was paid?" he repeated.

"Why don't you eat something, dear?" she asked. "Worrying does no good."

He pushed the plate away from him and rose.

"Why don't you answer?" he asked angrily.

He went to the mantelpiece, took a small tin box, and got a bundle of pawntickets out of it.

"I pawned the overmantle[2] to pay the rent the last time," he said as he ran over the bundle. "I can't think why you don't answer."

He picked out one at last, while the woman stood by the windows with eyes dilated by terror. He looked at the date and started.

"April the tenth!" he said. "Nearly six months ago."

Then he suddenly turned to the woman.

"How is it," he said' "how is it they haven't turned us out? Landlords don't let you live rent free for over five months. Where's the rent-book?"

"Behind the clock," she answered, mechanically.

He took it, opened it, and turned to her again.

"Paid!" said he, "paid! Every penny! Where did you get the money?"

"I didn't get the money," she answered.

"Who did?" he shouted.

She did not answer. He paced up and down the room for a few moments and then said, persuasively:

"Mary, how did you get this money? You can trust your husband. How was it paid?"

She was trapped, and she turned on him defiantly.

"The rent is paid. That's enough for you."

"But it isn't enough. I want to know how you paid it."

"With money," she said.

"You *had* no money. I want to know how you paid this."

She broke down and sobbed like a child.

"How was it paid?" he thundered into her ear as he shook her.

"I paid for it – with myself," she said in a dull, lifeless whisper.

He flung her from him, and picked up a knife.

"I could kill you," he said.

Then he flung the knife into the grate, seized his coat, and went out into the night.

* * *

From the "Evening Post": –

UNEMPLOYMENT TRAGEDY

The man found drowned in the Regent's Canal yesterday has been identified as Franklin Murdock, 15, Lower place, Shoreditch. He had been unemployed for some months, and it is supposed that he committed suicide in a fit of depression. The inquest will be held on Saturday.

SOCIALIST REVIEW

A. L. Grey, 'A Martian's Visit to Earth. Being a Literal Translation into English of the Preface to an Account by a Martian of his Visit to England', *Socialist Review*, November 1909, pp. 232–40.

Eric Dexter, 'Faith the Healer', *Socialist Review*, December 1910, pp. 266–75.

The *Socialist Review* (1908–34) was subtitled *A Monthly Magazine of Modern Thought* and was first published in May 1908. It was an ILP periodical that initially operated in London and then transferred to Salford in September 1909. There is no note of the original editor, but John Bruce Glasier took over editorial duties in January 1914. The periodical focused on socialist political theory, and in its first year it included articles by Labour Party members James Ramsay MacDonald and Philip Snowden, the Fabian H. G. Wells (1866–1946) and the French socialist leader Jean Jaurés (1859–1914).

There appears to have been a similar attitude towards the inclusion of fiction in the *Socialist Review* as in the ILP's weekly *Labour Leader*; in both periodicals, fiction was not a regular feature. There was only one short serial published in the *Socialist Review* between 1908 and 1914: Helen A. Forbes's (n.d.) 'Sir Aaron Ballyrag, M.P.'. There were two instalments of this fiction published in March and April 1908, the May instalment was missing due to a fire in the *Socialist Review* offices, and the serial was not recommenced in later issues. Short stories were published with a little more regularity, but there were only five stories included in the periodical between 1908 and 1910. There are no biographical details for either of the authors included in this selection, but Eric Dexter is the author of a short story entitled 'Derelict' that was also published in the *Socialist Review*.

A. L. Grey, 'A Martian's Visit to Earth. Being a Literal Translation into English of the Preface to an Account by a Martian of his Visit to England' (1909)

To those of my fellow Martians who hoped to learn something fresh in the domain of sociology, to add something to their science of politics, this account will certainly come as a disappointment. Instead of revealing an advanced, highly organised, highly differentiated civilisation from which we might construct new ideals I have to tell of a quite primitive state, to find a counterpart to which we must go back in our own history some thousands of years. To bring this fact home to my readers I need only refer to one fact, that upon Earth the "strife" age is still in progress. There have, it is true, been a few moments in history when a vision of a better state, in which help shall replace strife, moral strength replace cunning, and in which men shall recognise that the welfare of all is the highest good and rigidly entails, in the surest and best sense, the welfare of the individual – when such a vision has appeared to a select band whose philosophy surrounding influences too unfavourable, died an early death.

The etheroplane, which had cost us so many years' thought and labour, fully justified our efforts by a smooth and uneventful journey across the intervening ether. We chose for our destination the largest collection of habitations – a place called London, the metropolis of the British nations, as we considered that we should here be able to study society in its most advanced form. As we slowly descended upon this great collection of houses I noted a few particulars which I may as well describe here.

The first impression I got from the hurrying crowds of black-coated men in the streets, the knots of manual workers near the docks, upon the buildings, and passing to and fro in the factories and workshops, was that the whole was a great penal settlement where men were condemned to labour of varying degrees of irksomeness. Insufficient nourishment was betrayed by the pinched, pale faces of the sweating manual workers; worry, care, and anxiety furrowed the faces of the men in the streets, and even of the gaily-dressed crowds who were strolling about in the parks. The heaviest punishments seemed to be those of the manual workers, for they are at work long before other people are awake; they are exposed to many dangers to their lives, and frequently work without any protection against the rain or piercing cold. I concluded that they were the greatest criminals, probably murderers, for I could not conceive that for any less crime the State could condemn a man to pass the whole of his life in such discomfort and misery as these have to do. Those guilty of less, but still grave, crimes, I imagined, were the lowest grade of the black-coats who work nearly as long as the manual workers, sometimes even longer. They are cooped up in incredible numbers in badly lighted, comfortless rooms, where they spend nearly the whole of the day bent over books in which they write with a pen. I am informed that it is a very rare occurrence for one of these "clerks," as they are called, to be promoted to more responsible and better paid work. Compared with the first class, indeed, they were as regards physical well-being in even worse plight. The dull, unhealthy monotony of their lives of endless routine was expressed in the apathy and inertia of their minds and bodies. In prominent contrast to these was a small coterie of individuals who seemed to have been selected from the nation at large, set apart, and supported at what was in effect the State expense, either as a reward for great and meritorious services to the State, or because their transcendental mental and moral qualities marked them out as teachers and advisers of the fellows, or because they were in some way indispensable to the general welfare. Their dwellings were the most magnificent of all; their evenings were spent in feasting and gaiety; they dressed sumptuously and were attended by numerous personal servants who observed towards them the greatest deference. My first conclusion was that they were sacred personages or comprised some high religious caste, but when I observed that there was a separate priestly caste with which, indeed, they seemed to have rather less connection that the rest of the community, I was obliged to revise this opinion and formed the one I have already referred to. I was early brought, however, into contact with a considerable number of this leisured class; and to my surprise I was unable to detect any of the superiority I have imagined to be theirs. On the contrary, their moral and intellectual standard was undoubtedly below that of their fellows. One of my first inquiries was with regard to this anomaly. It appears that it is the custom on Earth for property and land to be parcelled out among individuals, and that a father leaves at his death almost the whole of his possessions to his children, only a small fraction passing to the State, the result being that a wealthy caste having no regular occupation other than that of disposing of possessions left to them has gradually come into existence. Now mark the consequences. In the course of generations the qualities which originally distinguished the members of this caste gradually atrophied through disuse, for it is one of the strange laws on Earth that, although a man can only amass wealth by his own efforts or by the efforts of other individuals, when he has got it, the continued possession of it is assured him by the State, an attempt on the part of another to deprive him of his possessions being an offence punished by the State; there is, therefore, no need for the possession by the son of the qualities of the ancestor who collected the wealth. In fact, at the time of my visit to London there were persons of notoriously weak intellect in the possession of vast wealth which had passed to them from a relative.

Not only is wealth transmissible in this way, but also, in this extraordinary country, the power of government! A certain section of the idle rich caste, known as the "titled nobility," inherit the right of taking part in the making of the law. There is, however, in the Legislature a House of elected representatives, and, as might be expected, the relations between the "Lower" House, as it is called, and the "Upper" House,[1] in which these persons of atrophied mentality and morality may sit, are often far from cordial. It is a significant fact that the progress of the nation has proceeded *pari passu*[2] with the decay of the power of the Upper House. Originally, the Upper House, or House of Lords, was a meeting of martial chieftains and men noted for their cunning or wisdom and prowess in debate, and was called as a rule for a council of war. As such it was indispensable, and even after its function as adviser to the head chieftain or king in matters relating to hostilities with neighbouring tribes or nations had undergone transformations and attenuations, the Council served a useful purpose in troublous times when each member or chief was the actual head of a band of warriors or retainers. A change, however, has taken place since the origin of this part of the Legislature in the social conditions of the race. In the case of the nation I studied the more especially, known as the English nation, this change, the change from the military state to the industrial state, was, perhaps, more complete than in any other terrestrial race, but such is their reverence for ancient institutions that they will retain them, not only after they have ceased to exercise their legitimate powers, but even after their influence is admittedly harmful. In no case is this more apparent than in the case of the British House of Lords. The Lords have ceased to be heads of bands of warriors; they are not necessarily warriors themselves; they have crests, but no helmets; armorial insignia, but no arms; territorial titles, but no consequent jurisdiction; in short, there is no vestige remaining of the right they once had, in the ages of physical strength, to govern their fellows – in the age of Intellect their only interest is for the historian, as Vestigial Rudiments.[3]

It will seem incredible, but it is nevertheless a fact, that all terrestrial nations who make any claim to civilisation are divided socially into two great classes, viz., workers, and capitalists or shareholders who own what the workers work with! And not only this, but under the present conditions the two classes are engaged in endless strife, each wishing to increase its share in the wealth produced at the expense of the other! Hence the social and political quagmire in which all parties are floundering. Most of the members of both classes may take a part in the election of representatives to the "Lower" Legislative House, called the House of Commons. At the time of which I write the electorate numbered 7,500,000, of whom 6,500,000* belonged to the classes of workers, so that they are an overwhelming majority at the polls. In spite of this, however, the special representatives who look after the interests of the "lower" classes form less than one-twelfth of the whole House![5]

There are very few constituencies in the country in which the shareholding class is sufficiently numerous relatively to be the dominant power on polling day. That this is recognised by the "upper" classes themselves is shown by the tone of the press, the addresses and speeches on such occasions of the political leaders, national and local, which are usually adroitly framed to inveigle the working man. Polling day is the one day in the year on which the working man feels that he is indeed a separate entity, and not an insignificant detail in the organism, which, like Sisyphus,[6] rolls the boulder of capital up the industrial mountain only for it to return for a fresh ascent. As will be already apparent, there were many features of the present civil and political life of a typical terrestrial nation which seemed out of date, anomalous, or ludicrous, but none more amazing than this, that though industrially the workpeople recognised clearly the consequences of the antagonistic nature of their relation to the shareholding or capitalistic class and had formed themselves into unions to strengthen their positions, politically this recognition had no existence. The workers have a majority at the Parliamentary polls; they have men of intellect and learning ready to come forward as their representatives; they have, collectively, the necessary funds; they have, in short, all that is necessary for them to reconstruct the industrial system on an equitable and rational basis, a basis upon which they will be able to enjoy the whole fruits of their labour. But they do not move; the handful of Labour Members in Parliament is impotent in the face of the number of the capitalist class arrayed against them. I looked around and saw the squalor and thraldom of the many, the luxury and license of the few, and marvelled greatly. But at last I saw the reason. Why is the elephant obedient to the prod of the mahout upon his head, whom he could crush to a lifeless pulp in a second's grip of his trunk or beneath the bulk of his mighty body? The man knows, the animal does not; that is the reason. So does the capitalist know, but the worker does not. But, unlike the elephant, the human worker has the capacity for knowledge, and once let him wake to it the time of the shareholder will be over, his place will know him no more.

I cannot better conclude this preface than by making a few reflections on more general aspects of this antiquated system and on the political state of Earth

---

* Mr. Chiozza Money[4] estimates that there are roughly one million persons in the receipt of incomes of £160 per annum and over. Making the large assumption that these have all a Parliamentary vote, and subtracting this number from the total number of electors, we arrive at the number above stated.

in general. The planet at present is divided among a large number of "nations," as they are called. Each nation has its little plot of land, which it considers to be its own inviolable property, and it is considered one of the highest virtues of man for him to do all in his power to render secure for the nation in which he was born the exclusive right to its particular plot of land, even to the extent of losing his life in its defence. Each nation guards its land with the utmost vigilance and jealousy, although its right to the particular area it occupied at the time of my visit seemed problematical in most cases, as it had often been previously taken by force from another race; this species of robbery had, indeed, on Earth at all times and by all races been considered to be creditable rather than otherwise, and those warriors who have plundered other nations most and driven them from their own formerly peaceful and often prosperous land into sterile and mountainous countries have been hailed as heroes on their return, and have received great rewards and honours. It is curious that while in the individual rapacity of this kind and the taking over of other persons' property by force is regarded as immoral, as a State, quite at liberty to seize the property of other States. Speaking generally, the morality of the State lags behind that of the individual. It so happened that the English nation, of whom I am speaking more particularly, governed directly from London, or indirectly at local centres, a greater portion of the land of the globe than any other nation, for the defence of which, as the territories in question were most easily or of necessity approached by sea, a tremendous navy was kept, at great expense both in men and money. With regard to this colonial question, affairs are rapidly approaching a critical stage. The population of the older and more congested portions of the globe such as Europe is increasing by leaps and bounds. England has millions of square miles of sparsely inhabited territory to which her surplus population may emigrate, and this is naturally regarded with covetous eyes by the other nations who have no outlet of their own. It will not be long, in my opinion, before there will be a world-wide upheaval, either peaceful or bloody, which will result in a more equitable distribution of the land as a preliminary to the final obliteration of the artificial division of the human races into hostile nations.

In many cases the annexation of territory has been peaceful, and has finally been acquiesced in by the minor nation upon which it has conferred many benefits. In such cases, of course, very little criticism can be made, but in other cases, when the conquest has been by the edge of the sword the wound has ranked[7] and produced an embittered, crushed people in whose midst the agitator, traitor, and anarchist have always found a home. The cases of Poland and Ireland come in this category, and in no case is the injustice of superior might more evident than in the case of Ireland, which has chafed against English rule for seven hundred years. To-day the wound is a sore as ever. The Irish race are the descendants of the primitive tribes who were expelled from England, Wales, and

Scotland by the Romans and Saxons. They belong to an entirely different stock from the Anglo-Saxons and have quite alien racial characteristics. It is probably this fact which has prevented anything like a reconciliation between the two peoples. Ireland was first brought under English dominion some seven hundred years ago, but it was not until several centuries later that the country was finally conquered – if it can be said ever to have been so in view of the numerous armed insurrections which have taken place at various times since. It is true that Ireland was in a turbulent state originally and was racked by internal dissensions between various independent chieftains. It is also possible that it would have remained in this state to this day if Irish soil had never received an English foot. But this is a question for the Irish and the Irish alone, and not for the English or any other nation. To say that Ireland is better off under English rule is no extenuation – the Irish are the best judges of their own happiness, and they want the English out. Possibly France might be better off under English rule, but (such is her blindness) she thinks otherwise, and the last vestige of English property on French soil disappeared four hundred years ago. I can find no justification at all for the continued occupation of Ireland by the English. It is an act of unprincipled aggrandisement. Surely the keeping of four and a half millions of people in a political yoke which is intolerable to them, by a nation alien in origin, in religion, in almost every racial characteristic, is an act of political immorality which a nation whose policy is supposed to be dictated by principles of justice and humanity should repudiate!

There are many aspects and problems of human life on Earth which I am unable to deal with in this short sketch, but those which I have touched upon will, I think, afford sufficient grounds for my general condemnation of the present system as cruel, wasteful, and, above all, aimless and vague. What is the object of the activity of the nations, *as nations?* Evolutionarily speaking, they are in the "amoeba" stage; their sole aim in life is existence; they seek to survive – that is all. They have yet to realise that they are only component parts of a higher organism, the world, and that strife between those parts reacts upon even the victors through the injury to that higher organism.

The same pathetic aimlessness marks the growth to maturity of the individual. His natural aptitudes and the needs of the State are often the last things considered in determining his life's occupation. The State maintains an attitude of indifference on the point of a boy's suitability for his occupation. He may wish, for example, to be an engineer (as many boys do), and may, or may not, have a genius for engineering, but his father, who is a doctor, wishes his son to join him in his practice. The State supplies no information as to the total number of medical men it requires for the efficient care of its sick or whether the supply already exceeds the demand; nor could it do so if it wished; it has no information, for it takes no interest in these things, being, as a rule, more intent on acquiring some desolate tract of land ten thousand miles away. The same vagueness applies to all human activities. A man's occupation, his make, his philosophy (if any), his outlook upon life, are all allotted to him by a process of which chance is the greatest ingredient and his own needs and the nation's needs the smallest. So long as those in power and affluence on Earth continue to lack the insight and moral stamina to prefer a happy community to a surfeited oligarchy, though the latter be themselves, so long will Earth be unable to progress toward the Marian polity in which, given an individual's mental ability, special talents (such as for art, music, engineering, scientific research, etc.), character, desires, and disposition, the State, acting on these data on the one hand and its own requirements for its most efficient equipment on the other, allots a definite career and prospect for that individual. On no other principle will it be possible to secure justice and contentment to the man and prevent the great loss to the State of intellect and talent which takes place to-day on Earth.

Eric Dexter, 'Faith the Healer' (1910)

Closing behind him the door of this cottage, the old Curé began to make his way down the eastern road, faced as he was by the full blaze of the new-risen sun. It was indeed the one road of St. Polliou, a straggling lane that ran between the cottages of his parishioners, few enough, and died away into a mere track on the outskirts of the village.

He was old, this priest of the solitary house of worship in that lonely place, and his progress towards his destination slow. People began to appear at the doors and to follow him; with them he exchanged benign words of salutation, using their names familiarly: address Pierre here, Antoine there, and joining in the talk that sprang up.

"When do you sail?" he asked one amongst them, to be told that the tide would serve at seven o'clock. "And it is now after six," added his informant, looking shrewdly at the sun. "The gale has gone down," pursued the man, with a glance behind him at the sea.

It shimmered in the level light of dawn, as though it had not wrought all day yesterday, flinging fold upon fold of its foaming coverlet about the rocks, in its long war of undermining and breaking down. The swell that lingered on it, like a smile on some treacherous face, evidenced its recent disturbance. But the wind was now light, and these sturdy men – women too – seafaring fishers all, were used to the sudden capricious death-bringing, life-bringing ocean; so they turned from it blithely enough on their way to Mass.

The church was large but broken-down. It had been roughly repaired here and there, and uneven patches of new fabric mingled with its ancient walls. Once this church has served a larger St. Polliou, and had even been filled at the local Pardon; but the sea had taken toll of a large section of the village, bearing away in one night of horror three-fourths of the houses perched hardily on the cliffs; and since then St. Polliou had languished. Its people were few. The one dream of the Curé – a dream that he never expected to see fulfilled – was that the village might recover its former population, and that many should join in the service at the grave of the Saint. It pained him to see how bare and empty the old church looked, even when most of his flock thronged, as now, to reverent service there.

He dismissed them with his benediction when the Mass was completed, and sauntered, as was his custom, to the tomb of Saint Polliou in the little crypt, rehearsing in his mind the simple story of the persecution and flight of the good Saint; of his finding peace and rest in the place now called by his name, and of his teaching and miracles. The Curé paused suddenly beside the great stone that covered the grave.

"How's this?" cried the Curé. "The stone is moved!"

It was pushed aside, as though by a violent hand; although no man living could have stirred unaided its ponderous weight. The Curé glanced around, and his eyes, then accustomed to the gloom of the place, made out that part of the inner wall had been thrown down, the plaster cracked and scarred, the earth about the tomb disturbed.

Meditatively the priest paced round the tomb. Had the storm done this, the beating of the furious wind on the shaky walls? Or was it such a sign from heaven as had been granted him more than once? The latter idea grew in the Curé's mind, and with it grew a pressing desire to push back the stone further, and see what it had guarded. Sacred relics! He spoke the words aloud; and the half-doubted prompting became stronger.

At that moment appeared in the doorway the form of a man, a bent, twisted man with one arm; the sacristan.[1] "Félix," said the Curé, "come here!"

"What do you make of that?" the Curé asked.

Félix paused. He was slow-minded, a little. After all one's wits are not improved by a fall over the cliffs; and such a fall had at one blow lost him his arm and his former strength. The Curé had nursed him back to life; not to complete life, however. A little cunning smile appeared on his lips. "What do *you* think, my father?" he temporised.

"The wind in the night," replied the priest; but his tone was too uncertain to deceive the other, in whom a knowledge of every thought of the Curé had been inspired by love. "No," said the twisted man, firmly.

"What then?"

"It is, perhaps," Félix hinted, his head thrown sideways in an implied suggestiveness, "that the Saint ...?" He paused there, and his eyes were watchful. What he saw in the priest's face confirmed him. "Saint Polliou indicates a wish: what do you say, father?"

"A wish?"

"Yes; that his tomb ... be restored?"

"Opened," returned the Curé, "and restored?"

"Without doubt!" cried Félix, with the air or a man who sees his way.

The priest's face lit up. "Catch hold of the corner, Félix!" he said, and bent with the other to lift. But they could not move the stone appreciably. They tugged again and again, but in the end they relinquished the task. "We must get some of the men," remarked the Curé, dusting his somewhat disordered dress.

"To-night," responded Félix, entering into the spirit of the thing: "to night I will get big Jean and Pierre and Henri, and we will see the inside of this!"

"Bring torches," answered the Curé in his turn, "and I will bring a reliquary.[2] Who knows, Félix, we may find the holy bones?"

They walked away together, gaily almost.

* * *

Big Jean, aforesaid, and Henri and Pierre and one or two more assembled in the crypt that evening. The flickering torches lit up the place with a vague illumination. Scared shadows fled in every direction from the glare, and seemed to find refuge in the corners and behind the pillars. The men themselves were not easy: but the presence of the Curé encouraged them.

They seized the corners of the great stone, and with much effort heaved it aside. Some stonework was then revealed, lining a hole some three feet deep; the supporting masonry had crumbled, however, and had at last collapsed under the weight of the heavy stone. A dank and cellary smell issued. They paused on the brink whilst the Curé sprinkled the cavity with holy water. Then they began to dig.

Vainly. Nothing whatever was unearthed. They went to a depth of five feet, and turned upon only earth, intermixed with stones of various sizes. If the place had been a tomb the body it contained had utterly decayed.

Reluctantly, as the torches burned down, they gave up their work. They had no time to fill in the hole.

The disappointment of the Curé was intense. He did not try to hide it; and Félix, who walked beside him, listening to his every word, was much downcast. During the day the priest had confided to him his hope that there might be found "one little bone of St. Polliou," so that worshippers might be attracted from the surrounding district. And now the dream was dispelled. If the Curé was sad when at last he bade Félix farewell, Félix was sadder because of the grief of his benefactor.

Next morning, however, there was a sensation in St. Polliou. For the Curé had gone down to the crypt at sunrise, and there had found a bone – a holy relic. The village hummed the news from end to end.

"I was bending over the hole," the Curé told everybody, with sparkling eyes, "and it occurred to me to move some of the stonework that had fallen in, and below I found – I found ..."

Reaching which point, excitement and reverence closed his lips; but he held up his old silver reliquary and in it reposed what an osteologist[3] would have told them was the femur of a man, badly worn at the lower end, and discoloured.

There were no osteologists in St. Polliou, however. There was not even a doctor. When people were ill there, they got well without more medical aid than was afforded by the herbal and surgical skill of the Curé and the old dames. To which remedial factors was added now another. The bone began to work miracles.

Big Jean's daughter, who limped on crutches for years, on kissing the relic threw away her crutch and was well. Henri Plougnard, hitherto an epileptic, had arisen from his latest fit when the relic was placed on his forehead, and was whole. Grand'mère Liardot, a martyr to rheumatism, had bathed in water in which the bone was for a moment placed and knew her pain no more. And so on.

A week after the relic was found, the cousin of big Jean, who lived in Triarnel, the nearest village, some eight miles away, walked over to St. Polliou, hearing of these miracles, and sought the relic for relief from a withered arm – not in vain. He spread the news.

A month later, an enterprising farmer rigged up an old waggon and drove it once a day to the nearest post-town, fourteen miles to the south-west. He brought visitors: some visitors brought crutches and slings, some of which were left behind.

Six months later, the enterprising directors of the *Chemin de Fer de l'Ouest*[4] projected and constructed a branch of their main line to St. Polliou. Visitors came from all over the Western half of France, and some even from Paris, seeking relief from pain and illness. Quite a reasonable proportion found it. The Curé had two assistants, and the old church had been repaired thoroughly.

A year later, there were five hotels in the place. Contractors were building houses further inland, and the original inhabitants prospered exceedingly. And – crowning glory – the latest volume of Baedeker's *Northern France*[5] devoted several lines to St. Polliou. Pictures of the town ("The Second Lourdes") appeared in the English *Daily Mail*.[6] There were almost too many visitors.

There was no end to the stream of cured people leaving St. Polliou and singing the praise of its Saint.

* * *

Now the Pardon of Saint Polliou occurs on the 28th of June. The second Pardon to take place after the finding of the sacred bone was a very successful fête; the church was overcrowded, and many people were compelled to remain outside during the service. Batches of visitors were conducted to the glorified tomb by Félix and his assistant; while other batches defiled before the altar, to see, to touch, and to be healed by the holy femur.

The merrymaking of the evening was over when the Curé made his way, in a complacent mood, to a favourite spot of his, a lofty, lonely headland. The flaming panorama of the sunset was reflected in a glassy sea on his right and on his left the melancholy twilit town, with its yellow lights and pleasant contours, took on a new aspect in the nightfall. Here the priest watched the descent of the sun behind the rocky islet of Tornoch, running over in his mind the gratifying incidents of the day. His heart warmed in thankfulness within him; and he was muttering a devout prayer, when a voice from the landward face of the cliff hailed him again and again.

He replied loudly; and, hurrying down the boulder-strewn path, met a tall fisher-lad, out of breath with climbing. The lad's red cap was in his hand at once.

"What is it?" cried the Curé.

"It is Félix Garnier, my father," said the boy, pacing at the other's side. "He is very ill."

"Why, what has befallen him?" the Curé asked. "He was at the Pardon."

"He has been struck down, my father," replied the lad; "he was walking with us all when he fell down in a swoon."

The Curé hastened his steps, for they had reached the road. "Where is he?" he demanded.

"We carried him home and put him in bed. He is very pale and weak; and, my father, he is crying out to see you. So I, knowing your walks, came quickly to seek you." The lad paused, then added in a low tone, "Félix is dying."

"Run, then, Mathieu, to the church," said the Curé presently. "Here is the key; bring hither the holy relic. Bring it to Félix's house. Quick, my son; for that will save him, if the good God wills."

The lad took the key, and ran off into the darkness.

Félix lay in bed, pale-faced and with closed eyes. He breathed slowly and with effort, and his one hand lay inertly upon the coverlet.

The Curé, admitted by the sister of the sick man, sat beside the bed, waiting. His entrance did not seem to disturb Félix; and it was some time before a fluttering eye-lid gave evidence that Félix was recovering consciousness. The priest bent over him and looked into the dark, restless eyes that stared so blankly.

"Félix!" cried the Curé.

The stricken man's lips moved, and his bosom heaved. His sister, almost in tears, held a cup of wine to his lips; he drank a little, and suddenly spoke, in such an altered voice, that it was not till after several repetitions that they thought they understood him. "He is asking for the relic," murmured Agnes.

The sick man shook his head and spoke again. "Leave me with the good father, Agnes," he whispered.

But here was Mathieu, all aglow, with the reliquary. He and Agnes retreated to the other room of the cottage, where the lad strove to comfort her.

Left alone with Félix, the Curé opened the reliquary, and reverently held it to the other's lips. "Say a prayer to Saint Polliou, my son," the Curé said, "and kiss this holy relic."

He put his unoccupied arm behind Félix, and lifted him into a sitting position. Whereupon the sufferer took the reliquary and threw it with calm deliberation into a corner of the room.

"Carrion!" cried Félix clearly. "Take it away!"

Unutterably horrified, the priest drew back from the bed. His face whitened; his knees trembled; his soul melted within him; and had a flame come out of the sky and licked clean the bones of the sinner, the Curé would not have felt surprise. But the sick man sat upright with glowing eyes. He beckoned with his one hand; and such was the power of his gaze that the priest was drawn nearer.

"I am dying, my father," said Félix; "and I will tell the truth."

Still silent, the priest regarded him in a kind of palsied horror.

"That thing there," went on Félix, pointing to the fallen treasure, "is not a bone of Saint Polliou."

At this last blasphemy the Curé found voice and strength. Rushing across the room, he fell on his knees, picked up the femur, now broken in two, and replaced it in the casket, repeating the while, in a tremulous moan, various comminatory sentences. Félix watched him calmly; but when the Curé fled to the door the sick man cried out: "Hear me; hear me!"

The priest paused. "Well?" he said, harshly. And then his native sweetness of disposition prompted in him the recollection that Félix – with whom he had been associated for so many years, whose life he had saved – was dying and probably distraught.

"Ah, Félix, Félix," said the old man, and fell on his knees beside the bed.

"You must listen, my father," murmured Félix, "for I have not long to live."

"Do you remember the night we opened the tomb of Saint Polliou? We found nothing, and you were sadly, sadly disappointed."

The Curé assented silently, with a hinted fear in his mind.

"I walked up with you from the church that night," Félix continued, "and it grieved me to think that you were so sorrowful. And as I walked home again all alone, a thought came to me. At first I resisted it; but I remembered how you saved my life, and how it would gladden you if you could have your wish fulfilled. After all, it could hurt no one."

He paused, and reached feebly for the wine, but the priest had anticipated him, and held the cup for him to drink. Félix thanked the Curé with a tender glance.

"So I got a torch," resumed Félix, "and in the graveyard I soon found an old bone. And then I went to the crypt. I saw that part of the stone lining of the tomb had fallen in, so I placed the bone under the stones, piling several more upon it. And there next day you found it."

The Curé stood erect, but did not speak.

"Pardon, father!" cried the sick man in an agonised voice. And so fell down flat in the bed.

Suddenly the priest's face beamed with joy.

"It must have been the bone of some saint, Félix," he cried, "for think of the miracles it has worked! Saint Polliou put the thought into your heart, my son, and led you to find this bone. It is a relic, after all." And the old man's faith warmed again.

Félix shook his head weakly. "I wish I could believe it, father," he replied, but I know better. I took the bone from the grave of Gaspard Rohan, who hanged himself one night, ten years ago."

In the act of recoiling, the priest saw a change come upon Félix. Sweat broke out upon the sufferer's brow; he gasped, and his hand beat restlessly upon the counterpane.

"Absolution!" murmured Félix. With which word on his lips he slipped peacefully out of this world.

"Félix, Félix, what shall we do?" said the Curé, bending over the bed. But he got no reply. Félix had left him to answer that question alone.

TEDDY ASHTON'S WEEKLY FELLOWSHIP/ TEDDY ASHTON'S WEEKLY

William Siddle, 'A Stormy Wooing. The Smart Young Man and the Smarter Woman', *Teddy Ashton's Northern Weekly*, 2 March 1907, p. 4.

Teddy Ashton, 'Bill Spriggs in the Pantomime', *Teddy Ashton's Weekly*, 4 January 1908, p. 5; 11 January 1908, p. 5.

The decline in sales of *Teddy Ashton's Northern Weekly* (1896–1908) continued, and the periodical, beset by debts, formally closed late in 1907. It had been renamed *Teddy Ashton's Weekly Fellowship* in April 1907, and later that year the title was shortened again to *Teddy Ashton's Weekly*, presumably in an attempt to widen the readership and separate the 'new' publication from the failed title. This remained the title for the remaining few months of publication until the final issue was published on 1 March 1908. The end of the periodical came amidst accusations from some in the movement that Clarke was personally benefiting from the money collected by the paper. This was strenuously denied by Clarke, and the paper, which had founded its popularity on fun and humour, ended on a very sour note.

Clarke maintained the high volume of fiction almost to the end, although the number of serial fictions declined; the final serial, which ended just before the final issue, was a re-publication of Clarke's early fiction 'A Curate of Christ's', originally published in *Teddy Ashton's Northern Weekly* in 1897. There was a similar decline in the volume of short stories, and there were fewer by Clarke and more by other authors, including Alfred H. Pearce (n.d.), Harford Willson (n.d.) and Ethel Carnie Holdsworth (1886–1962). There has been no biographical or publication details found for William Siddle, and full biographical information for Clarke is given in the headnote for the *Bolton Trotter* in Volume 1, pp. 1–2.

William Siddle, 'A Stormy Wooing. The Smart Young Man and the Smarter Woman' (1907)

"Good evening, Miss MacDonald. What a fortunate meeting! I am just on the way to Coltstone myself. You are bound for the same place, I suppose?"

The girl glanced with some amusement at the speaker, who stood behind a vast expanse of collar, smiling happily, and twisting his fair moustache.

"Unfortunately, yes," she said, ambiguously.

"Then we may walk together. How delightful!"

"Won't it be nice?" she returned, without enthusiasm.

"Er – you used the word unfortunately just now. I suppose from that you find Colstone dull in the evening? Much pleasanter in the town, isn't it?"

"Oh, I don't know. I don't find Coltstone dull."

"No? I can't think how you manage to exist there at all, you know – no amusements, no society, no anything."

"No society, indeed! You'd better not say so to the vicar's lady or the mistress of the Young Ladies' Academy. They'd wither you up with a look."

"Ha! Ha! How witty you are, Miss MacDonald. Really, though, speaking more of our own class, I think the young chaps at Coltstone are horribly rough and uncultivated. There isn't a gentlemanly fellow among them. Look at Harry Mayfield, for instance – a perfect boor I call him."

She tossed her head rather scornfully.

"And what's the matter with him, pray?"

"Oh, nothing much. He's all right, of course, only – well, I mean to say that he is – anyhow, not what you'd call polished, you know. No company for a girl of taste."

"Hum – no – I suppose not," said Helen slowly. "Now I come to think of it, it would be rather nice if he would polish himself up a little. How noble he would look in a white waistcoat, for example. I'm sure he'd be a better man if only he would take to gold-rimmed pince-nez[1] and practice the London accent."

"Er – yes," assented Lennis dubiously, wondering if she was laughing at him.

"And then – ah, yes, the very idea. How sweet of you, Mr. Lennis, to put me in mind of it. He must get a book of French phrases, and learn to say *rendezvous* for when he means meeting place, and *a propos* for by-the-way; not to mention *de trop* and *coup-de-grace* and all the others. If only he would flavour his conversation with these darling little foreign words, he would be stamped as a man of culture at once, and I'm sure we should all respect him three times as much. I must talk to him about it."

"Culture has its uses, anyhow," returned the little dandy, reddening and buttoning his coat over the obnoxious white waistcoat. "But that's hardly what I meant. It's his beastly manner I object to. The last time I met him he was giggling and grinning all the time I was talking to him. I don't know whether anything I said was very funny, but I thought he was showing horrible form. I was almost – Eh? – What? – Money? – No, you lazy vagabond. You should earn your money, like I have to do."

"Beggin yer pardon, sir,' said the tramp who had accosted him. "Me and my missus and the kid 'ere 'as tramped about for weeks a-seekin of work, an we can't get none nohow. We're pretty nigh famished, an – I wouldn't arsk it fer myself, but, gorblimy, I can't let the missus and the boy starve. You wouldn't miss a copper, sir."

"Bah! Get out of my way, man. You shouldn't have drunk your money when you had it. If you want food there's the workhouse open for the likes of you." He walked on, leaving the tramp muttering and grinding his teeth.

Helen MacDonald shot an indignant glance at him, and then turned back to the wanderer with her purse out. She stopped talking to him for some time, and when she returned to Tom Lennis there was a mischievous twinkle in her eye. He was soon to learn its meaning.

"Ah!" he said, 'the goodness of your heart runs away with your discretion. Yet how I honour you for it."

"How could you be so cruel?" she asked. "I'm sure the man was genuine."

"Maybe; but there are so many lazy rogues, it makes one suspicious of the whole crowd. But you are so different – so very womanly and sympathetic. Ah, Miss MacDonald, it is your sweet womanly impulsiveness which makes me love you so dearly. I would go to the world's end to win the privilege of calling you mine. Tell me, Helen, my beloved, may I hope for such happiness?"

"Oh, Mr. Lennis!" Helen's soft blue eyes spoke eloquently of real distress. "I – I had no idea of this."

"From the day when first we met,' he went on, encouraged by her blushes, "I have felt that we were made for one another. How much more delight would your refined soul find in intercourse with me than with rude, rough Harry Mayfield. I –"

"Stop," she cried indignantly. "You don't help your cause by insulting my accepted lover."

"Your *what*?" Phew! He had put his foot in it now.

"The man I marry must be a man," she said, stung. "He must be brave, honourable, strong, and kind-hearted."

"Ah," he said. Laying his little gloved hand upon that part of his brilliant waistcoat which covered the fifth rib. "You make the common mistake. Because a man spends his days sitting upon an office stool, therefore he is a coward and a weakling. Believe me, that for your sake I would go to the world's end. I would brave any danger to win your love. There is no peril by land or sea that --- Oh! Good heavens! Here's that fellow again."

They had turned down a narrow winding lane to the right, and the tramp, with his wife and fourteen-year-old boy, had apparently taken a short cut across the fields.

"Now, then, Poll," shouted the man. "You two look after the wench, an I'll show the little dandy whether 'e can blackguard me for nothink. I'll murder the little shrimp."

Helen screamed, and laid a trembling hand upon Tom's arm. Now was his chance. But the tramp advanced upon them, flourishing a huge stick. Lennis, pale with fright his scalp alive with a cold, prickly sensation, stood fixed to the spot. When the man was almost upon them, he gave one wild yell and bolted. Over the fence he blundered, and ran like a madman across the field, leaving the unfortunate Helen to her fate.

After him came the great, hulking, bearded brute, waving his bludgeon aloft. Lennis ran as had never run before, with long stumbling strides over the uneven meadowland. He could hear the laboured breathing of his pursuer coming near, nearer, ever nearer. His heart jumped fiercely against his side; in a wild madness of terror he strained until his surging arteries well-nigh burst; shouting murder as he ran. And then –

Oh horrid sight! There from the farther end of the meadow came a great bull, with head down and tail in air, charging straight for him. What could he do? A savage enemy pressed him behind, and a gory death awaited him in front. All the incidents of his past life crossed his brain in rapid succession and he vowed that if only Providence brought him safely through this, he would never touch another drop of shandy-gaff[2] as long as he lived!

Quick as lightning he turned at right angles and fled as though Beelzebub and all his train were after him. The thunder of the animal's hoofs sounded close behind him. Again he foiled the beast by turning at a sharp angle, but not for long. In almost the space of a second, as it seemed to him, the savage thing was again close behind him. The hat and stick he had long since lost, and oh, how he cursed his choking collar. No matter. Clutching wildly at his throat, his once irreproachable "quaff"[3] floating in the breeze, on he tore in a devious zig-zag to the fence. There, almost within touch of the bull's horns, he scrambled, he knew not how, over the top and souse![4] into the ditch below.

When, bedraggled and bemired, his once beautiful waistcoat stained with clay, he crawled out on dry land, the tramp and his family were in convulsions of laugher. Helen stood with laughter and pity fighting for the command of her countenance, until the rude, uncultivated Harry Mayfield arrived, when the pair walked off arm-in-arm.

Then Lennis remembered the mischievous light in her eyes after her talk with the tramp, and perceived that one part, at least, of his adventure had been arranged for him.

Teddy Ashton, 'Bill Spriggs in the Pantomime' (1908)

[4 January 1908]

Clinton Fields, the comic man in the pantomime of "Sinbad the Sailor" – he plays Sinbad – met Bill Spriggs one afternoon in the Stanley Arms, next door to the theatre.

"Bill," he says, "you famous old ichthyosaurus[1] –"

"Howd on, what's that?" said Bill. "If we're to have any bad language, let's ha' some gradely Christian cussin what we can aw understand, an' give a bit back on."

Clinton Fields laughed. "Bill," he said. "I want you to come and see me play to-night."

"Well, I wouldn't mind," said Bill, "it's a two-three year sin' I seed a pantomime. I gets enough to be gooin' on wi' awhum, yo' know"; and he grinned. "Still, I wouldn't mind seein' 'Sinbad' for a change. Is there th' same owd fairies i' tights, an' th' same owd jokes, an' th' same demon, an' aw that?"

"The same old things, but vastly improved. However, if you come I'll take you behind the scenes to have a peep at the fairies," said Clinton. "Will you come? I'll give you a free pass to the stalls – the front seats."

"Well, I wouldn't mind comin'," said Bill, "but there's eaur Bet. I rather fancy hoo'll object, especially if I tell her I'm going to have a look at th' fairies behind the scenes; but I'll say nowt abeaut that. Eawr Bet's rather jealous, yo' know; I'm such a handsome felly, yo' see" (and Bill grinned again) "that hoo weren't let me goo eaut by mysel."

"Bring her too, then," said Clinton. "Give the old girl a treat."

"Ay, that met do," said Bill. "I'll try her."

"Here's tickets for the pair of you," said Clinton, "reserved seats, front row."

"We'll be there," said Bill, and off he went with the tickets, to tell Bet the news, while Clinton Fields unwrapped a small parcel of window bills he had, and read the following:

GRAND PANTOMIME OF "SINBAD THE SAILOR."
BENEFIT OF CLINTON FIELDS – SINBAD.
ON THIS NIGHT ONLY, THE IMMORTAL AND NOTORIOUS BILL
AND BET SPRIGGS, OF TUM FOWT, WILL APPEAR.

"That'll do," said Clinton Fields. "I'm glad I've persuaded Bill to come. I guess he wouldn't if he saw one of the bills, which are now out all over the town. But there's little chance of that. Ah, there'll be some fun to-night; though exactly in what shape it will come on the programme I don't know. I shall have to trust to chance for that. But I'll get Bill Spriggs on the stage, somehow, and then I'm pretty sure Bet will follow."

Bill and Bet turned up at the theatre all right. Bet had insisted on Bill going in a tall hat, so he hunted up the old one in which he was married; it looked contemporary with Noah's ark.

"Theau owt to have a big white shirt-front, too," she said, "an' a weskut aw oppen at they chest, seein' as we're gooin' a-sittin' among th' aristocracy. There is a big dickey[2] here –"

"I'd sooner go i' my scarf an' be comfortable," said Bill.

"Theau's no pride abeaut thee," said Bet. "Let's see if we cornt manage to mak thy front show like a white flag," and she unbuttoned his waistcoat, turned the edges in, making it wide open, and fastened only one button at the bottom.

"Theer, that looks better," she said. "But theau'll ha' to keep quite still, or else th' edges o' th' weskut ull come eaut. Is there owt else we want? Ay, we owt to have an opera glass."[3]

"Well, we have noan," said Bill. "But that theer sixpenny spy-glass as eaur Baccarat[4] bowt will happen do."

"Ay, bring it," said Bet, "it'll be better than noan at aw."

So they set off for the theatre, Bet attired in her daintiest, with a hat as big as a frying-pan.

"If we're in th' front row theau'll ha' t' poo that hat off," said Bill, 'Or nobody behind will be able to see owt."

"I'm noan pooin' my hat off," said Bet. "I've noan done my hair for takkin' my hat off. I'm noan decollected, nor dishybill,[5] as polite society says."

The seats for the Spriggs were almost in the middle of the front row, behind the band and conductor.

The house was full, and there was some tittering at Bill and Bet, who, however, sat quite unconcerned.

A fashionable woman, with a great display of bare neck and half her back, sat next to Bet, though she evidently wasn't pleased to have such a grotesquely garbed neighbor.

Bet looked at this lady's powdered, nakedness for a while, and then said: "Missus, durn't yo' think yo'll get cowd? I'll lend yo' my shawl to cover yore shoulders if yo' like. I con do beaut it neaw, I'm quite warm"; but to this kindly offer the lady's only acknowledgement was to turn her head away in disgust.

Oh, aw reet," said Bet, "I'm as good as yo if I durn't mak a penny show o' my neck."

When the band came in, and the conductor took his seat, right in front of Bet, she said to Bill, "is that mon beaund to sit theer aw th' time?"

'I gouse he is," said Bill; 'he's th' band conductor."

"He con be a tram conductor for aw I care," said Bet, "but I'm noan gooin to have him sittin' theer. He blocks aw my view eaut."

When the curtain went up, Bet poked her finger in the back of the conductor, and he turned round, wondering who had dared to touch him.

"I cornt see," said Bet. "Yo'd better get a bit lower deawn, or else shift awtogether. I durn't see that yo're any use. Yo're doin' nowt but wave a bit of a stick abeaut, an' takkin' th' attention o' them other chaps off their instruments. They're doin' aw' th' wark, an' they'd get along better if yo'd nobut stop flirtin' that twig abeaut. If yo' want to be i' th' band, get howd o' summat, an play it."

The conductor glared at Bet, but said nothing.

"If he doesn't be shiftin' I'll knock him off his bloomin' peearch," said Bet. So to prevent hostilities Bill diplomatically changed seats with his spouse.

"Ay, that's better," said Bet; "but if I were thee, Bill, I wouldn't ha' that mon obstructin' my vision. Give him a shove, and he'll tumble into th' piano."

At this point some men behind Bet cried, "Hats off in front."

"Ay, theau owt to tak thy hat off," said Bill.

"I'st do nowt o' th' soart," said Bet.

"Pull that hat off," shouted somebody.

Bet turned round. "I'll poo thy yead off, if theau down't shut up," and the theatre roared; while Bet calmly put the sixpenny toy spy-glass to her eye and surveyed the stage, where a crowd of sailors and nymphs were dancing at the port prior to Sinbad's embarkation. At sight of the spy-glass everybody smiled and laughed, and somebody bawled, "Oh my, look at the opera-glass!"

[11 January 1908]

Presently one of the programme boys came to Bill and whispered, "Mr. Fields wants to see you behind."

"Aw reet," said Bill, "which road? Leead on."

"Here, where are ta gooin'? Corn't I come too?" asked Bet.

"That mon as gan us th' free tickets wants to see me a minute," said Bill, "an' it would be gradely bad manners not to goo an' thank him for the treat he's gan us."

"Very weel," said Bet, "theau con goo. But durn't be above two minutes. An' let's ha' no tricks. Sithee!" And she showed the rolling-pin under her shawl.

"Whatever has ta browt that wi' thee for?" said Bill.

"Well, one never knows what'll happen," said Bet, "an' it's allus best to be prepared for emergencies. So be careful, an' behave thyself."

The programme boy led Bill to the side of the theatre, and opened a little door, which led to the stage. In three seconds Bill found himself in the midst of a number of nymphs and fairies, attired in the usual pantomime costume – sweet but scanty.

"Eh, by gow!" said Bill, "it's a good job eaur Bet didn't come wi' me behind th' scenes, or some o' these nice wenches would ha' geet a bonny dressin' deawn – an' they look as if they needed a dress o' some sort. But not for me – I con stand such giddy seets – I'm weel content wi' 'em as they are! Oh laws, but aren't they scrumptious! I wonder if I dar touch one!"

And Bill looked yearningly at the Queen of the Fairies, who, seeing his glance, winked at him, and – having been put up to the proceeding by Clinton Fields – tickled him under the chin and said, "Oh, you nice old thing! I've half a mind to kiss you till your whiskers drop off!" And she gave Bill a frolicsome little push which shaked his tall hat to the back of his head, so that he looked a regular gay old sport.

"Neaw, steady," said Bill, dazzled by feminine beauty, "durn't tempt me or I'st be puttin' my arm reaund thee. Eh laws, am I in heaven or Jerusalem,[6] or where? Wheer's Clinton Fields gone?"

Though Bill could not see him, the comedian was on the stage, saying "Bring forth Bill Sprigs and his harem. Bring forth the henpecked hero of Tum Fowt, that we may take him a trip to the Valley of Diamonds. Bring forth the bucolic Bill Spriggs."[7]

While Fields was thus declaiming, the ladies of the ballet had surrounded Bill and put their hands on his head and over his ears to prevent him hearing the words on the stage, Bill gaily crying out, "Neaw, durn't – durn't if yo' keep ticklin' me I'st get howd o' some on yo – I'st noan be responsible for my conduct – neaw give o'er. By gow, I'll stop thee, theau minx." And Bill grabbed at one of the girls, whereupon the rest of them surrounded him and pushed him through the wings on to the stage, where his tall hat rolled friskily off, just as Clinton Fields shouted, "Ha, here he comes – the noble Bill Spriggs and his harem."

Bill hardly knew where he was or what he was doing as he stood in the glare and dazzle of the scene, with the lime light on him, and the girls dancing merrily round him, pulling his hair and twisting his nose, while the packed house thundered laughter, and Bet Spriggs, amazed, enraged, gazed, for a bewildered moment, at her husband frolicking in the midst of these sportive damsels on the other side of the footlights.

Then Bet rose, angry and combative – as Clinton Fields had hoped she would – and, producing the rolling-pin, and brandishing it ominously , bawled out,

"Oh, Bill Spriggs, theau desateful villain! So this were they dodge, were it? Laws, heaw they're cuddlin' him an' clippin' him! Come off that stage this minute, Bill Spriggs – come off or I'll massacre thee!"

But Bill could not hear a word. The "fairies" were shouting and the band was playing, and the audience was exploding hilariously.

"By gow, I'll fotch thee off!" shouted Bet, and she tried to climb up the wooden partition enclosing the band, but only succeeded in knocking the conductor off his perch and tumbling him upon the piano.

The spectators fair chinked again; they had never seen such a pantomime as this.

Bet, finding that she could not scale the barrier behind the conductor, ran to the side of the stage, where she managed to scramble over into the orchestra. For a minute, after desperate exertion, she sat, paused on the top of the frame, then – to the huge and screaming delight of the "house" – wobbled, tottered and went head first into the big drum, the musicians scattering for their lives.

"By gow!' shrieked a woman in the gallery, tears of fun rolling down her face, "hoo's tumbled i' th' big drum and brasted it. Oh, dear me, – I'm brastin wi' lowfin! There never were sich doins sin' Eve fawd off th' appo-tree!"

Meanwhile Bet, with the rolling-pin in her left hand, by standing on the top of a fiddler she had knocked prostrate, managed to get half-way up the front of the stage, where she hung, desperately suspended, puffing and panting, unable to get any further, and unwilling to drop back, till the big drummer gave her a whack with his drumstick and pushed her headlong on to the stage, at the end of the footlights, while the audience split its sides at the sight.

Soon as she was on the stage Bet, with the rolling-pin raised for destruction, rushed upon her husband and the fairies. The latter immediately scattered, leaving Bill alone on the stage. Poor Bill, dazed, paralysed, turned to flee, but too late. Bet gave him a mighty whack that sent him sprawling into the wings, where Bill gathered himself up as quickly as he could, and looked for ways of escape. But he did not know his whereabouts, so ran, unintentionally, back upon the stage, Bet following him with the rolling-pin. Bill tuned and ran back again, Bet still pursuing; and this game was kept up for some time, to the vast amusement of the audience, till Bill caught sight of the door by which he had come behind the scenes, darted through it, and out of the theatre.

And Bet followed with the rolling-pin.

EDITORIAL NOTES

Blatchford, 'The Sorcery Shop. An Impossible Romance'

1. *gold-rimmed pebbles*: spectacles; the lenses within the gold rims are referred to as 'pebbles'. Jorkle is the archetypal capitalist, displaying his wealth ostentatiously through his physical being and material accoutrements.
2. *sabreur*: one who fights with a sabre; one who fights without skill; *OED*. Although the General is described in negative terms – vicious, arrogant, obtuse – Blatchford, the ex-soldier who later described himself as a 'Tory Democrat', indicates that the General is redeemable by interweaving positive attributes between the negative: the General is also brave and had defended his country. While Jorkle, the Liberal, is without any redeeming features, the Tory General suggests the possibility of hope.
3. *House*: House of Commons, the elected half of the British Houses of Parliament. The House of Lords was, and continues to be, made up of unelected bishops, and hereditary and life peers. Neither Jorkle nor the General can imagine a working-class man being an effective Prime Minister, as both are immersed in the entitlement of the wealthy and landed.
4. *black satin stock and Gladstonian collar*: Stock may refer to a stocking worn with knee breeches, a close-fitting neckcloth, or an article of material worn around the neck and chest by clergymen. A Gladstonian collar is a starched neckcloth worn with a collar, which stood vertical from the shirt, with the tips folded back to protrude away from the chin. This form of collar was popularized by British Prime Minister William Ewart Gladstone (1809–98). The image is of a man dressed in the fashions of the past.
5. *Nathaniel Fry, of Wells and Wells, in Simmery Axe*: very probably a reference to the Gilbert and Sullivan comic opera *The Sorcerer*, which opened in 1877 at the Opera Comique in London. 'The Sorcerer's Song', which introduces the eponymous character to the audience, names him as 'John Wellington Wells', who lives at 'number seventy, Simmery Axe'. Blatchford was a keen theatregoer and had lost money financing a comic opera with his cousin Clarence Corri (n.d.).
6. *Maskelyne and Cooke*: former watchmaker John Neville Maskelyne (1839–1917) and his friend, former cabinet maker George Alfred Cooke (1825–1904), were stage magicians and illusionists who have been credited with devising some of the most famous illusions, including levitation. The reference anticipates the difficulties both Jorkle and the General have in imagining a socialist reality.
7. *on the halls*: working as an act in the music hall variety shows.

8. *parqueterie*: usually spelled parquetry; a wooden floor covering made of individual blocks of wood placed in a geometric pattern. The art of inlaid wooden blocks could also be used in the decoration of wooden furniture, and the description is reminiscent of William Morris's (1834–96) Arts and Crafts movement and the pared-down style of Art Nouveau.
9. *No. 70, Simmery Axe*: St Mary Axe is a street in the City of London running parallel to Bishopsgate and is most famous in the twenty-first century for being the address of the Swiss Re Building, also known as the Gherkin because of its shape, at 30 St Mary Axe. The men are entering the socialist utopia through the heart of capitalism in London.
10. *from the West End to the City*: The Directorate Club, from which the characters have travelled, is a fictitious club, but it is possibly meant to be located in Pall Mall, which had many gentlemen's clubs in the nineteenth century, including the Reform Club, which remains there today. Pall Mall was the scene of a disturbance after an address by the SDF at Trafalgar Square in 1886. See Bramsbury, 'A Working Class Tragedy', Chapter XXVII, *Justice*, Volume 1 for a fictional representation of the disturbance. The distance between Pall Mall and St Mary Axe is around 6 km or almost 4 miles.
11. *Penally*: a coastal village in southwest Wales near Tenby. There has been an army training camp near the village since 1860. If the General was there in 'the sixties', he would have been one of the first to use it in training after the Crimean War (1853–6).
12. *Philistines*: can be read as either the modern use of the word, meaning an ignorant and unenlightened person, or as Matthew Arnold's description of the middle classes in *Culture and Anarchy* (1869). Jorkle and Storm can only appreciate nature for what they can extract from it: money and violent entertainment.
13. *campanile ... golden crown*: A campanile is a free-standing bell tower usually found in Italy, and the golden crown is reminiscent of the golden roofs and towers of mosques such as the Dome of the Rock in Jerusalem. The overall image is of a multicultural architecture.
14. *Paradise regained*: Like Milton's 1671 poem of the name, Blatchford sets out his socialist utopia through a series of juxtapositions and reversals of reality.
15. *Hulme Town Hall*: Hulme was one of the worst slums in Manchester in the nineteenth and early twentieth centuries. It was described by Friedrich Engels (1820–95) in *The Conditions of the Working Class in England* (1845) as 'approaching ruin' and being 'generally sunk in filth' (London: Penguin, 1987), p. 99. Blatchford's conversion to socialism began when he was conducted around some of the slum dwellings in Hulme by his socialist friend Joe Waddington. Blatchford later examined the Ancoats slums before reading the pamphlet *What is Socialism* by Henry Mayers Hyndman and William Morris: 'That, as the boys say, "tore it." I had thought out an economic scheme for myself; but directly I grasped the collective idea I saw that it was what I wanted'; R. Blatchford, *My Eighty Years* (London: Cassell and Co., 1931), p. 191.
16. *pro bono publico*: literally for the public good or benefit. One of the few issues on which most socialist groups agreed was the necessity of public landownership as the basis for an equal society and the foundation for socialism.
17. *Life Guards*: a senior regiment in the British Army and a part of the household cavalry guarding the monarch. Originally the household cavalry would be staffed only by gentlemen, and Fry's point is that these ordinary men in New Manchester are akin to the fitness and quality of the elite in capitalist Britain.
18. *Lascelles*: an allusion to Ferdinand Lassalle (1825–64), the German philosopher and socialist who promoted state socialism and believed that the workers were the driving force of humanity and humanitarian society. Blatchford and the *Clarion* group declared

that they had never read Marx but had developed an ethical, rather than economic, socialist ideal.
19. *a whole station*: the full regiment. Mrs Lascelles is distractingly beautiful and would captivate the heart of every soldier.
20. *hod-man*: a brick carrier on a building site. Storm's point is that a manual labourer would not be expected to live well, have an attractive wife or afford to give away food.
21. *do not drink ... in the country*: Blatchford advocated teetotalism but was also fond of drinking whisky himself. He did not impose abstinence on others, but he did argue, in *Merrie England*, that it was more important for the alcohol to be pure and of a better quality than that which was sold in public houses at the time. He also argued that given healthy work, alternative leisure activities and more leisure time, levels of drunkenness in the working classes would decline.
22. *precious good job ... whisky and soda*: Like many of the ruling class who attempted to impose abstinence on the workers, General Storm does not lead by example.
23. *What is meat?*: in Chapter 5 of *Merrie England*, Blatchford states: 'I am much inclined to think that a vegetarian diet is the best, and that alcoholic liquors are unnecessary'.
24. *Dorothy Suthers*: Robert Suthers (1870–1950) was one of the founding members of the *Clarion*. Dorothy Violet was the name of his youngest daughter, born in 1905.
25. *whiskey peg*: could either refer to an Indian form of fluid measurement or to a mixture of whiskey and soda. The General qualifies the term 'peg' by 'whiskey' here because a 'peg' usually refers to a mixture of brandy and soda
26. *given up ... philistinism*: In later life Blatchford claimed he had always been a Tory Democrat, and so here he leans toward the Tory soldier as the hope for change while dismissing the Liberal capitalist as too narrow-minded and self-concerned to understand the wider implications of socialism.
27. *her face ... without a name*: Sir John Suckling (bap. 1609–c. 1641), the Cavalier poet. The quotation is from the drama *Brennoralt, or the Discontented Colonel*, Act 3. Suckling's plays were not as well received as his poetry, but this play – about a disillusioned Colonel aware of the King's failings, and thought reflect the personality of the author – has been deemed his work with the most potential. In this quotation Brennoralt is describing his love's face as he watches her sleep.
28. *the 'Shining Ones' in Bunyan's dream*: John Bunyan (c. 1628–88), *The Pilgrim's Progress* (1678). Christian recounts meeting the three Shining Ones at the foot of the cross after leaving the Interpreter's house. The sight of the crucifixion relieves Christian of his burden, and the Shining Ones forgive his sins, replace his rags with an embroidered coat and give him hope. Here, the women in New Manchester are the hope and comfort of the future.
29. *sweetness and light*: a term generally meaning pleasing and educational, but may also refer to the title of Chapter 1 of *Culture and Anarchy. An Essay in Political and Social Criticism* (1869) by Matthew Arnold (1822–88), where Arnold argues for the improving qualities of art and culture over the preoccupation with production and profit propounded by the philistine Liberals. For Fry, the women of New Manchester are the heart and soul of the community, bringing beauty and kindness to life.
30. *Under the greenwood tree ... sweet bird's throat*: William Shakespeare (1564–1616), *As You Like It*, Act 2, scene v. In the play, Amiens's song brings a call for more from Jaques to indulge his melancholy at the expense of Amiens's throat; the audience in New Manchester is invigorated and uplifted by both the performance and the music.

31. *Vronsky ... Mildred Thompson*: Vronsky is perhaps a reference to the lover of Tolstoy's eponymous Anna Karenina (1873–9), whose reciprocated love for Anna causes them both chaos and disaster in strictly ordered Russian society. Metin is a Turkish name meaning strong. Miss Mildred Thompson was the name of Blatchford's friend and *Clarion* co-founder Alex. M. Thompson's daughter, who would have been about nineteen at the time of writing. She is listed on the 1911 Census as 'chorister', so Blatchford has promoted her to composer in his utopian society.
32. *churchwarden*: a form of pipe with a long slender stem. The longer stem cools the smoke and keeps the bowl at length from the smoker's face. This form goes some way to reducing the intake of tobacco and reinforces Blatchford's/Fry's opinion that less smoke is better, as evidenced in the utopian's attitude towards smoking.
33. *not our Hoxton*: Hoxton is a district in East London in the borough of Hackney next to Shoreditch. In 1902 Charles Booth described the district in *Life and Labour of the London People* as having 'a considerable admixture of the very poor and vicious'. In Fry's New Britain, one of the worst parts of Britain becomes one of the most attractive.
34. *The children ... What do the men say to that?*: Until the case of Caroline Norton (1808–77) and her separation from her violent husband, the law had declared that all children were the property of their father. Norton campaigned against this law and was effective in the introduction of the 1839 Infant Custody Act, giving the mother custody of children under the age of seven if she had not been found guilty of adultery. The General appears to favour the old division of awarding automatic custody to the father.
35. *Mrs. Glasse ... hare*: Hannah Glasse (bap. 1708–70), author of *The Art of Cookery Made Plain and Easy ... by a Lady* (1746), is misattributed as the originator of the phrase 'first catch your hare', as is Mrs Beeton. The phrase is used to warn against making plans without having created the means to carry them through, or not to get ahead of oneself. Fry is warning Jorkle to remember this society is based on matriarchal power.
36. *noblesse oblige*: the obligations and duties that come with the benefits of aristocracy. Here it refers to the responsibilities of men to women in this New Britain.
37. *Some Socialists ... such a fear*: The discussion of 'free love', meaning unmarried sexual relationships, was not limited to the socialist movement; but, as Karen Hunt notes, it was 'easy for the association of apparently subversive behaviour and subversive politics to become a strong one in the public mind'. Karl Marx's daughter Eleanor lived unmarried with Edward Aveling, as Aveling was unable to obtain a divorce from his wife; others, such as Edith Lanchester and James Sullivan, made the decision to cohabit a political one. See K. Hunt, *Equivocal Feminists* (Cambridge: Cambridge University Press, 1996). Blatchford was often criticized by female *Clarion* workers for his conservative views on the gender question.
38. *Aspasia*: Aspasia of Miletus was the mistress or hetaira of Pericles and was one of the most influential women in fifth-century Greece. She was highly intelligent, and Pericles treated her as an equal despite fierce criticism from his peers. Fry's point is that the General – and the rest of British society – appreciates the intelligent woman, but the physical and sexual side of relationships between the genders often overwhelms this. For all Jorkle's puritan attitude, his first thought is sexual, as Fry goes on to point out through his reference to Venus, and even the General's broader view of women is perceived through the filter of sex.
39. *Honour bright*: a protestation, or interrogation, of honour; *OED*. The General is asking Fry if this is really true.

40. *In our highly moral ... Socialist State*: Fry extends the issue of morality beyond sexual relations and social mores and questions the morality of a society that keeps some of its citizens in poverty and destitution.
41. *a question of facts*: an allusion to Charles Dickens's (1812–70) character Gradgrind in *Hard Times* (1854) and his inability to see the beauty of things beyond the bare facts of the matter.
42. *unwise to be rude to the equator*: No source has been located for this quotation.
43. *Who shall walk ... Spring is calling*: There is no evidence of this song being published outside of this fiction.
44. *Reminds me ... the General*: The General recalls being beaten for playing with children below him in the social hierarchy. His sense of class distinction is learned behaviour passed down the family's generations, therefore emphasizing the natural equality between children before they are conditioned by adults. Bideford Green now abuts Leighton Buzzard in Bedfordshire.
45. *importing Socialist ideas ... uniform citizens*: a reference to the ideas on education promoted by Friedrich Engels, who advocated the uniform and equal education of all children by the state.
46. *bairns*: a Scottish term for children, also found in northern English dialect.
47. *the three R's*: a term for the basic foundations of learning, referring to reading, writing and 'rithmetic (arithmetic, mathematics). Utopian England has an equal standard of education between the genders and across all citizens, so mothers are able to pass on their knowledge and begin their child's education.
48. *the universal language*: Esperanto, a language created by Ludwig Lazarus Zamenhof (1859–1917) with the intention of creating an easily learned universal system of communication, was published in 1887. The *Clarion* carried advertisements for Esperanto groups, classes and books and, for a short time, included an Esperanto column.
49. *some are allowed ... a year or two later*: The official school leaving age of ten, set by the 1870 Elementary Education Act, was raised to eleven by the 1893 Elementary Education (School Attendance) Act. The 1893 Act was in turn amended in 1899 to set the leaving age at twelve. Blatchford's utopia extends childhood freedom and eases the child into work.
50. *repousse work in copper*: repoussé, the art of ornamenting metal by hammering an image on the reverse side to raise a scene or pattern on the visible side.
51. *off-drives ... William Gunn*: In cricket, off-drives are when the ball is hit through a long arc, which can send it in a number of possible directions into the 'off' side (the half of the field in front of the batsman, as opposed to the 'in' or 'leg' side). William Gunn (1858–1921) played cricket for Nottinghamshire and England between 1880 and 1904 and football for Notts County, Nottingham Forest and England. Lascelles is a talented and experienced sportsman as well as an artist. None of the citizens of New England are forced into undesirable work while their talents lie dormant, nor are they expected to give their life to a single role or type of work.
52. *explained the nature of spiral nebulæ*: The nature of spiral nebulæ was a cause of much astrological debate in the early twentieth century, culminating in the Shapley-Curtis Great Debate in 1920, when two astronomers, Harlow Shapley (1885–1972) and Heber Doust Curtis (1872–1942), presented opposing opinions. Shapley argued that the nebulæ were gas clouds that were part of the Milky Way, and Curtis asserted that the nebulæ were clusters of stars and planets similar to, but outside of, the Milky Way. Joseph Norris, the tile painter, has anticipated the conclusion of the nebulæ debate by thirteen years.

53. *sit in the woods, and moon*: To moon means to daydream. Bernard is a dreamer and unsuited for the usual methods of learning in New England.
54. *Drake and Dampier breed*: Sir Francis Drake (1540–96) began his seafaring life as a pirate before gaining royal acceptance and becoming a national hero. William Dampier (1651–1715) was a seaman and buccaneer whose tales of his exploits made him famous. His knowledge of the South Seas provided the foundations for later scientific discovery and theory, including that of Charles Darwin (1809–82). The General's point is that both Drake and Dampier had inauspicious beginnings to their fame and fortune.
55. *Jack Robinson*: a colloquialism meaning to be speedy or to do something very quickly: before you can say Jack Robinson.
56. *turning an Afghan flank*: a reference to the Second Afghan War (1878–80), when Britain invaded Afghanistan from Pakistan. The General's point is that Jorkle's concern with rote learning is useful neither for the individual nor the nation.
57. *ambassadors from Norway*: a reference to *Hamlet*, Act 2, scene ii, where Polonius presents to the king and queen the Danish ambassadors Voltemand and Cornelius, who have returned from Norway in an attempt to dissuade Fortinbras from attacking Denmark. The use of the phrase here does not suggest that Norris sees the group as a potential threat from an external source, but rather that he recognizes them as strangers from another land.
58. *wisdom is better than rubies*: Proverbs 8:11: 'For wisdom is better than rubies; and all the things that may be desired are not to be compared to it'. The inhabitants of New Manchester prefer knowledge to material wealth and, despite there being no evidence of Christian religion, use Biblical quotations to reinforce their statements.
59. *nebulous suns in the Pleiades*: newly formed or forming suns and galaxies in one of the closest star clusters to earth. Tomtit Lemon is interested in the as-yet unknown causes and consequences of nebulæ. The point is that children, given freedom of learning, will develop interests suited to their own tastes and achieve more than children forced into rote learning and strictly regimented educational atmospheres.
60. *played for safety*: The General puts the general term 'playing it safe', meaning to take no chances, into cricketing terms. Jorkle needed to change the subject to maintain his critical position on the utopian form of education.
61. *Goathland Moor*: common land in North Yorkshire, southwest of Whitby.
62. *"I suppose ... human*: Again, Blatchford's Tory leanings are evident as he positions the Tory General as the appreciator of human enjoyment and pleasure against the rigid puritan views of Jorkle. See Patrick Joyce, *Visions of the People: Industrial England and the Question of Class, c.1848–1914* (Cambridge: Cambridge University Press, 1991) for more detail on the divisions between Tory and Liberal ideologies.
63. *"I'm not a feminist myself*: The General is using the word in its older sense, referring to the attributes and character of the female rather, than its more modern use, referring to a political movement that aims to create equality between the sexes. In the bound version, this comment is made by Jorkle.
64. *dancing Dervishes*: A Dervish is a practising Sufi Muslim who leads an austere and ascetic life. The whirling dance performed by some Sufi Muslims is a physical form of meditation that sought to achieve heightened senses and bring the practitioner closer to God and the self. Mr Jorkle associates the enjoyment of dancing with non-Christian (and therefore unacceptable) religions.
65. *navvy*: an abbreviation of navigator, a construction worker employed in the building of roads or canals; *OED*.

66. *break a ball from the off*: a particular form of bowling that sends the ball towards the batsman's offside after bouncing on the pitch. The reference is to the skills of cricket as a sport that the British workman does not have time or opportunity to develop, as well as the other skills listed.
67. *Charles Darwin ... new thought*: Charles Darwin, naturalist, geologist and author of *The Origin of Species* (1859). Darwin's quiet contemplation in his home at Down in rural Kent produced one of the most revolutionary works of science of the nineteenth century.
68. *Nelson, Wellington, Gordon, and Clive*: Horatio Nelson (1758–1805), naval officer and hero of Trafalgar, 1805; Arthur Wellesley, first Duke of Wellington (1769–1852), army officer, Prime Minister, victor of the Battle of Waterloo, 1815; Charles George Gordon (1833–85), army officer who held Khartoum against a siege by Egyptian nationalists in 1884–5 and who was eventually killed when the siege was ended by surrender; Robert Clive (1725–74), first Baron Clive of Plassey, army officer for the East India Company and administrator of India who expanded British rule in India. Fry's point is that although these men gained renown and recognition for their achievements, none were motivated by financial gain but acted for the good of the nation.
69. *dismal science*: from the subtitle to Blatchford's 1898 Clarion pamphlet, *Altruism: Christ's Glorious Gospel of Love against Man's Dismal Science of Greed*. In this pamphlet, Blatchford argues that 'Altruism, indeed, is more important than Socialism itself. Given universal love of man for man, and we have something better than Socialism itself. We should have Communism of the purest and most durable kind'.
70. *volunteers and yeomen ... South Africa*: The volunteer force were a corps of part-time citizen volunteers who first saw active service during the Second Boer War (1899–1902) and who later became the Territorial Army; the yeomen were originally formed from the landed gentry and nobility during the 1790s to defend Britain against a possible invasion by Napoleon. They also fought in the Second Boer War. Both sets of volunteers were willing to sacrifice their lives for their country and not for financial gain.
71. *Socrates ... Nelson*: Fry's wide-ranging list, encompassing army and naval officers, poets, playwrights, scientists and inventors, is compiled to support his argument that people will work to create startling change or to make revolutionary discoveries without the motivation of money.
72. *What shall ... own life*: Mark 8:36 and Matthew 16:26. Blatchford replaces the original word 'soul' with 'life'.
73. *Brummagem jewels*: Brummagem is colloquial term for Birmingham and is used in this instance to suggest something of inferior quality or counterfeit.
74. *Chicago packer of diseased meat*: a reference to Upton Sinclair's *The Jungle*, serialized in the American socialist periodical *Appeal to Reason* in 1905 and published in book form in 1906. Sinclair's novel about poverty and working practices in the Chicago meat industry was researched by his incognito employment in meatpacking plants. The book led to the passage of the Meat Inspection Act and the Pure Food and Drug Act in 1906.
75. *Jesus Christ to Darwin*: Blatchford's juxtaposition of Christ with Darwin raises the arguments he aired in the *Clarion* in 1903 after reviewing Ernst Haeckel's *The Riddle of the Universe*, where he provocatively stated that the book 'demolishes the entire structure upon which the religions of the world are built'; 'In the Library', *Clarion*, 23 January 1903, p. 3. Blatchford's subsequent book *God and My Neighbour* (1903) drew together his arguments and the rebuttals he published in the *Clarion* during the debate. Blatchford denied the accusation of infidelity levelled at him, arguing that a truly Christian

country would not allow the poverty and suffering evident in Britain in the early twentieth century.

76. *Irwell*: The River Irwell is one of two rivers that run through Manchester, the other being the River Medlock. Both rivers were polluted through the dumping of human and industrial waste over the course of the nineteenth century and the rapid growth of urban and industrial Manchester. The opening of the Manchester Ship Canal in 1894, which developed Manchester and Salford as trading ports, added to the levels of pollution. It was not until the mid-twentieth century that efforts were made to clean the rivers. In 1907 it would have been impossible for fish to survive in the water and for people on the riverbank to see the bottom of the river.

77. *in wavering morrice*: John Milton's (1608–74) *Comus (A Mask Presented at Ludlow Castle, 1634)*, a celebration of chastity as Comus attempts to force the Lady into sensual pleasures. Here, lovers join together in dance; 'morrice' usually spelled Morris, is a traditional English folk dance. It is unlikely that Blatchford, who recorded a conversation with W. T. Stead on the joys of physical love, is referring to the poem as a criticism of dance and pleasure, but rather as an image of the fish moving away from the centre reminiscent of Morris dancing.

78. *L.S.D.*: shorthand for pre-decimal British currency, meaning pounds, shillings and pence. The abbreviation stands for the Latin *librae, solidi, denarii*, referring to Roman currency. *Librae* was a Roman pound, *solidi* was a gold coin worth twenty-five denarii, and *denarius*, the singular form of *denarii*, was a silver coin worth ten asses. Fry is asserting the disparity between genius and money and the importance of respect and honour.

79. *James Watt ... Beethoven*: James Watt (1736–1819), engineer and scientist who invented the condenser, which made steam engines more efficient; Christopher Columbus (1451–1506), explorer and discoverer of the 'New World'; Sir Francis Drake, see above, p. 336 n. 54; George Stephenson (1781–1848), railway engineer and inventor of the steam locomotive; Lord Clive, see above, p. 337 n. 68; William Caxton (c. 1415/24–1492), merchant who introduced the printing press to England c. 1476; Rembrandt Harmenszoon van Rijn (1606–69), Dutch painter and etcher; Ludwig van Beethoven (bap. 1770–1827), composer. All had a significant effect on human knowledge, power or culture through working in areas they were interested in and enthused by, rather than for monetary reward.

80. *Gold ... love*: Algernon Charles Swinburne (1837–1909), poet and literary reviewer. Swinburne's short poem of 1878 sets out the worthlessness of gold in relation to human pleasures and emotions.

81. *Bruno ... Darwin*: Giordano Bruno (1548–1600), mathematician and astronomer executed for heresy because of his cosmological theories; Galileo Galilei (1564–1642), physicist, mathematician and astronomer imprisoned by the Inquisition for his proposition that the earth circled the sun; Nicolaus Copernicus (1473–1543), mathematician and astronomer, the first to propose the earth orbited the sun, whose ideas were followed by Bruno and Galileo; Martin Luther (1483–1546), priest and theologian who was instrumental in the Protestant Reformation; St Paul or Saul of Tarsus (AD c. 3–10–c. 63–7), early Christian missionary; Oliver Cromwell (1599–1658), parliamentarian and Lord Protector of England, Scotland and Ireland; Charles Darwin, see above, p. 337 n. 67. Fry gives a list of people who have been execrated for their ideas or discoveries that opposed the status quo but which eventually came to be accepted as progress.

82. *milkmen ... letters*: Fry is juxtaposing the waste of resources through competition with the efficiency of the nationally owned postal service.

83. *Mr. Atkinson, an American statistician*: Edward Atkinson (1827–1905), American economist and advocate of free trade. It is possible that Blatchford found this argument in Atkinson's pamphlet *Cheap Cotton by Free Labour* (1861), published at the beginning of the American Civil War, which sets out the necessity of production on principles of political economy rather than on the basis of slavery.
84. *professional strap ... proper things*: In *Unsentimental Journeys* (1867), James Greenwood describes the dress of the navvy, including 'leather harness-to wit, the straps that preserved the hitch of their trousers above their mighty calves and the broad brass-buckled belt by which their loins were begirt'.
85. *done by a girl!*: This statement seems to contradict the earlier suggestion, in Chapter VII, that there is equality between the sexes in utopian New England.
86. *Beachy Head*: a chalkstone cliff on the East Sussex coast. The cliff is renowned for suicides, and the loss of Maria near to the cliff may suggest that her fall was not accidental.
87. *Sir Gorell Barnes*: John Gorell Barnes (1848–1913), a judge and an advocate of divorce reform, argued that his work in the Probate, Divorce and Admiralty Division had revealed to him the necessity of radical reform. He was made chair of the 1909 commission on divorce and matrimonial causes, the report of which recommended 'extension of the grounds for divorce to include desertion, cruelty, incurable insanity, habitual drunkenness, and penal servitude for life in commutation of a death sentence'; J. E. G. de Montmorency, 'Barnes, John Gorell, first Baron Gorell (1848–1913)', rev. H. Mooney, *Oxford Dictionary of National Biography* (Oxford: Oxford University Press, 2004), at http://www.oxforddnb.com/view/article/30604 [accessed 17 October 2012].
88. *the Guest House*: echoes of William Morris's Guest House in *News from Nowhere* (1890; London: Penguin, 1993), p. 53: 'There were no windows on the side opposite to the river, but arches below leading into chambers, one of which showed a glimpse of a garden beyond, and above the a long space of wall gaily painted (in fresco, I thought) with similar subjects to those of the frieze outside'.
89. *hermitage*: a wine produced in Valance, France.
90. *Dionysus*: Greek god of wine, fertility and art; also known by the Roman name of Bacchus. Dionysus has two sides to his nature, the provider of the 'mellow joys' Fry describes, and also the bringer of rage and madness. Both Fry and the General acknowledge and celebrate the beneficial uses of alcohol in moderation.
91. *Mr. Faith-and-works*: a theological debate within Christianity that asks if Christians attain salvation through their faith in the existence of God or by works that promote and spread the Christian religion. The General is annoyed by Jorkle's accusation of his being a pagan.
92. *Smite-the-Amalakites*: 1 Samuel 15: Amalekite, a warlike race who were the adversaries of the Hebrews. Samuel's order to Saul to slay them is ignored as Saul and his army bring people and livestock back for sacrifice against God's wishes. This reference shows Jorkle as a dogmatic stickler for rules and standards and unable to imagine the necessity of flexibility or the pleasure of enjoyment, which the General proceeds to elucidate.
93. *Wilt thou ... before death*: 'Hymn to Proserpine: After the Proclamation in Rome of the Christian Faith' (1866) by Algernon C. Swinburne. The narrator is a pagan worshipper of Proserpine, also known as Persephone, who has decided to die with the pagan religion now that Rome has declared Christianity as the state religion. Fry and Storm are worshippers at the 'pagan' alter of enjoyment and bonhomie in the 'state religion' of Puritan capitalism.

94. *American colonies ... replacing his Government*: Mr Fry gives two examples of successful revolution producing a republican democratic state, without descent into anarchy at the point of overthrowing the old order.
95. *Mr. Birrell, Mr. Lloyd George, and Mr. John Burns*: Augustine Birrell (1850–1933), Liberal politician who entered the House of Commons in 1889; David Lloyd George (1863–1945), Liberal politician elected for the first time in 1890; John Burns (1858–1943) was elected as Labour MP for Battersea in 1892 but gradually moved towards the Radical wing of the Liberal Party, taking the post of Minister of the Local Government Board in 1906. Fry mentions these men as successful politicians whose family backgrounds were neither aristocratic nor historically political.
96. *quieter means of establishing Socialism in this country*: Blatchford did not advocate revolutionary socialism but stated in *Merrie England* his belief that '[s]ocialism will not come by means of a *coup*. It will grow up naturally out of our surroundings, and will develop naturally and by degrees. But its growth and its development may be materially helped'; *Clarion*, 10 June 1893, p. 2.
97. *The Earth For All*: possibly a reference to Henry Mayers Hyndman's pamphlet *England For All* (1881), which was published for the inaugural conference of the Democratic Federation in the same year; the group became the SDF in 1884 and the SDP in 1907. Blatchford and Thompson, and others in the *Clarion* group, favoured Hyndman's Tory socialism over what they referred to as the ILP's and Keir Hardie's 'Puritanism'.
98. *Sir William Blackstone, Sir Edward Coke, and Sir Frederick Pollock*: Sir William Blackstone (1723–80), judge; Sir Edward Coke (1552–1634), lawyer and politician; Sir Frederick Pollock (1845–1937), jurist. All three men were influential legal writers.
99. *Accurately ... the King*: 'This allodial property no subject in England had; it being a received, and now undeniable, principle in the law, that all the lands in England are holden mediately or immediately of the king'; W. Blackstone, *Blackstone's Commentaries: With Notes of Reference, to the Constitution and Laws, of the Federal Goernment of the United States; and of the Commonwealth of Virginia* (Philadelphia, PA: William Young Birch, and Abraham Small, 1803), p. 105. Blatchford misspells 'alloidal', which should be 'allodial'.
100. *All lands ... not holden*: 'all lands and tenements are holden either mediately or immediately of the king, for originally all lands and tenements were derived from the crown'; E. Coke, *The First Part of the Institutes of the Laws of England or, A Commentary upon Littleton* (Philadelphia, PA: Robert H. Small, 1853), Sect. 139.
101. *'No absolute ownership ... on record'*: Sir Frederick Pollock, *The Land Laws* (London: Macmillan, 1883), p. 12. This quotation is verbatim.
102. *Fourteen years*: The duration of a patent in the United Kingdom was extended to twenty years under the Patents Act 1977.
103. *The author ... period be the longer*: The 1842 Copyright Act set the copyright period at forty-four years from the date of publication or seven years after the author's death, whichever is the longer period. This act was repealed in 1911 and replaced with the 1911 Copyright Act, which extended the period to life plus fifty years. The term was extended again to life plus seventy years by the implementation of the Duration of Copyright and Rights in Performances Regulations 1995 (SI 1995/3297).
104. *one acre and half a cow*: The slogan 'Three Acres and a Cow' was used by Joseph Chamberlain in the promotion of his Radical Programme and had originated with the land reformers of the 1880s, who argued for equal distribution of land and resources. Fry

explains that socialism would make every citizen the holder of land and means of production rather than 'sharing out' the country to individuals.
105. *Society flourishes ... atoms*: Herbert Spencer (1820–1903) argued that human beings were controlled by immutable natural laws and that the role of the state was to protect individual freedom. Fry's argument is that, rather than society being motivated by antagonism and individualism, a society that recognizes the necessity of harmony and equality will achieve much more.
106. *The Right Honourable H. Campbell-Bannerman, our present Prime Minister*: Sir Henry Campbell-Bannerman (1836–1908) was Liberal Prime Minister between December 1905 and April 1908. He was responsible for moving the Liberal ideology from *laissez-faire* to a more collectivist position.
107. *Marquis of Salisbury, then the Tory Prime Minister*: Robert Gascoyne-Cecil (1830–1903), Prime Minister 1885–6, 1887–92 and 1895–1900. Salisbury argued that working men should not have a preponderance of the vote over other classes. Fry's point in raising these two men is that, despite differences in political ideology and no socialist interests, they both recognized the problem of poverty and want in Britain.
108. *444 persons ... dangerous*: statistics taken from *In Darkest England and the Way Out* (1890), which was published under the name of William Booth (1829–1912), founder of the Salvation Army, although much of it was written by W. T. Stead (1849–1912).
109. *The ordinary conditions ... social system*: Joseph Chamberlain, the Annual Meeting of the Severn Street Adult School, 10 November 1874.
110. *William Smith ... Scotch carpenter*: William Smith (1769–1839); Sir William Herschel (1738–1822); Michael Faraday (1791–1867); Humphry Davy (1778–1855); James Watt and George Stephenson, see above, p. 338 n. 79; Richard Arkwright (1732–92); John Hunter (1728–93). All came from inauspicious backgrounds.
111. *convinced against his will*: Benjamin Franklin (*c*. 1705/6–90), 'A man convinced against his will is of the same opinion still'. No one can have their mind changed for them.
112. *Straight mine eye ... rivers wide*: John Milton's *L'Allegro* (1645), an idyll.
113. *silk purses and sow's ears*: an idiom: 'you cannot make a silk purse out of a sow's ear', meaning that something of quality cannot be made out of inferior materials. The General is lamenting the state of society evidenced by its individuals.
114. *six to four*: betting odds. The General states his belief that there is more chance of meeting an ass, or a cad, or a man on the make than there is of meeting a stranger who is good and true. According to the odds, the General thinks a person is two-and-a-half times more likely to meet a cad than not.
115. *jerrymanders*: also gerrymander, originally it meant to weight an election to a particular party by moving the boundaries to their favour. Jerry-built means something which is poorly made from cheap materials and sold at the highest price. The General sees British society as poorly constructed and not built to last.
116. *a dozen natives*: an oyster reared in British waters. Jorkle's order also suggests the image of the employer consuming the lives of the British workers.
117. *There is a Happy Land*: a hymn by Andrew Young (1807–89) and Leonard P. Breedlove (1803–64). The lyrics continue, '... far, far away'. The marchers sing about heaven while the General adjusts after his return from New Manchester, far, far away from the realities of early twentieth-century London.
118. *hansom*: a horse-drawn carriage used as a method of public transport.
119. *the Rag*: the Army and Navy Club, an exclusive private members club, in Pall Mall, London. The General's destination adds further ambiguity to the ending of the serial: he

has separated himself from the Guinea Pigs and moved down to street level to meet the marchers, but he once again removes himself from the workers, first by entering a hansom cab and then by entering his exclusive club.
120. *Damn*: the bound version ends 'God! God!'
121. News from Nowhere: William Morris's utopian fiction, published in the *Commonweal* January–September 1890. Morris's fiction might have been vague on the issue of how the revolution was effected, but there was a great deal more detail and nuance than Blatchford brought to his utopian story.
122. vipers ... above the rest: from *Sartor Resartus* (1831) by Thomas Carlyle (1795–1881). Here the Professor describes the crowded struggle for individual survival, even at the expense of others. It is a similar image to that given by Fry of the maggots in a grease-pot in Chapter XVI. Both images illustrate the violent struggles of individualism that would be alleviated by the equality of socialism.

McGinnis, 'An Idyll of the Dover Road. A True Story'

1. *Arcady*: meaning poet. The narrator is chiding the churchman for wanting to hear secular songs.
2. *Goats of mine ... among the artintus*: a series of quotations from Theocritus, *The Fifth Idyll*. Comatas and Lacon are two rural peasants who accuse each of stealing from the other, and settle the difference by a battle of pastoral song. The version quoted is the Andrew Lang (1844–1912) translation *Theocritus, Bion and Moschus* (1880). Blatchford replaces 'Lacon' with 'McGinnis' in the accusation, and 'artintus' should be 'arbutus'.
3. *When Britain ... tricks*: a pastiche of the crier's nationalism, making a medley of 'Rule Britannia' (When Britain – first – at heaven's command – arose from out – the azure – main), a mnemonic nursery rhyme about Guy Fawkes (and gun – powder – treason was plot) and the national anthem (confound their knavish – tricks, which should read 'frustrate their knavish tricks').

Potter, 'He Was a Valuable Dog'

1. *chou of chiffon*: a knot of material worn as an ornament; *OED*. The chou in this reference would refer to an ornamentation signifying the occupation of maid or servant.
2. *Murray Hill district*: a wealthy district in Lower Midtown, East Manhattan, New York City. Today it is the area where Grand Central Station, the Chrysler Building and the United Nations are located.

Lyons, 'Little Reggie Writes Home. A Childish Document, Edited'

1. *pads*: cricket pads, protection for the shins when playing cricket.
2. *Alphabet Cake Shop*: possibly meaning the Aerated Bread Company (ABC), which was founded in 1862 and opened the first chain restaurant in the mid-1870s – the exact date is unknown. There were 678 restaurants by 1891, but by the turn of the century the ABC tearooms were facing competition from the J. Lyons chain. See G. Shaw, L. H. Curth and A. Alexander, 'Creating New Spaces of Food Consumption: The Rise of Mass Catering and the Activities of the Aerated Bread Company', in J. Benson and L. Ugolini (eds), *Cultures of Selling: Perspectives on Consumption and Society Since 1700* (Aldershot: Ashgate, 2006), pp. 81–100

3. *some girls and ladies ... dinner-bells and flags*: a demonstration by the Women's Social and Political Movement, formed by Emmeline (1858–1928) and Christabel (1880–1958) Pankhurst in 1903, and renowned for their noisy protests demanding womens' right to vote.

Grayson, 'The Myopian's Muddle'

1. *Coma*: in this context, a reference to the blurring of an object under a microscope due to an aberration in the lens.
2. *Myopians*: Myopia is a condition of the eye that prevents distant objects from being seen clearly. The naming of these people suggests that there is no long-term vision for their lives or society.
3. *Thews and sinews*: Thews and sinews in this context refer to the bodily vigour and physical strength of the individual, as if the person consists of muscles or tendons alone. Thew is also an archaic term for a slave or thrall and an apparatus of punishment; *OED*.
4. *yclpet*: to name.

Grayson, 'A Dead Man's Story'

1. *self-murder*: suicide. The act of taking one's own life was deemed a criminal offence in Britain based on Biblical teaching, and 'self-murder' was the legal term for suicide. The act of attempted suicide was criminalized in 1854. While some of the penalties against suicide were lifted during the nineteenth century – burial only in unconsecrated ground was revoked in 1823, burial at night repealed in 1882, and the restrictions on inheriting from suicides removed in 1870 – there was still a cultural stigma attached to suicide. Suicide or attempted suicide was only decriminalized in Britain with the passing of the Suicide Act in 1961.
2. *the make-weight or 'jockey'*: a piece of bread added to a small loaf to make the correct weight. The girl has dropped this small piece of bread, and the narrator is accused of trying to steal it.

Lyons, 'My Lady's Chariot'

1. *teal and woodcock ... Bishops Bury Hall*: Smithers is a poacher, and the narrator is buying stolen goods in the form of game birds caught on the fictional aristocrat's land.
2. *anderions*: andirons, sometimes called 'fire-dogs', are usually a pair of elongated 'H'-shaped, often ornamental, iron bars to support burning wood in a fireplace; *OED*.

Everard, 'The Eternal Feminine'

1. *St. Stephen's*: St Stephen's Hall, on the site of the Royal Chapel where the House of Commons sat until 1834, when the chapel was destroyed by fire.
2. *the shrieking sisterhood*: a derogatory term for women demanding suffrage. The origin of the term is a cartoon published in *Punch* 17 January 1906 entitled 'The Shrieking Sister'.
3. *Rome was saved by the cackling of her geese*: The cackling of geese woke sleeping Roman soldiers when Rome was attacked by Gauls.
4. *exults over a Boer War ... foot the bill*: The successes of the British Army in South Africa during the Second Boer War (1899–1902) were celebrated with excessive exuberance, but the £200 million cost to the country was not so well received.

5. *Chinese Slavery*: After the Second Boer War had ended, British companies were importing indentured Chinese labour, who were paid considerably less than British workers would have expected to receive.
6. *Manchester school*: advocates of free trade, opponents of war and imperialism, and the protection of consensual contract between peoples.
7. *Stirling Burghs*: a United Kingdom parliamentary constituency in Scotland, which, until 1918, consisted of Stirling, Dunfermline, Inverkeithing and Culross.
8. *Herbert Spencer ... Or Machiavelli*: Herbert Spencer, see above, p. 341 n. 105; Niccolò Machiavelli (1469–1527), author of *The Prince*, which showed pragmatic politics based on cunning and duplicity.

Clarke, 'The Red Flag'

1. *Glimpses into the Abyss*: Mary Higgs (1854–1937) published *Glimpses into the Abyss* in 1906, having already published *Five Days and Five Nights as a Tramp among Tramps* in 1904 under the pseudonym 'A Lady'. Her investigative work – following that of James Greenwood (bap. 1835–1927), author of *A Night in the Workhouse* published in the *Pall Mall Gazette* in 1866, and Jack London (John Griffith, 1876–1916), author of *The People of the Abyss* (1903) – involved dressing up as a tramp to report on the experience of the female tramp. She was influential in the Vagrancy Reform Society and was awarded an OBE for her work in 1937. *Glimpses into the Abyss* contains *Five Days ... as a Tramp*, and Clarke's fictional account of the experiences of Mrs Wilkinson and May very closely resembles the real accounts of Mary Higgs.
2. *"tay"*: tea. One of the signifiers of working-class status is the names given to the meals of the day: middle- and upper-class families were likely to refer to the meals of the day as breakfast, lunch or luncheon, dinner and supper, with high tea inserted between lunch and dinner in some circles; working-class families would often use the terms breakfast, dinner and tea for the morning, noon and evening meals, with regional variations on the midday meal if eaten away from the home, for instance, bagging in Lancashire, snap in Nottinghamshire and take-out in north-eastern England.
3. *Christian temples ... Salvation Army captain*: A citadel was the name for the building where members of the Salvation Army would gather for religious services. The Salvation Army was a Christian Methodist movement founded in 1865 by William (1829–1912) and Catherine (1829–90) Booth in Whitechapel, London. Members of the group were organized in a hierarchical fashion similar to that of the army, and men and women were sent into urban slums to convert the inhabitants to Christianity. There was also some relief work carried out to alleviate some of the sufferings of poverty, but generally the socialist movement was critical of the Salvation Army for elevating the soul above the body's material sufferings and therefore distracting the poor from working towards social, political and economic change. See, for instance, the exchange between Henry Hyndman and John Law [Margaret Harkness] in *Justice*, March 1888, after the publication of her novel *Captain Lobe: a Story of the Salvation Army* (1888; republished in 1890 under the title *In Darkest London*).
4. *lodging-houses*: The common lodging house, also known as a doss house or kip house, was a private house where a bed – or a shared bed – could be bought for between four and sixpence a night.
5. *gay girls*: a euphemism for prostitutes and morally 'loose' women.

6. *No tick here*: a humorous play on words, as 'tick' also means to defer payment. To have something 'on tick' is to have or consume goods with the promise to pay sometime in the future. Nobody stays in the lodging house without paying first.
7. *in the wars*: a Lancashire phrase meaning something that looks abused, broken or battered; may refer to both inanimate objects and human beings.
8. *St Crispin*: the patron saint of shoemakers.
9. *The mender of shoes ... reader of books*: There is a history of association between shoemakers and literacy, often leading to radicalism. George Fox (1621–91) founder of the Quakers, was apprenticed to a shoemaker; Thomas Cooper (1805–92), the Chartist, also trained as a shoemaker. See A. McShane, '"Ne sutor ultra crepidam": Political Cobblers and Broadside Ballads in Late Seventeenth-Century England', in P. Fumerton, A. Guerrini and K. McAbee, *Ballads and Broadsides in Britain, 1500–1800* (Farnham: Ashgate, 2010), pp. 207–28.
10. *Prometheus Unbound*: Percy Bysshe Shelley's (1792–1822) four-part lyrical drama published in 1820. The work has been described as 'Shelley's most consistently optimistic expression of the revolutionary purpose of writing'; A. Leighton, *Shelley and the Sublime* (Cambridge: Cambridge University Press, 1984), p. 73. The quotation is from Act I and should read: 'Ione: And who are those with hydra tresses / And iron wings that climb the wind, / Whom the frowning God represses / Like vapours steaming up behind, / Clanging loud, an endless crowd – / Panthea: These are Jove's tempest-walking hounds, / Whom he gluts with groans and blood, / When charioted on sulphurous cloud / He bursts Heaven's bounds'.
11. *With their trousers out behind*: The cobbler's wife is reminding him that, while the trades may give the workers time to think and talk, there is little money to be made by either trade or talk. Hence the reference to ragged clothing – the seat of cobblers' trousers being worn out.
12. *Burns too, and Byron*: Robert Burns (1759–96), son of an Ayrshire gardener and tenant farmer; Burns was known as the ploughman poet and was the first to popularize vernacular poetry. His poetry was popular with both Chartists and the later socialists. His poem 'A Man's a Man for a' That' was a favourite with British socialists for its egalitarian sentiment. 'The Beggars Cantata', also known as 'The Song of the Jolly Beggars', are six songs by the beggars at a revel. The six songs are by the old soldier, his woman, a tinker, a fiddler, a pickpocket and a fool, celebrating the abandonment and lively existence of those at the very bottom of society. George Gordon, Lord Byron (1788–1824), aristocratic poet and friend of Percy Shelley.
13. *bottom dogs*: as opposed to the 'top dogs', meaning the successful and powerful. Also, possibly, a reference to Robert Blatchford's *Not Guilty: A Defence of the Bottom Dog* (1906).
14. *moucher*: sometimes 'moochers', people who survive without working by battening on to others; the professionally unemployed. The *OED* defines 'moucher' as one who eats voraciously, and it is used in this sense as one who devours the money of another.
15. *man's inhumanity to man*: Robert Burns, 'Man was Made to Mourn, a Dirge', stanza vii; 'And Man, whose heav'n-erected facce, / The smiles of love adorn, / Man's inhumanity to Man / Makes countless thousands mourn!'
16. *'Venice Preserved' – Otway's play*: Thomas Otway's (1652–85) *Venice Preserved* was first staged in 1682. The play, a tragedy, creates a web of intrigue and deceit between high and low members of society, including noblemen, courtesans and soldiers. The cobbler's point here, and on Charles II, is that the working classes are condemned for doing what the upper classes do without censure.

17. *gay*: in this context meaning wanton, lewd, lascivious; *OED*.
18. *I'm thinking ... above their betters*: *Venice Preserved*, Act I, scene i. The first two lines are spoken by Pierre Jaffier's friend, the rest by Jaffier, husband of Belvidera, a noblewoman.
19. *Oliver Goldsmith*: (*c.* 1728–74), Anglo-Irish poet and playwright, son of the curate at Kilkenny West. *The Deserted Village* was published in 1770 and is an elegy on the destruction of an ancient fictional village he named Auburn.
20. *Byron's satire ... precautious benches*: Byron's long and unfinished poem *Don Juan*; the first canto was finished in 1818 and the last was written in 1823. Byron hoped the poem would be remembered as a criticism of the state and its abuses, but it became notorious for its bawdy comedy, hence the cobbler's differentiation between 'ladies' and 'women' readers. The quotation is taken from stanza lxiii of canto xvi.
21. *It is all a mystery... as before*: *Don Juan*, canto v, stanza xxxix.
22. *"Swell"*: The *OED* defines the word as a description of someone dressed handsomely, suggesting distinction, but the quotation marks around the word in this context suggest someone dressing to suggest a higher social station than they inhabit in reality. See also the character of Linnis in Siddle's 'A Stormy Wooing' in *Teddy Ashton's Weekly Fellowship* in this volume.
23. *cabalists ... Wheel of Fate*: The Cabala is the Jewish tradition of interpreting the Old Testament; *OED*. The wheel of fate is a concept explaining the randomness of life, as the goddess Fortune spins the wheel to decide a person's fate. Clarke became interested in spiritualism and the afterlife after the death of his first wife, Lavinia (Vinnie).
24. *Though the future ... slumberless head*: *Prometheus Unbound*, Act I.
25. *Nil desperandum*: do not despair.
26. *cig.*: cigarette. The popularity of cigarettes over pipe smoking increased significantly in the early years of the twentieth century as the mechanization of manufacture made the product strong and cheap, and the popularity of the match meant the cigarette could be smoked anywhere.
27. *Morecambe*: a Lancashire seaside town four miles from the county town of Lancaster and forty-one miles from Blackpool. The town was developed as a seaside resort after the railway had made the village of Poulton-le-Sands popular with bathers. While Blackpool was primarily associated with tourism from the Lancashire cotton mills, Morecambe had better railway connections to Yorkshire and Scotland and so drew its tourism from these areas.
28. *Piecer*: usually children employed in the cotton factories who would repair broken threads. The work was arduous and poorly paid: a little piecer in Bolton in 1906 would earn 10*s.* 7*d.*, while the spinner in charge of the machine would earn 45*s* 9*d*. Jim Campbell's complaint is that he was unable to progress from this occupation usually carried out by children.
29. *Life is all a variorum*: Robert Burns, 'Beggar's Cantato'.
30. *terrible trade unionists ... leading spirits*: Clarke's attempt to begin a piecers' union in Bolton, with J. R. Clynes and James Haslem, had been given the same reaction by the Bolton spinners.
31. *cops*: the conical ball of thread wound onto a spindle or tube in the spinning machine; *OED*.
32. *Not only ... parting with brass*: Clarke expressed his criticism of trade unionism in *The Effects of the Factory System*, ed. P. Salveson (Littleborough: George Kelsall, 1989), p. 143: 'though trade unionism has been a fairly good shield, it is but a narrow one; and, further, though the workers have often used it for purposes aggressive as well as defensive, it has never been anything but a shield, never a sword'.
33. *listed*: enlisted in the army.

34. *quoting Shelley ... Victory*: *Prometheus Unbound*, Act IV, scene i.
35. *the party in Scripter*: The legend of the Wandering Jew – a homeowner who refused to let Christ rest at his door while carrying the cross to his crucifixion at Calvery and was cursed to roam the earth until Christ's return – is a Christian legend rather than biblical story. Scholars have pointed to Matthew 16:28, 'Truly I tell you, some who are standing here will not taste death before they see the Son of Man coming in his kingdom', or to the story of Cain in Genesis as possible origins for the story, but there is no figure in the Bible similar to that of the Wandering Jew.
36. *the tramp-ward skilly an' stone-breakin'*: The original 1834 Poor Law Amendment Act had no provision for the houseless poor, but a regulation was added in 1837 which stated that the workhouse must give food and shelter to the destitute in return for a certain amount of work, usually picking oakum or stone-breaking. The food was usually a lump of bread and a bowl of gruel, which was also referred to as 'skilly'. The tramp ward, also known as the casual ward or the 'spike', was a separate building from the main workhouse because it was thought that vagrants would be more likely to carry disease.
37. *togs*: clothes.
38. *Father O'Flynn*: a popular song in the Irish dialect celebrating the virtues of 'Father O'Flynn' by Alfred Perceval Graves. The character is remembered by Bloom in James Joyce's (1882–1941) *Ulysses* (1922), and the poem was included in W. B. Yeats's (1865–1939) *A Book of Irish Verse* (1895).
39. *Sandunes, near Brightpool*: probably Lytham, a seaside town on the Lancashire coast roughly eight miles south of Blackpool ('Brightpool'). Clarke regularly changed the names of Lancashire towns – for instance, he would refer to Bolton as 'Spindletown' in reference to the proliferation of cotton mills in the town. The 'swell' (see above, p. 346 n. 22) has already named Morecambe as the seaside town where Mr Langdon lives, but Morecambe is not known for its dunes, as Lytham is, and the forty-one-mile distance between Morecambe and Blackpool is 'near' only relative to the rest of Lancashire. Chapter IX locates Langdon's home on 'the road from Friartown [Preston], by way of Leythorpe-on-the-Sea [Lytham-St.Annes], to Brightpool [Blackpool].'
40. *Solomon ... concubines*: 1 Kings 11:3: 'And he had seven hundred wives, princesses, and three hundred concubines: and his wives turned away his heart'.
41. *suicide had been left hanging ... police came*: This appears to have been a common belief, and there are records of jurors at inquests asking why bodies found hanging were not first cut down before the discoverers left to inform the police. In the case of a man who found his mother-in-law hanging in 1876, 'the coroner observed that it was a prevailing belief, to which he did not subscribe, that when a dead body was found, it was best to leave it where it was until the police or someone had seen it'; V. Bailey, *This Rash Act: Suicide across the Life Cycle in the Victorian City* (Stanford, CA: Stanford University Press, 1998), p. 42. For the history of suicide as a criminal act, see above, p. 343 n. 1.
42. *garter ... thick string*: a band worn around the leg to prevent a stocking falling down; *OED*. The woman was unable to afford anything delicate or rubberized, and so her poverty provided the means for suicide.
43. *Peace, peace ... strife*: *Adonais, An Elegy on the Death* (1821), stanza xxxix; an elegy for John Keats (1795–1821) where Shelley claims Keats's death was caused by a bad review.
44. *Whence are we ... to sorrow*: *Adonais*, stanza xxi.
45. *"The Sensitive Plant" ... mockery*: Shelley, 'The Sensitive Plant' (1820), conclusion, ll. 128–9.

46. *Light after Darkness ... with Me*: 'Light after Darkness', words composed by Frances Ridley Havergal (1836–79) and music by Ira David Sankey (1840–1908); 'Jesus, Lover of my Soul', words composed in 1740 by Charles Wesley (1707–88), music in 1879 by Joseph Parry (1841–1903); 'Lead, Kindly Light', words composed in 1833, by John Henry Newman (1801–90) and music in 1865 by Edward Bickersteth, Jr (1825–1906); 'Abide with Me', words composed in 1847 by Henry F. Lyte (1793–1847), music in 1861 by William H. Monk (1823–89). The following extracts are from each of the last three hymns respectively.
47. *nightly pitch their moving tent*: a line from the hymn 'Forever with the Lord' (1835) by James Montgomery (1771–1854), set to the traditional English melody 'Terra Beta': 'Here in the body pent, / Absent from Him I roam, / Yet nightly pitch my moving tent / A day's march nearer home'.
48. *tramp wards ... dosshouses*: see above, p. 344 n. 3.
49. *the touch ... voice that is still*: 'Break, Break, Break' (1834) by Alfred Lord Tennyson (1809–92), one of the mourning poems for Arthur Hallam.
50. *shekels*: an ancient unit of currency. Doolan is wishing for money of any kind.
51. *The Cruiskeen Lawn*: a traditional Irish song that celebrates life and alcohol: 'And when grim death appears, after few but happy years, / And tells me my glass is run; / I'll say, begone, you slave, for great Bacchus gives us leave / To drink another cruiskeen lawn'. The original Gaelic is cruiscín lán, meaning a little jugful.
52. *Colborough*: possibly a reference to Tipton-on-the-Hill, next to Colborough Hill to the east of Leicester.
53. *stoving*: Clothes thought to be infested with fleas or other insects were hung in a room that would be heated and filled with sulphur to kill the infestation. The *Lancet* for 1841–2 records attempts to fumigate human beings in a similar way, but with fatal consequences.
54. *Churcham*: probably a reference to the Fylde workhouse at Medlar-with-Wesham, which was begun in 1903 and opened in 1907. Readers would note the irony of Jim (and workers generally) being forced to take work building the workhouses that caused them such suffering.
55. *not the only tenants ... by dozens!*: The bed is infested with fleas, ticks and bed bugs.
56. *"stoved"*: see above, n. 53.
57. *the workhouse committee*: The Visiting Committee was made up of members of the Board of Guardians – annually elected members who were ratepayers of £25 per year or members given a post on the Board through their work as magistrates – who administered the Poor Law for their parish. The Visiting Committee would visit the workhouse weekly to check on the running of the establishment and to hear any complaints.
58. *stay two nights ... oakum*: The requirement for inmates of the casual or tramp wards to work for the cost of their food and shelter meant that by the time they had completed the required amount of work, there was little time other than to make their way to the next workhouse. The Casual Poor Act of 1882 required casual inmates to stay two nights, working throughout the day in between, and to leave at 9 am after the second night, which would allow time to find employment that day.
59. *bathing flannel*: a woollen cloth, squares of which were used for washing the body or general cleaning. The cloth is neither substantial enough to be warm nor large enough to be modest.
60. *Jane*: There is no indication of who 'Jane' is, so the name is presumably either a mistake or a misprint for 'Lucy'.

61. *scarlet fever ... croup*: scarlet fever, a fever that produces a reddening of the skin; pneumonia, inflammation of the lung; croup, a deadly inflammation of the throat and trachea.
62. *Rock of Ages*: written by Augustus Monatgue Toplady (1740–78). He published the first verse in the *Gospel Magazine*, which he edited, in 1775 and the completed hymn in 1776. It was set to music in 1830 by Thomas Hastings (1784–1872) and became one of the most popular British hymns.
63. *ironclad*: a wooden warship clad in iron. Advances in naval ordnance in the mid-nineteenth century made the construction of warships from stronger material than wood a necessity. There had been experiments with the cladding of ships with metal for centuries, but the first successful design was produced by France and demonstrated in *La Gloire*, 1860.
64. *Pilgrims of the night*: an English hymn with words by Frederick William Faber (1814–63), first published in 1854, and often sung to Henry Thomas Smart's (1813–79) composition 'Pilgrims' (1868). The hymn is often known by its first line, 'Hark! hark, my soul! Angelic songs are swelling'.
65. *oakum picking*: oakum picking, or tow picking, was an occupation prisoners and workhouse inmates were set. Picking oakum meant either the separation of the woody fibres of tow from the finer fibres of hemp or flax, or the unravelling of old hemp rope; *OED*. The prepared fibre was then used for spinning or for the repair of wooden ships.
66. *electric tram as well as railway*: The Blackpool, St Annes and Lytham Tramways Company ran gas-traction trams between Blackpool and Lytham from 1896 until 1903, when the route was converted to electricity. The last tram ran in 1937.
67. *the course*: the Royal Lytham and St Annes Golf Club. The prestigious club was founded in 1886 and has hosted ten Open Championships (the latest in 2012) and two Ryder Cup tournaments. Mr Langdon is a member of a very exclusive club.
68. *Sims Reeves*: John Sims Reeves (1818–1900), famous English tenor who married his twenty-two-year-old student Lucy Richard after his wife's death in 1895. His *ONDB* entry does not mention offspring from this marriage.
69. *Blondin*: French tightrope walker, born Jean-François Gravelet (1824–97), married his nurse, Katherine James (1864/5–1901), in 1895, when he was seventy-one and she twenty-nine/thirty. She had nursed him after he injured his back performing at the Crystal Palace. The *ONDB* does not mention offspring from this marriage, either.
70. *navvy*: see above, p. 336 n. 65.
71. *River Ripple*: presumably the River Ribble.
72. *the priest and the Levite of old*: the parable of the Good Samaritan, Luke 10:30–7. The priest and the Levite walked past the beaten traveller as the Christian worshippers passed the starving Jim Campbell. The spirit of Christianity in Edwardian England is to be found not in the churches but in the socialist movement.
73. *righteousness of getting on*: see Law [Harkness], 'The Gospel of Getting On', *To-Day*, Volume 1.
74. *Church ... humbug*: Clarke, like many socialists – and Chartists before them – differentiated between the spirit of Christianity and the attitudes and practices of the Church of England. He had a strong belief in spiritualism and the afterlife, wrote extensively on life after death (including *The Eternal Question* (1899) and his fiction *With Ghostly Eyes* (1899)), and believed in reincarnation and in God as a 'vitalising intelligence'. His biographer describes him as having 'had no time at all for religious "humbug" and veered towards anticlericalism'; Salveson, *Lancashire's Romantic Radical*, p. 38.

75. *"Trilby" hat*: a soft felt hat with a narrow brim and indented crown; *OED*. The hat is named after the eponymous character of George Du Maurier's (1834–96) phenomenally popular novel published in 1894.
76. *The People's Flag ... flying here*: Jim Connell (1852–1929), a member of the SDF, regularly published poetry in *Justice*, the official paper of the group. 'The Red Flag' was published in the issue of 21 December 1889. Connell later complained about his words being sung to the traditional German tune 'Tannenbaum': 'There is only one air which suits the words of *"The Red Flag"*, and that is the one that I hummed as I wrote it. I mean *"The White Cockade"*. I mean moreover the original version known to everybody in Ireland fifty years ago. Since then some fool has altered it by introducing minor notes into it, until it is now nearly a jig. This latter version is the one on sale in music shops today, and it does not, of course, suit my words. I suppose this explains why Adolphe Smith Headingley induced people to sing *"The Red Flag"* to the air of *"Maryland"* [an American Confederate song set to the tune of 'Tannenbaum'] ... Every time the song is sung to *"Maryland"* the words are murdered'; Jim Connell, 'How I Wrote "The Red Flag"', *The Call*, 6 May 1920.
77. *Salvation Army*: see above, p. 344 n. 2. The Salvation Army flag is red with a yellow star at the centre.
78. *Churchman ... Nonconformist ... agnostic*: Churchman, a member of the official Church of England; Nonconformist, a member of one of the Dissenting sects of Protestant Christianity in England, for instance, Methodist, Congregationalist, Quaker, etc.; agnostic, one who believes in the material because nothing can be known about the immaterial. The socialist lecturer does not declare his acceptance of atheism, i.e. one who denies the existence of God.
79. *Lord Salisbury ... selfish*: In 1894 Salisbury had led a majority of peers in insisting that employers should still be able to 'contract out' of the statutory Workmen's Compensation Benefits in the Employer's Liability Bill. He had accused trade unionism of being 'a cruel organisation' for opposing this 'contracting out' after fierce campaigning by the Trade Union Congress. Salisbury sees the trade unions as selfish for wishing to place restrictions on employers; Joe sees them as selfish for not allowing the same benefits of collective action for workers.
80. *gasometer*: a large tank or reservoir for storing gas; *OED*. The use of the image is apt, not only to conjure up an image of a large receptacle for the butter, but also a reminder that there were some utilities that were already municipally owned and organized. This was known colloquially as 'gas-and-water-socialism'.
81. *"puffer"*: a childish name for a train.
82. *coll*: The *OED* defines one use of the word 'coll' as an embrace around the neck. This use may suggest a feeling of entrapment by indicating an irremovable harness around the necks of the working class.
83. *world without end, Amen*: the final line of the Catholic prayer Glory Be. The prayer celebrates the everlasting glory of God: 'Glory be to the Father, and to the Son, and to the Holy Spirit, as it was in the beginning, is now, and ever shall be, world without end. Amen'. The caretaker, though, is referring to the conservative teachings of the Christian church, which persuades followers of the everlasting form of social order that benefits the rich at the expense of the poor and offers happiness for some only after death.
84. *The man that got the idea ... aggrandisement*: as Langdon freely admits in Chapter IX.
85. *Whack in ... enjoy himself*: The caretaker is encouraging Jim to begin eating and satisfy his hunger.

86. *Two hours' pay for the man – eight hours to the master*: Marxist economics. In *Das Kapital*, Volume 1 (1867), Marx calculated that the length of the working day and the intensity of output through the industrialization of production meant that the portion of the day spent by the worker recouping enough wages to subsist was far exceeded by the surplus value taken by the capitalist. Clarke's socialism was wide-ranging and liable to change (although he did not cease to adhere to some form of socialist thought), and this fiction was produced at a period when he was more open to the theories of Marx.
87. *Jew's harp*: a Jews' harp, a metal instrument played in the mouth by using the tongue. The association with the Jewish faith is only made in England, but the *OED* conjectures it may have been sold by Jewish traders. The caretaker's description of the Nonconformist Christian is one who does not practice Christ's teachings but who is concerned with selfish notions of personal salvation and will be receive a lesser reward than that promised through the church's teachings.
88. *Labour Church*: *Labour Church*: The Labour Church was founded in Manchester in 1891 by John Trevor (1855–1930) after he heard a speech by Ben Tillett criticizing the abandonment of the working classes by the existing churches. The Labour Church reached its peak in 1895 with fifty-four churches, and it was closely associated with the ILP. Trevor began publishing the movement's periodical, the *Labour Prophet*, in 1892. Trevor was not a strong leader, and there was a division in attitude as to what role the Labour Church had in the British socialist movement. As Leonard Smith notes, 'The reason for the decline of the movement is not altogether clear, but suggestions have included the internal struggles between those, like Trevor, who regarded it as essentially concerned with the personal regeneration of Labour supporters, and those, like Fred Brocklehurst, its second General Secretary, a Cambridge graduate and former Anglican ordinand, who saw it as little more than an extension of the ILP's electoral machine'; 'Religion and the ILP', in D. James, T. Jowitt and K. Laybourne (eds), *The Centennial History of the Independent Labour Party* (Halifax: Ryburn, 1992), pp. 259–276, on pp. 260–1.
89. *I.L.P. ... religion as a sop*: The ILP took an ethical approach to socialism, which was projected through the lens of Nonconformity; James Keir Hardie and Katherine Bruce Glasier were Congregationalists, Katherine's husband, John Bruce Glasier, was a Calvinist, and John Trevor – the founder of the Labour Church in 1891 – was a Unitarian. Clarke's rejection of organized religion leads him to similarly reject organized worship through socialism. Historians have lately critiqued the notion of religion as a conservative weight on working-class radicalism that needed to be shrugged off, instead viewing Nonconformity as providing an atmosphere of dissent that reaches the material as well as the spiritual world. Mark Bevir argues, 'The Labour Church was less a part of a process of secularization than an expression of ... ethical socialism'; *The Making of British Socialism* (Princeton, NJ and Oxford: Princeton University Press, 2011), p. 280.
90. *Mrs. Wilkinson*: a mistake in either Clarke's writing or the typesetting. Jim is searching for his mother, Mrs Campbell, and at this point he is unaware that she has shared a tramp ward berth with Mrs Wilkinson and May.
91. *been through the mill*: a phrase meaning someone who has had troubles in their life. The original meaning of being crushed by the mill-stones that grind flour has a further relevance in Lancashire, with its proliferation of cotton mills, their harsh working regimes and the number of accidents caused by tiredness or unfenced machinery.
92. *great Socialistic writer ... path to progress*: Blatchford's *God and my Neighbour* (1903); see above, pp. 337–8 n. 75.

93. *cycling club ... places of Britain*: Clarion cycling clubs were originally founded by *Clarion* readers to take the periodical and its pamphlets across the local countryside and spread socialist ideas. The clubs grew in popularity and spread across the country; see the General Introduction.
94. *God scrape their selfish souls*: a reference to Psalm 106:15, where God sent food to the Israelites, who had begun to take God's kindness for granted, but with the food He also sent 'leanness'. Their souls were 'scraped', or wasted away. Blythe hopes God will punish those workers who have caused the bodily 'leanness' of their fellow workers.
95. *Independent Labour Party ... Trade Unionism*: see above, p. 346 n. 32 for Clarke's attitude to trade unions.
96. *antagonistic ... election times*: The antagonism between the executives of the ILP and SDF was not always drawn through to their membership, and Clarke was joint SDF/ILP candidate for Rochdale in the 1900 general election.
97. *Ben Brierley*: (1825–96), dialect author famous for his character 'Ab-o'th'-Yate' and his Lancashire sketches.
98. *infernal machine*: an explosive device made to look like something harmless. Fordham is manipulating the more extreme members of socialism for his own selfish and greedy ends. Clarke, like H. J. Bramsbury in his serial 'A Working Class Tragedy' in Volume 1, is positioning the originators of violence carried out in the name of socialism with individuals who have ulterior motives and are not true socialists.
99. *Birmingham police ... police themselves*: the Walsall Anarchists, who were sentenced to prison under the Explosives Act in 1892 on the instigation of Auguste Coulon, who was suspected of being a police spy.
100. *Jim rejoiced ... his own sphere*: Unlike some of the more sentimentalized stories of apparently inter-class relationships, Jim does not find out he is unexpectedly the true offspring of a higher class. Instead, he is relieved that the woman he loves, and who he has assumed is of a higher class than him, is revealed to be a member of his own class.
101. *many more tramp journeys than I*: Mary Higgs published *A Tramp among Tramps* (1904), *The Tramp Ward* (1904), *Three Nights in Women's Lodging Houses* (1905), *London Investigations* (1905) and *Glimpses into the Abyss* (1906). During the investigations for *A Tramp among Tramps* and *The Tramp Ward* she was accompanied by 'a friend'.
102. *Board of Guardians*: local ratepayers who were responsible for the running of the workhouse.
103. *twit*: a light censure or taunt; *OED*.
104. *old Pendle*: Pendle Hill, Lancashire, a hill on the east side of Lancashire surrounded by the towns of Colne, Nelson, Burnley and Clitheroe. The area is most famous for the Pendle witches, twelve people (ten women and two men) who were tried and executed during the Lancashire witch trials of 1612.
105. *Harrison Ainsworth's romance*: Harrison Ainsworth (1805–82) was a solicitor-turned-novelist who wrote many novels based on real-life events. *The Lancashire Witches* was published in 1848.
106. *spirit-kettles*: a kettle that can be used outdoors. Set on a stand, the kettle is heated by a reservoir of alcohol (spirit) under the kettle.
107. *The trouble is always with us*: a re-phrasing of Matthew 26:11: 'For ye have the poor always with you; but me ye have not always'.
108. *Tennyson ... creation moves*: the final lines of *In Memoriam* (1850) by Alfred, Lord Tennyson, 'That God, which ever lives and loves, / One God, one law, one element, / And one far-off divine event, / To which the whole creation moves'.

109. *too many in the world*: a paraphrase of 'Father Time's' suicide note, 'Done because we are to menny', after he murdered his half-siblings in Thomas Hardy's *Jude the Obscure* (1895). While 'Father Time' imagines he will relieve the poverty of his father and common-law stepmother by removing the burden of their children, the tramp couple take a similar view of their place in society. They do not consider that their poverty is caused by wealth distribution rather than overpopulation.
110. *compensation*: The Workmen's Compensation Acts of 1897 and 1906 had allowed for compensation claims by workmen for all injuries caused at work unless caused by serious or wilful misconduct. Section 2.1. of the 1906 Act placed a statutory time limit of six months after the accident in which a claim should be made; 'as soon as practicable after the happening thereof and before the workman has voluntarily left the employment in which he was injured'. The success of the man's claim lay with his knowledge of his entitlement of the law, and his employer's voluntary aid until the time limit had passed ensured the workman did not seek to find information about his employment rights.
111. *Whitsuntide*: The seventh Sunday after Easter, Whitsun is celebrated across the northwest of England with parades and Whitsun Walks to herald the beginning of summer. The history of the Whitsun holiday goes back to feudal society when the lord would allow his serfs time away from work.
112. *As a man sows*: that shall he also reap; Galatians 6:7.
113. *go 'sick' for me*: May has arranged for another weaver to take her place while she is away.
114. *Cottage Homes system*: This was an alternative system to raising children in workhouses. The children would be located to purpose-built cottages, often set out around a 'village' green, where they would be raised by foster parents in 'families' of up to thirty children. The cottage system was growing in popularity in the early years of the twentieth century, and by 1903 it had twenty-five sites across the country, including Hornchurch, Bolton, Gateshead and Swansea. The 'villages' would have a school and lessons for the children in trades that would make them employable when they left. Jim's support for the system suggests his sympathy for the lives of the children and for their prospects as adults. Critics, however, argued that by removing children from towns and cities, they were not being prepared for life after they left the system.
115. *provender*: food, provisions; OED.
116. *England Arise*: by Edward Carpenter (1824–1929). Subtitled 'A Socialist Marching Song' and published in 1886, it was written specifically for singing at socialist meetings. The song looks forward to a new life and opens with the line 'England, arise! The long, long night is over'. No record has been found for the song 'For all the Little Children'.

Hartley, 'The Man in the Street. High Rates, Officialism and Socialism'

1. *three-cornered fights*: an election contest with three candidates from different parties. Mr Blank is noticing that Labour candidates are becoming a regular part of elections and are affecting the previous bi-partite divide of electors between Liberal and Conservative parties.
2. *we are all Socialists now*: a comment made by Sir William Harcourt (1827–1904), Liberal politician speaking in the House of Commons on the Labourers' Allottments Bill of 1887.

Smith, 'Socialist Red'

1. *massive gold albert*: An Albert chain is a watch chain with a t-bar that would be tucked into a button hole, from which would hang another length of chain to which charms would be attached.
2. *hotel boots*: the servant in a hotel who cleans guests' boots; *OED*. The man is giving himself the air of one who considers himself lowly.
3. *Uriah Heep-wise*: Uriah Heep, a character in the Charles Dickens's novel *David Copperfield* (1849–50), is infamous for his hypocritical statement of being 'ever so 'umble'.
4. *S.A.U. organisers*: the Shop Assistants' Union or the National Union of Shop Assisstants, organized by Margaret Bondfield (1873–1953) and Lady Emilia Dilke (1840–1904) in 1898.
5. *domestic servants*: the terms 'domestic servant' and 'shop assistant' were generally listed together on official documentation such as census data, and the registrar-general classified 'shop assistant' as semi-skilled.
6. *unkindest cut of all*: a personally devastating injury. The phrase is taken from Shakespeare's *Julius Caesar*, Act 3 scene ii: 'For Brutus, as you know, was Caesar's angel. / Judge, O you gods, how dearly Caesar lov'd him! / This was the most unkindest cut of all'.
7. *law is a hass*: Mr Bumble's famous declaration from Dickens's *Oliver Twist* (1838) on the law, presuming Mrs Bumble acted under his direction. The additional aspiration to the word 'ass' indicates the narrator's impersonation of the assistant's 'proper' English.
8. *margarine ... living-in system*: Shop assistants would often be required to live in dormitories over the shop, and the food provided for them would often be of very poor quality. The workers would be provided with the cheaper alternative of margarine rather than expensive butter. The plight of shop assistants was addressed in fiction by H. G. Wells's *Kipps* (1905) and Émile Zola's *Au Bonheur des Dames* (1883).
9. *Blatchford's "Britain for the British"*: *Britain for the British* (1902) was one of many socialist polemic pamphlets and books written and published by Robert Blatchford, none of which matched the phenomenal popularity of *Merrie England* (1893).

Laycock, 'The "Retired" Street Sweeper'

1. *middin'*: midden, a dunghill, dung heap, refuse heap; *OED*. The superintendent maintains his distance from the workers through clothing, regardless of the demands of his employment.
2. *supe.*: abbreviation of superintendent.
3. *prepare a place for us*: John 14:3: 'And if I go and prepare a place for you, I will come again, and receive you unto myself; that where I am, *there* ye may be also'. Christ goes to prepare a place in Heaven for his followers, while Billy leads the way into the deprivations of the workhouse.
4. *shops*: meaning employment generally, and not strictly limited to the retail trade.
5. *locus standi*: Literally meaning 'place of standing', the narrator laments his loss of social and economic standing when demoted from foreman.
6. *steyl*: handle.

Rosamund, 'For the Syndicate'

1. *windlass*: the old-fashioned mechanism of drawing water up from a well using a winding roller and chain.
2. *Syndicate*: Farmers in the United States had struggled with low food prices and high debt since the end of the Civil War, and farmers formed alliances and cooperative groups to stay afloat. The earliest alliance was the Grange or Patrons of Husbandry, formed in 1867. The Greenback Party in the 1880s and the Populist Party in the 1890s grew out of this cooperative inclination. The story presents the negative side of these growing alliances, as the ploughman is overworked despite having been given a vote in the proceedings, and the multiplicity of individual farms have been overwhelmed in the process of industrial agricultural practices.
3. *took up the lines*: took hold of the reins to start the horses and begin ploughing again.
4. *not with life-taking explosives*: The narrator supports the methods of the Socialist Labour Party, who focused on political action rather than the trade union route or the 'propaganda by deed' attitude of the anarchists. The anarchist branch of American socialism had been expanded with the arrival of German revolutionaries emigrating to avoid the Anti-Socialist Exception laws.

Mérimée, 'The Capture of the Redoubt'

1. *Ilna*: In the Oxford University Press edition, this is translated as Jena. The Battle of Jena was part of the Napoleonic Wars and was fought between the French and the Prussians in 1806. See P. Mérimée, *Carmen and Other Stories*, ed. N. Jotcham (Oxford: Oxford University Press, 1998), p. 67.
2. *redoubt*: an entrenched stronghold or refuge; *OED*. The original title for the story is 'L'Enlèvement de la Redoute' and has also been published under the titles 'Storming the Fort' and 'How the Redoubt was Taken'.
3. *'a garbled form of the name Shvardinó.'* Carmen, p. 345: This annotation to 'Cheverino' makes note of Mérimée's licence with historical facts, evident here with the Captain's statement of his friend's death yesterday from a wound sustained at Ilna/Jena, a battle fought six years earlier.
4. *cuirass*: body armour covering the front and back to the waist; *OED*.
5. *skirmishing order*: in this sense, meaning irregularly in small bodies of troops; *OED*.
6. *shako*: a cone-shaped military cap with a plume or pompom; *OED*.
7. *skirmishers*: in this sense, meaning small groups of soldiers sent to the edges of the battle; *OED*.

Pitcairn, 'Because They Understood Not'

1. *Cook's tourists ... six thousand years*: Thomas Cook (1808–92), travel agent. Cook had begun his excursion business by organizing railway trips, but by the 1860s he conducted parties to Italy, America and Egypt. The image of Cook's tours in this fiction is not one of the democratizing of travel but of wealthy philistines who litter areas of man-made wonder and have little interest in the history of the sites they visit.
2. *a little child to lead them*: Isaiah 11:6: 'The wolf also shall dwell with the lamb, and the leopard shall lie down with the kid; and the calf and the young lion and the fatling together; and a little child shall lead them'.

Maynard, 'Unemployment: A Tragedy in Little'

1. *lithograph*: a printed image taken from stone or zinc plates. Lithography was a popular medium for artists in the 1890s.
2. *overmantle*: a large ornamental piece, often made of either wood or plaster and containing a mirror, which would sit on the mantelpiece surrounding the fire.

Grey, 'A Martian's Visit to Earth'

1. *"Lower" House... "Upper" House*: The House of Lords and the House of Commons in the British parliamentary system, as the Martian goes on to explain. The Martian's account of the House of Lords' history focuses on the 'Lords Temporal' members – peers and noblemen, who in the feudal period would raise and command armies. The House of Lords is also attended by the 'Lords Spiritual' – bishops and archbishops. Parliament in Britain became the two distinct Houses in the fourteenth century. In 1909 the Lords rejected the Liberal government's budget, also known as the 'People's Budget'. This budget was to introduce new taxes rates (including heavy land and property taxes), tax allowance for poor families with children, health and unemployment insurance for workers, and old age pensions. The unelected Lords' rejection of the budget, desired by both the electorate and their representatives in the House of Commons, caused a constitutional crisis and led to the passing of the 1911 Parliament Bill, which removed the Lords' right to veto any Commons Bill other than the extension of Parliament beyond five years.
2. pari passu: side by side, simultaneously and equally; *OED*.
3. *Vestigial Rudiments*: something remaining from an earlier, less developed period.
4. *Mr. Chiozza Money*: Sir Leo George Chiozza Money (1870–1944), Swiss politician and author who changed his name from Leone Giorgio Chiozza in 1903. He developed a reputation for economic, political and statistical journalism. He was elected as Liberal MP for North Paddington in 1906 and East Northamptonshire in 1910. He argued for the redistribution of wealth through taxation.
5. *one-twelfth of the whole House*: In the 1906 general election, twenty-nine Labour candidates had been elected to the House of Commons out of a total of 670 constituencies. This makes the proportion nearer to one-sixteenth.
6. *Sisyphus*: In Greek mythology, Sisyphus is condemned to rolling an immense boulder uphill for eternity.
7. *ranked*: i.e. become rancid.

Dexter, 'Faith the Healer'

1. *sacristan*: the sexton, one charged with maintaining the sacredness of the church.
2. *reliquary*: a receptacle for holding religious relics, usually highly ornamented; *OED*. The Curé begins to consider how capital might be made out of this event.
3. *osteologist*: an expert in osteology, the study of bones.
4. Chemin de Fer de l'Ouest: a French railway company that was responsible for one of the worst accidents on French railways in 1842, when fifty-five people were burnt alive because the doors to the carriages were locked.
5. *Baedeker's* Northern France: tourist guides, this particular one giving information on northern France. Baedeker's was a business founded by Karl Baedeker (1801–59) in 1827 and run as a family company until 1984. The guides were popularized in Britain

6. Daily Mail: newspaper founded by Alfred Harmsworth (later Viscount Northcliffe) (1865–1922) in 1898 and still published today. The paper had a reputation for imperialism and war-mongering in the years leading up to the First World War. The naming of the paper in this context suggests that English visitors were the credulous readers of a scurrilous paper.

Siddle, 'A Stormy Wooing. The Smart Young Man and the Smarter Woman'

1. *pince-nez*: a pair of spectacles clipped onto the nose rather than held by earpieces. Mr Lennis is affecting the dress habits of the upper classes and making himself a figure of humour by rejecting his own class.
2. *shandy-gaff*: a mixture of beer and lemonade, usually shortened to shandy; *OED*. Lennis shows his hypocrisy, after having accused the tramp of being in his poverty-stricken condition through drink, by being partial to alcohol himself.
3. *quaff*: his hairstyle, presumably a phonetic spelling of coif, meaning to dress the hair; *OED*.
4. *souse*: a sudden or deep plunge; also to prepare food by steeping in tart liquor; *OED*. Lennis is suddenly covered by dirty ditch water.

Ashton, 'Bill Spriggs in the Pantomime'

1. *ichthyosaurus*: The ichthyosaur was a dolphin-like marine vertebrate that first appeared in the Triassic period and was most prevalent during the Jurassic. Archaeology became an established science during the nineteenth century, and the first ichthyosaur had been found by Mary Anning on Dorset coast at Lyme Regis in 1809. Clinton Fields is making fun of Bill's age.
2. *big dickey*: a shirt-front giving the impression of the person wearing a full shirt. There are many meanings for the word 'dickey', and the reader may have been expected to know that the word is also applied to a donkey or he-ass; *OED*. This double entendre perpetuates the comic stupidity of Bill.
3. *opera glass*: originally a short telescope, now a small pair of binoculars used at the opera or theatre to aid sight of the stage. The Spriggs' use of their son's 'spy glass' not only gives a comic vision of working-class aping of aristocratic leisure but also reinforces the sense of their having outdated ideas of what is considered 'upper class'.
4. *Baccarat*: Bill's son is named after a card game that was illegal in Britain at this time, although it was brought to public prominence in 1891 with the Royal Baccarat Scandal. Alternatively known as the Tranby Croft Scandal, William Tranby Croft was accused of cheating during a weekend house party with a group of aristocrats, including the Prince of Wales. The Spriggs naming their son after a royal scandal is further evidence of their inability to understand what it is they are aspiring to emulate.
5. *decollected, nor dishybill*: decollected, a misunderstanding of décolletage, meaning the exposure of the neck and shoulders by a low-cut bodice; dishybill, a literal pronunciation of dishabille, meaning to be partially undressed or dressed carelessly; *OED*. Again, Bet's aspiration to be taken for upper class is comically mistaken.

6. *heaven or Jerusalem*: New Jerusalem, heaven on earth. Revelation 3:12: 'and the name of the city of my God, *which is* new Jerusalem, which cometh down out of heaven from my God'.
7. *bucolic Bill Spriggs*: meaning both rural or rustic through its association with the pantomime fairies, and a humorous term for a peasant; *OED*.

SILENT CORRECTIONS

Blatchford, 'The Sorcery Shop. An Impossible Romance'

p. 17, l. 3	ancient or] ancient nor
p. 46, l. 32	seeking] seeing
p. 53, l. 2	England] England many
p. 65, l. 35	The genius] "The genius
p. 70, l. 32	"The] "Then
p. 77, l. 29	mets] meets
p. 79, l. 8	Mr. Fry] Mr. Jorkle
p. 97, l. 6	Sir Humphrey] Sir Humphry
p. 101, l. 2	children congenial] children, congenial

Clarke, 'The Red Flag'

p. 154, l. 23	meant most more] meant more
p. 156, l. 24	he] he said
p. 156, l. 24	on errand] on an errand
p. 248, ll. 12–13	"you] "when you

Pitcairn, 'Because They Understood Not'

p. 292, l. 22	ecstacy] ecstasy